THAT TIME
OF YEAR

Also by Garrison Keillor

The Lake Wobegon Virus, 2020
Living with Limericks, 2019
The Keillor Reader, 2014
O, What a Luxury, 2013
Guy Noir and the Straight Skinny, 2012
A Christmas Blizzard, 2009
Pilgrims, 2009
Life among the Lutherans, 2009
77 Love Sonnets, 2009
Liberty, 2008
Pontoon, 2007
Daddy's Girl, 2005
Homegrown Democrat, 2004
Love Me, 2003
In Search of Lake Wobegon, 2001
Lake Wobegon Summer 1956, 2001
ME, 1999
Wobegon Boy, 1997
The Old Man Who Loved Cheese, 1996
The Sandy Bottom Orchestra (with Jenny Lind Nilsson), 1996
Cat, You Better Come Home, 1995
The Book of Guys, 1993
WLT, 1991
We Are Still Married, 1989
Leaving Home, 1987
Lake Wobegon Days, 1985
Happy to Be Here, 1981

THAT TIME OF YEAR

A MINNESOTA LIFE

Garrison Keillor

Arcade Publishing • New York

First Edition

Arcade Publishing books may be purchased in bulk at special discounts
for sales promotion, corporate gifts, fund-raising, or educational purposes.
Special editions can also be created to specifications. For details, contact
the Special Sales Department, Arcade Publishing, 307 West 36th Street,
11th Floor, New York, NY 10018 or arcade@skyhorsepublishing.com.

Arcade Publishing® is a registered trademark of Skyhorse Publishing, Inc.®,
a Delaware corporation.

Visit our website at www.arcadepub.com.
Visit the author's site at garrisonkeillor.com.

10 9 8 7 6 5 4 3 2 1

Library of Congress Cataloging-in-Publication Data is available on file.
Library of Congress Control Number: 2020943449

Cover design by Brian Peterson
Cover photograph: Benjamin Miller, copyright © by Prairie Home Productions

ISBN: 978-1-951627-68-3
Ebook ISBN: 978-1-951627-70-6

Printed in the United States of America

To all the musicians, words cannot express
The happiness you made with the songs you played
In the long parade. God bless.

CONTENTS

The Keillor family tree is located on page 22.

THAT TIME
OF YEAR

I grew up in a northern town
Ground was flat for miles around
We were fundamentalist
Underwear was in a twist
Aloof, avoiding those in sin
Expecting Jesus to drop in
I was staunch and rather pure
Riding on the Brethren bus
And then I read great literature
Lusty, longing, humorous
Telling us to seize the day
Before the flowers fade away
We were taught obedience
To the Word, God's Holy Book
But Mother loved comedians
And that was the road I took
And so I bent and smelled the roses
Which God intended, one supposes
And now as life slips away
Just as Scripture said it would
I write this little book to say
Thank you. So far, so good.

1

My Life

IT'S BEEN AN EASY LIFE and when I think back, I wish it were a summer morning after a rain and I were loading my bags into the luggage hold of the bus and climbing aboard past Al, the driver, and the bench seats up front to the bunks in back and claiming a low bunk in the rear for myself. We're about to set off on a twenty-eight-city tour of one-nighters, two buses, the staff bus and the talent bus (though actually the tech guys, Sam and Thomas and Albert and Tony, have most of the talent and the rest of us just do the best we can). I kiss Jenny goodbye and she envies me, having been on opera and orchestra bus tours herself and loved them. The show band guys sit in front, Rich Dworsky, Chris, Pat and Pete, Andy, Gary or Larry, Richard, Joe, Arnie the drummer, Heather the duet partner on "Under African Skies" and "In My Life" and Greg Brown's "Early." Fred Newman is here, Mr. Sound Effects, and we'll do the Bebopareebop commercial about the meteorite flying into Earth's atmosphere about to wipe out an entire city when a beluga in heat sings a note that sets off a nuclear missile that deflects the meteorite to the Mojave Desert where it cracks the earth's crust and hatches prehistoric eggs of pterodactyls, which rise screeching and galumphing toward a tiny town and a Boy Scout camp where a lone bagpiper plays the Lost Chord that pulverizes the pterodactyls' tiny brains and sends them crashing and gibbering into an arroyo, and I say, "Wouldn't this be a good time for a piece of rhubarb pie?" and we sing, *One little thing can revive a guy, and that is a piece of rhubarb pie. Serve it up nice and hot, maybe things aren't as bad as you thought.*

At the table sits Janis or Katharine or Jennifer, who has the cellphone that Sam or Kate or Deb will call if there is a crisis. If they called me about a crisis, then they'd have two crises. I sit at a table so I can write on a laptop, but the show is written, the Guy Noir sketch, the commercials, the news from Lake Wobegon about the pontoon boat with the twenty-four Lutheran pastors, the canceled wedding of the veterinary aromatherapist, the boy on the parasail who intends to drop Aunt Evelyn's ashes in the lake when the boat towing him swerves to avoid the giant duck decoy and he is towed at high speed underwater, which tears his swim trunks off, then naked he rises on a collision course with a hot-air balloon.

The boys on the bus. Pat Donohue Andy Stein, Arnie Kinsella, Gary Raynor, and Richard Dworsky.

The bus is home; everyone has a space. You can sit up front and listen to musicians reminisce and rag on each other or you can lie in your bunk and think your thoughts. The first show is the hardest, a long drive to Appleton, then sound check and show, breakdown, drive to Grand Rapids and arrive at 4 a.m., a long day, and then we get into rhythm, Cedar Rapids, Sioux Falls, Lincoln, Denver, Aspen, Spokane, Seattle, Portland, and on. The bus pulls into a town around 4 or 5 a.m. and you stumble out of your bunk and into a hotel room and sleep and have lunch and head to the venue midafternoon, and each show is mostly the same as the night before, you walk out and sing "Tishomingo Blues"—

O hear that old piano from down the avenue.
I smell the roses, I look around for you.
My sweet old someone coming through that door:
Another day 'n' the band is playin'. Honey, could we ask for more?

And the show ends with the crowd singing "Can't Help Falling In Love With You" and "Auld Lang Syne" and "Good Night, Ladies" and whatever else comes to mind, and they go home happy, and the bus is sociable, and there is beer and tacos and ice cream bars. You belong to a family engaged in a daring enterprise and you're on the road and all your troubles are behind you. Sometimes late at night, I imagine climbing on the bus at Tanglewood, past the band guys noodling and jamming and the game of Hearts, and I lie in the back bottom bunk and we pull away, headed for Chautauqua, near Jamestown, New York, and I fall asleep and wake up in Minneapolis and it's years later.

I was not meant to ride around on a bus and do shows, I grew up Plymouth Brethren who shunned entertainment, Jesus being all-sufficient for our needs and the Rapture imminent. (The Brethren originated in Plymouth, England, it had nothing to do with the automobile—we were Ford people.) God knew where to find us, on the upper Mississippi River smack dab in the middle of North America, in Minnesota, the icebox state, so narcissism was not available, I was a flatlander like everyone else. We bathed once a week, accepting that we were mammals and didn't need to smell like vegetation. By the age of three I could spell *M-i-ss-i-ss-i-pp-i*—one hard word I'll always get right—and that started me down the road to writing. I had eighteen aunts who praised what I wrote, and they prayed for me, and I have floated along on their prayers. I recited my verse in Sunday School and they praised me for speaking nice and loud and clear, which eventually led to radio. My parents didn't hug me but my aunts did, Elsie and Jean and Margaret—I stood next to Ruby's wheelchair and she clung to me, Ruth held me to her great bosom and pressed her wire-rimmed glasses to my head, Eleanor and Bessie hugged, Brethren men didn't deal in affection but I was rich with aunts and never lacked for love. I was born in 1942, early enough to see the last Union Army veteran, Albert Woolson, in his blue forage cap riding in a parade, and in time to be moved by Jerry Lee Lewis who shook my nerves and rattled my brain. Gettysburg on one side, "Great Balls of Fire" on the other, half of American history in one swoop. I felt destined for good things, thanks to my aunts and because I was 1 person, the son of 2 parents, their 3rd child, born 4 years after my sister and 5 years after my brother, in '42 (four and two equals 6), on the 7th day of the 8th month in 19—nine, ten—42. I never revealed this magical numerology to anyone; I held it close to my heart. It was a green light on the horizon.

M-i-ss-i-ss-i-pp-i.

I'm a Scot on my mother's side, so I come from people who anticipate the worst. Rain is comforting to us, driven by a strong wind. My Grandpa Denham came from Glasgow and never drove a car lest he die in a flaming crash. Mother warned me as a child never to touch my tongue to a clothes pole in winter because I would freeze to it and nobody would hear my pitiful cries because the windows are all shut and I would die, hanging by my tongue. So I imagined I'd die young, which prodded me to make something of myself until now I'm too old to die young and can accept myself as I am, a tall clean-shaven man of 78 who escaped alcoholism, depression, the US Army, a life in academia, and death by hypothermia while hanging by my tongue. My people were Old

Testament Christians who believed that God smites people when they're having too good a time and so, doing shows, I was the stiffest person you ever saw on a stage, I looked intense, solemn, like a street evangelist or a pest exterminator. Laughter doesn't come easily to me; it's like bouncing a meatball. Strangers walk up to me and ask, "Is something wrong?" No, I'm a happy man but I come in a thick husk, like sweet corn.

From the age of nine or ten, I was determined to be a writer and didn't waver from it. This is due to having grown up in a tiny utopian sect that due to its separatist tendencies kept getting smaller. Whatever the opposite of "ecumenical" is, we Brethren were that. We considered Lutherans to be loose. I grew up believing that the Creator of the universe, the solar system, the Milky Way and the Way beyond it had confided in a handful of us, the Faithful Remnant. The whole of Christendom had slid into a slough of error and our little flock of twenty-five or thirty in this room on 14th Avenue South in Minneapolis was in on the Secret. When you believe that, it is no problem to imagine you'll grow up to write books and be on the radio. Most Brethren preaching sailed over my head but I loved the stories: Noah and his boatload of critters, Jonah and the whale, Daniel and Nebuchadnezzar, Bathsheba, the drunken Herod who is seduced by the young dancer who asks the head of a holy man as a favor, Thomas the doubter, Peter the denier. To all appearances, we were normal Midwestern Americans, we wore clean clothes, spoke proper English, took small bites and chewed with our mouths shut, mowed our lawn, played softball and Monopoly and shot baskets, read the paper, were polite to strangers, but in our hearts we anticipated the end of the world. Meanwhile supper was sloppy joes on Monday, spaghetti on Tuesday, chow mein on Wednesday, tuna casserole on Thursday, hamburgers on Friday, fish sticks on Saturday, pot roast on Sunday. We sat down to meals under a wall plaque, *JESUS CHRIST IS THE HEAD OF THIS HOUSE, THE UNSEEN GUEST AT EVERY MEAL, THE SILENT LISTENER TO EVERY CONVERSATION.* This didn't encourage loose talk at meals, so we didn't: conversation was sparse. Philip, Dad, and I sat on one side, Judy, Mother, and the twins on the other, and baby Linda in a high chair at the end. I spooned oatmeal into her and she ate applesauce with her fingers off a plate. *Please pass the potatoes* and *What's for dessert?* was about the extent of conversation. We certainly didn't talk about bodily functions: diarrhea was "the trots." We didn't pee or poop, we "went to the bathroom." We avoided the expression of personal preference, such as *I want to watch TV tonight*, and anyway we didn't have a TV. We had a radio, a big Zenith floor model with stately columns in front and vacuum tubes that gave off heat and a tuning knob the size of a grapefruit. I lay on the floor and listened to Fred Allen and Jack Benny, and sometimes when nobody was around I stood in the hall closet among the winter coats and pretended I was on the radio, using the handle of the Hoover upright vacuum cleaner for a microphone. One day I took the Hoover behind the drapes in the picture window and imagined I was onstage, about to come through the curtain and say, "Hello, everybody, welcome to the Gary Keillor show," and my older sister knocked on the window. She was outside, weeding the flower bed, laughing at my white Fruit of the Loom underwear. I was so excited about doing the show, I forgot to put on my pants.

My folks were Depression survivors, so they squeezed the toothpaste hard to get the last molecules out of the tube. Mother darned the holes in our socks. Dad was a farm boy and grew up with a big garden and loved fresh strawberries, tomatoes, and sweet corn and couldn't imagine living on store-bought, and so he purchased an acre of farmland north of Minneapolis and built a house on it and kept a half-acre garden. Mother would've preferred a bungalow in south Minneapolis, but Dad got his way and so I grew up a country kid. I was a middle child and was left to my own devices and became secretive, devious, never confided in anyone. As a city kid, I would've adopted a gang and become socialized, but instead I was a loner, had very little adult supervision. Mother was busy with the little kids. I could leave the house unnoticed, sit by the river or ride my bike among the cornfields and potato farms, ride for miles into the city past warehouses and factories, penny arcades and cocktail lounges, independent at the age of ten. Nobody told me the city was too dangerous for a kid to ride around on a bike, so thanks to ignorance, I was fearless. I learned to smoke by the age of twelve.

My parents loved each other and stayed in the background as we children worked out our identities. There was no alcohol, no dark silences, no shouting, no slamming doors. I was never struck, though sometimes Mother said she wanted to. Once in a while she said, "You kids are driv-

ing me to a nervous breakdown." And let it go at that. I don't recall
Mother or Dad praising me ever—that was left to Grandma and the
aunts. I was a quiet, bookish kid who liked to stand off to the side and
observe, which back then people took to mean I was gifted. Today they'd
say "high-functioning end of the autism spectrum," but autism hadn't
been thought up yet so I was free to imagine I was gifted. I was crazy
about girls, they were all fascinating, the way they talked, their boldness.
Once, when I was eleven, I walked past Julie Christensen's house and she
said, "Do you want to wrestle?" and so we did. She took hold of me and
threw me down and pulled my shirt up over my head and sat on me. It
was thrilling. She said, "Let's see you try to get up." I didn't want to get
up. She kissed me on the lips and said, "If you tell, I will beat the crap out
of you." She was a freethinker. She taught me to sing the Doxology to the
tune of "Hernando's Hideaway." (Sometimes I look at my wife and think
of Julie. I never was in therapy—you are the first person I've told this to.)

I was an indifferent student in high school and college, which served
to limit my career possibilities, which were further limited by having no
social skills thanks to growing up Plymouth Brethren, who taught us to
avoid defilement by standing apart from those in Error, i.e., everyone
on Earth. But I had good jobs—I washed dishes and I was a parking lot
attendant and then a classical music announcer, which is like parking
cars except you don't yell at anybody. For a few weeks one summer I ran
a manure spreader and did it about as well as a person could. The next
summer I was a camp counselor and led three canoeloads of thirteen-
year-olds across an enormous wilderness lake, a black sky above, lightning
on the horizon, and I instilled confidence in them even as I was shitting
in my shorts. Back then, a state university education was dirt cheap, and
I incurred no debt so I could entertain the notion of becoming a writer.
I wrote dark stories, Salingeristic, Kafkaesque, Orwellian, O'Connorly
(Flannery, not Frank), exhaled cigarette smoke with authorly elegance
and looked down upon engineers in their polyester plaid shirts with plastic pocket protectors who were busy designing the digital world we live
in today. I was in the humanities, where existentialism was very big back
then though nobody knew what it was exactly nor even approximately,
which made it possible for even an ignorant twerp to expound upon it.
At the U, I identified as a liberal Democrat for protective coloring but I

had conservative leanings, was scornful of bureaucracies, unions, popular movements, and venerated the past and intended to make my own way and create work that would earn money on the free market, preferably satire that goes against the prevailing tide. I am still a Brethren boy. A little profanity I can tolerate but obscenity turns me away. I have agnostic friends but I don't tolerate intolerance of religious faith. Scripture is clear about how to treat strangers and foreigners, any race or creed or gender, they are brothers and sisters. Life is a gift and we need be wise in the knowledge of death.

My true education was the deaths of four of my heroes, all four not much older than I, earthshaking deaths. My cousin Roger drowned at seventeen, a week before his high school graduation, diving into Lake Minnetonka to impress Susan whom he wanted to be his girlfriend, although surely he knew he couldn't swim. I admired him, a sharp dresser, a cool guy, his slightly lopsided grin, his disregard for sports, his fondness for girls. Two years later, Buddy Holly crashed in a small plane in Iowa. I heard the news on the radio. It turned out that the young pilot was not qualified to fly by instrument at night, but, unable to say no to a rock 'n' roll star, he took off into the dark and flew the plane into the ground and killed everyone in it. Two years later, Barry Halper, who hired me for my first radio job and became my good friend, who was smart, stylish, Jewish, had been to Las Vegas and met famous comedians, drove one afternoon east of St. Paul and crashed his convertible into the rear of a school bus and died at the age of twenty. And a year later, my classmate Leeds Cutter from Anoka, a year older than I, the smartest guy at our table in the lunchroom, who talked about why he loved Beethoven, how he'd go to law school but make a life as a farmer and raise a family, who was in love with my friend Corinne, who said, "I never do easy things right and I hardly ever do hard things wrong," was killed by a drunk driver while riding home from the U. He was nineteen.

I felt the wrongness of their deaths, the goodness lost, the damage done to the world, and felt responsible to live my life on their behalf and embrace what they were denied, the chance to rise and shine and find a vocation. They didn't know each other, but I see them as a foursome, Barry, Buddy, Leeds, and Roger. They were my elders and now they're my grandsons. They each died in swift seconds of violence and the thought of them gives me peace. I promise to love this life I was given and do my best to deserve it. I carry you boys forever in my heart. You keep getting younger and I am still looking up to you. Life without end. Amen.

After college, I was hired by a rural radio station to do the 6 a.m. shift Monday to Friday, because nobody else wanted to get up so early. I worked alone in the dark and learned to be useful and clearly imagine the audience and do my best to amuse them. In my twenties I sent a story by US mail to a famous magazine in New York, as did every other writer in America, and mine was fished out of the soup by a kind soul named Mary D. Kierstead, who sent it up to the editors and they paid me $500 at a time when my rent was $80 a month and that was the clincher, that and the radio gig, my course in life was set, everything else is a footnote.

A few years later I went to see the famous Grand Ole Opry radio show in Nashville and decided to start something like it of my own. My boss, Bill Kling, against all common sense, approved of this. I had lost a short story about a town called Lake Wobegon in the men's room of the Portland, Oregon, train station, and the loss of it made the story ever more beautiful in my mind, and, thinking I might recall it, I told stories about the town on the radio and also wrote books, including one, *Pontoon*, about which the New York *Times* said, "a tough-minded book . . . full of wistfulness and futility yet somehow spangled with hope," which is no easy thing for an ex–Plymouth Brethrenist, to get the wistful futility and also spangle it, but evidently I did.

My great accomplishment was to gain competence at work for which I had no aptitude, a solitary guy with low affect who learned to stand in front of four million people and talk and enjoy it. I did this because the work I had aptitude for—lawn mowing, dishwashing, parking cars—I didn't want to get old doing that. I preferred to tell stories. My first book, *Happy to Be Here*, published when I was forty, earned the money to buy a big green frame house on Goodrich Avenue in St. Paul. People noticed this. A renter for twenty years, I wrote a book and bought a house. In warm weather, I sat on the front porch and people walked by and looked. That era is over. Now you can get an unlimited Kindle subscription for pocket change and a successful book will buy you an umbrella tent. I am lucky I lived when I did.

I also became the founder and host and writer of a radio variety show of a sort that died when I was a child, for which I stood onstage every Saturday, no paper in hand, and talked about an imaginary town for twenty minutes. It was the easiest thing I ever did, easier than fatherhood, citizenship, home maintenance, vacationing in Florida, everything. I wrote five pages of story on Friday, looked it over on Saturday morning, went out onstage and remembered what was memorable and forgot the fancy stuff, the metaphors, the subjunctive, the irony, most of it at least.

Lake Wobegon was all about the ordinary, about birds and dogs, the unexpected appearance of a porcupine or a bear, the crankiness of old men, the heartache of parenthood, communal events, big holidays, the café and the tavern, ritual and ceremony, the mystery of God's perfection watching over so much human cluelessness. The tragedy of success: you raise your kids to be ambitious strivers and succeed and they wind up independent, far away, hardly recognizable, your grandkids are strangers with new fashionable names. The small town is strict, authoritarian, and your children prefer urban laxity and anonymity. There was no overarching story, few relationships to keep track of; it was mostly impressionistic. The ordinariness of a Minnesota small town gave me freedom from political correctness, no need to check the right boxes. In Lake Wobegon society, ethnicity was mostly for amusement, and Catholic v. Lutheran was the rivalry of neighbors.

I did Lake Wobegon pretty well, as I could tell from the number of people who asked me, "Was that true?" The Tomato Butt story was true and the homecoming talent show. The stories about winter were true. The story about being French was not true. Or the orphanage story. But I did have an Uncle Jim who farmed with horses and I rode on Prince's back to go help him with the haying as Grandma baked bread in a wood-stove oven.

I never was a deckhand on an ore boat in a storm on the Great Lakes, the Old Man at the wheel, water crashing over the bow and smashing into the wheelhouse, running empty in thirty-foot seas, navigation equipment lost, and the Old Man said to me, "Get on the radio and stay on the radio so the Coast Guard can give us a location," and I went on the radio and sang and told jokes for two hours and the ship made it safely to port, and that was how I got into radio. That was my invention, to demonstrate my facility. Hailstones the size of softballs smashed into my radio shack on the rear deck as I told Ole and Lena jokes. A story about a lonely guy in marital anguish wouldn't have served the purpose.

One true story I never told was about Corinne Guntzel, whom I met when we were six years old and rode a toboggan down a steep hill and onto the frozen Mississippi River. It was thrilling. Later, she got the same excitement from beating up on me about politics. She was a college socialist and smarter and better-read and I argued innocently that art is what changes the world, which she scoffed at, of course. I loved her and thought about marrying her but feared rejection, so I married her cousin instead and then her best friend, after which Corinne killed herself. It's not a story to be told at parties.

But the best story is about the day in New York I had lunch with a woman from my hometown of Anoka and had the good sense to fall in love with her. I was fifty, she was thirty-five. I am a Calvinist, she's a violinist. We talked and talked, we laughed, we walked, we went to the opera, we married at St. Michael's on 99th and Amsterdam, we begat a daughter. Now, twenty-five years later, she and I live in Minneapolis, near Loring Park, across from the old Eitel Hospital where my mother was a nurse, near the hotel where I worked as a dishwasher the summer after high school and learned to smoke Lucky Strikes, a block from Walker Art Center, where Suzanne Weil produced the first *Prairie Home Companion* shows. My old apartments are nearby and fancy neighborhoods I walked in back in my stringency days. I like having history around to help keep my head on straight and ward off delusion.

I had relatives who used outhouses and now I walk into a men's room and pee in a urinal and step back and it automatically flushes. I walk around with a device in my pocket the size of a half-slice of bread and I can call my daughter in London or read the *Times* or do a search for "Success is counted sweetest by those who ne'er succeed. To comprehend a nectar requires sorest need." It's a world of progress.

When I go live in the Home for the Confused, I'll sit in a sunny corner and tell stories to myself. When my time is up, they'll wrap me in a sheet and truck me back to Anoka and the Keillor cemetery fifteen minutes north of where I was born and plant me with my aunts and uncles on whom the stories of Lake Wobegon were based. I got a lot of pleasure out of writing them up, and so it's right I should lie down there in a cemetery where Aunt Jo used to send me over to mow the grass and trim around the gravestones. Dad's cousin Joe Loucks is here, who drowned in the Rum River in 1927: a dozen boys formed a human chain into the river to rescue him and he slipped from their grasp. Now they are here too. Old farmers are here, also an astrophysicist, a banker, a few salesmen, a cousin who died of a botched abortion by a doctor in town. Some had more than their share of suffering. My cousins Shannon, Philip, William, and Alec are here, all younger than I. When I was young, I was eager to escape the family, but death is inescapable and I'll be collected into their midst at last. A brief ceremony, no eulogy, no need to mourn a man who had an easy life. Lower him down and everybody grab a shovel. Either there will be a hereafter or I will be unaware that there is not. I believe there will be. *I am convinced that nothing can ever separate us from God's love. Neither death nor life, nor our fears for today nor our worries about tomorrow, nothing in all creation will ever be able to separate us from the love of God that is revealed in Christ Jesus our Lord.* Amen and amen.

2

My People

James Keillor, 40, a skilled carpenter turned farmer, 1900.

MY LIFE WAS HALF LAID out before I existed. My great-grandfather William Evans Keillor was walking home in Anoka one night in 1910 and heard an invisible crowd of people around him in the dark, walking with him, talking in low unintelligible voices, who, as he neared his house on the hill, faded into the night. A Brethren preacher had recently come through Anoka and Great-Grandpa assumed the voices were Plymouth Brethren, and so he led his family down the narrow rocky road of Brethrenly separation. Episcopalians can be unintelligible, so can Methodists or Mennonites, but he chose Brethren and our family history hangs on this ghost story. Grandpa James married Dora Powell, who was a progressive Methodist at the time, a proponent of women's education and racial equality, and she became a loyal farm wife and Brethreness, though she made her sympathies known to her grandchildren. She advocated for scholarship and science. She said, "Don't be a five-dollar haircut on a twenty-nine-cent head." A $5 haircut was fairly extravagant back then.

Denhams were city people. Grandpa Denham was the son of a Glasgow street sweeper and grew up in a tenement, no toilet, no bathtub. His poor overworked mother died young and his father married her nurse, Martha Whiteside, a censorious woman. Grandpa never attended a movie or read a novel. He was not a storyteller. He sailed back to Scotland in 1920, to visit his dying father and kept a meticulous diary of his trip, what he ate for breakfast, what he saw aboard ship, right up to when the ship docks in Glasgow and then the diary ends, not a word about his father, Martha, none of it. I suppose it was too painful and confusing for him to leave a record. I wanted to be a Powell, or a Keillor, but I have Denham in me too, and I have painful chapters too but shall tell my story as honestly as I can without causing too much pain to those I love. The Denhams appeared in the Lake Wobegon saga, their name changed to Cotton, and they were renowned for caution and a tendency to apologize. Their letters often begin, "I am so sorry it has taken me all this time to sit down and write to you. I've thought of it daily but then get busy with one thing or another. Please forgive me. I shall endeavor to do better in the future."

Brethren instilled perfectionism. A band of dissenters, led by the Irish curate John Nelson Darby, who around 1831 left the pomp and hierarchy of the Establishment Church to create an assembly of saints gathered in simplicity, as instructed in Scripture. God is perfect and everything we do or say must meet His standard, which is impossible, as we Brethren could see, looking around the room at the few survivors. I still live with perpetual failure. I attend an Episcopal church now and that is a magnificent pageant, but no show is ever good enough, no piece of writing is ever finished. When I lie in hospice care, on oxygen, catheterized, I will whisper to the nurse: *Bring me that book, the chapter about the luncheonette, I forgot to put in the salt and pepper shakers and the napkin rack.*

I chose my parents well. John Keillor and Grace Denham, a farm boy and a city girl, loved each other dearly and I grew up in the warm light of that love. She missed him when he was on the road, sorting mail on the North Coast Limited. He liked it when she came over and sat on his

John and Grace, 1936.

lap. She baked pies for him and beautiful pot roasts. She had little bouts of jealousy; he felt completely out of place among the Denhams. He and she disagreed about Christmas; he was laconic and she was excitable. Whenever Mother left the house, she imagined she'd left the iron on and the house would go up in flames and we'd come home to a basement full of ashes. She never left it on, but she kept thinking she had. When a big storm moved in, she went to the basement and begged him to come but he liked to stand in the front yard and watch it.

Dad came from a family of eight, she from thirteen. Her mother died of a blood infection when Grace was seven, and she was brought up by sisters. She and John laid eyes on each other at a Fourth of July picnic on the Keillor farm in Anoka in 1931, a month after he graduated from Anoka High. She was a slim lovely girl of sixteen, born on May 7, 1915, the day the *Lusitania* sank, and he was eighteen, born on Columbus Day, the handsomest boy in the Brethren. His father James's birthday was July 4 and he was on crutches, suffering from a mysterious wasting disease, and Grace was solicitous and took his arm, and John noticed. She sent John a birthday card in October. They met again in a carload of

Brethren young people going to the Minneapolis airport for a plane ride. She was frightened and he put an arm around her in her white summer dress. Both families were opposed to the romance, on the grounds the two were too young and had no money and he was needed on the farm—his father died in 1933. Grace went into nurse's training and got a job as a caregiver. He visited her often and sang hymns to her with the word "grace" in them. On Sunday, May 10, 1936, he wrote her a long letter:

> *Friday morning after breakfast, I was instructed to haul manure over to a field north of Aunt Becky's place. We put all four horses on as it was a long hard pull. After duly getting ready, I mounted the driver's seat and left for the field. Everything went fine until the homeward trip for the second load. At the top of Aunt Becky's hill, the horses started acting up, kicking and jumping around, as the spreader had run against their heels. I eased them almost to the bottom of the hill when they became unmanageable, and broke into a terrifying gallop. As they did, I dropped one rein, but bent forward and picked it up. I then crawled back in the main part of the spreader so I could stand up and brace myself. I thought of jumping out but decided to stick by it and try to stop the mad rush of horseflesh.*
>
> *In no time at all they had covered the distance from Aunt Becky's to our place with my efforts to stop them of no avail. As they neared our driveway, they tried to turn in, but could not make the turn. They ran across the ditch between the paper box and a telephone pole and on into the yard. As they crossed the ditch, the tongue on the spreader broke and plowed about four feet into the ground, breaking in three pieces. As it did so, it threw the machine to one side and I pitched out the other onto the broken pile of tongue.*
>
> *My mother being a witness to the scene ran over and asked if I was hurt. I said no and ran after the team, which had become tangled down the road in the ditch. It was then I started to feel faint and hurt, but nothing serious as it could have easily been, for which I am truly thankful. It is no fun to be hauled behind four wild horses at breakneck speed to be thrown lord knows where.*

Jo brought her bedroom suite home yesterday and is it ever swell. I feel sort of jealous of her because I wish I or you and I could get things like that, don't you, Honey? Perhaps our time will come when we can have the fun of picking out our furniture and things for our home. I have been thinking of you and realize more and more that you are more to me than any earthly or natural ties and yet I cannot as yet claim you for my own. I can only say I hope in the near future to make such a claim.

Until then, I am lovingly
Johnny
P.S. May I come down sometime? Love, Johnny

That was his way of proposing marriage, a reminder of his mortality followed by intimations of intimacy. *I wish that I—or you and I—could get a bedroom set, don't you, Honey?* They feared losing each other in those unsettled times, and a few months later, he borrowed his brother Bob's Model A and he and Grace drove to a secluded spot—let's say the Pioneers and Soldiers Cemetery at Lake and Cedar in Minneapolis—and lay a blanket in the grass and held each other close and made love. In November, in fear and trembling, Grace rode the streetcar to the Medical Arts Building downtown, accompanied by sister Elsie, and the doctor said that yes, it was so, as Grace suspected. She was starting to show.

She and Johnny faced her father, William Denham, in January. She was unaware that her father and his sweetheart, Marian, had been in the same situation in Glasgow years before—Marian was pregnant for several months before they married, and William's stepmother took a harsh view of this, even after the young couple married and had six children, and that was one reason they brought their brood across the Atlantic, to escape her disapproving eyes and sharp tongue. The old man, unable to reveal his own story, sat before the young couple and wept. And they lied and told him they'd married secretly on August 8, 1936, but it was not so. They were not married until January 6, 1937, by a justice of the peace in Stillwater, and my brother Philip was born in May. Not out of wedlock but not nearly far enough in. The fiction of the August marriage was maintained to the end of their days. The marriage certificate was

Grace, 18, and Elsie, 16.

kept secret. In later years, when we children inquired about their wedding and who was in attendance and was it in a church or where?, we got vague answers, and if we persisted, Mother got testy. They never observed their wedding anniversary until 1986, supposedly their fiftieth, and over Mother's opposition, we children insisted on giving them a quiet dinner in August in Anoka. Mother agreed to it on one condition: only immediate family, no guests who had been around in 1936 except the two lovers themselves, and no publicity. It was a small, quiet dinner at Mary Helen Cutter's restaurant in the Jackson Hotel. A nice wine was served. Philip offered a toast. Mother was relieved when the whole thing was over and done with. Years later, when a granddaughter brought forth a baby out of wedlock, Mother wrote a tender letter to her, assuring her that the crisis would pass and she would be happy again and grateful for the child, and then Mother did not mail it, for fear it would expose her own secret. It was found in her papers after she died.

The four crazed horses gallop toward home, the young man bracing himself, and the spreader crashes into the deep ditch and he's thrown onto the wreckage and somehow doesn't break his neck, but jumps up and runs after the team, and the crash lends urgency to his passion for Grace and he makes his claim and she accepts him in her arms. Their families weep over them, preach at them, but then accept them, and the secret is kept. Two large families and there must've been whispers but none of it ever reached us children. Philip, the scandalous child, was well-loved as were we all.

Thinking back, I remember Dad's agony when he took his turn preaching the Sunday night gospel meeting and ascended the platform like a man going to the gallows—his sermons had no conviction or spirit and were extremely brief—and we felt great relief on the drive home and he stopped at the Dairy Queen on Lyndale for sundaes, a root beer float, whatever we wanted, hang the expense. I wonder now if, on those Sunday nights, his own adventure of 1936 was on his mind, the drive in the Model A, the walk into the cemetery, the spreading of the blanket, lying next to her, the breathing. It's hard to preach when you are distracted by your own vivid memories. The Pioneers and Soldiers was only a few blocks north of the Gospel Hall.

The pain of the scandal made John and Grace merciful to a fault and forgiving, as we children discovered as we went off in our various directions: they could be disappointed but they never condemned, they never raised their voices, never spoke ill of anyone in my hearing. I was their rebellious child—somebody had to be—and I drew heavily on their forbearance. Both were brought up evangelical, under hellfire preaching, in a flock of contentious Christians, but scandal freed them to be loving and gentle all their lives. We lived next door to angry couples. I remember people yelling. A woman cried out, "When are we ever going to get out of this dump?" I babysat at neighbors' who came home drunk and cursing each other. I only saw one serious argument: Dad left for work at the Railway Mail and Mother looked out the kitchen door and said to herself, "One of these days, that man and I are going to come to a parting of the ways." I was fourteen. I was floored by that, I turned and went upstairs and threw myself on the bed and I wept, and Mother came up and apologized and said she didn't mean it. I grew up in a house of love, my parents holding hands, whispering to each other, so I looked upon happiness and contentment as ordinary and natural, and I still do. It took me longer to find that happiness but when I did, I recognized where I was. Jenny walked into the room and sat on my lap and put her head on my shoulder and I felt a sweet abundance. I would do the same for her but I weigh 240 and she weighs 114.

Family Tree

James Crandall Keillor = *Dora Edith Powell*
1860–1933   1880–1964

Ruth, 1907–1962

Robert, 1909–1971

James, 1910–1970

Josephine, 1912–1979

John, 1913–2001

Lawrence, 1915–1997

Elizabeth, 1918–1991

Eleanor, 1921–1996

William Denham = *Marian White McKay*
1877–1957   1874–1923

Marion, 1898–1995
Mary, 1899–1991
Ruby, 1901–1962
Margaret, 1903–1968
Jean, 1904–2002
William Jr., 1908–2002
James, 1909–1992
Ina, 1911–2002
George., 1913–1967
Grace, 1915–2012
Elsie, 1917–1991
Dorothy, 1919–1923
Joan, 1922–2011

John Keillor = *Grace Denham*
1913–2001   1915–2012

John Philip Jr, 1937–2009

Judith, 1938

Gary, 1942

Steven, 1948

Stanley, 1948

Linda, 1951

All You Need To Know

I'M OLD ENOUGH NOW TO see that my life was woven of the benevolence of aunts and a series of crucial failures before the age of twenty.

1. A botched robbery
2. Cowardice in the face of Darwinism and learning the art of invisibility
3. Green teeth
4. A fall from a haymow headfirst onto concrete and into the bull's pen
5. Demonstrated incompetence at the power saw
6. A flunked physical at age thirteen, due to mitral valve prolapse
7. A schism in the Plymouth Brethren that rendered our Minneapolis Assembly weak and listless and left a blockhead in power, thus making it easy for me to jump ship and wend my way back to the Anglicans whom the PBs had revolted against.

Seven failures that closed off certain avenues and opened others, all when I was too young to have a will of my own, and thus I went bopping along a circuitous path to wind up traveling around doing *A Prairie Home Companion*, telling stories that made intimate friends of complete strangers. I owe a great debt to failure, though I do feel I've gained enough benefit from it and would like to coast for a while.

The green teeth episode sticks with me. I was ten and a boy named Bob told me they were green and rotten and said it with authority, looking closely into my mouth. We were standing by the swings on the playground of Benson School. The school was torn down long ago, but I remember the exact spot where he said it. I looked in a mirror in the lavatory and saw no greenness but believed him because he sounded so certain. I didn't mention it to my mother or anyone else. It was my terrible secret. I was horrified. Pictures of me from that time afterward show a solemn, tight-lipped boy. The muscles around my mouth forgot how to smile. Even today, people look at me and ask, "Are you okay?" Yes, I'm fine; when your teeth are green, you don't smile, that's all. Thanks to this somber face, I never went into retail sales or politics, but it was no handicap for a writer or a radio guy, so that's what I did instead. My tormentor who said my teeth were green once took hold of my wrist and said, "Your wrists are so thin, like a girl's. It's good you didn't go out for football, you would've gotten killed." Which drove me to wear long-sleeved shirts, to hide this deformity. He was a big confident guy, an excellent student, was elected president of our senior class, and he bestowed his contempt whenever he laid eyes on me. I was an indifferent student but was admitted to the University of Minnesota and worked in a scullery and in parking lots to pay my way. My tormentor saw me there and said, "I never thought you'd make it to college, you're such a freak." He saw my poems in the *Ivory Tower* magazine and told me how worthless they were, and probably he was right.

I took a hodgepodge of English lit courses and stayed in college as long as I could, and in 1969 I went to work in radio, twelve-hour days, writing at night at home; meanwhile my tormentor graduated from medical school and did his residency and ran into me at a reunion and asked, "So what are you up to now?" like a dog sniffing my résumé. I muttered something. He was married and had a family and was on an upward trajectory when one day, repairing a water pump at his home, he stuck a screwdriver into the works, thinking the circuit was broken and it was not and he was electrocuted. He was entering the best years of his life, and a flash of powerful voltage passed through him and he fell into a coma and died three days later. It happened as I was finding my vocation and embarking on a happy career. Since then, I've forgiven him over and over, and also I've avoided trying to repair any electrical appliance, I don't even replace burnt-out lightbulbs. I am fearful of this story winding up in symmetry.

Despite my best efforts, I was spared alcoholism, lung cancer, carpal tunnel syndrome, high blood pressure, and death by stupidity. I once got my car up to 100 mph on a straight stretch of northbound Highway 47 just to see if it could and a pickup truck pulled out of a driveway ahead of me and I steered around behind it as it pulled into the southbound lane, thus avoiding death at 22. My brother Philip and I went canoeing around the Apostle Islands on Lake Superior and paddled into a deep cave under one of the islands, and explored it for a while, ducking our heads under the low rocky ceiling, and then paddled out to open water a minute or two before the wake of a distant ore boat came crashing into the cave, four-foot waves that would've splattered us on the cave ceiling, no need for EMTs, the turtles would've feasted that night. We sat in the canoe and watched, no need to say a word: death was in the cave and we had eluded it. Once a mattress that I was hauling home fell off the roof of my car and landed in the center lane of the freeway fifty yards back and I ran to drag it to safety as my wife screamed and a semi whooshed past, horn blasting, and I got to experience the Doppler effect up close. I horsed the mattress back up on the car and we drove slowly home. She thought about saying something and then did not. I've often stepped off a curb in New York thinking my thoughts and heard shouted Chinese, and a deliveryman on a bicycle raced by so close I could smell the garlic sauce. I once ran on a slippery dock at Cross Lake and slipped and instead of landing on the dock and breaking my neck and starting a new life as a paraplegic, I landed in the water (which covers three-quarters of the world, so statistically your chances are good) and was spared an endless amount of self-pity.

I survived these close calls and the Saturday night show, *A Prairie Home Companion*, launched in 1974 and, with a break in 1987, ran until 2016, and through no fault of my own became a box-office success in the public radio sphere, a porpoise among the hippopotami, and I was launched onto a writer's dream—I wrote and hosted the show while smarter people, Margaret, Christine, Kate, and Sam, ran the business. I played the detective Guy Noir (*It was November. Gray day. My landlord, Doris, had just turned on the radiators, which are on the National Registry of Historic Heating Systems and I looked out the window and saw a gray cloud that looked like someone I knew and then realized it was my face.*) who waits for a big case involving Louie B. Louie or some other slimeball with a bulge under his jacket and instead in comes an old man who's lost his glasses and needs a detective to retrace his footsteps. I played the cowboy Lefty in search of his Evelyn and I played a dullard named Duane, and now and then I got to stand next to a woman and sing a love song with her, and this was considered *work*. I have a picture of Grandpa Keillor in his farmyard on a bitterly cold winter day, earflaps down, denim jacket buttoned up, a sweater over his coveralls, pitchfork in hand, tending his animals, and he looks truly happy, as was I doing the show or sitting down to write with a fine black pen on the white cardboard the dry cleaners put into my shirts. It is too small for a story and the right size for a sonnet.

> *Frankie and Johnny were lovers and swore to be true*
> *To each other and it didn't take him all that long*
> *Before he went to the hotel with You Know Who*
> *And got busy doing Miss Frankie wrong.*
> *He was her man, a good lover, handsome*
> *In his bowler and spats, but not so astute,*
> *Which led to her looking over the hotel transom*
> *And pulling out the .44, which went rooty-toot-toot.*
> *And the rubber-tired hearses came and poor Frankie*
> *Was locked up in a dungeon cell. They threw*
> *Away the key. She lay and wept in her hanky*
> *But mostly she felt like a fool. Wouldn't you?*
> *People had warned her, again and again and again.*
> *And she knew it too. There is no good in men.*

We sang "Frankie and Johnny" in Mrs. Moehlenbrock's fourth-grade classroom out of our blue *American Harmony* songbooks and we loved the lines *the first time she shot him he staggered. The second time she shot him he fell. The third time there was a southwest wind from the northeast corner of hell.* We sang it loud. And we sang about *the E-ri-e was a-rising and the gin was a-getting low and I scarcely think we'll get a drink till we come to Buffalo.* It was joyful to sing about gin, a Brethren boy who had sat under Brother Tomkinson's preaching as he shouted, "There are people here who are going to hell and they don't know it!"—it made for a vivid and varied life. Bullies stalked the schoolyard, and I slipped away from them.

Brethren preached separation from worldly pleasures, but my mother laughed at comedians, particularly Gracie Allen, who said, "My mind is so fast, sometimes I say something before I even think it." To Mother, this was hilarious. And also, "If it wasn't for Thomas Edison, we'd be listening to radio by candlelight." Other Brethren frowned on jokes. Dad was indifferent to them and I never heard him tell one. Mother claimed she couldn't remember jokes, but when I told one, she just laughed and laughed. And so, from the time I could read, I looked for jokes to tell my mother and it made me happy to hear her laugh. It's just that simple.

Years later, working on a screenplay for Disney, a very funny movie that never got made, sitting through production meetings attended by fourteen men in short-sleeved white shirts who talked about the Narrative Arc and the Hero's Quest and what is the Gift that he brings back from his Journey, I went for a walk one foggy afternoon and passed a Hertz office, and got an urge to rent a car. They offered me a convertible; I took it. I cruised along Sunset Boulevard, the top down, traffic juking and bopping around me, through a canyon of flashing lights and people wearing sunglasses and billboards with faces of famous celebrities I never heard of, and then lost my bearings and circled for a while in strange neighborhoods. Whenever I drive around for fun, I think of my dad who loved driving around. There was some teenage boy left in my dad, though he worked so hard, doing carpentry work, sorting mail in the swaying mail car hurtling through the night, his .38 snub-nose revolver at his side. My dad came home weary from his shift with the Railway Mail Service and after supper he fell asleep in his chair reading the *Star*, and Mother had to wake him up to go up to bed. I didn't want to ever work that hard. So I aspired to be a freelance writer and achieved that, thanks to the virtues I rebelled against that my dad had tried to instill in me: to buckle down and tend to business and to thrive on work, the old middle-class virtues of persistence and attention to detail. Jokes made my mother happy so I went into radio to do a show that had died long before but in my Brethrenly isolation I didn't notice and if I live to be 100 I'll ride in a parade in a convertible with a big sign, AMERICA'S LAST LIVING LIVE RADIO SHOW HOST. The idea of radio will be as foreign to them as the telegram or mimeograph, but there will still be good manners and people will applaud as I go by.

4

Luncheonette

I WAS CONCEIVED IN LATE fall, their third child, in their rented house on Jefferson Street in Anoka. They had been forgiven for the scandal of 1936 thanks to their having produced two obedient, truthful, well-behaved children in Philip and Judy, and now here came a third. I'd like to say I was conceived in patriotic fervor on December 7, 1941, the night of Pearl Harbor, but actually it was November 7, and I appeared August 7, 1942, at 6:40 a.m., Gary Edward Keillor, eight pounds, seven ounces, in Dr. Mork's maternity hospital at 1841 Ferry Street, near where the Rum flows into the Mississippi. The long wall across the street by the Caswell house was built by my great-uncle Allie around 1911, of rock from the Rum, he who in his eighties went with his wife, Millie, to buy a new mattress at Thurston's in Anoka and told the clerk, "I don't like the firm mattress—I can't get a good purchase with my knees," and Millie blushed. My great-uncle Lew's Pure Oil station was around the corner, and John worked there, pumping gas in his smart Pure Oil uniform with an officer's cap, waiting to hear about his application at the post office. He had no fondness for farming, but thanks to his upbringing he knew about carpentry and auto repair, and was patient and soft-spoken by nature, having herded cows. He was hired by the post office and then drafted into the Army. America was at war. Anoka was a town of 7,000 with a classic Main Street, two banks, two newspapers, a county courthouse with a high steeple in a grassy square, a Carnegie library with dome and pillars, the county fairgrounds with dirt racetrack and the State Hospital for the Insane on the north side of town. The big news of the day was the landing of the 1st Marine Division on the beach and rainforest of Guadalcanal in the Pacific, the first land offensive against Japan after Pearl Harbor.

We moved around during the war, living with Grandma and then Aunt Jean, and when I was four and Daddy came home from the war, we lived in a duplex apartment at 39th Street and Bloomington Avenue in south Minneapolis for a couple years while he saved up to build us a house in the country north of the city. America had won the war and saved the world. Boys on the Bancroft School playground sang: *Hitler had just one ball. Goebbels had two but they were small. Himmler had something similar, and Goering had no balls at all.* My first dirty songs. I didn't completely understand the words but I knew to sing it only to myself, not at home. Dad bought a movie camera and shot a scene of his children emerging from the front door on Bloomington one by one—"Don't look at the camera and smile," he said—so we looked down at the sidewalk and frowned, Philip, nine, with curly hair, and Judy, eight, straight and tall, and me, Gary, four years old, almost five, in a blue peacoat, and as I walk out the door, a streetcar passes, and I look up and smile.

I liked to sit on our front steps and watch the big yellow streetcars go by, the conductor clanging his dishpan bell, the long upright arm in the rear with the little wheel that rode on the electric overhead wire, sparking as it rolled. Mother and I often rode the Bloomington car downtown and she gave me coins to drop into the glass farebox, the coins dinging on the little metal flanges, and we sat in the woven-straw seats and women smiled at me, chubby-cheeked, and once the conductor in full uniform saluted me and called me Winnie—I was a dead ringer for Winston Churchill. And we rolled downtown to the department stores smelling of new clothes and perfume and floor wax and soup from the basement cafeteria, the elevators operated by uniformed women with white gloves, visions of elegance and comfort, and a man in a suit who knelt at my feet and slipped shoes on them, one after another, until Mother saw what she liked. And then we walked to the library.

One day, while Mother was visiting Mrs. Lindahl up the street, I stole money from her change jar so I could ride the streetcar downtown. Having ridden it with her, I had seen how it was done. You simply climbed the steps, grabbing onto a pole, and dropped your money in the glass box and took a seat. The motorman would throw the big wooden lever and the car would roll north and we'd wind up on the avenue of Powers and Donaldson's and Dayton's department stores, from which I could find my way to the public library and climb the stairs and look at the magnificent enormous picture books, of which they had hundreds at the library, spread across long tables, free for the looking. That was the extent of my plan.

Before leaving for Mrs. Lindahl's, Mother told me to swat some flies and I had swatted them. The change jar was shaped like a strawberry, sitting on the counter by the toaster. I lifted the lid with the stem and grabbed a fistful of change. I headed down the back stairs and walked down the alley to catch the streetcar at 38th Street.

My mother told this streetcar story now and then, even as she got into her nineties, and once in Scotland, in Pitlochry, I went for a walk and got a powerful sense of the past, smelling coal smoke, and the acrid tang brought back Bloomington Avenue, the alley, the luncheonette. The past brought vividly to life by air pollution. My streetcar adventure was a large event in my life, maybe not so important as the apple that fell on young Isaac Newton's head, but important.

So I stuck my hand in the strawberry-shaped change dish, stole a fistful of change, scooted out the back door and down a wooden staircase and up the alley past the little white garages lining either side. I was afraid of dogs, but none came after me. I got to 38th Street, intending to catch a streetcar, and walked by a luncheonette just as a strange man opened the door. He held the door open. He said, "Good morning."

It was simple synchronicity. The friendly man said hello and held the door open for me and, politely, I entered. On a minor turn of fate hangs a lifetime. I walked into the luncheonette, a storefront the size of a one-car garage, and climbed up on a stool at the counter, and the cook asked what I wanted and I said, "A cheeseburger." I put my change down on the counter and he took a few coins and put the patty on the griddle and it hissed and flames flared up. A man sat a few stools away, gazing out the window. The cook was smoking a cigarette, and the smell of tobacco smoke was new to me. Dance music played on the jukebox. It was all quite new. The cook set the patty in a bun on a white plate, and I noticed he'd forgotten the cheese and I pointed this out just as I felt a big hand on my shoulder. It was Dad. He pushed the plate away. I said to the count-erman, "But I wanted cheese." Dad led me out by the hand. I said, "But I paid for it!" I tried to go back, and Dad pulled me along back home. Mother was waiting by our garage, looking distressed. She handed Dad a yardstick and told him to give me a whipping and marched up the back stairs and into the kitchen. He and I sat in the garage on the bumper of our 1941 Ford sedan not looking at each other and he said something mournful about my having caused Mother worry and after a while he stood up and I followed him up the stairs to the kitchen. Dad was not a whipper. I was sent to my room, an enjoyable little closet with my books, my pencils and paper. Philip and Judy came home from school and were told what I'd done and they looked at me with, I thought, new respect.

(Had the man at the luncheonette not opened the door, maybe I catch a streetcar and ride downtown, get lost, maybe I step into the street, a truck honks, a man shouts, a big dog barks, I stand, weeping, and a policeman takes me home and my terrified mother, stricken with guilt, is watchful of me ever after and I grow up sensing the world as hostile and perilous and I take a cautious course in life, a job as a stock boy at Day-ton's from which I retire at 65, single, childless, and move into a high-rise and watch a good deal of television, but it didn't turn out that way.)

Dad sang me a song that night as I lay in bed. He loved old sad songs and he sang:

Where is my wandering boy tonight,
The boy of my tenderest care?
The boy that was once my joy and light,
The child of my love and prayer?
My heart o'erflows for I love him he knows.
Oh where is my boy tonight?

I was touched by the song. My dad never said he loved us, but there he had sung it in a song. I'm sure he told Mother that he loved her, but men back then kept their affections to themselves lest they betray weakness. Brethren men spoke of God's love, of course, but none of them ever looked at me and said, "I love you" and I would've been embarrassed if one had. This is still rare in Minnesota. My friend

George Latimer said, "I love you" to me not long ago, but he was 85 and it was the cocktail hour and it was over the phone during a pandemic and he was feeling blue and it was snowing and George is a liberal Democrat.

The next day was Sunday, and we walked to the Grace & Truth Gospel Hall at 3701 14th Avenue for Sunday School and the Remembrance Meeting. Aunt Marion saw me and put a hand on my shoulder and said, "I understand you like cheeseburgers. If you want one, you can come to my house and I'll make you one. With cheese. For free." And she laughed and laughed and so did Uncle Bill. Aunt Elsie said something similar. My bad deed was amusing to them. My dad had told them the story. The thief was now a character in a humorous story. Even my mother

Elsie and Don (Myrna and Earl).

laughed about it. She loved the Lord and yet she enjoyed comedians like her rascally brother George, who had left the Brethren for ungodly Lutheranism, but he could make her laugh out loud. My uncles weren't so amused by the cheeseburger, but the aunts remembered it for weeks. They loved me and their laughter was proof of it. It was as simple as that.

A delicious confection of love and comedy, tasted when I was almost five. And so the die was cast. Brethren were opposed to shows, but thanks to Dad's lenience and my aunts' appreciation I grew up and became a show myself. Many years later, doing *Prairie Home* at the State Fair grandstand, knowing they were in the crowd, I put Aunt Elsie and Uncle Don into the Lake Wobegon monologue as Myrna and Earl, a story in which she entered her apple pie in the Fair's baking contest held at the grandstand, and while the judges looked at the finalists, Myrna stood and modestly disparaged her pie, the crust especially, as Elsie tended to do, and so she won a red ribbon instead of blue, though the winner was more pudding than pie.

Eleanor and Grandma Dora, 1949.

Don and Elsie came backstage afterward and were clearly delighted though also faintly embarrassed at being made much of, even under pseudonyms. She asked if I remembered the luncheonette, and I did and I still do. She was my mother's closest friend. They spoke every day on the phone until Elsie died, and that phone call was Grace's steadying pleasure. She and Elsie were the younger, more ebullient sisters in the midst of Brethren austerity, two slender girls grinning at the end of the panoramic photograph of hawk-faced men and bearded preachers and their dour wives. She was my beloved aunt, jittery on the outside, strong on the inside, and she and Don went into the Lord's work and ministered to far-flung isolated Brethren. When she lay dying, Don cared for her at home until the very end and was put off by suggestions that she go into hospice: "Of course I'll take care of her," he said. "I love her." When I need to clear my vision as a Christian, I don't read St. Augustine, I just think of Elsie and Don on my way to St. Michael's, arriving late this morning just in time for confession, and there's not room in the pew for a tall man to kneel comfortably so I twist into position, which reminds me of trying to make love in the back seat of an old VW—not where my mind should be right now—her name was Sarah, she had a laughing fit, which let the air out of the moment so there is no sin to repent of there, only the memory of a failed attempt, and in the prayers I whisper her name, and in the prayers for the departed, I envision the two girls in summer dresses in the photograph and I say their names, Grace and Elsie, Elsie and Grace.

5

At the Farm

AFTER THE LUNCHEONETTE, I WAS sent up to Grandma Keillor and Uncle Jim's. I was put on the Zephyr bus to Anoka and Uncle Jim picked me up by the Baptist church and drove me out to the farm and there was Grandma in the doorway, smelling of lavender, her silvery hair pinned up in a proper bun. She hugged me and commented on how tall I was. I adored my grandma. A few years later, when I needed glasses, I picked out a pair of octagonal wire-rims just like hers.

We sat in the kitchen where she was baking bread, flames flickering in the woodstove when she lifted up a lid and tossed in a log. She said she'd heard that I liked to read and she approved of that. The farm was a long step back into the past: kerosene lanterns, no running water but a hand pump in the kitchen where I caught cold water in my hands and splashed it on my face and washed with Lava soap and rinsed. Chickens ran loose in the yard, and an evil goose lay in wait for a child to snap at, cows grazed in the pasture between the big red barn and Trott Brook. It was dark at night. No yard lights. The outhouse out back. Everything was a lot like it had been in the 1880s, and if you awoke in the middle of the night needing to do your business, there was a nice enamel pot with a lid under the bed, no need to go to the biffy. No radio, so there was plenty of silence. For entertainment, we stood around the pump organ and sang about the little rosewood casket sitting on a marble stand with a package of love letters written in a faded hand.

Grandma whistles under her breath, a tuneless music. She cuts me a slice of warm yeasty bread and pours me a cup of Salada tea. Her fingers are knotted at the knuckles. She is a woman of firm beliefs. If you leave

35

your windows open at night, you won't get sick. Chew your food thirty times before you swallow. There's no need for herbs if the ingredients are good. You catch more flies with honey than with vinegar. And once I heard her say, "The colored are better looking, more intelligent, more talented, harder working, more honest, and more loving toward their families than Caucasians." I was impressed. Her grandfather had been a federal administrator in the South after the Civil War, during Reconstruction, and she got her ideas about people of color from him.

The schoolhouse where Dora Powell taught and James Keillor went to court her.

She had taught in the big frame schoolhouse across the road forty years before, and there Grandpa had gone to court her. He was on the school board. They married and had eight children: Ruth, Robert, James, Josephine, John, Lawrence, Elizabeth, and Eleanor. He was strict, and at supper each child was required to stand up and give an account of his or her day, for their father's reproof or commendation. People remembered that about him, and also his love of books, seeing him raking hay, the horses' reins in his left hand, a book in his right. He died in 1933 of a neurological ailment exacerbated by smoke inhalation the day the house burned down. At his funeral, the preacher chose as his text, "For all have sinned and come short of the glory of God," and some neighbors were offended that he'd speak of James Keillor that way.

The school across the road wasn't a school anymore so my cousins Susie and Janice and Rachel and I played school there. The Brethren held Meeting there on Sunday morning and we sat in formation, facing the table in the middle with the pitcher of wine and loaf of bread, me next to Grandma next to Uncle Jim, the tall regulator clock tick-tocking on the wall. A Model T Ford was parked in the yard and the cousins and I liked to sit in it and rock back and forth and sing, "Go tell Grandma the old gray goose is dead" and the song about the death of a cat and tears ran down our cheeks.

After lunch, Uncle Jim hitched up Prince and Ned to go bring in the hay. He put his hands under my arms and hoisted me up on Prince, my legs spread wide on the broad back, arms around the neck, my face pressed against the mane, the two great ears twitching above. Jim boarded the hayrack and chucked to the team and they trotted across the yard, the hayrack creaking and groaning, harness jingling. They paused at the gate and Jim jumped down and unlatched it and swung it open, and the team and I went rocking along down the lane and into the meadow where the hay lay in windrows where he had mowed it that morning and they stopped. I swung a leg back over Prince's back and slid down his flank and climbed up on the rack to do my job. The horses started forward at a slow walk and my gentle uncle, shirtless in his blue coveralls, forked billows of hay up on the rack and I stomped on it to pack it down and make a nice firm load, no words between us, each with his work to do. We did four windrows; the load was four feet high and fairly firm, and he spoke to the team and they headed back for the barn. He gave me two ears of dried corn from the corncrib, and I held them up to each horse in turn who wrapped his horse lips around it and with great delicacy took it in his teeth and crunched it.

Years later I wrote a song about them, changing their names to Brownie and Pete, for the rhyme, and Chet Atkins and I did it on a tour: *Oh the harness jingled on Brownie and Pete, two big Belgians with their dancing feet, pulling a hayrack down the pasture lane—I was six years old and I got to hold the reins. Uncle Jim up beside me, standing up on the rack. "Hold onto the crossbar, boy, push the branches back." Their big feet dancing and their big backs shone, and they tossed their heads like thoroughbreds as we headed home.* Chet's drop-thumb style was perfect for the nobility of workhorses, their gait, the grace of their big hooves. It was one of the better songs I ever wrote, but you had to have ridden a workhorse to appreciate it and not many people have.

The horses pulled the hayrack up close alongside the barn, and I clambered up and opened the doors to the haymow and jumped into the great cathedral of barn, beams of sunlight from holes in the roof, golden motes of dust falling through the beams, some piles of hay across the floor of the mow. I took a pitchfork from near the door and went to work spreading the new hay around as Uncle Jim pitched it into the mow, and when he was done, he excused himself to go use the outhouse and I stood on a high promontory of hay and recited a poem to hear my voice reverberate under the arch of the roof. *Breathes there the man with soul so dead who never to himself hath said, "This is my own, my native land"—whose heart hath ne'er within him burned as home his footsteps he hath turned from wandering on a foreign strand,* and in my admiration of my own voice, I didn't notice the open trapdoor and I dropped down into the cow pen below and bounced off the hindquarters of a cow in its stanchion and landed on concrete and skidded on fresh manure under the gate into the bull's pen. He sniffed me and pushed at me with his great slimy nose as Uncle Jim came on the run. He whacked the bull's hindquarters with a shovel and carried me into the house and lay me on the sofa. I touched my head. I was bleeding. Grandma brought wet brown paper to put on my wound—it had some medicinal value—I lay very still and didn't cry and she put her face down next to mine and held my hand and sang to me a favorite song about the babes lost in the woods:

And when they were dead, the robins so red
Brought strawberry leaves and over them spread,
And all the night long, the branches among,
They mournfully whistled, and this was their song:
Poor babes in the woods.

I loved her whispery voice. She asked if I was all right. Yes, I said. She was worried and looked me in the eyes and said things for me to repeat back to her. Uncle Jim went to town with big bags of corn to have them ground up for chicken feed. I wanted to go with him, but she wouldn't let me. To make sure I hadn't suffered brain injury, she asked me to recite a poem and I recited, *Birdie with a yellow bill sat upon my windowsill, cocked his shining eye and said, "Wake up, wake up, you sleepyhead,"* which she thought indicated no brain injury though in truth I did feel odd, but didn't mention it. Something jarred loose in my brain. Years later, Mother said she worried about me from that time on, that I seemed elusive and quiet and developed the habit of hiding from the family. Perhaps hitting my head on concrete knocked something loose. The more I think about it, I do feel something loose up there, so I try not to think about it.

I went to the barn to help Uncle Jim with evening milking. He milked twelve cows, one by one, by hand, putting his forehead to the cow's flank just ahead of the hind haunch and reaching for the immense udder and drawing the milk pinging into the steel pail squirt by squirt. I emptied the pail into the milk can and he moved to the next cow. The fresh milk smelled sweet and warm. When the can was full, he and I took it to the milk house and lowered it down into the cistern, into the cold water, to await the milk truck next day. Milk was his livelihood; the land was too poor for row crops. Other uncles were employed in shops and offices, and my dad on the mail car of a train; Uncle Jim raised hay, fed it to cows, and harvested their milk. He was of another world from ours, carrying on the past, a heroic burden. Farming wore my uncle out and he eventually found a job in town, working in a kitchen. He and I had the same hereditary heart problem, and he died of a heart attack at 59. My heart was surgically repaired at age 59, an operation that didn't exist thirty years before when he had needed it. I hardly knew my soft-spoken uncle at all, but I feel connected to him, having gotten twenty years that were denied to him.

6

Liberation

JOHN WAS DRAFTED INTO THE Army in 1943 and boarded a train to basic training in Virginia, and to Mother's great relief, was not sent to Europe but to New York, to sort mail in the Army post office. Dad wrote to Mother, "Dearest, Remember that sweet smile you gave me as I went through the door to the train tracks? That has never left my memory." She got $100 a month from Uncle Sam, and we four lived on the farm with Grandma for a year and then with Aunt Jean's family in Bettendorf, Iowa, and then moved to Bloomington Avenue and then to Jean's on Hubbard Street in St. Paul while Dad saved up to build a house north of the city. No wonder family meant so much to Mother. She was friendly to neighbors, polite to strangers, but family was who you could count on in time of need. Years later, when Dad fell off a barn roof and fractured his skull and contracted spinal meningitis, Aunt Eleanor put everything aside, left her children in Grandma's care, and came straight-away to nurse the patient and stayed a month until she felt no longer needed. We knew she would and she did. Mother and Elsie spoke on the phone daily; they had been in cahoots since childhood, and Jean had been their surrogate mother, so she was very tight with the two of them. Dad and I drove up to Anoka once after his brother Lawrence had become president of the First National Bank. Dad stopped to visit him, and I said, "Do you have an appointment?" He said, "I don't need an appointment, he's my brother." And walked into the bank and was shown in and sat down and visited. Family took precedence over social standing. A schism in the Plymouth Brethren left Dad on one side and his siblings on the other, but it didn't change their feelings for each other. Jo or Eleanor or Lawrence or Jim, Dad could knock on their door and then walk in, feeling at home in their house.

The house that Dad built, 1947. 2 BR up, 1 down, 1 in bsmt.

In the summer of 1947, Dad bought an acre of cornfield in Brooklyn Park Township north of Minneapolis from a farmer, Fred Peterson. We all drove out to watch the bulldozer slice through the corn down into black dirt and gray-green clay. The next week, a big truck with revolving tank lowered a long chute and pumped wet concrete into the pit for the slab and Dad and his brother Lawrence started laying the concrete-block walls and framing partitions of two-by-eights and two-by-fours to make interior walls. I went along to help, but they didn't need me. The two brothers were best friends and worked easily together, mixing mortar in a trough, cutting boards for the forms, the whine of the circular saw, and they didn't notice me walking away, down a dirt road toward the river. It was a good feeling to be on my own. I followed a path that led to a fence with a sign, KEEP OUT, and I climbed over it and there, down a slope, was the great Mississippi, a row of mighty trees along its shore. I walked along the bank to where the water was shallow, flowing over rocks, and I took off my shoes and waded in. I was stunned by the bigness of the Mississippi. I'd never stood in moving water before and there was so much of it. God had created this and I could imagine Him admiring His own work.

I skipped flat stones into the V of the current moving through the rapids, on its way to the Gulf of Mexico. Nobody had shown me how to skip flat stones, it came naturally. I tossed in a chunk of branch, and it floated away heading due south down the middle of America. It was rather majestic, the splash of the rapids, bird cries in the great hush, no sounds of motors or voices. You could imagine it was wilderness. I put on my shoes and walked back the way I had come. Dad and Lawrence paid no attention to me. I had discovered the Mississippi River and stood in it, and I alone knew this. It was a good feeling.

That summer, Dad and Lawrence finished framing up the walls in the basement, did the wiring and plumbing, insulation and drywall. They dug a cesspool, planted a few maple and birch saplings and a row of apple trees, and on Labor Day we left the city and drove out in our Ford, the five of us, towing a trailer full of cast-off furniture, me in the back seat by the window, telephone poles flashing past, and Dad turned down the dirt road and there it was, our concrete bunker, flat roof covered with tar paper, surrounded by mud and scraps of lumber. Mother studied it for a moment, said nothing, and led us down the steps through the laundry room with the water pump and into the kitchen and living room and two little bedrooms. A historic moment. After squatting with relatives through the war years, now we had a home of our own, underground, a hideout. Bunkbeds for Philip and me, a daybed for Judy, a double bed for our parents, nail kegs for chairs, orange crates for cupboards. Kerosene lamps. An icebox in the kitchen, lined with tin, a block of ice in the upper compartment, bought from a vending machine at the lumberyard. Eventually Dad built a house atop the basement with a proper front door and an upstairs with two bedrooms, but we were content in our burrow. Across the dirt road where our mailbox stood was a big cornfield. A few neighbors' houses along the road. Judy and I trotted around and met the Andersons, Coutures, Welches, and Streges. We were going to give them gospel tracts (*Where Will You Spend Eternity?*) but were too shy to hand them out directly, so we slipped them into mailboxes instead. Telling people they were liable to go to hell did not seem like a neighborly thing.

In our dim burrow, the little basement window wells soon filled up with snow that winter as Mother grew so enormous she could barely move from room to room. I asked Dad what was wrong with Mother. He was putting up heating ducts, and he said that she was expecting a baby. He kept hammering as he said it. He said, "They say there may be more than one." He looked worried, but then he always did.

In the spring, Dad planted hills of corn, set tomato plants in and a melon patch. The apple trees were skinny as your finger, and over the years they gave up a bounty that made him feel prosperous. In April, twin baby brothers appeared. They just happened, without explanation, and were laid on Mother's yellow chenille bedspread for relatives to come gaze upon one Sunday afternoon. They were a carnival show. I stood in a forest of legs of aunts and uncles and felt a total eclipse. Mother dressed them in identical outfits. Dad took movies. Hundreds of pictures of them were pasted into scrapbooks. Two boys, Steve and Stan, sitting, lying down, bouncing in their bouncy chairs. They were a wonder of the modern world.

The twins and the sister, Linda, who came along three years later were my liberators. Mother had her hands full, Dad worked two jobs, so nobody ever asked me, "Where are you going?" when I got on my bike, I was free, no supervision. Mother worried about the river after Frankie Renko tipped over in his kayak and drowned, but the river was boys' territory. We were free there. So down to the river I went. Once four neighbor boys and I floated on a truck inner tube, heading for the island with the abandoned stone house, but the tube caught the current and we were swept miles downstream and had to walk home dripping wet. I was missing a shoe. Even so, Mother was too busy to notice. I swam in the river, canoed it, skated on it, holding my jacket open for a sail. I joined up with Kenny and Chuck and Jim and Billy and roamed along the river, shooting each other with cap guns, fighting the Civil War, taking captives, holding trials on charges of treason, enacting deeds of valor, chasing Stonewall Jackson through the valleys of Virginia. The ravine and river shore were a boy sanctuary. No adult ever came around to ask what we were doing. Fathers worked at jobs or worked on their yards, mothers kept house, the woods belonged to us. When we tired of drama, we lay on the shore and discussed great questions. What if you found out you had one day to live? What if you found a big bag of money, thousands of dollars, lying in the ditch? We talked about life on Mars: would the arrival of Martians mean the Bible was untrue? When we're old enough to drive, will cars still run on highways or will they fly through the air? We debated, "Would you rather be blind or deaf if you had to choose?" I chose deafness; I wanted to read. What if the Communists took over and demanded we renounce Jesus Christ or else drink a pitcher of warm spit? We came home for supper and then played Capture the Flag in the dark. Our mothers called our names from far away, and I knew my mother's voice so I knew when she was only warming up and when she really meant it.

In the summer, our kitchen turned into a canning factory, billows of steam from a pressure cooker, and Mother filled Mason canning jars with dill pickles, beets, beans, peas, tomatoes, peeling and slicing and stewing them, apple butter, and corn—every year, a bumper crop of sumptuous sweet corn, feasts of corn, the ears husked as I walked from field to kitchen where the water was boiling. Four minutes in boiling water, then buttered and salted, the freshest hot corn in Hennepin County. This was what Dad had in mind when he bought the land from Mr. Peterson: pure decadent pleasure. Six ears of corn apiece, chewing it off the cob like horses did. Then fresh raspberries for dessert.

I started school the fall after the twins were born. Benson School was a quarter-mile south on the highway, a handsome 1917 brick edifice, named for Elmer Benson, the last Farmer-Labor governor of Minnesota and a supporter of Henry Wallace in 1948, with three classrooms, two grades to each room. We first-graders sat on the sunny side of the room, near the windows, and the second-graders near the wall, and we listened to each other's lessons. Washington and Lincoln stared down at us from the wall, like wife and husband, Washington prim and disapproving, Lincoln sympathetic. High windows looked out at a sandlot field and swing set and monkey bars and grove of oaks. We sat at wooden desks with iron scrollwork on the sides, a shelf below for books, lumps of petrified gum stuck to the bottom of the shelf, initials carved in the sides. Great canvas maps like window shades mounted on the side wall, Europe, The World,

The United States of America. Mrs. Shaver, her white hair tied in a bun like Grandma's, wrote words in big loopy letters on the blackboard, and we copied them, the curve of the tail of the *g* and *j* and *y*, the delicious curves of *b* and *d*, of *m* and *n*. I was a slow reader and she kept me after school to read aloud to her on the pretense that I was doing her a favor, entertaining her as she graded quizzes, so I stood before her desk, book in hand, and read aloud. "Listen to him," she said to Bill the janitor mopping the floor. "Doesn't he have a wonderful voice?" And I swelled with pride. I got remedial help and at the same time felt privileged. That winter, watching a movie in class, I could read the text faster than it scrolled up from the bottom of the screen—"Once upon a time, in a land far away, in a beautiful castle in the forest"—and I took this to mean that I was smart, which came as a relief.

The Darwins, David and Daryl, on the other hand, were hooligans and dumb as could be. They lived in a ramshackle house with rusted-out cars in the yard, and they were eager to beat up other boys. The playground was strictly segregated: the girls played kickball and stoop tag on the grass in front of the school, and the boys played pom-pom-pullaway on the gravel. No teachers watched over us, it was open season, and the Darwins loved to be It and chase boys down and pound on them. In the lavatory, they liked to yank on your pants as you stood at the urinal and make you wet yourself. They liked to go after Ronnie, a boy who was large and slow and fearful and who'd been held back in school, what we called "retarded." They snuck up behind him and punched him in the gut and kicked him when he fell, or they went after Sheldon Herdine, a girlish boy with pretty blond hair. They were evil. Two scrawny knuckleheads with flat noses and small feral eyes, bruised hands, torn clothes, who roamed the playground, eager to jump someone, no provocation needed. I was appalled, but Billy Pedersen stood up for Ronnie and told the Darwins to leave him alone. "Who's going to make us?" they said, and he went at them, fists swinging, and connected with a Darwin's snout and blood appeared and the bully yelped and ran away as his brother back-pedaled toward safety. Men in my family weren't battlers. Mother had told me: "If someone hits you, tell a teacher, don't hit back," but what worked better was to hide. I developed keen peripheral vision to keep track of the bullies' whereabouts so I could avoid them. I became evasive.

I retreated. I never raised my hand in class; Corinne Guntzel did, waved her hand eagerly, I kept my thoughts to myself. I didn't talk in the lunchroom. Once a boy threw up, a big york and a splash, and Bill the janitor had to come with a mop and a bucket of disinfectant and I resolved never to throw up at school: too much attention. And I never did.

Lovely Mrs. Carroll taught third grade, and we were thrilled when she told us she was expecting a baby, and then she was promptly dismissed— pregnancy was grounds for dismissal then—and Mrs. Fern Moehlenbrock took her place, a kindly woman who allowed me to spend recess in the school library, safe from Darwins, reading Richard Halliburton's adventure stories, and *Little House in the Big Woods, The Three Musketeers* (*Sacré bleu!! Mon Dieu!!*), a relief from cruelty. Books became my family, the Ingalls family on the prairie, Heidi, Hans Brinker. I read about Black Beauty, Penrod, Tom Sawyer and Huck Finn. I loved a book, *Runaway Home,* by Elizabeth Coatsworth, about an artist and his wife and their three children who migrate cross-country in a house trailer from Maine down the East Coast and across the South and up to the state of Washington. Every morning, a new place in which to eat breakfast. You make friends and then leave them. Fixing lunch as the landscape slips past. Domestic life and adventure, all in one vehicle. The absolute ideal life. I discovered *Roget's Thesaurus,* which opened up glittering pools of lingo, jargon, argot, patois, officialese, idiom, and phraseology of all sorts and made me feel like a scholar, sage, savant, well-armed to scuffle, skirmish, scrap, confront, and combat any scoundrel or rapscallion. The Darwins knew nothing about synonyms. Billy Pedersen and I vied for supremacy in the weekly spelling bee. I read the dictionary to study spelling, which got me thinking about words. *Sausage* has the word "usage" in it: this interested me. *Librarian* contains a bra. There is a *turd* in Saturday. Billy thought I was smart because I told him that "fatigue" is pronounced *fa-teeg* and not *fat-i-gew.* So he lent me his comic books with ads in back for "love pills" and a pair of binoculars that could see through clothing. A man's eyes bugged out as he stared at a buxom beauty in her undies, beads of sweat popped from his brow. And an ad for Dynamic Tension exercises developed by Charles Atlas, a former 97-pound weakling who became the World's Most Perfectly Developed Man. There was a picture of him and his enormous biceps. He appealed to me because I'd suffered the humiliation of dropping an easy pop-up, running in from right field, the ball in easy reach and then it bounced off my chest. A turning point. It was the summer Grandpa Denham died in a nursing home. I was ten. I was allowed to attend the funeral. My only previous encounter with death was staring at the Egyptian mummy in the Public Library. His funeral, seeing the tears of my aunts, the stolid faces of his sons, George and Jim and Bill, was a high point amid the crushing boredom of that summer, mostly spent sitting on the riverbank, hurling rocks at sticks floating along, too old to play cowboys, too young for everything else. I took an eye test and had to get glasses, and after that I stayed clear of organized sports and stuck to the disorganized; instead of the respect of my peers, I sought the approval of teachers and aunts. My best friend, Billy Pedersen, who wasn't afraid of bullies and was a good speller, caught pop flies one-handed. I didn't know until many years later that a congenital condition called Duane's syndrome causes my eyes to lose focus when looking up, a splaying apart, a divergence, and suddenly everything became clear: I dropped the fly ball, and the humiliation drove me to hide in the library, read books, turn inward, become a writer. I was 78 when Dr. Chaiken told me. Why go to a shrink if you have a great ophthalmologist?

New houses sprang up here and there, but we were still surrounded by truck farms and open country. Every summer, Billy Pedersen and I earned money hoeing corn, picking radishes, strawberries, onions, peas, and pumpkins. We worked in the afternoons so the goods would be fresh for the farmers' market in the morning. The farmer counted my harvest and paid me a dollar, some of which I spent at Yaldich's store on a Pearson's Nut Roll. I didn't get an allowance, I was on my own.

I biked west past Fred Peterson's farm to Victory Memorial Field with the empty hangar and the wrecks of abandoned Piper Cubs, tires flat, engines gone, an Army training camp during the war. Charts and papers strewn in the office. We boys chose our planes and flew them against German Messerschmitts coming in low over the cornfield and blew them out of the air, and then I biked home around suppertime, and Mother looked up and said, "Where were you?" and I said, "Riding my bike." That was sufficient explanation. I went where I felt like going and stayed as long as I liked and nobody needed to know the details. Other boys were interested in baseball, but I was a loner. Riding quietly away from potential problems and disappearing became the formative experience of my boyhood. I was briefly in Scouts at the Izaak Walton Lodge and then quit, having failed to reach Tenderfoot rank. I avoided 4-H entirely. My only organized recreation was the war against Hitler and his Nazis. My city cousins lived with strict supervision under the eyes of grownups, played Little League, wore uniforms, but my friends and I played catch, shot hoops and played HORSE. On hot days we cooled off in the river.

It was rather idyllic. Nobody paid attention. We played hockey on backyard rinks with wheelbarrows for goals and rolled-up magazines for shin pads and we kept playing even when our feet had lost all feeling. No fathers came around to try to coach us. We lived independent of the adult world. Adults had no fun, from what we could see. If someone's parent called your name, it meant you were in trouble, so we kept our distance. And when I was ten, I dared to ride my bike into Minneapolis to the big library downtown. I knew the way because Mrs. Moehlenbrock's class took a field trip to Franklin Creamery to watch milk bottles jiggle along on a conveyor belt to be filled and capped and then to the *Star & Tribune* to watch the giant presses roll out a roadway of paper to be cut and folded, stacked and bound. In the newsroom, pale bespectacled men smoking cigarettes did not look up from their typewriters as we children filed by, and I was impressed by their coolness, ignoring our admiration.

I set out on my bike, a couple bucks in my pocket, without a word to Mother, who was occupied by the little kids, and headed south toward downtown Minneapolis twelve miles away, down Washington Avenue past a busy sawmill and lumberyard, auto salvage yards, printing plants, a barrel factory, a slaughterhouse where men stripped to the waist loaded trucks with beef carcasses hanging on hooks from little wheels on overhead rails, their shoulders to the beeves, flesh on meat. Nobody paid me any attention, a slight boy with wire-rimmed glasses, crew cut, yellow nylon shirt, new jeans, black-and-white Keds. I turned up Hennepin past flashing lights of cocktail lounges and a penny arcade and the Alvin Theater offering GIRLS GIRLS GIRLS in their underwear. I knew the route well; we drove it every Sunday morning on our way to the Grace & Truth Gospel Hall, I sat in the back seat, my hair slicked down, in a pressed white shirt and dark pants and a tie, with a Bible on my lap, memorizing a verse for Sunday School—"The wages of sin is death but the gift of God is eternal life"—and now I looked up Hennepin and saw people earning their wages, men drunk in doorways, loose women, beggars with hats in hand, tough guys, hoodlums, lunatics.

The library was on Hennepin at 10th Street. I leaned my bike against the stone wall and walked in, through a big room full of old buzzards in overcoats poring over newspapers, and rode a cage elevator up to the second floor where an Egyptian mummy lay under glass in a sarcophagus, his belly and innards exposed. I stopped and paid my respects to the deceased and walked up half a flight to a replica of the Declaration of Independence, under glass in a marble case, and up to the third floor and the Children's Reading Room and an enormous table covered with fresh-smelling books. A wealth of books. Stacks of books, piles of books on the floor. A dreamy place to spend an afternoon. I looked at a book I found exciting, something of a biological nature with illustrations, and a librarian said, "Isn't that a little advanced for you?" and I closed the book but resolved to find it again someday. I stayed at the library for hours and rode my bike back on Washington Avenue and was late for supper. I told Mother I'd been playing at Bergstroms' and she was satisfied with that. I had ridden my bike twenty-four miles on busy streets through bad neighborhoods, including Hennepin Avenue, the street of iniquity, and I had gotten away with it. A day to remember. A day to serve as a model for the future.

7

Poverty

ONCE I SLIPPED OUT THE door, nobody knew what I was up to. I rode down to the river or west to the uplands. In winter, we built forts and tromped out a big circle in the snow, with spokes, and played Fox and Geese. We dammed up the spring melt in the ravine. We raced bikes on a dirt road down a hill and practiced skidding and if we fell and skinned our elbows and tore our pants, it was a badge of honor. I roamed freely, and at suppertime, I heard Mrs. Forsberg crying, "DON-ald! JAN-et! JUU-dee!" and the Guntzels ringing a bell for Corinne, and I headed for home and looked in the window and there was my family in the midst of supper, an empty chair waiting for me. They had not noticed my absence. They were busy watching the twins dipping their tiny hands in their Cream of Wheat. I watched them, like a TV show, an interesting cast, Philip next to Dad, Judy next to Mother. They were a story and I was their reader. *Who were these people? How did I come to be in this story?* I wanted to skip ahead and be fifteen.

One morning, sitting on the railing in front of Benson, waiting for the bell to ring, my tormentor asked, "How much money does your dad earn?" I had no idea but I thought up an enormous number and said, "Three thousand dollars!" and he said, "You're poor." He said it as a fact and as I thought it over, he seemed to be right. Mother saving raggedy old clothes in a cardboard box and ripping them into strips to weave into rag rugs. The little storefront we bought our clothes at, run by the old Jew who displayed the goods in cardboard boxes spread out on the floor, and Dad bargained with him. And then there was Mother's fascination with

Gold Bond stamps. You got them with your purchase at SuperValu and pasted them into books, which then you traded for valuable premiums such as TV trays, a brass planter, a lazy Susan. She believed in the Gold Bond motto: *Each purchase pays a dividend, you're saving money as you spend.* Pasting stamps into booklets struck me as a poor person's game.

We rarely ate out but one Sunday after Meeting, we trooped into Bill's House of Good Food on 38th Street, sat down, looked at the menu, Dad looked at Mother, shook his head, and we all stood up and walked out. Too expensive. Other diners stared at us as we piled into the car and drove to the downtown YMCA for the Sunday buffet in the cafeteria, which was cheaper.

We lived in a new house as nice as the neighbors'. On the other hand, every spring, Dad and Philip and I drove north to Lake Superior near the mouth of the Lester River, where a crowd of men in waders walked into the water with landing nets to haul up pounds of smelt, little fish heading in to spawn, and take them home to fillet and freeze for eating over the summer. Poor people food, free for the taking. We used margarine instead of butter. Mother was a mender of clothes, a darner of socks. I wore hand-me-down clothes, some from cousins, or my older brother, and once from my sister Judy, jeans that zipped up the side. I flinched at going to school in girls' jeans. "They're perfectly good jeans," said Mother. "If it bothers you, leave your shirt tails out." (But this shirt was a girl's blouse, with pearly buttons and darts on the side.) Dad bought cans of food at Red Owl marked down 50 percent because the labels had come off. On long car trips, Mother made sandwiches on a cutting board across her lap and passed them back to us children, to save on expenses. One day, coming home from SuperValu, I carried two big glass jugs of milk down the stairs to the back door and tripped and fell, dropped the two jugs, which smashed on the concrete steps, I fell against the door and went straight to my upper bunk and lay in it, sobbing at what I had done. Mother came and put an arm around me and said, "It's okay. You couldn't help it." But I had caused expense to my impoverished family and I wept over it. We were poor; I had destroyed gallons of milk.

And then there was the drama of Christmas. Mother adored Christmas, began her shopping before Thanksgiving, studied the Montgomery Ward catalog, roved around Dayton's bargain basement, and aimed for perfection—of tree, stockings, gifts, and wrapping: the ribbon and bow, the paper precisely folded—because the appreciation of the perfection makes the recipient delay the opening, which prolongs anticipation, which heightens pleasure. Dad, however, looked on the day as a pagan festival modified with Christian images but not blessed by Holy Scripture—we were to celebrate the Lord's death, not His birth. If we had the Lord in our hearts, we would not need these candles to feel reverence. And he dreaded the expense. They enacted this argument year after year, and she wound up in tears ("Why do I go to all this trouble when it isn't even appreciated?") and he put an arm around her and sort of apologized. It was like having Scrooge and Mrs. Cratchit under one roof, married to each other.

Mother had grown up in a family of thirteen children, whose mother died after a long illness when Mother was seven, and Christmas was a burst of festivity in an austere and fearful world. And so the stockings were hung, milk and cookies put out for Santa Claus, and she sat at the piano and we sang "Silent Night." Dad did not sing but he listened. Mother's gifts tended toward the practical, underwear, socks, a tablet and pencils, but one year I got a Lionel model train and an oval of track and was engrossed watching it go around and around through the town I'd made of boxes, and I noticed my mother watching me and the pleasure in her face was that of a child. I unwrapped a miniature garage with gas pumps and a hoist and another one, a printing press with movable rubber type. My father tried to look pleased.

On Lyndale Avenue, in north Minneapolis, stood a large brick building with barred windows and a fence around it, and I got the idea it was the Poorhouse and that we poor people might someday have to live there, as Dad sang in an old song:

> I am growing old and feeble
> And the days of my youth have gone by,
> And it's over the hill to the poorhouse
> I must wander alone there to die.

And it stuck in my mind that prison might be our destination.

One summer, Dad fell off his cousin Harold's barn roof while nailing shingles and landed headfirst on concrete and fractured his skull, which eventually led to spinal meningitis, and he was never so agile or able again. The three younger kids were farmed out to relatives, and we three older ones boarded the school bus in the morning and sat down to a quiet supper with Mother at night. She didn't say much, but we knew that it was bad. She warned us that there might not be Christmas this year.

One Sunday, at Meeting, I noticed a shoebox on a table in the coatroom, wrapped in white paper, a slot in the top, and marked "For the Keillor Family," and I felt ashamed to be the object of charity. And then Christmas began to appear. A smaller tree than usual, a few presents, the smell of baking. And then our father came home. Pale, withdrawn, slow afoot, holding onto railings, but still himself. He lay on the sofa, a blanket over him, and Mother sat at the piano and played "Silent night, holy night, all is calm, all is bright," and we sang and he was moved by the beauty of the song and wept a little, and Mother knelt by the sofa and lay her head on his chest and wept with him.

Forty years later, thanks to a best-selling book, I embraced extravagance, hoping to expunge the memory of walking out of Bill's House of Good Food. I bought box seats at the opera, a pair of emerald earrings at Tiffany's, paintings, rare books, we dined at La Reserve and La Côte Basque and flew to London and Jenny and I stayed in a suite at Claridge's where the bellmen wear tails like footmen of the Duke of Earl's and the chambermaids treat you like movie stars, the price of which would have brought my dad to the point of physical collapse. Jenny enjoyed it, she who knew actual poverty from her freelance years—she loved opera so elegant costumery and bowing and curtsying were right up her alley. In one week, I made peace with the years of potato picking, home haircuts, jeans that zipped up the side, meatloaf suppers, and Melmac dishes on TV trays bought with Gold Bond stamps. Poverty was not our problem. We weren't poor, only frugal, and my childhood sense of deprivation and Brethrenly strictures became a golden thread in the Lake Wobegon saga that paid for the voyage and the lovely hotel room. You create a fiction based on your family's pinching of pennies and it appeals to a readership that experienced the same and you use the proceeds to get a hotel room that makes your wife happy: there is a rightness about it.

All feelings of deprivation vanished when our family gathered around our Zenith radio, and the dial lit up and we listened to WCCO, the Good

Neighbor station, and KSTP, home of the *Sunset Valley Barn Dance* on Saturday nights with Pop Wiggins ("Says here that radio's gonna take the place of newspapers. I doubt it. Y'can't swat a fly with a radio."). The horror shows with footsteps on gravel as the monster approached the deserted cabin in the woods where the lost children had taken shelter, whimpering in terror as the hairy beast tore the door off its hinges. Radio could turn your blood cold, space aliens invading a small town and eating somebody's grandpa but mostly we stuck to comedy. It was the comedians whom Mother loved. I already knew about horror from gospel preachers, descriptions of eternity in the Lake of Fire: what was remarkable was George Burns and Gracie Allen (*I got a full-length mirror for my father so he wouldn't catch pneumonia. Oh? Before, he only had a half-length mirror so when he went outside he forgot his pants.*) and Jack Benny, the cheapskate who sawed on his violin and claimed to be 39 (*Mary and I have been married forty-seven years and never have we had an argument that made us consider divorce. Murder, yes, but divorce, no.*) and Slim Jim and the Vagabond Kid singing "Yonny Yonson's Wedding" in a soft Scandihoovian accent.

O the meatballs and the herring and the aquavit and beer
And for Lutherans, don't you know, it was a festive atmosphere
And when I cut the cheese, O they'll be talking 'bout that all year
'Twas a heckuva time at Yonny Yonson's wedding.

I raised my hands for silence and then I told a joke,
'Bout Ole and Lena, not meant for decent folk.
And Pastor Larson laughed so hard I thought he'd have a stroke.
And he blew some tapioca out his nostrils.

As Brethren we were to abstain from worldly pleasures and cling to the promise of His return, but we came home from Meeting and I lay on my belly in my Sunday clothes, reading the funny papers, Dick Tracy and Little Iodine, Jiggs and Maggie, Skeezix and the gang on Gasoline Alley. They didn't proclaim the gospel but I loved them still.

We had true saints in our family, beautiful Aunt Ruby in her wheelchair, stricken by multiple sclerosis, delighted to see us. I felt sorry for her but Mother told me, "Those who sow in tears shall reap in joy." Uncle

Duncan and Aunt Ruby had preached the gospel, driving across Canada in a van with Now is the Day of Salvation and Prepare to Meet Thy God in large letters on it, and now here she was, holding out her arms to us. Mother played the piano and we children sang to her, "Heavenly Sunshine" and "I'm on the Faith Line," and Ruby clapped her hands. The other saint was Aunt Margaret, whose husband had betrayed her with a schoolteacher and she accepted her plight with gladness of heart. Brethren believed that suffering purifies the spirit—those whom God loveth, He chasteneth—give thanks for tribulation—masochism as the road to righteousness—the deep root of Minnesota stoicism. I worried about polio and didn't want to catch it. I prayed to be spared. It came on suddenly, a weakness in the limbs, then you were paralyzed, maybe needed to be placed in an iron lung to respirate. One should stay away from beaches and swimming pools, breeding grounds for polio. Avoid crowds. The best prevention: stay by yourself. Which was easy for me, being a loner. You won't catch polio sitting in the basement reading a stack of books from the library. And I didn't.

8

Aunts

William and Marian's brood in chronological order, Grace is third from right.

MY MOTHER, GRACE, WAS THE tenth of thirteen children of William and Marian Denham, who emigrated from Glasgow in 1906, and the signal event in my mother's childhood was the death of her mother in 1923 when Grace was seven. The youngest child, Dolly, died soon thereafter. Aunt Jean wrote in her family history ode:

> *Things didn't go well for Mother*
> *Who had a setback and got an infection*
> *It went all through her system; she was ill over a year . . .*
>
> *We thought Mother was coming along pretty well*
> *But blood poisoning set in and she went to be with the Lord.*
> *We were a saddened, subdued household.*

About a month after God had called Mother home
The family was ready to sit down to dinner—
"Oh, where's little Dolly?" someone asked
And we called her and went out to find her.

We found her asleep on the couch on the porch
A hot little girl, face puffy and red—we carefully put her to bed
The doctor was called, when he saw her he said
'Twas a case of scarlet fever . . .

In just a few days, little Dolly got worse
As spinal meningitis complicated her illness
She became unresponsive and just semiconscious
And a few days later she fell asleep
And was gently carried by the angels to Jesus.

In later years Grace had no memory of her mother, which troubled her deeply. She remembered the death of Dolly but could not picture Marian in her mind. She studied a photograph of herself, six years old and seated on a photographer's pony, her mother standing, haggard, nearby, and Mother tried to recall the sound of her voice, the smell of her hair, her touch. Grace was raised by her sisters in a house of dark furniture, daily chores, no daydreaming, but she and Elsie and Jean had some lively times together, chattering and laughing, and they stayed close all their lives. It was a Brethren home, but Elsie and Grace snuck away to football games and even to movies. We often went to Elsie's or Jean's for Sunday dinner, seldom to any others'.

The signal event in Dad's life was the death by drowning of his cousin Joe Loucks in the Rum River when Dad was a teenager and, with other cousins, tried to rescue Joe and could not, a playful moment turned terrifying, and several of the boys, including Dad, were moved to confess Jesus as their Savior in the aftermath.

The crucial fact of my childhood was that I had eighteen aunts, a rich and varied plenitude of auntliness; wherever I looked, there were two or three of them, smiling down on me. They comforted me and excused my shortcomings and praised my letter writing and my penmanship. They brought me up to be mannerly, helpful, to not be a lazybones but not a braggart either, to avoid bad language, the vulgar kind and the ungrammatical. They listened to me when I spoke up. My uncles did not engage in conversation with children; they formed a fortress of moral authority and I shrank in their presence. The aunts, on the other hand, paid attention to me from the time I could form words, so naturally I gravitated toward them. They asked what I was up to and I told them—reading books, riding my bike, and writing stories. "About what?" they said. "About our family," I said. I liked to imagine what my greatgreat-greatgreatgreat-grandfather Elder John Crandall was like in Puritan Massachusetts in the 1600s. Grandma said he could speak Iroquois and that he was a friend to Indians so I imagined him in the woods in deerskin leggings and breech-cloth and a blanket and dancing with them around a campfire.

My uncles held to strict principles and you went against them at your peril; if you diverged from the path, you were watched carefully. Women forgave, over and over. They believed that, more than appearances, what matters is what's in your heart. Some men ridiculed women for their delicacy, but Keillor women were farm girls, had driven horses and handled guns and slaughtered chickens, they showed great *capability*. In 1942, the year I was born, a violent storm hit Anoka and our cousin Florence Hunt ran out of her house with a baby in hand as a tornado blew the roof off and blew mother and child into the limbs of a tree. Thenceforth, Anoka High School teams became the Anoka Tornadoes to suggest devastation. Florence was a strong, confident farm woman like my aunts and had a cheery disposition, and once she'd been blown into a tree, she was liberated from anxiety. If she'd ever been a worrier, she wasn't one anymore.

My aunts thought I was of interest, so I gravitated to their kitchens, not to the garage or barn, and I chopped as they cooked, I dried as they washed, I told them what I'd read and seen and done, and they paid attention. I said, *Our neighbor Mr. Birk doesn't believe in God. He says that when you die you go in a hole in the ground and that's it. He drinks beer. He hit his wife once and Mother went next door and told him to stop or she'd call the police. Our neighbor on the other side, Mr. Couture, shot our dog Skeezix because he got in their garbage, and Dad had to go over and get his body off their front lawn and bring it home and bury it in the garden. The Andersons live on our road and they fight all the time and he gets drunk and their mom is extremely fat and I saw her underwear on the clothesline once and it's size 48. The Welches are rich: they have two cars. They've been to Europe. I've never been in their house. Behind us are the Forsbergs. She has the loudest voice of anybody: you can hear her a quarter-mile away. Les Michaelson is my age and he is an only child. The other only children near us are Dianne Mattson and Jim Olmscheid and Corinne Guntzel. Her family owns a horse and a cabin up near Brainerd. She said I can go there someday if I learn to swim. It's lonely being an only child, they watch you closely all the time, I wouldn't like it.*

I tried to amuse them as they worked. I felt useful, talking to them. They liked to hear stories about school, what we studied, so I obliged. Aunt Eleanor said, "We are all islands in the sea of life and seldom do our peripheries touch," but my aunts were an archipelago that my island nestled among comfortably. I wrote her a poem: *God smiled down on Aunt Eleanor/Who, guided by Him, did quite well in her/Choice of a man, though he couldn't be called rich/Was wise in the Lord, Uncle Aldridge.* She had a passion for gardening, raised Angus steers for meat, was an accomplished letter writer, had a good throwing arm and could swing a bat, and out of the goodness of her heart tended to a bachelor farmer neighbor. Aunt Josephine was tall and majestic, black hair tied in a bun, the handsomest of the family, who tended her flock of chickens and her immaculate garden and sang as she hung the wet laundry on the line, "It Is Well with My Soul." Bessie was the Keillor family historian and knew everyone going back centuries. Aunt Margaret told me I was her favorite nephew. Ruby wanted to hear all about our car trips out West, so I stood in front of her and described Montana and Idaho. Elsie was ever lighthearted, Mother's confidante, who snuck away with her to movies and football games. Aunt Frannie would swim with us in the Rum River and dive underwater and stand on her head, her two legs high in the air. Marion spoke with a Scottish lilt and had a pool table in her basement. Jean wrote poems. They all liked to tell stories. Eleanor wrote letters in a minimalist style all her own. She wrote, not long before her death:

> *Dear Gary,*
> *You must have given up on me a long time ago. You wrote me*
> *a letter last winter and never had an answer and now another*

and I'm sure you have given up hope. Letter writing is something that I can put off forever. And I am embarrassed writing to a writer. This I can truthfully say, that I think of you much more often than I write.

I would enjoy very much a visit with you this month but the truth of the matter is that I have a husband. He is perfectly capable of taking care of everything so long as I am here but if I so much as leave the house, he falls apart at the seams.

I spent the week primarily in hauling wood and stacking it, which makes me feel like an ant trying to move the beach. I am moving wood because I am selling it. We are inundated with wood and it will not remain in a saleable state much longer and Mother was half Pennsylvania Dutch and she brought us up to abhor waste. At the same time we butchered the six roosters that have been waiting since spring. They were not chickens that I had raised so I had no particular attachment to them and I had not trained them so they were hard to catch. We put them in jars hoping to use them for chicken and dumplings. The bony pieces are dedicated to broth for persons suffering from colds.

We had a very strong wind on Thursday, which took the remainder of the willow tree. There was one gust that went through here that I thought was going to take us, too. I was feeding the animals and heard a roar coming through the woods, and I didn't know whether to run for the house or step into the barn. I did take shelter in the barn until it quieted down a little.

We had an experience the day the wind died down. The doorbell rang one noon and when I went to the door there was a young bushy-haired, bushy-bearded man with a gun in a holster on his hip and a shotgun cradled in his arms. In the split second that I had to consider my options, I wondered if I should slam the door and lock it but then I said to myself, "Oh, don't be a coward!" I walked out the door and asked if I could help him. He was furious and said, "You shot my dogs!" Of course, we hadn't but it was next to impossible to convince him. He finally cooled down enough to tell me that he had followed

*their tracks and the tracks came into our yard. Eventually he
settled for trying to follow their tracks further. I was not impressed with his intelligence—he lives up on the corner in that
old schoolhouse that was converted to a house.*

*I feel I have not covered much ground in this letter but it is
suppertime and I must stop. Thank you for the book you sent
that defines old English terms. I read it and realized how old I
am because I knew most of them. We have had numerous very
favorable reports of your lovely wife, Jenny. Someday you will
stop running around and Jan and I will come to your house
and introduce ourselves.*

Very much love from your Aunt Eleanor

Her letters were a precious gift—a busy woman taking time to pen an
account of her doings—and so the letter (or column, essay, blog) became
my favored genre. Writing columns for *Time, Salon,* the New York *Times,*
or "Talk" pieces for *The New Yorker* or a Lake Wobegon monologue, they
all originated in the pleasure of an envelope from her and the page within,
the writing style in which I could hear her voice. My uncles didn't tell
stories lest they betray weakness or frivolity. They discussed the correct
way to lay concrete or the meaning of the verse in Deuteronomy where
it says God will set us above all the nations of the earth. They were not
comedians. Uncle Don was the exception; he'd tiptoe into the bedroom
where his boys and I lay in the dark, and he leaned over us and whispered, *I'm going to find out who's sleeping and who's playing possum,* and he
put his head down by mine and growled like a bear, and it was thrilling.
Aunts wanted to be friends. Aunt Ina once told me how, at age 21, she
took the streetcar to a Ford dealership on Harmon Place in Minneapolis
and bought a Model A and, though she had never driven before in her
life, she and two girlfriends drove from Minneapolis to Yellowstone Park
on dirt roads across South Dakota and Wyoming, saw the geysers and
the mountains, sold the car, and came back by train, and then she took
a job in an office and settled down as a proper young lady. The story
was counter to Denham cautiousness, about allowing yourself a dramatic
adventure and I was honored to be confided in. Mother and Elsie, fixing

Sunday dinner, told me about the summer of 1931 when they took the trolley up to Anoka to the Keillor farm, and Elsie and Mother both were taken with young John, eighteen, and they were fifteen and sixteen, and admired his handsome good looks and his kindness, and they recalled his fun-loving sisters, the ailing father, the ride on the hayrack behind the big horses, the odd house of fireproof concrete, the brook nearby, and suddenly it occurred to me that Elsie, not Grace, might've won John and then who would I be? The beauty of the story and how it might've turned out otherwise.

Uncles did not tell such stories. They didn't confide in me. Why should they? I was a child, I knew nothing. But I wanted to hear how they happened to meet my aunts and had fallen in love, the whole story, leaving nothing out, and now I wonder if maybe I should've asked.

Aunt Ruth was a Saturday night regular at our house. She had no children, so she treasured her nieces and nephews. We sat by her ankles as she told about Thomas Keillor, at the advanced age of 45, leaving Yorkshire, taking his wife, Mary Ann, and twelve-year-old son John to sail to Nova Scotia on an overcrowded ship that was under-provisioned, the ship's owners knowing that many passengers would die anyway and why carry food for the doomed? They wound up near Dorchester, New Brunswick, and intermarried with the Crandalls, who had fled from Connecticut when violence broke out there in 1776. They had taken the side of law and order, which was the losing side. With other Loyalists, they left their houses and property and fled north. Thomas Keillor died three years after landing in Canada: the perilous voyage was for his children's sake, not his own. His son married a Trenholm girl who bore a son, Robert, whose son William had a son James Crandall Keillor who became my grandfather.

James was a hewer of timber in a shipyard in Chatham, New Brunswick, had been hewing since he was fifteen and was skilled at the craft when he got word from his sister Mary in Anoka that her husband, Mr. Hunt, was dying and he came on the train by way of Albany, arriving just in time to attend Mr. Hunt's funeral, and so his course was decided for him. He didn't care for farming, but he switched from shipbuilding to farming, helped raise Mary's three children, and might've returned to shipbuilding, but he was entranced by the schoolteacher across the road. Dora Powell was a progressive and a Methodist, like her father, and she believed that every woman should have an education and a career, so that she would never have to depend on a man. She had begged her father to take her and her twin sister, Della, to Chicago to the Columbian Exposition of 1893 to see the wonders there, the moving walkway and Ferris wheel and motion picture theater, but they were only thirteen and he thought that was too young. She and Della had learned Morse code so they could share answers in school and they became two of the first female railroad telegraphers in the United States. At the Anoka depot, they had posed as one person named D. Powell. One worked the morning shift, came home for lunch, changed clothes with her twin who then worked the afternoon. In her early twenties, she came to teach in the school across the road, and she boarded with James and his sister Mary. James served on the school board. She liked that he knew history. She admired his ancestor Elder John Crandall, the Baptist cleric in colonial Rhode Island who befriended the Narragansett Indians and learned their language, and Prudence Crandall the abolitionist and women's suffrage

Dora and Della, 1886. They learned Morse Code so they could talk in class.

activist, so his heredity passed muster. She was 25, he was 45, they married in St. Francis.

Grandma told Aunt Ruth: *He was a tall handsome man with a brushy mustache and I was told he was part Indian and I liked that. He was very good to Mary and he raised her three children and then he started paying attention to me. He crossed over the road to the schoolhouse after the children had left and followed me around washing the blackboards and clapping the erasers, and I moved away from him but not so fast that he couldn't catch up and then he kissed me. I hadn't been kissed like that before and back then it meant something. I agreed to go with him to town and get married, and as soon as he told Mary, then we got in his wagon and went away and did that.*

Mary Hunt moved to her sister's up the road, and James and Dora came back to his house, and he carried her into the house and left the horses standing hitched to the wagon, their reins hanging down, until morning. He had attended to his sister's family for twenty years and now he intended to start his own. He doted on Grandma. She was the only farm wife around with a serving girl to help her with chores. He called her "My Girl" and sang to her in a clear tenor voice and until he was very old carried her up the stairs at night to bed. He fathered eight children. He bought the first Model T in Ramsey Township. He drove it home and went to turn in at the yard and forgot what he was dealing with, and he pulled back hard on the wheel and shouted "Whoa!" and the car went in the ditch and he had to hitch up his horses and pull himself out. He was laughing when the car went into the ditch, and he was laughing as he towed it out.

She told about Grandpa Keillor rousing his brood from their warm beds on a winter night and bundling them up and leading them up the road to the pasture to see, on a nearby ridge under the full moon, a silver wolf, sitting on his haunches, gazing back at them. She was scared and asked, "What if the wolf attacks us?" and he said, "He won't so long as we stay close together." She told about the day the house burned down—the children looking out the schoolhouse windows and seeing their house in flames. Ruth was home sick from school and she and little Eleanor heard Grandma cry out and ran downstairs, and one wall of the house was in flames. Ruth pumped a kettle of water and threw it at the flames as Grandma hauled an armload of bedding and books and pictures out on the lawn and was about to go back for Grandpa's desk drawers, but he grabbed her, he'd run up from the field, and he wouldn't let her go back in. The children formed a bucket brigade, but it was too late. A chimney fire. "I never saw him so sad. He and the neighbors shoveled out the debris and Uncle Allie built us a new fireproof house with concrete walls, covered in stucco. Mother missed the old house so much. But Dad wanted one that was fireproof."

Philip and Judy and I lay on the floor mesmerized. The house fire was part of a Keillor saga that begins with James Hunt's death from TB and James Keillor's journey to help his sister, whereupon Grandma Dora leaves her job as a railroad telegrapher in Anoka when her twin sister, Della, marries Frank, and Dora takes a teaching job at that country school in Ramsey Township and boards with Mr. Keillor and his sister Mary. She sits across the table and they talk night after night about all sorts of things and he chases her around the schoolhouse and kisses her and thus our family gains the sensible influence of progressive Methodism to temper the Brethren idealism. Everything I knew about our history came from my aunts, nothing from my uncles.

Aunt Elsie wrote:

Granny McKay had lived with her son Jim for years who'd been seeing a lady, Louise, but felt he couldn't leave Granny. He was Christian Science. He was going to be best man at George's wedding and then suddenly Jim died and everyone felt so awful that he missed out on marriage. Mary made a blueberry pie for his funeral and your mother and I were doing dishes that morning and taking our time as we always did, that's how your mother and I became so close, I washed and she dried because she was taller and could reach the cupboards. She sat on the windowsill, drying a platter, and the blueberry pie was sitting on the sill, cooling, and she knocked it off and it crashed to smithereens and she felt so bad, but Mary just made another one. We went to his funeral and afterward we snuck away to a movie, which was strictly forbidden, Dad didn't want us to set foot in a theater, but we enjoyed the movie until there was a lightning storm in the movie and we spotted our brother George

*sitting two rows away, and we snuck out and never saw the
end. Your mother was seeing your dad around then. Our dad
had pulled her out of high school because he thought she was
boy crazy and sent her to live with Jean and Les and she went
into nurse's training and got a job for the Quinlan family, who
owned the department store, taking care of their old uncle who
couldn't walk. He told her one morning he wanted the Journal
so she ran down to the corner to get a copy of the Journal and
came back and he'd wet his pants. He wanted a urinal. Oh,
she had stories. That's why she loved nursing, you got to know
people. But mostly she talked about your dad.*

There is a whole novella in that paragraph with my tall mother drying a
platter and knocking a pie off the sill, and going to the forbidden movie
after Jim's funeral, and looking for the newspaper when the man needed
to pee. No uncle of mine would've written a letter like that, admitting
to having tasted the pleasures of life. Life was about struggle, fidelity,
devotion to the Lord, not about conversation and jokes and going to the
movies.

My aunts were circumspect, but if you asked pointed questions, they
would tell you that Aunt Margaret's husband, Paul, had abandoned her
and run away with their kids' schoolteacher in Cottage Grove. Margaret
sat in front of me in Sunday morning Meeting, and Paul's sisters Leila and
Pluma sat across the room, facing us. If I leaned to one side, I could see
the three of them in a triptych, the whole story. Aunt Margaret bore her
trials without complaint, putting her faith in the Lord. After she died, her
two surviving children, now mature adults, located their father and his
lover in Seattle and made a trip there to grant him their forgiveness. He
wept when he heard of his younger boy's death by drowning and Margaret's hardship. This was a haunting story, like the house fire story and the
death of Joe Loucks. But I also heard stories about Halloween pranks that
my uncles may have been involved with, or not, but the aunts described
them in some detail, a story about boys disassembling a Model T Ford and
reassembling it on the roof of a machine shed, and a story about tipping
over outhouses on neighboring farms with the farmer inside the outhouse,
trousers around his ankles, sitting on the hole, his bowels opening, as the

vandals pushed the outhouse over on its door so that the victim had to evacuate through the hole he'd been emptying his bowels through and perhaps landing in the pit on top of his own waste products. It was cruelty beyond my imagination, carried out as a joke, but only permissible on October 31st. Any other day, you'd be thrown in jail.

Some stories were out of bounds: Uncle Lew had been in trouble at the Post Office for stealing money, and the family loved him dearly and kept his wrongdoing secret so that we children could love him too and not judge him. And then of course there was my parents' late marriage, a secret carefully kept for sixty years, no whispers leaked.

The only uncle who told stories was Lew, Grandma's brother, and he was more like an aunt in that way. He visited us, bringing boxes of sugar wafers and bags of peanut brittle from his company, Ada Claire Candies, named for his wife. He loved to tell about his grandfather David Powell, a restless farmer, born in Pennsylvania soon after the Louisiana Purchase, married Martha Ann Cox, they started having babies and, though a farmer, he kept moving the family west, to Ohio, Michigan, Illinois, Iowa, Missouri, begetting ten children all told, including a set of triplets, and he then took off with a group of men he organized in 1859 to look for gold in Colorado, leaving his wife and children behind. It was the nineteenth century when irresponsibility was called *pioneering*. A reporter for a Chicago paper followed them from Iowa to the Mormon Trail to Laramie and then into the mountains and the land of the Cheyenne. David wrote in his diary:

> *June 2nd: Hard rain & wind storm. Rain poured in torrents. Cattle stampede & we had to be on horseback all night. Awful night. Men all tired and want to leave. Horses all gave out & men refused to do anything. Wet all night. We found the cattle all together near camp at daybreak. Worked all day hard in the river trying to make the cattle swim & did not get one over. One in our party drowned (Mr. Carr) & several had narrow escapes and I among the number. Had to turn back sick and discouraged. Am not homesick but heartsick. Have not got the blues but am in a Hell of a fix.*

He got to Fort Collins, Colorado, and then to Denver, where thousands

of prospectors had arrived before him and all claims were taken, so he
gave up on gold and took up politics, and got himself elected mayor of
Canon City and then representative to the Colorado Assembly, where
he helped write the state constitution, but that didn't satisfy him. He
returned to Missouri to sweet-talk Martha Ann into moving west. She
would not be persuaded, but she still loved him and bore one more child,
whereupon David headed for Oklahoma Territory and settled on a claim
near the Cherokee Strip. He wrote to his children:

> *I built a house 21 x 24, one-story of pickets, shingle roof, 6 windows
> and 2 doors, divided and will be when finished one like my house in
> MO. Dug a well 20 feet deep, plenty of water, and put up a stable for
> 10 head of stock, covered with hay. I am very comfortable in OK. We
> would like to see you all once more in this world, but it is hard to tell.
> It is not likely that we shall all meet again. If the Strip is open up for
> settlement this summer, you may come down and take a claim as I am
> a mile and a quarter from it. If I intend to take a claim joining OK.
> There is fine land on Turkey Creek joining OK. We are 5 miles NW
> on the west side of Turkey Creek, Sec. 5, Town 18, R8. Hennessey will
> make us a fine town I think as there is in OK.*

And there David died, in the Land Rush of 1889. He could not stop
himself, he rode to the Strip, found a tract of land to claim, leaned up
against a tree to defend it against claim-jumpers, and died a few days
later, at the age of 62.

This was a long story, and Lew was a slow talker and loved to digress. I
heard him tell the whole story twice, both times exhausting. By the time
he got to Fort Collins, I wished David would give up and go home to
Missouri. But I loved the line "I do not have the blues but I am in a hell
of a fix." Uncle Lew never swore but when a man has tried to drive cattle
across a big river in a raging storm, he has a right to. It was clear to me
that David was in the grip of an obsession bordering on insanity—selling
his farm every few years and packing up the wagons and heading west
over the objections of his sensible wife—and so his children grew up with
a desperate craving for stability. Wherever along the route they reached
maturity, in Ohio, Michigan, Illinois, Iowa, or Missouri, they stayed put.

PLOP. But David refused to settle and saw something brighter ahead and set out to find it. This was not the lesson our parents tried to teach us. I admired his craziness and suspected Uncle Lew did too by the fact he told the story in detail, no comment. He let the story speak for itself: *Don't be afraid to take big chances. Live boldly. Don't mind what others say. Do what you feel you were put here to do.*

Denhams were different. Grandpa Denham grew up in a Glasgow tenement, married Marian, and sailed away to America to raise his thirteen children. He was a bookkeeper for the Soo Line Railroad, wore starched shirts with satin armbands and black high-top shoes. He was strict and watched his children closely for signs of worldliness. I remember him as a fretful old man warning children not to dash out in the street, but there was more to him than that. I was glad to come across a picture of him hoeing strawberry beds in a large garden, looking up at the camera and grinning. This is Anabel Wright's garden near Hastings. Grandpa's wife, Marian, had died a few years before, and now Grandpa is courting this tall cheery woman who owns a farm. He takes the train out to Hastings, and she picks him up in her electric and he hoes her garden, grinning at the lady holding the camera, Anabel. That is romance on Grandpa's face. He hopes to marry her and he does. A man who fathers thirteen children is a man of enthusiasm. The picture is a revelation.

9

You Are Welcome

We don't drink liquor or come near it:
The body is the temple of the Holy Spirit.
No movies, dancing, or libations,
We get our thrills from revelations.
The Lord will come, perhaps tomorrow,
Bring an end to all our sorrow.
We'll rise to meet Him in the air
And you guys won't be there.
Everything we say is reliable,
We have read it in the Bible.
Rapture's coming in a minute,
Sorry but you won't be in it.

EVERY SUNDAY MORNING, WE DRESSED up and drove to Meeting, passing the billboards—I had learned to read by saying *Murray's Silver Butter Knife Steak for Two* and *Ewald's Golden Guernsey Milk*—the heads of two light brown cows protruding from the sign—and came to the Gospel Hall in Minneapolis and walked up the steps, past the sign that said:

GRACE AND TRUTH GOSPEL HALL
  LORD'S DAY
Worship Meeting 10:30 A.M.
Sunday School 9:30 A.M.
Gospel Meeting 7:45 P.M.

YOU ARE WELCOME

Theoretically you are welcome, but as an outsider, you'd be an amazing phenomenon, like a blind man holding sparklers, and we'd have to figure out how to deal with you. Inside, past the cloakroom, was a large plain white meeting room, no imagery, no crosses or candles, with chairs arranged in six rectangles facing the little table in the middle with a pitcher of wine and a loaf of bread, covered with a white cloth. Men in dark suits, women in dark modest dresses and head coverings, no lipstick or jewelry, everyone sitting exactly where they sat every Sunday. Our family in a row behind Grandpa and Grandma Anabel, with Aunt Ina and Bill and Marion, and Aunt Margaret, Shirley, cousin Roger. Sun streaming in the big windows, long silences as the Saints wait upon the leading of the Spirit. We sing from *The Little Flock* hymnal—no musical accompaniment, because no pianos are mentioned in Scripture. (No cars or washing machines either, I point out, and Mother gives me a look.)

There used to be more of us. Our numbers shrank in 1947 with the split between the Anoka assembly and us over a question regarding separation principles, but the root of the split was a rivalry between two preachers, Brother Ames and Brother Booth, who couldn't bear the sight of each other. Two male buffalo locked horns. We were Booth Brethren, and Anoka cut us off from fellowship and one Sunday morning, with some Anoka people in our midst, Jim and Dorothy Hunt and Florence and Harold and Rozel and David, our relatives, and people weeping, we sang, *God be with you till we meet again. By His counsels, guide, uphold you*, and we parted. Anoka thrived and grew, thanks to loving elders, and Minneapolis shrank, thanks to a blockhead elder whose bullying drove the younger members from the flock. But Mother couldn't leave her family, and Dad couldn't leave Mother. Aunt Eleanor was Dad's best friend, and though they were on opposite sides they were even closer after the split. They never argued about it. They sat in her kitchen and laughed and laughed—he was a changed man around her, not the silent man he was with the Minneapolis people—and clearly, family was more important than correct doctrine. Years later, our assembly having dwindled to a handful, our Gospel Hall was sold to a charismatic Black church. Our mournful remnant disappeared and the Holy Spirit moved in, and there was rapturous singing and shouting, people crying out Alleluias and Amens.

After Meeting, the eight of us ride over to Don and Elsie's for Sunday dinner, a big adventure because they have a TV and we do not. I'd seen TV—at school, we watched the inauguration of Dwight D. Eisenhower and the coronation of Queen Elizabeth II—but we couldn't have a TV "because it's Hollywood," Mother explained. In 2005, when the movie *A Prairie Home Companion* held its premiere in St. Paul, Mother was given a seat of honor in the balcony. I sat behind her, and I could see she was enjoying the movie. I leaned forward and said, "I hope Grandpa Denham didn't see you walking into this theater," and she told me she had done it as a favor to me, but she laughed. Eventually, everything becomes humorous. Almost everything.

Uncle Don didn't care about movies; he was a football fan, having played in high school in Wausau, and the Green Bay Packer game started around noon on Sunday, so the TV got turned on the instant they arrived home from Meeting, and Don took his place on the couch. He got intensely involved with the game and tended to move laterally with the play. Sometimes he crouched up close. If the Packer quarterback faded back to pass on third down, short yardage, Don threw himself at the screen: *You gotta be kidding.* When a ref called Holding on a Packer lineman, Don rose to his feet. "Holding! You call that holding? He stuck out his hand and the other guy ran into it. Open your eyes!" he yelled, and then he demonstrated to me how holding differs from sticking out your hand as the other guy runs into it. My dad sat quietly nearby, ignoring him: he cared nothing about football but was obliged to sit with us males in the living room; the kitchen was a sanctum of sisterhood. So he sat, looking at the paper, which didn't interest him either. He liked Uncle Don but didn't understand how a grown man could get excited about a *game.* I, on the other hand, was delighted to see a Brethren man in a state of excitation about anything. Grim solemnity was the standard, but here was Uncle Don, who an hour before stood up in Meeting and prayed a long Brethrenly prayer, now yelling at a referee on TV.

Aunt Elsie put the pies in the oven, apple and lemon meringue, and the pot roast came out, and she made gravy, and when dinner was ready, if the Packers were on the march, dinner might need to be delayed for a few minutes. Then we trooped in around the table and the TV sound was turned down as Uncle Don thanked the Lord for the food before us and for His death on Calvary's cross, and we dug in, while Elsie quietly disparaged her cooking so as to ward off compliments. The potatoes were dry, she said, and the meat overdone, the creamed corn too salty, but of course the dinner was sheer perfection. If the Packers took possession, if they came within field-goal range, Don kept an ear out and was apt to slide over a few feet to where he could see the screen. He was a man besieged by conflicting forces. A perfect dinner, powerful Packer loyalties, his wife's patient disregard of the game, the holiness of the Lord's Day, and wretched officiating.

Once a month, Brethren gathered to mail gospel tracts to the survivors of people listed in the obituaries, telling them they should accept Jesus as their Savior or else wind up in the Lake of Fire. I pointed out to Mother that this seemed cruel, to suggest to the grieving that their loved ones had maybe wound up in hell, but she felt it was an act of mercy. I asked if we knew of any people who'd been converted by the tracts we mailed. "It's not for us to know," she said, "it's for God to know." Our next-door neighbor, Mr. Birk, was an atheist who said, "When you're dead, you're dead. They stick you in a hole and you don't come out. Anything else is a fairy tale." (Though when Mrs. Birk said she wanted a new couch for the living room, he said, "People in hell want ice water.") Dad was friendly with him, but they only talked about carpentry and cars, not the Last Judgment. It was Mother who once went next door and testified to him about the Lord and he laughed at her. She stood in his doorway, hands on her hips, and told him that Jesus had died for his sins. I was impressed by her gumption. Mother was moved by Mrs. Birk's having to endure her husband's drunken tirades and wanted him to know that God was watching, and so was Grace Keillor.

One morning in late May, the phone rang in our upstairs hall and Mother set down her clothes basket and answered. There was a long silence and then she said, "Oh no." My cousin Roger Hummel had drowned in Lake Minnetonka. He was seventeen, about to graduate from Central High that week, a tall boy with a crew cut, a sharp dresser with a sweet smile. He had rented a rowboat with a girl named Susan, whom he had a crush on, and she dove into the water from the stern and he dove after her though he could not swim a stroke. Perhaps he thought it would come to him as a natural reflex, but he sank and panicked, arms and legs thrashing. Susan grabbed him by the hair, but his crew cut was too short to get hold of and he pulled her under and she had to fight free. She called for help and swam to shore and Roger disappeared. A couple hours later, sheriff's deputies dragged the bottom and brought his body up.

Thirty years later, a woman approached me at the airport and said, "I'm Susan. I was with your cousin when he drowned." We stood and talked. That day was still vivid to her. She had taken a lifesaving course and there was Roger, terrified in the water, and nothing she had learned could save him in that horrific minute. She was shaken, describing his wild panic, her attempt to get hold of him, and also the fact that she felt responsible: he had a crush on her and that's why they were there, but she was not attracted to him. She was starting to realize, way back then, that she was attracted to women, and didn't know how to tell him. He died for unrequited love, of a mysterious kind.

The funeral was at Albin Chapel on Nicollet, a beige-colored room, draperies, perfumy, squishy organ music, his classmates weeping. We trooped in past the coffin banked with flowers where the body lay in a gray suit, white shirt, and tie, his prominent Denham jaw, his crew cut. Aunt Margaret and cousin Shirley sat in an alcove, behind a transparent curtain. Roger's brother, Stan, was stationed in Korea and couldn't get leave to come home. Roger's father, Paul, had run off with the other woman when Roger was a baby, and the story was that Paul had almost taken the baby with him, and so we contemplated how the baby's kidnapping might have saved his life. Some of my aunts wept, and we all sat in shock. Aunt Margaret sat, composed, silent. Mother wept at the graveside and later I asked her why, since now Roger was in heaven with the Lord, and she said, "We don't know that. He went to a dance at school."

The next week, Mother enrolled me in swim class at the YMCA downtown. It met daily for three weeks; Monday morning I waited on the highway by Mrs. Fisher's asparagus field and caught the bus into town, disembarked at the Public Library on 10th Street and walked over to the Y on LaSalle and through a side door down the steps into a locker room reeking of chlorine where an old man handed me a key and told me to take my clothes off and put them in a locker. I stripped down to my undershorts. "Those too," he said. I grew up in a proper home and when

I stepped out of my shorts, I crossed a line I'd never crossed before. He pointed me to a large dank shower room and turned on the water and I stepped under it. Cold. He pointed me to a steel door marked POOL and I went through. Forty other boys, all naked, sat around the long pool, feet dangling down into the water, and I joined them. A couple of fat ones, the others spindly like me. The instructor strode in, holding a clipboard. He was lean and muscular and wore black swim trunks. He called off our names and we answered *Here* except one boy said *Present*. The instructor glared at him. And he told us to jump in the water, hold onto the side of the pool, and kick our legs. Then he told us to float by pushing away, take a deep breath, facedown in the water, hands at our sides, as he stood on the side, holding a long pole for us to grab onto if we started to sink. I tried to do what he said but it was so strange, an act of faith, and I got scared and tried to stand up but the pool was eight feet deep, and then I got really scared and he jabbed me with the pole and I grabbed it. "What's the matter with you that you can't follow simple directions?" he yelled. "Try again!" I clung to the pole, trying to lie back in the water as he'd told me to do. "Let go!" he said. "We don't have all day."

I was scared of water, and the instructor was a sadist. He enjoyed his superiority. He strode around behind us and explained swimming as if this were as simple as walking and then sent us into the water, five at a time, and told us to swim, and belittled those who couldn't. "Come on, ladies, put your faces in the water," he yelled. "What are you scared of? Follow directions!" I stuck it out for two days and on the third I could not make myself go down those steps and strip naked. I turned around and went to the library instead. Spent two hours looking at books, then went to the WCCO studios on Second Avenue to watch *Good Neighbor Time* with Bob DeHaven and Wally Olson and His Orchestra, a live show at 11:30 with a studio audience. Ernie Garven played the accordion, Burt Hanson sang, and Cedric Adams came in and read the news at noon. My mother read his daily column in the Minneapolis *Star* and loved his reminiscences of boyhood in his hometown of Magnolia. After the news, I got on the elevator and there he was, smiling, in his blue pinstripe suit and shiny brown shoes, and I stood next to him and felt the greatness of the man, fame exuding from him, and smelled his cologne. He was the most famous man in Minnesota. Airline pilots reported that when Cedric said good night at the end of his 10 p.m. newscast, lights dimmed all across Minnesota. Occasionally he substituted for Arthur Godfrey on his CBS morning radio show in New York, a native of Minnesota heard nationwide, and there I was standing next to him on an elevator, a profound moment, a corn picker from the sticks brushing up against a national celebrity, and then the door opened and we stepped out together and I heard his gravelly voice and famous chuckle up above. Mother admired him because he made her laugh.

Every morning I boarded the bus to downtown, intending to be brave and instead went to the library and then to WCCO for a brush with greatness. I didn't imagine Cedric Adams was afraid of water. I imagined him diving off the stern of a big yacht and swimming to shore and shaking himself like a dog. He was a great man, and I was a sneak and a coward and a liar. And every day downtown was a fresh lie—"How was swim lesson?" *Fine.* "What did you learn?" *We learned to float.* "I really want you to learn to swim." *I will.* "You're not afraid of water, are you?" *No.* "Are you sure?" *Yes.*

I asked Mother why the Y required nudity in swim class and she asked the Y, and they told her it was so the instructor could better observe the boys' leg movements. This satisfied her. To me, it felt like pure humiliation. I spent the next three weeks traversing between the library and WCCO, and at the end of July, one day at Twin Lakes, when Mother asked me to swim for her, I walked out in water up to my armpits and pantomimed swimming and that satisfied her.

I did not bother my parents with my problems—did not complain about the Darwins or the tormentor who made fun of my green teeth—didn't ask permission to ride my bike into the city—never ever confessed to feeling sad or troubled—I kept my troubles to myself. Mother had the little kids to worry about without me adding to her problems. This did not strike me as peculiar. It still does not. Shut my mouth; put a lid on it. This worked pretty well for me. Keep moving. If you feel sad, get on your bike and ride. Don't get fascinated by your problems. Tomorrow is a new day. I still feel this way.

10

The Trip to New York City

I PICKED STRAWBERRIES FROM OUR strawberry beds, tithing some into my mouth, same with raspberries. I read in a book that men on their way to fight at Gettysburg picked strawberries and ate them before going over the hill to die. I burned our trash in a wire-frame incinerator and put an empty whipped-cream aerosol can that said *Danger: Do not put near flame* into the fire and watched it explode. A dump truck drove along 77th and dumped asphalt scraps from a shingle factory on the road and the cars driving by pressed the pieces into somewhat solid pavement. New houses arose near us, yellow and green and pink ramblers. Trucks hauled rolls of sod that men spooled out to make lawns. Skinny saplings were planted and watered with a hose. The mail van came by around noon.

One day I heard my parents arguing in the kitchen about a trip to New York City. Uncle Lew's neighbor Mrs. Palmquist asked Dad if he could drive a Pontiac to New York and put it on a ship to Germany for her son-in-law, a captain in the Army, and this struck my dad as an excellent opportunity. My mother didn't see it that way. She was wary of Mrs. Palmquist for whom Dad did some carpentry and who fixed him lunch and sometimes he quoted her interesting opinions, which made Mother jealous. She felt that the father of six young children should not go gallivanting off alone on a vacation and she was wary of the fact that Dad planned to visit two young women, Nancy and Betty Kirkwood, who had befriended him back in his Army days in New York—young Christian women, yes, indeed, both now married, but nonetheless. Mother was jealous, and she informed Dad that he would be taking me along on the trip on general principle, as a ball and chain. He was not happy about this, but he knew she was right. It was wrong to leave her with the house, garden, children, nobody to help her. She nominated me because I was spending time down by the river with bad companions. I monitored the discussion closely. He argued that the city was dangerous, what with hoodlums like Lucky Luciano and Legs Diamond, shootings, street gangs, people getting shoved off subway platforms into oncoming trains, the danger of contagious disease in crowded places, he mentioned the dread word "polio," but Mother held firm. No Gary, no trip. And so it was decided. Dad was gracious in defeat. Mother bought me a mustard-colored shirt and matching pants for the occasion.

He and I got in the brand-new Pontiac on an August morning and headed east through Wisconsin on two-lane roads, I sat with the map on my lap, holding my hand out the window like an airplane wing to feel the lift of the air, and I read from the *Federal Guide* book I got from the library.

7m SE of Pepin is the village of Lund, site of the log cabin built by Charles Ingalls in the early 1870s, which became the setting of Laura Ingalls Wilder's Little House in the Big Woods. *The cabin still stands as part of a granary.*

Four-lane roads looped around Chicago and we made it to Sandusky, Ohio, the first night and Valley Forge, Pennsylvania, the second, spent a morning examining the log huts in Washington's winter encampment, then plunged into the city through the Lincoln Tunnel. On the trip out, I was surprised at how Dad, so reserved at home, liked to chat up waitresses. *How're you doing today? Good. That apple pie sure looks good. You wouldn't happen to have some cheese with that, would you? Apple pie without the cheese is like a hug without the squeeze.* And the old waitress in the hairnet chippered up at his greeting. I was even more surprised by his excitement at seeing New York again and how he became almost effusive with Nancy and Betty and their husbands. He was a new man in New York. His Brethrenly solemnity disappeared, and he became a man about town, eager to mingle in the crowds, the traffic, the bright lights, eager to see the sights.

We delivered the Pontiac to a dock in Brooklyn and took a taxi to Manhattan, my first cab ride, and got a room in the Aberdeen Hotel on 32nd and Broadway, where he had been quartered with other Army postal workers during the war. A sergeant had made them march in formation from 32nd to the Post Office. "It was pretty ridiculous," he said. But his war years had been enjoyable. "People treated us like heroes," he said. "Free tickets to things, free meals." *Free tickets to what?* "Shows," he said. My Brethren dad had attended Broadway shows, women with bare legs dancing, high kicks, jazzy tunes. This was a revelation. Now he seemed to be in no rush to get home. We went to Radio City Music Hall and saw the Rockettes dance and jugglers and a trained dog act followed by a movie. ("This is a secret between you and me," he said.) We rode the Cyclone at Coney Island and ate chili dogs, rode the Staten Island Ferry and the subway, packed with people, many of them speaking foreign languages. We took an elevator to the 86th-floor observation deck of the Empire State Building, where Dad pushed me into a little recording booth and told me to say something to my mother. The door closed. He put quarters in a slot. People stood staring at me, waiting. A red light flashed on, and because I could think of nothing else, I sang a verse of "Jesus Wants Me for a Sunbeam" and recited John 3:16. He showed me the magnificent Post Office with columns and the inscription ("Neither snow nor rain nor heat nor gloom of night . . .") where he'd spent the war sorting mail for the Army, and I loved the words (". . . stays these couriers from the swift completion of their appointed rounds"), but what was so surprising to me was the thought that the war had been very pleasant for him, entertaining even. It was not what I'd been taught in school, that soldiers made heroic sacrifices. My dad had enjoyed a wonderful time, admired for his uniform, free tickets to shows. I was stunned.

Four days in New York, threading our way through oncoming crowds, Dad holding my hand. I thought, *He does not want to lose me. Because he loves me.* This had not been so clear to me before. It was very companionable. I still think of this sometimes in New York, that this is where once I felt close to my dad.

We stayed our last night with Don and Betty in their Brooklyn

apartment, one bedroom, a kitchen alcove, a small living room with a
round claw-foot dining table. We sat down for supper, and Don asked me
to say grace, and I looked pleadingly at Dad who explained that I was shy
and he prayed instead. Dad and Betty reminisced about the fun of the war
years, shows they'd seen, parties, and Don was quiet. It was a hot night in
Brooklyn—and hours later, when they went to bed, Dad lay on the couch
and I lay awake on the floor. I could hear Betty and Don laughing in
their bedroom ten feet away, and then it sounded like she was crying and
he was grunting from physical exertion. Dad said, "Let's go for a walk,"
and we got dressed and walked to a candy store and bought cream sodas.
They were very cold. The man behind the counter was a hunchback with
orange hair; he chomped on a cigar and wore a yellow silk vest. Dad and
I perched on the curb at the corner and drank the sodas. Across the street,
in a park, families sleeping on sheets and blankets spread out on the grass,
hundreds of people, little kids nestled against their mothers, and on the
benches around the perimeter men sat smoking and talking in the dark.
An encampment on a hot night in Brooklyn.

   We walked back to Don and Betty's and Dad spread sofa cushions on
the fire escape and we lay down, five stories in the air, headlights passing
below, the elevated train rumbling a block away. I could see the escape
was designed with the last segment of stairs suspended twenty feet above
the sidewalk, too high for an intruder to jump up and reach, suspended
so that someone descending would lower the stairs simply by walking
down them. Your weight would carry you gently to the sidewalk. Dad
fell asleep and I lay awake, listening to him snore. I got up from the
cushions and I dared myself to go down the stairs, though I knew it was
a bad idea. I went down a flight, and two, and a man walking below
looked up and said something I didn't understand. He seemed to be
inviting me to come down, but I didn't understand the words. I considered descending—it was exciting to contemplate—what would happen?
Where would we go?—But I climbed back up and lay down, curled
against Dad, who did, after all, love me, and then I woke up and it was
morning.

   We rode the Greyhound back home in time for Brethren Bible conference at Lake Minnetonka, and my aunts asked me about New York and
I told them about some things, but not the Rockettes or the fire escape.

At the end, after the Sunday night gospel meeting, the Saints stood and sang their hymn to the Rapture:

Then we shall be where we would be,
Then we shall be what we should be.
Things that are not now nor could be,
Soon shall be our own.

They were deeply moved by the imminence of the Second Coming, so many signs and portents all around. And I realized I did not wish for the Rapture. I wanted to grow up, get a driver's license, a job, a girlfriend, and go back to New York and find the happy life Dad found there in wartime, which didn't exist in Minnesota. Late that night, I walked out of the house and crossed the road to Fred Peterson's cornfield to be alone with my thoughts. I had worked for Mr. Peterson, hoeing his corn, tedious work, and I dared myself to take my clothes off. A crazy thing to do, but I stripped naked and ran up and down the rows for the pleasure of leaves brushing against my body. It was sinful and I did it anyway. I could imagine Mother suddenly appearing and asking, "Why are you doing this?" Probably the answer is: *Certifiable Insanity.* Normal people do not do this. Nevertheless, it felt good. I ran a hundred yards to the end of the row and turned and ran back and did it again. A few porch lights in nearby houses, the stars overhead, the corn all around, and I was naked, and it felt good.

That summer, I was picking tomatoes with my older sister and I threw a couple of them at a pile of rocks by the incinerator to hear them splat and she reproached me for wasting good food and said, "I'm going to tell," so I found a rotten tomato lying on the ground, mushy, filled with white organisms swimming around, and I picked it up, all smelly and liquidy, and there she was bending over and working, my industrious sister, her womanly hindquarters in the air, and before I could stop myself, the tomato was flying through the air and as it splatted on the seat of her pants I was dashing for the house, my sister in pursuit, and I slowed down to duck under the clotheslines and she leaped on me like a jaguar on an eland. I crashed to the ground and she was about to pound me and Mother called her name from the kitchen window and the good sister hissed at me, "You'll be sorry for this someday," and retracted her claws. Mother asked me why I would throw a tomato at my sister, and I said, "I didn't mean to. It slipped out of my hand."

Mother shook her head but said no more. She was busy. She had a little girl and two five-year-olds to look after. I was a free man. On my own, I had quit Boy Scouts, seeing no reason to learn semaphore code with wig-wagging flags or recognize weasel tracks from raccoon. And the Boy Scout Jamboree at the Minneapolis Auditorium was ridiculous. A couple hundred of us Scouts lined up naked in the basement to be sprayed with brown paint to make us Indians and red and white stripes painted on our faces and chests, all under the supervision of men in uniforms, some of whom later scrubbed us off in the showers. I found this very weird. I didn't ask Mother's permission to quit Scouts, I just stopped going. A great revelation: *do as you wish and be prepared to make up a story.* Nobody cared. It was a laissez-faire world: the word "parenting" did not exist then. Anyway, they were busy. I was free. I went to the library and because my mother had said disparaging things about Hemingway, I pulled him down off the shelf and had a look.

When I babysat at the neighbors' on Saturday nights, I sent the kids to bed and scrounged around in ashtrays for cigarettes and lit one and took a couple puffs. Watching a movie on TV of high-society people twirling on the dance floor and drinking cocktails, a cigarette felt very stylish between my index and second finger, and the plume of exhaled smoke was dramatic in the mirror, I felt like a famous author.

Our family went to the State Fair every August, took a picnic, ate it on the grass by the Conservation building, but that year Mother was too busy, so Dad took Philip and Judy and me and gave us $3 apiece and set us loose at the foot of the Grandstand. I was eleven, I'd never wandered free in a big crowd before but I felt no fear. The *Star & Tribune* booth was nearby and Cedric Adams was chatting with a crowd of fans so I joined the crowd looking at the great man, balding, suit and tie, horn-rimmed glasses, his famous voice. He was rich, he chummed with Bob Hope and Arthur Godfrey, he had a big powerboat on Lake Minnetonka. He was smoking a cigarette and asking people about their hometowns, and I thought if he asked me, I'd step up and say that Anoka was the Halloween Capital of the World and that my family had been there since 1880, but he didn't notice me. I wandered the Midway, watched the barker at the freak show tent bring out his wares, the Penguin Boy, the sword swallower all skinny and leathery, the lady snake handler with a boa constrictor wrapped around her, the Tall Man who looked rather sad, and Popeye who could pop his eyeballs out of their sockets, first one, then the other. I watched the couples holding hands, boarding the Ferris wheel. I looked at the big tent of the Harlem Revue with canvas posters of colored girls in their underwear and I knew that a Christian boy should not want to go in there, but I stood behind the tent hoping that a flap would open and someone of interest emerge. The stock cars roared around on the dirt track, clouds of dust, the low moan of the crowd when a car skidded into the retaining wall. I bought a hamburger, gazed at fish in tanks and giant swine. I found my way back to the parking lot beyond the enormous Lee coveralls hanging from a high wire and stood by our car, waiting, until the others returned. Dad said, "Are you okay?" as if I might not be, but I was. I liked being on my own, without family, nobody guiding, no cautionary advice. An interesting discovery at the age of eleven.

Sixth grade was an idyllic year. Due to booming population growth, our class—Corinne, Billy, Elaine, Dianne, Judy, Rosemary, and all—rode the bus to Sunnyvale, a little one-room country school with a pond nearby and a hill around it. We left the Darwins behind; they simply disappeared from my life forever, a remarkable development, on a par with the polio vaccine, which came along the year after. We sat in ancient desks, and I learned that I was the only one who'd been to New York City. Not even our teacher Mr. Lewis had been. Corinne had been to Washington, DC, but I had New York all to myself. It was a big leap in status. I wrote a report about it and read it aloud to the class, about riding a train underground, a train crowded with many Negroes, Chinese, people speaking strange languages. The Empire State Building. Swimming in the Atlantic Ocean at Jones Beach. Sitting in the studio audience at Rockefeller Center for the NBC quiz show *Beat the Clock* with Bud Collyer. It was the first time I had amazing firsthand experience to offer to an audience.

There was some skepticism among the boys. *Weren't you afraid in New York?* No, I was not. *Yes, you were.* I was not. *Ha.* Ha, yourself. It was a good year. That winter, we laced on our skates at recess and skated round and round the pond or we slid down the hill on cardboard and Mr. Lewis allowed recess to go on for an hour. Christmas decorations went up. We exchanged valentines. Without Darwins, there was no fighting. It was a perfect world and gym class included two weeks of dance instruction, and Mother sent a note to school: "Please excuse Gary from dancing for religious reasons." Which I sent to a wastebasket. Would God, with all the cosmos to worry about, really feel offended if I danced the polka? I learned to polka, dancing with the marvelous Karen Brown, and also the schottische and the Virginia reel. We laughed, we held hands, I put an arm around her waist and she put hers around mine.

I was the only Brethren in my class and I never told a soul. On a questionnaire, where it said "Religion," I wrote *Protestant*. My tormentor who saw my green teeth asked what church I belonged to, and I hesitated and he said, "You belong to a weird one. I know about you." I didn't want to be weird. From the road, our Cape Cod house looked normal, the lawn mowed, the driveway paved with asphalt, the garbage can and incinerator in back where they should be. But there was our Ford Fairlane with the sticker on the rear bumper: FOR ALL HAVE SINNED AND COME SHORT OF THE GLORY OF GOD. People who saw it thought, "Stay away from those people, they're *odd*." In all the years I lived at home, I never invited a friend into the house for fear Mother would ask them if they had accepted Jesus as their personal savior. I didn't want to be odd. I was curious about normality. I wanted a TV like other people did because at school, kids tossed out lines from favorite shows—"One of these days, Alice, *pow*, right in the kisser!"—and everyone laughed but me. Jack Benny and George and Gracie and Bob Hope were on TV, comics that Mother liked on radio, but out of respect for Grandpa Denham who felt that television was pernicious, we abstained even though he was dead. I sat in Sunday night gospel meeting, looking out the window at the family next door watching Ed Sullivan on TV as we listened to Brother John Rogers preach that the Last Days were at hand when Christ would come to take us home to heaven. Meanwhile, on TV, a man and a woman were singing about their love for each other. Brethren never spoke of romantic love, not in my hearing. I looked forward to romance. Our songs were about the necessity of suffering, being persecuted by the worldly, and looking forward to our reward in heaven.

I wanted to enjoy life in the world with the least amount of suffering: I wanted to live a life of comedy.

And then Mother happened to see *I Love Lucy* one night when she dropped in next door to borrow a cup of bleach and she was gone a long time. She said she'd gotten "stuck," but the truth was that she adored Lucille Ball, and on Monday nights after supper Mother made a habit of going next door to the Birks'. We could smell cigarette smoke on her clothing when she returned. When our Baptist neighbors, the Sundbergs, got a TV, Mother switched to their house to avoid the smoke. Were Ricky and Lucy and their goofball mishaps with Fred and Ethel to the glory of God? I didn't think so. I loved to point out these inconsistencies to my mother and make her feel guilty for loving Lucy.

And then Grandpa went into the nursing home and was too confused to care about pernicious influences and soon after he died, when the three littler kids were in bed miserable with the mumps, Dad went to the hardware store and bought a TV set so the kids could watch *Howdy Doody*. It happened just like that, no discussion, like young David putting down his slingshot and inviting Goliath in for lunch. The TV sat on a swivel stand by the piano, and Mother set up her ironing board and watched shows. "I only watch while I'm ironing," she said by way of justification. Soap operas didn't interest her, or detective shows or Westerns—she loved the sarcastic Henry Morgan, the mild-mannered George Gobel ("I feel like the world is a tuxedo and I am a pair of brown shoes"), Jackie Gleason stammering, "Hamana hamana hamana hamana," the big squints of Buddy Hackett, Jack Paar, and Charlie Weaver ("We had a fire in the bathroom but luckily it didn't spread to the house") and George and Gracie ("You've buttered your bread, now sleep on it"). Mother had no time for TV evangelists, but she loved a Jewish comic doing a routine about his mother—*My mother made dinner, there were two items on the menu: take it or leave it. My mother was very practical. When she got old and she bent down to tie her shoes, she thought, "What else can I do while I'm down here?"*

The Brethren were dead set against fiction, preferring Scripture, but to be admitted by way of narrative into the secret unwrapped lives of men and women seemed to me a great privilege. Brethren separated themselves from the world; fiction gave you intimate knowledge of how people thought and conducted themselves and what they talked about. I wanted to know these things. How could you not?

My pretty classmate Karen Brown asked me to go to the spring dance with her, and I said yes, and for the occasion I brought two Pall Mall cigarettes stolen from the Andersons. She and I stood outside in the dark and I lit one of them and took a drag and blew smoke out. She was impressed. I put my hand on her bare shoulder and it was a beautiful experience. Only a shoulder, but it was hers.

A month later, I sat in Gospel Meeting behind a girl in a sleeveless dress, the left armhole revealed her white bra and the slight curvature of her breast. The preacher came down from the pulpit and cried, "There is one here tonight who God is talking to and I beg of you, do not harden your heart against the Lord." His gaze was on me. I thought I was saved, having grown up among the saved, but wasn't sure if God knew this or not. The preacher walked back and forth in front of us, in full cry. "I knew of a young man just like some who are here tonight, who was taken to a revival service just like this one, heard the message of salvation, and he was moved but he decided, *Not yet. I want to live a little first. I want to enjoy music and dance and movies and comedy. Comedy! Think of it! For the love of a joke—a joke!!!* He went out of that place without accepting the Lord and that night, heading home, his family's car was struck by the Evening Express and he was ushered into eternity to meet the judgment of a righteous God. Think of it. Eternity. In a burning fire. Burning but never consumed. All he had to do was say, *Yes, Lord, I come.* This may be your last chance. You may never have another."

He was a powerful preacher and I wanted to respond, but I doubted my own sincerity. Shouldn't I be crying and on my knees? I was not. I'd heard this sermon before, having grown up Brethren, and it did not shake me to my depths as a person convicted of sin should be shaken. This is not a business transaction, this is a struggle with the powers of darkness, so where is the anguish? I wondered. Why am I not falling on the ground? And the crowd sang *Softly and tenderly Jesus is calling, calling for you and for me. See on the portals He's waiting and watching. Watching for you and for me. Come home, come home. Ye who are weary come home.*

And that night, I spoke to Brother Tomkinson and he prayed with me. I told him I wanted to make my testimony that I belonged to the

Lord. I just thought it was something I should do. The next day, in front of a crowd of Brethren, I walked into Lake Minnetonka, the same lake Roger drowned in, and was baptized by Brother John Rogers, as people on shore sang: *When I survey the wondrous cross on which the Lord of glory died, My richest gains I count but loss and pour contempt on all my pride.* I wore a white shirt and white trousers and he a dark blue suit, white shirt and tie, wading into the water up to his waist. I was impressed that a grown man would walk into a lake in a suit and tie, and he put one hand on my chest and the other behind my head, and down I went in the name of the Father, the Son, and the Holy Ghost, and I arose dripping wet, a skeptical believer who hoped baptism would wash away his doubts, and it did not.

I lived a divided life: I knew I should stand in downtown Anoka and hand out tracts, *Where Will You Spend Eternity?* and I did not. The baptism was to please the Brethren and would not be divulged to my school friends. One never knew the other. Corinne never set foot in my house. I told nobody at school about the gospel service. The two were incompatible. I never confided in my parents. No information was offered except under direct questioning. I made a tiny niche of my own, Anoka Boy of Letters, and carried myself in a serious literary manner and went on to the U where, if you could write lines that sounded like a translation from the Japanese, you were considered a poet. I was a failure in marriage, avoided the unhappiness of my wife by going into a small room with a typewriter and closing the door. My first wife, Mary, hoped we'd find a comfortable domestic arrangement as her parents had done, but I ducked away from misery and the silence between us got heavier. I dodged the military draft and never suffered the consequences. I escaped into books, reading them and then writing my own. I created a radio circus in which I was ringmaster and solo writer and nobody cracked the whip. I shunned meetings, committees, movements. I followed this strategy of evasion all my life, joining nothing, living in fictions. When *Prairie Home* started, I had no more idea how to manage an organization than I knew how to build a house or butcher a pig. Other people had to manage things, and I sat in a room and made up things and tried not to get in their way.

11

The Amazing Year, Part 1

THE SUMMER I TURNED THIRTEEN, my dad swung the car onto High-way 10 and headed west with Mother and us four kids to visit our cousins in Idaho. Philip and Judy, the trustworthy ones, eighteen and seventeen, stayed home to work at jobs they'd found and guard the house and tend the garden. I sat in back by the window, landscape rolling by, Dad maintaining a steady 65, edging up to 70, as eastbound semis blew past like ICBMs and my mother shuddered at each one. *Johnny, could you please slow down?* I read a book across North Dakota and we stopped for the occasional historical marker (IN MEMORY OF OFFICERS AND SOLDIERS WHO FELL NEAR THIS PLACE FIGHTING WITH THE 7TH UNITED STATES CAVALRY AGAINST THE SIOUX INDIANS ON THE 25TH AND 26TH OF JUNE, A.D. 1876) and I said to myself the beautiful names of Montana and the Bitterroot Valley, the Sapphire Mountains, the Mission Range and Rattlesnake Creek, and finally got to Idaho and Edith and Edmund's farm jammed up against mountain slopes on the banks of the St. Joe River. I was a little too well dressed but tried to blend in with my cousins, and one afternoon, while the grownups were away visiting, cousin Chuck told me to take the wheel of the Allis-Chalmers and I did, a terrifying pleasure for a city kid, driving a big tractor up a twisting dirt road through stands of tall trees, the great black treads throwing up dirt, the engine throbbing beneath me and, far beyond, the forested peaks mounting into the sky and the road curving into the folds of the foothills. I took deep breaths of the balsam air, putting my sneaker down on the gas pedal, shifting up to second gear, the tractor tipping, bouncing, going up a steep slope, Chuck standing behind me, hanging on, me feeling wildly alive and also on the verge of violent death. It was a burst of freedom. My cousins were fearless. They drove hard and fast on mountain roads and took a rifle, hoping to see a mountain lion. When they wrestled, they meant it. They talked about saving up money to buy an old plane and flying it home, learning to pilot it by trial and error. Their mother, Edith, was a farm girl, she let her boys run free. I survived my tractor run. We came back to Minnesota. The tractor ride was remembered.

The day after Labor Day, 7 a.m. I stood on the highway and waited for the yellow bus to start seventh grade. For the next six years, I rode the bus for twelve miles to Anoka High School every day, a bus kid, in snow or rain or bitter cold—school was never canceled ever. I waited for the bus knowing it would be full of kids who didn't want to sit next to me. Mine was the last stop. Six years, anticipating rejection. The bus appears, stops, the door swings open, I climb up the steps past the unhappy driver, and I face forty kids avoiding eye contact. The boys in back are braced to defend their seats. The bus driver watches me in his mirror. "Find a seat and sid-down," he says. In the front sit the girls, who do not give me the time of day, except Corinne Guntzel sitting with Elaine Ness in the third seat on the left. Corinne smiles at me and moves over, and I sit with my right arm across the back of the seat and thus is formed a lifelong bias in favor of women. I trace my heterosexuality to the offer of a seat on the bus at the age of thirteen. Boys defended territory. Girls were civilized and shared.

The bus ran up the West River Road and around the sharp curve by the Coon Rapids Dam where, in winter, if the road was icy, the boys in back flung themselves to one side and then the other, trying to throw the bus into the ditch. We crossed the river to Anoka and along Ferry Street, past the big white house where I was born, and pulled up in front of the old high school. We piled off and entered through an arch and past a plaque listing the dead of two world wars and into a grand central hall thronged with town kids and farm kids, the two easily distinguishable. The prim and studious girls with books held against their bosom and the social girls gathered in gaggles, poking at each other, the oddball boys all too aware of themselves, and the jocks who'd all been on teams together, and the black-leather hoods fixing their hair to look like James Dean's. We Benson School kids were aliens; the town kids ruled. A few deformed misfits with an odd gait, slurred speech, a drooping arm, an off-kilter eye, suffering from some disability for which we then had no name other than "feeb" or "retard," and we shunned them lest it be contagious. I climbed the great staircase to the second floor, old floorboards creaking underfoot, to the library, where Mrs. Goodner stood in her pulpit of a circulation desk and surveyed the four long study tables, students bent over their work, gossiping. I discovered *Webster's Unabridged* here and Civil War histories. I read Sinclair Lewis's *Babbitt* and stories of F. Scott Fitzgerald, two Minnesotans who made the grade. And, wonder of wonders, the Gershon Legman collection of limericks, including filthy ones, the young man of Antietam who loved horse turds so well he could eat 'em and the young man of Madras whose balls were made out of brass— he could clang them together and play "Stormy Weather" as lightning came out of his ass—I laughed so hard, involuntary gasping and snorting at the thought of metallic testicles and electrical flatulence, it hit me in a deep and visceral way. But the book that struck me most deeply was Anne Frank's diary. I read it over and over. I felt closer to the Franks in their attic in Amsterdam than to my own family. Anne opened her heart to me, my family did not. I wrote a story in high school, in which she came to Anoka as an exchange student and I became her best friend. Mr. Hochstetter gave me a B, saying it was very well-written but pointing out that the assignment was to write about a personal experience, not an imaginary one. Frankly, I didn't see the difference or why it mattered. She was real and so was my feeling for her.

In choir, I stood with the altos and Miss Hallenberg raised her pencil baton and we sang, *April is in my mistress' face,* a*nd July in her eyes hath place.* And in Latin, Helen Hunt taught us *Amo, amas, amat, amamus, amatis, amant.* In gym, Mr. Ziegler insisted we do chin-ups and the impossible rope climb and run and dive over the horse and do a forward roll, though I was nearsighted and timid, and then there was the misery of showering in the nude, gangly boys with tiny penises shrunken by self-consciousness, other boys stroking their penises and displaying them to rivals. I didn't care for nakedness, I simply wanted to be normal.

Brethrenism was not, it was like driving a Studebaker. I hid my Brethren light, such as it was, under a bushel. A true Brethren wouldn't laugh at the young man of Madras—he'd go to Mrs. Goodner and ask that the book be removed from the library. I did not do that. A good Christian would not say, to a classmate who asked for help in Latin, "Go to Helen Hunt for it." And that was what happened to me at Anoka High School, I found out I was going to leave Us and become one of Them. I was a dodger, I avoided trouble.

I made an attempt to be normal in eighth grade when my friend Billy Pedersen went out for football; I tried to join him and went to Dr. Mork for the required physical. He put his stethoscope up to my chest and heard in the *badadum badadum* a click and, though the term "mitral valve prolapse" was not in his vocabulary because echocardiography wasn't around yet, Dr. Mork looked at me and said, "I can't sign your permission. You have a clicky heart." So, on the authority of a doctor who was only guessing, I skipped football. I had a pair of leather shoes with steel cleats, handed down from a friend of my brother, and I threw them away. Two days later I got up the nerve to walk into the Anoka *Herald* and ask the editor, Warren Feist, if he had a sportswriter (knowing he did not) and if he did not, could I have the job? He hired me. Two dollars for a home game, three for an away game, copy due on Monday, the paper came out on Thursdays. He hired me, thinking I was the son of my uncle Lawrence Keillor, who was head cashier at the First National Bank, an important *Herald* advertiser, so I got the job on false pretenses. But I was hired. My name was on the masthead: *Gary Keillor . . . sportswriter.* And on Friday night, as the Tornadoes ran onto Goodrich Field and the crowd sang *Fight, fight, Anoka, fight. Go, go, Tornadoes. Win, win, Maroon and Gray, we're with you tonight, Tornadoes,* I sat in the little press box perched at the top of the grandstand with a notebook and a couple sharp pencils.

I sat next to Chuck McCartney and Rod Person, broadcasting the game on KANO, and thanks to them, I got an idea what was happening on the field. I had no money for the bus, so I hitchhiked after games and the ride home was often more interesting than the game itself. After one game, I stood out on Ferry Street and a man in a Cadillac stopped and between Anoka and my house twelve miles away, he told me never to get married and to enlist in the Navy, not the Army. He'd been in the Army and was on a ship heading for Japan when the war ended. "I would've been in the invasion of Japan getting my head blown off but Uncle Harry dropped the big one." I asked him what the Army was like and he said, "It was hell. None of us wanted to be there. We were expendable. They would've sent us ashore in Higgins boats until the Japs ran out of ammo." The men who picked me up were not idealists. They knew that politicians were a bunch of damn crooks and the game was rigged in favor of the rich. Roosevelt was a drunk, Eisenhower cheated on his wife, and both parties were full of damn liars and soon there'd be another crash like the one of 1929 except even worse, so only an idiot'd put your money in the bank, buy gold coins and put them in a Mason jar and bury it in your flower bed but don't tell your wife. My rides had a view of the world not found in history books or the Minneapolis *Star*, and it struck me again and again that teenage boys playing a game was of far less importance than the conversation of lonely men late at night, but I was assigned to sports so I wrote sports.

The Anoka *Herald* was the lesser paper in town, the *Union* was twice as thick, owned by the lordly Arch Pease who honked when he spoke, and the kindly Mr. Feist was scraping along, hoping that Arch would buy him out (which soon happened) so he could get a job with a salary (which he did), but meanwhile I was a professional writer at the age of fourteen and my aunt Eleanor read the paper weekly and thought I was a better writer than Jack Blesi who wrote for the *Union*. I went to the *Herald* office after school on Monday and sat at a desk in the front window and pecked out a thousand words on a Royal typewriter and turned it over to Red and Vernell who sat at the Linotypes and batted out my copy, line by line into hot lead in a tray, both of them sipping straight gin out of coffee cups. I came back on Tuesday to read galley proofs, then on Wednesday to watch them print the *Herald* on a flatbed press, Red lifting one side of the 8 x 12-foot sheet of paper atop the stack and flipping it off the pile and onto the bed like setting a cloth on a table and pulling the lever and the roller rolled over it and it slipped down into the trimmer to be folded. I pulled a copy out of the stack and saw my name in print and that was it—instead of a fourth-string B-squad end, I was a person of consequence, a writer. I wanted to be one so I could see things and describe them. When Frankie Renko drowned in the Mississippi, we heard the sirens and I wanted to go see, but Mother said, "There's no point in a bunch of people standing around gawking." She said it was immoral to look upon the sufferings of others unless you could do something to help. She said rubberneckers only got in the way, and sometimes the traffic jams of the morbid kept ambulances from reaching the victims in time. I didn't argue, but I knew that somebody needed to write about Frankie's death. It shouldn't be ignored. A boy my age had fallen into the river near where we boys played and his life came to an end. This demanded attention. When the Morrow house burned one winter day, I rode my bike past the smoking ruins. Chuckie Morrow was my classmate.

I once overheard a Brethren elder tell Dad how he'd been listening to his police radio one night and heard about a big grain elevator fire and got out of bed to go see it. "Flames five stories high and heat so fierce it bent the train tracks, fire engines from all over the city. You don't get to see a fire like that very often," he said. It astonished me that a grown-up could have the same exact fascination as I had. Dad thought it was juvenile. Mother thought it showed a real moral flaw. I shared his curiosity.

The summer after I joined the *Herald,* the notorious O'Kasick brothers went on a crime spree that ended in the woods north of Anoka where they were gunned down by a posse. A man came by the *Herald* office with photographs of the bodies lying face-up in tall grass, mouths open, bloodstained, and Mr. Feist glanced at them and said, "No, thank you." I got a good look, though. I had only seen dead people in coffins, prettied up, and this was the real thing. I felt sheepish about looking, but it certainly was worth a look. Three tough guys like the Darwins who robbed a drugstore, killed a cop, hid in the woods, and met their end in a blaze of gunfire. A story waiting to be told.

This was a large year in my life, me a writer, old printers drinking gin, a drunk at the wheel pouring his heart out about the invasion of Japan, dead men in the weeds. This was the year Mr. Orville Buehler ushered me out of his shop class. I had flunked ball-peen hammer, was hopeless at sheet metal and couldn't make a good flour scoop, and now he watched me cut plywood on a jigsaw while joking around and the plywood slipped and it scared Mr. Buehler, imagining me growing up with a prosthetic arm, and he switched off the saw and took me aside

and said, "All you do is talk here, so I'm going to send you up to speech."
And up to Miss LaVona Person's speech class I went. Life pivots on such
small events. I was destined to become an incompetent factory worker
and then lose an arm, but Orville Buehler sent me into radio instead.

Miss Person was a recent graduate of Gustavus, blond ponytail,
ruffled white blouse and plaid skirt and loafers, a brilliant welcoming
smile, a smile of theatrical quality but it was genuine, it felt like she was
handing you a thousand dollars. I was a string bean, almost six feet tall,
148 pounds, geeky half-rim horn-rimmed glasses, homemade haircut
with a big shaved arc over each ear, and a pair of hand-me-down jeans of
my sister's with the zipper on the side. I wore my shirttails out to cover
it, but the shirt was hers too, with darts on the sides, which I was keenly
aware of. I took a seat and a week later I did my oral interpretation
assignment, reciting "Annabel Lee" about the lost love who winds up in
the sepulchre, which I pronounced "sepulcree," which Corinne kindly
corrected, and then I balanced it off with three original limericks (clean),
one about a young person of Blaine who stood all day in the rain and an
old man of Ham Lake who lost his pants by mistake, and then the one I
was truly proud of:

> *There was a young man from Anoka*
> *Who wanted to write a good limerick.*
> *He tried and he tried*
> *And some were not bad*
> *And yet something seemed to be missing.*

Miss Person laughed, standing in the aisle, beaming her thousand-dollar
smile my way, and that gave the class permission to laugh and they did.
For a brief moment, I was a cool person, a new sensation for me, one I
cherished.

Soon after I met LaVona, my English teacher, Mr. Frayne Anderson,
handed me a copy of *The New Yorker* one day as I walked into his classroom and said, "I thought this might interest you." I'd never seen the
magazine before. We were a *Reader's Digest* family. The cover drawing
was of a housemaid removing her master's boots, pulling on one boot,
his other boot pushing her rear end. Inside were Richard Rovere, Janet

Flanner, Wolcott Gibbs, Sylvia Townsend Warner, and John Cheever, a fine cast of writers, each stunning in his or her own way. I read that issue many times over. He'd given it to me as a rich compliment, and I soaked up the goldenness of the writing, the urbanity. I read it with the devotion I was supposed to feel for St. Paul's epistles. I could hear in Cheever something I wanted that I had none of myself, the liquescent splendor, the shadowy wit and knowingness, the flourishes of feeling, the jazzy syntax, the beautiful sufficiency. I loved him. (I never met him, it would've been too much.) I read all the *New Yorkers* I could find, read Liebling, Thurber, Calisher, Angell, White—and all the minor deities, Audax Minor, Edith Oliver, Andy Logan. The very type font was significant, the columns wending around cartoons, the contention between the columns of prose and the glassware and tweed and ocean liner cabins in the ads alongside. Wanting to write for it was like wanting to play second base for the Yankees, much too extravagant to be said aloud to anyone, but still I wanted to.

These miraculous events occurred in one calendar year and clued that clueless kid in on the path to being a contributing citizen rather than a jerk or a nitwit. Grandma Keillor expected her descendants to pay attention and give a good account of themselves. And it wasn't the Baccarat crystal I craved, it was the writing, which allowed itself liberty and subtlety denied to Midwestern speech. Plain speech was imposed on us by social pressure, the obligation to not show off, but the language itself is a capacious castle of glittering splendors so why not visit it since it belongs to us? Why not try to make a life out of turning these splendors to the service of my people?

I didn't shine in high school. I was a B-minus student, thanks to my perfect pitch on multiple choice tests. The correct answer tended to be C. If you went with C, you could probably get a B and B was good enough. And I found a path in life there. I shied away from competition—speech contests, sports, honor roll—I didn't care if I were 3.0 or 3.6—I wanted to be unique and so turned to writing. I needed a pen name. Gary was a lame name compared to William and James, my grandfathers, or my great-uncles Albert and Llewelyn. We called Llewelyn Lew, but I would've used the whole name. *Llewelyn Keillor:* I considered it. In the name *Gary* you sensed the low expectations of your parents: they hoped you'd be a gas station attendant or a mailman. I intended to be an author. So I searched the dictionary under *gar-* and found *garbanzo, gardenia, garland,* and *garrison,* a place where soldiers are quartered. So I became Garrison. Eventually it wound up on my driver's license and tax return—my girlfriend Mary married me as Garrison. In my heart, however, I still am Gary: Garrison feels like a fake mustache. Like a Roy calling himself Royalton or Gene becoming Genet. I wish I had become Llewelyn and written crime novels and gone to live in Zurich, but that's another story.

I started out playing with ambiguity, a fine way to disguise ignorance. "To be great is to be misunderstood," said Emerson, so, in search of greatness, I wrote poems that couldn't be understood because they made no sense. Writing poems that pushed the reader away came naturally to a Brethren boy. But deep down I wanted to make my mother laugh. Dad smiled at jokes and Mother had an innocent girlish laugh. She was fond of a particular kind of silliness. *I saw two houseflies in the kitchen today. Both females. I knew they were females because they were on the phone.* My father might smile at that. My mother laughed, hard. She didn't care for riddles or knock-knock jokes. Puns: not really. She preferred plausible preposterosity. *The old Norwegian was struck by lightning and died with a big smile on his face. He thought he was having his picture taken.* She laughed at that. She didn't care for Helen Keller jokes or jokes about cripples or dumb blondes. But she laughed and laughed at the one about the two missionaries caught by cannibals who put them into a pot of boiling water to cook and after a while one missionary started laughing—The other said, "What's so funny?"—He said, "I just peed in their soup." A joke with the little leap into unreality. But a natural sort of unreality. Hot water would naturally relax the urethra, a nurse would know that. A martyr is amused to get revenge. Why not?

12

The Amazing Year, Part 2

I HAD GOOD TEACHERS AT Anoka, that wasn't my problem. Mr. Charles Faust taught American history, the first teacher I had adult conversations with, about history and how it comes crashing down on good people. He was marked by the Depression, brought up by his grandma and older brother after his family fell apart. He wept, telling about it. Mr. DeLoyd Hochstetter taught English, pacing back and forth in front of the class, talking long twisting sentences like grapevines about Martin Luther, Freud, the myth of Sisyphus, Tolstoy, the Volstead Act, small-town life in South Dakota, the meaning of *agapé*, the vacuity of pop culture, the discrimination faced by German families during the World Wars, a steady drumroll of talk interrupted every fifteen minutes or so by his sudden disappearance to (someone said) go to the lavatory and wash his hands and then he'd return and resume his monologue. We didn't know about obsessive-compulsive disorder back then, so we admired Mr. Hochstetter as a crazed genius. Maybe not a good teacher of English but a man of fortitude and powerful recall. He wrote to me years later from a hospital bed, suffering from deep depression, and said he was proud of me and would I do a benefit performance at his church, Central Lutheran, so I did. He was there, happy to see me but a wreck of a man. I introduced him as my old English teacher and he got a big ovation. It struck me that night how little I know about human suffering. He had been pushing his burden a long way down a steep uphill road, I could see it in the face of his wife, her anxiety.

Helen Story was an English teacher who became a friend. I ate supper in Cully's Café on nights when I covered games for the *Herald*, and she invited me to sit with her. She ate a big salad and a slab of pie. She was a Minnesota farm girl who became a teacher so she wouldn't have to marry a farmer. She landed in Anoka in 1946 and boarded with a family, as unmarried women teachers were required to do, and ate supper at the café, arose early in the morning and took a shower at school. She was a tall birdlike woman, keen eyes behind her horn-rimmed glasses, who gave us *Macbeth* and *Romeo and Juliet*, correcting our wild attempts to impress her. She saw through me easily, my fake sophistication. She was the genuine thing; she truly loved theater, it was her life. "I could go every night of the week and someday I hope to," she said. She and her friend Lois Melby often took a bus to Minneapolis to see Shakespeare, Shaw, or Oscar Wilde, at the Lyric or Guthrie, and watched the last act from the door, waiting as long as possible before dashing to catch the last bus back to Anoka. She said, "Talent is worth about twenty percent and all the rest is experience. You *are* a writer. I know it and you know it." I hadn't known it, but when she said it I devoutly hoped it might come true.

Years later I got to speak at LaVona's retirement dinner and say how much her smile meant to me. Later I visited her at the hospice where she lay dying of breast cancer. She said she listened to my show and admired the Lake Wobegon monologue. She took my hand and said, "I'm going to beat this thing." She was so disfigured by chemo I hardly recognized her, but her voice was clear. I recited the *Young man of Anoka* limerick to her and she laughed. I helped her down the hall to her PT workout. That wonderful woman had given me the first dazzle of big possibilities. We have all sinned and come short of the glory of God, but I did make the class laugh out loud and Miss Person gave me encouragement, which I was desperate for, a boy with bad hair and wearing girl's clothes. Her gift was to help self-conscious youngsters step out of the bubble: *It's not about you. It's about the material. Work on the material. Don't make the performance be about you. Let yourself be a vehicle for something greater than yourself.* In the sixty years since, I've never had to multiply fractions or distinguish maple leaves from elm or birch, or talk intelligently about *Moby-Dick*, but her teaching—"It's not about you, it's about the material"—sticks with me. Shyness is not a trait; it's a shtick, and when it gets in your way, you should drop it. When she told me on her deathbed that she enjoyed my monologues on the radio, I felt complete. She was the last word. If she was proud of me, it is enough.

I thanked DeLoyd and LaVona, and I wished I'd thanked Hilmer and Helen, Corinne's parents. All through high school and during breaks in college, their house was open to her friends; all of us would-be intellectuals held forth in the lofty living room with the tropical fish drifting around their tank, the picture window overlooking our old sliding hill and the Mississippi, arguing about Injustice and Free Enterprise and Race, while the parents sat pleasantly, saying nothing, Helen on the couch with a glass of sherry, Hilmer in his big chair by the door with a bourbon in hand, smoking a Lucky. Christine was there, Thatcher, Tom, kids with big opinions. Corinne wasn't sheepish about her parents: she was resolutely loyal. She could denounce big corporations and the nuclear arms race, and she also attended the national plumbers' convention to make her parents happy. Those evenings looking out at the river were all about good manners. You could denounce capitalism with conviction, and the plumber and his lady listened with interest, smiling, made gentle inquiries, said, "I'll have to read more about that." All was easy and pleasant and *Help yourself to more cookies* and *May I warm up your tea?*

The 1950s gave birth to the term "teenager," but I looked forward to 1963 when I'd be 21 and could vote. In 1972, I'd be thirty, by which time I should have done something distinguished like maybe write a novel—that was the plan. Somewhere in the future, though I couldn't imagine it, a woman waited. None had shown interest so far but I hoped that one would appear.

In my junior year, our Anoka Tornadoes basketball team, a cinch to go to State, played little St. Francis in the first round of the district tournament—and in the fourth quarter our team froze and a bunch of awkward farm boys with bad hair beat us 53-50. There was profound grief at school the next day, cheerleaders weeping in the lunchroom. I wrote a poem about it: *The sky was cold and remorseless, a day to end romances—* which rhymed with St. Francis. I showed it to a girl who sat behind me in English, and she invited me to come over to the house where she was babysitting that night, so I did, and after we put the three children to

bed, she and I slipped into the parents' bed and she scootched up close to
me. I once found a book in my parents' dresser, *Light on Dark Corners*, a
marriage manual where I learned the word "coital," which I pronounced
COY-tle and which involved the *PENN-iss* and *VAGG-in-ah*, and now
I imagined something profound was about to happen but we heard a
car in the driveway and leaped out and straightened the bed. It wasn't
the parents, only someone turning around, but the mood was gone. We
laughed. We sat and held hands and watched TV. I went home. Still,
a girl had shown interest in me. This overshadowed the tragedy of St.
Francis completely.

One June night the Class of 1960, 300 strong, filed out of the cafeteria in our long blue gowns and down the hall past the band room and out
the back door of the high school and onto Goodrich Field as flashbulbs
popped in the grandstand and we marched under the goalposts to sit in
ranks of folding chairs set up between the twenty- and forty-yard lines,
and we heard a speech by someone about the great debt we owed to our
community for educating us, though we knew by now it wasn't a very
good education, and then we lined up to go forward to receive our diplo-
mas and be marched out into the real world. We returned our caps and
gowns to the cafeteria and I noticed classmates huddling to talk about
which parties they were going to. I hadn't been invited to any and had
no idea how to wangle an invitation, so I went home with my parents.
Among the shining stars of the Class of 1960, I was a small dim moon.
I was reading Emerson, Aristotle, the Bhagavad Gita, and *The Compassionate Buddha,* making my parents very uneasy, but it was like trying on
shirts, one after another. Fortunately, I had been pushed by four impressive teachers, who put a few ideas in my head, and I was allowed my
illusions and kept ignorant of the difficulties ahead. Ignorance was my
strong suit for a long time to come.

Two days later, I landed a job as a dishwasher in a residential hotel for
women in Minneapolis, running racks of dirty dishes through a steaming
hot machine as women brought their plates and bent and set them down
on a low ledge, the open necklines of women bending low so they could
say hi. It was inspiring. Stepping out of the steam and heat and into the
green world, I lit up a smoke, walked into Loring Park, practiced expres-
sive exhaling, figuring smoking to be a basic requirement for a writer.

Working hard in a hot steamy room makes the rest of a summer day very pleasant. My boss, the cook, was an ogre, but the graciousness of women made it all bearable. I didn't miss Anoka at all, not for a minute, and I never would, one advantage of being a nobody. I was free of the ignominious past and happy to be.

I saw my first movie, *Elmer Gantry* with Burt Lancaster as the corrupt evangelist and Jean Simmons as the godly woman he loves. I identified with Burt. I had applied to the University but wasn't confident, so I wrote to a Trappist monastery in Iowa, asking to visit and maybe join—I liked the idea of silence, which the Trappists practiced, and if you were silent, who would care if you were Catholic or not? The Trappists wrote back and suggested a visit, but Mother was distressed to see a letter from the Abbey of Saint Melleray. She said she was praying for me. "I love you, you know," she said.

I was surprised to hear her say it. We didn't talk like that in our family. To us, it came under Flattery, like saying "You are so smart." It moved me that she said it. I was glad when the U of M (*Omnibus Artibus, Commune Vinculum*) opened its arms to me, a B-minus student with a wistful ambition to be a writer. The acceptance letter came in late August. I went to campus and paid $71 for a quarter's tuition. My dad took me aside that night and told me he couldn't contribute money to help pay for college. I felt liberated by this. It meant that I was free to do as I pleased, no need for permission.

13

Radio

ON THE SUNDAY NIGHT BEFORE classes started at the U, I boarded a Greyhound to Isle to pick up a car from my uncle's Ford dealership. I was sitting on the bus, halfway back on the left side, window seat, a stream of southbound headlights passing, people heading back to the city from their lake cabins. I was reading Thoreau's *Walden* and suddenly there was an explosion of light up ahead and I was pitched forward and into a standing position as the bus went careening into a deep ditch and up onto a hayfield. There was some screaming, then silence. A few men and I stepped out past the driver who sat in shock, the windshield shattered, the dashboard crunched in, the steering wheel in his lap. I walked across a hayfield freshly mown, back to the highway, long lines of headlights, cars stopped north and south, and I saw the station wagon we'd hit, the hood in a sharp upward V, and the bodies, a man and a woman lying on the road, the man convulsively raising his head, the woman dead, her skirt up over her head. The body of a young man in the back of the car, shirtless, another man's body in the ditch. A Catholic priest bent over the woman, praying. The driver was the man raising his head. We onlookers treading on broken glass, talking in whispers, the smell of oil and gas in the air. A man said, "He passed me going eighty and I made room for him and he kept going. I thought he was out of his mind." Flashing red lights, a sheriff's car, an ambulance. Greyhound sent a spare bus to take us onward. I got to Isle, found my Uncle Aldridge up and awake though it was almost midnight. I told him the whole story, and he, a small-town doctor who'd seen drownings, gunshot wounds, suicides, car crashes, sat and patiently listened. I picked up the Ford and drove back home and slept on the couch for a couple hours and drove to campus to report for work.

I pulled into the parking lot at 5, put on a white smock, sat in the shack with my co-workers. I didn't know how to say that I'd been in a crash, seen the dead on the highway, and in the split second they were killed, I was thrown to my feet and I was happy to be on the bus and not in the car, profoundly grateful to be where I was, a parking attendant, eighteen, starting college. Thoreau said that the mass of men lead lives of quiet desperation but I was not one of them, I was happy and grateful. But they were strangers and one of them was grousing about summer having ended and they all seemed to be in agreement on that, so I said nothing.

The parking lot was on the river bluff, twelve acres of open gravel. My job was to direct incoming cars to the exact right parking spot, creating straight double rows, though there were no painted lines on the gravel, keeping fifteen-foot lanes, no easy task, especially when the big rush came at 7:30 (classes began at 8). Three ticket-sellers stood in the street and sold tickets (15 cents), and all the drivers were running late and nobody had correct change. One man, the infielder, stood mid-lot and directed traffic toward the two outfielders (me and another guy), whose job it was to look each car straight in the windshield, no waffling, and signal authoritatively so the driver knew that *no deviation is allowed here, sir, and do not test me even for a moment—No sir, not there, back that up, right there, you, right there.* Each car had to go to its one true and correct space in a parallel double row. Some people tried to park ironically or close to the bridgehead for personal convenience. *NO. Not today.* It was instructive, confronting the headlights of freethinkers. If individualism were to rear its head, chaos would ensue, lines go cockeyed, lanes get blocked, people be late for class, and we'd face frustration and rage—I had to fix my gaze on the driver and bark, *HEY, back that up, sir,* and they obeyed me. *Thank you, sir.* The exercise of power for the common good. As an eighteen-year-old I was in favor of freedom, and as a parking attendant I cracked down hard on it. Someone said the test of a great mind is the ability to embrace opposite ideas at one time. I became a genius.

The lot was full by 8 and we six attendants sat in the shack and listened to Steve Cannon on KSTP. My colleagues were a rough lot; you couldn't imagine women loving them at all, but it felt very chummy, listening to Cannon talk to his sidekicks Ma Linger and Morgan Mundane, who were Cannon himself. He was cool. He played against the Minnesota Nice model, doing Sarcastic Cantankerous. He was brilliant. Having just bullied hundreds of cars, I loved Steve-O, a guy from the Iron Range, married to Nanook of the North, no pushover. I imitated him, dealing with difficult drivers trying to cut a better deal for themselves, and when I yelled at them, they did as directed. I was an invisible middle child, I'd never been in command before. I enjoyed it.

And at 9 a.m. I crossed over the old iron-truss bridge to campus, looking down on the junky yards and shacks called Bohemian Flats on the flood plain below, a place you might wind up in if you failed to apply yourself, and over to the U on the east bank, the majesty of the Mall, the arched footbridges over Washington Avenue, the stately Library, the pillars of Northrop Auditorium and the inscription above, FOUNDED IN THE FAITH THAT MEN ARE ENNOBLED BY UNDERSTANDING, DEDICATED TO THE ADVANCEMENT OF LEARNING AND THE SEARCH FOR TRUTH, DEVOTED TO THE INSTRUCTION OF YOUTH AND THE WELFARE OF THE STATE. Passing under the canopy of elms, Sikhs in turbans, more black faces than ever I had seen before, Africans from Africa, the sound of Hindi and Chinese, women in saris with red dots on their foreheads, Korean War vets in fatigues, lovely intellectual girls in tweed skirts and horn-rimmed glasses descending the front steps of the library, books in satchels, a mathematician with wild Einstein hair. And a bunch of very black men speaking perfect French: it astonished me. And fraternity boys in three-piece plaid suits, boys my age impersonating downtown clothing salesmen. My uniform was blue jeans, leather boots, blue work shirt with a pack of Luckies in the pocket, corduroy jacket with leather elbow patches. This was how a writer should look, down at the heels but distinguished. I had little money but I splurged on a season ticket to the concerts in Northrop and saw Isaac Stern, Arthur Rubinstein, Andrés Segovia, the Royal Danish Ballet, the Swedish tenor Jussi Björling, the Cleveland Orchestra, Glenn Gould, a balcony seat, ten concerts, fifteen bucks. I was from artless Anoka where the only culture was agriculture. I wanted to see it all.

Northrop Auditorium, U of M.

Most of my classes were in Folwell Hall, an Elizabethan castle with balustrades and parapets, porches and gables, high chimneys, and class-rooms full of loose talk and tobacco smoke. James Wright chain-smoked through his elegant lectures on *Oliver Twist* and *Little Dorrit* in his Dickens class. In Richard Cody's Composition: The Essay class, elbow to elbow at sidearm desks, we studied prose architecture in the work of Addison, Chesterton, Emerson, and Mencken, smoking, using tuna fish cans for ashtrays. Asher Christensen smoked a pipe through his American Government course. He was a slim man with a beautiful voice who spoke in whole paragraphs without notes; his great theme was the Constitution as a device of checks and balances to force antagonists to deal with each other civilly. One day that fall, he went to the faculty club for lunch, lay down for a nap, and died of a heart attack. He was 57.

Maggie Forbes's Latin translation class was the big challenge, despite my two years of high school Latin, I was a bona fide tabula rasa, tried to be incognito, committed many errata, had no alibi, only mea culpas. English was my terra firma, my sine qua non. Maggie gave me a B-minus, which was more than generous. Pax vobiscum.

Across University Avenue from Folwell was Dinkytown, a neighborhood squashed in between the Como freight yards and the main line of the Burlington Northern on which, four times a day, the Silver Zephyr raced to or from Chicago, a few feet behind McCosh's bookstore, owned by the anarchist Melvin McCosh, with radical slogans on index cards pinned to the shelves ("The last capitalist we hang shall be the one who sold us the rope") and Al's Breakfast, a hole-in-the-wall joint with four-teen stools at the counter, where you ate your eggs and sausage with mathematicians, med students, maybe a medievalist. A coffeehouse, the Ten O'Clock Scholar, where in the evening someone sat on a stool in the front window, singing about the plight of miners, sailors, sharecroppers, hoboes, people in short supply in Minnesota. Bob Zimmerman, who had lived around the corner in a rented room with a mattress and a hotplate, had recently left for New York to become Bob Dylan, and I heard people complain about the money he owed them. Across the street was a gro-cery, Virg 'N Don's, where people shopped for the sound of the name. Around the corner on Fourth Street was the Varsity Theater where I saw Godard's *Breathless*. A rats' nest of a bookstore called Heddon's whose snowy-haired proprietor, after pondering a moment, could reach into the third orange crate from the bottom and pull out the very book you asked for. In Perine's Books, a few years later, I invested in a copy of John Updike's brand-new *The Centaur* and got swallowed up in it and realized that I would not become a novelist. Updike, only ten years older than I, was a genius. I was not and there was no point in pretending. A novelist is a boatbuilder, and what I do is make model airplanes. So radio comedy would have to be enough.

I got into radio two weeks after arrival. I was in Westbrook Hall tak-ing a written psychological test, required of incoming students, with questions like *Do you sense that people whom you do not know are conspir-ing to cause you harm?* and *Do you sometimes feel there are insects crawling all over your body?*—I glanced out a window and saw, fifty feet away, in a dressing room at Northrop Auditorium, a young naked woman looking at herself in a long mirror. She was tall and lean, black hair tied in a bun, delicate breasts, long exquisite fingers, extending a leg, lifting an arm, as she struck dancerly poses. She was a dancer with the Royal Danish ballet performing that night at Northrop, and I wanted to meet her. I had had a crush on Ulla, the Danish exchange student at Anoka, my unattainable date. Now, looking at the dancer, I got the bright idea of finding a tape recorder and meeting the dancer and doing a *radio documentary* about a Dane's impressions of America—yes!—and sending the tape to Ulla, so I hiked down the Mall to Coffman Union and the WMMR studio and walked into a crowded room, a staff meeting in progress, and a tall guy in a trench coat shook my hand, the program director Barry Halper, who showed me around the studios, and told me I had the voice of a newscaster. He was very friendly. I did not mention the naked dancer. That idea petered out.

Barry was very enthused about radio. We walked into the control room. Three big felt-covered turntables, a mixing board, a glass window looking into the announce studio beyond. He needed a newscaster, he said. He showed me an Associated Press teletype clattering in a closet, continuous yellow paper spilling out the front, and he ripped off about forty feet of it, and asked me to put together a newscast. So I assembled a stack of stories and the engineer, a kid named Harvey, pointed me toward the studio, a tiny room with green acoustic tile walls and a felt-covered table, an RCA microphone suspended over it, a gooseneck lamp, a clock on the wall, and a small metal box with a cough switch. A red light came on, and I said, "This is Garrison Keillor with the news." And I was in radio. I got in by wanting to interview a naked ballet dancer and thereby impress someone I wished would be my girlfriend, and I became a newscaster because Brethren sermons had taught me how to speak with solemn authority. I read the news in the voice of Brother Rogers talking about the Tribulation.

The next day Barry called to ask if I could do a noon newscast, daily. No pay, but it'd be fun. I said yes. I had a job as a parking lot attendant, 5 to 8 a.m., and four classes to attend, but sure, of course, why not?

The next Saturday, there was a WMMR beer party on the riverbank. It was a football Saturday and the U of M Marching Band came parading down University Avenue past Folwell toward the stadium, the drum major Mr. Dicky Johnson of Anoka in his blazing white uniform and grenadier's hat strutting ahead of them, pumping his baton as they burst into the *Minnesota Rouser* and you could feel the pride for blocks around, old alumni in their thirties and forties standing and singing, *Minnesota, hats off to thee.* I went to the library and studied that day and saw the Danish ballet that night—the dark-haired dancer was prominent on stage and fully clothed—and around ten o'clock I went down to the river to the party. I met three girls, one of them passing a pint of rum around, all of them jazzed at having pledged a good sorority. Barry wasn't there, but some engineers were, one of whom said I was a good newscaster. One of the girls said, "We ought to go skinny-dipping!" and the other two squealed. A couple boys heard this and joined us. The girls dared us to go in the water and said if we did, they would too. We declined, but they pleaded, and they said, "We'll follow you in. Promise." I didn't want to be taken for a prude. So I stepped forward and took off my jacket and shirt, shoes and socks, and dropped my trousers and shorts, and slid down the bank and jumped in the river. It was a steep drop-off and I tried to stay upright, but the current swept me off my feet and I floated, arms thrashing, and thought, "This would be a ridiculous time to drown." I wasn't a good swimmer, having skipped swim class years ago at the Y, but I stayed afloat for a couple hundred yards and passed under the Franklin Avenue Bridge and grabbed hold of a branch on shore and climbed up the steep slope. Little paths wound through the trees, and as I followed one up the bank, I was aware of several older men wandering around in a furtive way. I had stumbled on an old cruising area for homosexuals, I who did not even know the word. A man asked me what I was looking for, and I said, "My clothes." I walked naked along the East River Road back to the parking lot and found the girls guarding my clothing. The party had broken up. They were terrified that I might've drowned and they ran to meet me, holding out my jeans. One of them was crying. She had dark hair cut very short, white blouse hanging loose, bare arms. She put her arms around me and noticed I was shivering. She led me to her car and we got in. As soon as the door closed, she kissed me, tears on her cheek. We drove to White Castle and bought a sack of burgers and fries. She took my hand and kissed it. She was trembling. She told me that if I had drowned, she would never be able to forgive herself. She drove me across the bridge to the big parking lot where my car was parked. We sat in her car and talked. Her name was Lynne and I thought of a limerick, *I once met a woman named Lynne with whom I was tempted to sin. I opened her shirt, thought "What can it hurt?" and carefully put my hand in.* She laughed in a way that suggested anticipation. So I did. I was nineteen and had never touched a girl there. She had big eyebrows and a chain around her neck with not one but two crosses, so I guessed she was Catholic. I had heard things about Catholic girls and was curious to know if they might be true. I thought of my cousin Roger. Probably this was exactly what he wanted. He risked death to be able to touch that girl's breast, he knew he couldn't swim and he dove into the water after Susan expecting her to throw her arms around him and hold him up, he dove in anticipation of her embrace, he never imagined the violence of panic, he only wanted to hold her. I thought of this, my hair wet, having floated down the river. Now he lay in a grave in Lakewood Cemetery and I was a year older than he. She kissed me. She said, "You're so different." She said, "I hope I see you again." I wrote the limerick on a slip of paper and she wrote down her phone number, but the paper was gone when I got home. Still, I went naked into the river and might've drowned but climbed out through a motley band of forlorn men and found tenderness in a woman's arms in a White Castle parking lot. No wonder they are still my favorite hamburgers.

I did my daily newscast in hopes of meeting Lynne again. Barry said she was the sister of a DJ who'd dropped out of school. He promised he'd find her for me, but he left WMMR and was busy looking for a job. To my amazement, he had become my friend. He was twenty, he'd already been to Los Angeles and Las Vegas, had personally met Buddy Hackett, Shelley Berman, Shecky Greene, Joey Bishop. He collected *Playboy* magazines, he was a man of the world, he invited me to his house in St. Louis Park, took me to Lincoln Del and bought me a Reuben, taught me the words *mishegoss* and *schlock,* explained the difference between a *schlemiel,* a *schmendrick,* and a *schlimazel.*

WMMR was a closed-circuit radio signal transmitted by cables strung through steam tunnels to transmitters in the basements of student dormitories. Out the studio window as I did my newscast I saw Comstock Hall, a women's dorm, and I imagined young women listening to me and it was inspiring. Other WMMR boys aimed to be DJs at Top Forty stations and practiced the growling, gulping jacked-up style of rock 'n' roll radio, which was too Holy Roller for me. I aimed for a mature dignified sound. Barry said I sounded good.

I did the newscast daily from October through May, when I was informed that due to a dreadful mistake, the WMMR circuitry had failed the summer before. Nobody had realized it, but 730 AM had gone dead. I'd been reading the news for seven months to myself. Nobody knew why. It meant nothing to me, though, because a few days earlier Barry

Halper had died, driving his white convertible on Highway 12, heading home from his newscaster job at KDWB around 3 p.m. He must've looked away for an instant, maybe to light a smoke, and drove into the rear of a school bus stopped to pick up kids and was killed instantly. The next day's *Tribune* ran a picture of the wreck on the front page. I bought a yarmulke and went to his funeral at Mikro Kodesh Synagogue and sat next to his mother, Ida. He was her only child, she was frozen in shock. I held her hand. She leaned on me, weeping. Her husband sat on the other side of her, he looked furious, wanting it to end, the whole bad joke, and life to resume. The casket was closed. "You wouldn't want to see," she said. "I saw, I can never forget." There was nothing to say, no comfort to give. The rabbi chanted the Kaddish and people around me chanted along from memory. Barry was the coolest guy I knew, generous with praise, a fan of comedians, and he had befriended me, an evangelical kid, out of the goodness of his heart. I visited the Halpers twice that summer and once the year after, and she wept and hugged me and his dad, Paul, sat stone-faced and silent, inconsolable, wishing I'd go away, wondering *Why Barry? Why my son? Why not this schlemiel?* I put WMMR on my résumé—no mention of my newscast having been a private one—and it got me another radio job two years later. I thought of Barry often: a young guy starting out in radio, distracted for a moment, and crashing into the high rear bumper of the bus, the hood of his car shoved into his face, dead of a crushed chest and a broken neck, I saw this in my mind a hundred times. I owed it to him to stay in the business. And after seven months of practice, imitating Edward R. Murrow, I didn't sound bad, even if nobody else knew it.

14

Newspapering

My sophomore year was a lost year. I enrolled in English Lit courses, Shakespeare and Eighteenth Century and Milton, and grew a beard for the scholarly look, and published a few abstruse (obtuse? refuse?) poems in the *Ivory Tower*, but I was lackadaisical, indifferent, lost in class, having skimmed the text lightly if at all. I sat under the gentle drizzle of learned lectures and wrote term papers stringing together critical monkey talk, but nothing took, nothing interested me. I drifted along, learning nothing until I took a course in journalism taught by Robert Lindsay, a former Marine with a big dent in the top of his head. (Oddly, none of us journalists ever asked him how he got that dent. We sat and studied it and formed theories but never sought the facts.) He cared about facts and not so much about fancy writing. He circled it in red: "Too lit'ry." Mr. Lindsay was gruff but good-hearted—his motto, *Endure. Hang in.*—and he was a good teacher. The difference between him and English Lit teachers was that they spoke to impress and he to engage. They spoke to the ghost of a long-ago mentor and he met us on the ground where we stood. On the first day of class, he announced a simple rule: one misspelling in a written assignment and you got an F, regardless of literary merit. We rolled our eyes at the unfairness of it, but he was serious. As a Marine, he believed that pain could change minds. Once you wrote an assignment for him and got a big red F, you paid closer attention to your work and saw up close what was on the page, word by word. We students had plenty of attitude, but he gave us a competence: after Lindsay's class, you were a copyreader for the rest of your life on earth. You looked at your manuscript and the mistakes flickered like fireflies. A good writerly habit, *pay attention,* from which other good habits may derive.

One day I saw a notice on the J-School bulletin board for a temporary job at the St. Paul *Pioneer Press* and drove over to St. Paul and was hired as a reporter and dropped out of school. It was a morning paper, so I worked 3 p.m. to midnight in the city room, the big presses rumbling down below, and reported to the city editor, Walt Streightiff, sitting at the head of the horseshoe desk facing the copy editors and rewrite men to his left and right. He was a bulldog of a man, bald, starched white shirt with sleeves rolled up, suspenders, a bark that could be heard fifty feet away. He put me to work writing obituaries. It was a classic newsroom: reporters' desks piled high with papers around black Royal typewriters, clouds of smoke in the air. Everyone smoked more or less steadily. Don Del Fiacco did human interest, Nate Bomberg had the police beat, Don Giese covered major crime, Don Riley did sports. I was in charge of death.

I felt useful, picking up the phone, talking to a widow. Her man had died, and she wanted the world to pay attention. She had a story to tell about his knowledge of local history or his love of Scouting or fishing, his carpentry and the fact that he made her happy for fifty-some years. The man had his merits.

Mr. Streightiff liked his obituaries straight and simple, four graphs— name and address and DOD, church and club memberships, survivors, and funeral arrangements. "We can't get into feelings and how much someone was loved, otherwise it turns into a contest. Just bury the stiffs and leave the eulogy to the priest," he said, but I tried to add personal detail, as told to me over the phone—the man who, until he was seventy, swam across White Bear Lake every summer, the woman who could speak the alphabet backward quickly and perfectly, the man with the enormous model-train layout in his basement, the woman whose peach pie was envied by others. Some of these Mr. Streightiff sniffed at but tolerated; others he crossed out. "Every woman in St. Paul has a pie recipe," he said. "If we start putting recipes in obits, there'll be no end to it." That was fifty-five years ago and he was in his fifties and a chain-smoker, so I suppose he is gone now. If I were writing his obit, I'd mention the stiffness of his starched white shirt and how he picked up a phone and said, "YEAH?" into it: Mr. Heaberlin, the press foreman in the basement, a copyboy, Mrs. Streightiff, every caller was equal. The "YEAH" was to discourage small talk and it did. Disaster, crime, government and politics were our principal crops, followed by sports and weather. Opinion was not his province. He was loud but not a bully; he didn't play favorites, he paid no compliments because he didn't look back at yesterday. He was in charge of weights and measures, what goes at the top of page one, what goes back by the want ads.

My hero was Irv Letofsky, who covered politics. He was from Fargo, had a beautiful smile, a knack for putting people at ease. Now and then he and I had supper at the Lowry Hotel. He wrote satiric sketches for the Brave New Workshop nightclub in Minneapolis and had a reporter's innate contempt for big muckety-mucks. He said, "Politicians are all desperate to be loved, and the worst are Democrats because they pretend to care about the common man. Republicans don't pretend." He said, "Liberals get it wrong over and over. Joe McCarthy was a blowhard but he was small potatoes. Eisenhower was not a dolt and Stevenson was no giant. He had the luxury of high-minded talk because he knew he was going to lose." He said this over a steak dinner at the Lowry and then he said, "You wouldn't happen to have twenty bucks, would you? I left my wallet at the office." I reached into my pocket and he said, "Just testing. Good to know who I can count on." He gave me a big grin. He was the coolest guy at the paper, and I followed him around like a puppy dog. Years later, when I was a best-selling author, and the editors of the Los Angeles *Times* invited me to lunch, there was Irv, grinning at me—he was their entertainment editor—and he leaned over and said, "I knew you when you were just white trash. It's great that the publisher invited you to lunch but don't shit in your pants." It was a Fargo guy's way of making me feel at home.

As the death correspondent, I called up hospitals to find out if the victims of car crashes had perished or not, so I could update the highway death toll. In my spare time, I was sent to interview minor celebrities: a classical pianist, a sportscaster, Robert Frost's daughter, nobody really big came to St. Paul. Irv referred to the celeb beat as "the garbage run," but I liked it, the slight brush with minor greatness. I asked if I could go out on a fire or cover a murder trial—"We haven't had a good murder in years, and anyway that's Giese's department," Mr. Streightiff said. I was offered a slot in the copy desk doing rewrite, but one look at the pallid faces in the smoky haze of the horseshoe told me all I needed to know about rewrite—it was a cemetery—so I left.

The pleasure of newspapering moved me to disappoint my aunts and leave the Brethren, a simple matter of preferring a wide-ranging life to strict adherence to the letter of doctrine. God gave us eyes and the men around me watched each other closely to make sure their blinders were tight. My brother Philip left for a nondenominational Christian fellowship, my sister Judy married a Baptist, eventually the three youngers would depart as well. Our Assembly had lost its spirit in the division of 1947, we were a militant remnant clinging to a life raft and it made sense to float free, and swim. There was a hospitable shore not far away, trees, gardens, friendly strangers.

The Brethren was a great education however. It said that the material world is not All, that human institutions are susceptible to severe moral judgment, and that one day the mighty will be brought low and the low exalted. It was like a superhero comic except you knew it was true. And Brethren exclusivity stuck with me, a rich inheritance, the gift of scorn. You get attached to the wrong things, and it wastes whole parts of your life unless you can break away without remorse. Thanks to a Brethren upbringing, I could quit jobs, some of them cushy, and walk away from two marriages and several romances, drop burdensome friends. When I heard that Tina Brown would be taking over *The New Yorker,* I packed up my office and got in a cab and went home.

I am an Escape Artist; avoidance is my specialty. I quit smoking and put away alcohol and gave up writing incoherent poetry that sits on shelves and is never read. An artist needs to believe in God, whether he can say the Lord's Name or not. There is no art without Someone who looks at your work and says, *It is not good enough, not even close.* Other people tell you you're a genius, but He knows better and you must pay attention to Him whether you call Him Jehovah or George. And a writer needs arrogance to get him through the scrappy years until he acquires a name and can afford to be humble. I acquired arrogance as a child, reading the Brethren prophet J. N. Darby and looking at Brother Booth's *Chart of Time from Eternity to Eternity,* a map of the dispensations of human history from the Garden of Eden to the Judgment Throne and the Lake of Fire, which gave me the feeling that I was in possession of the secrets of the universe. It was a wonderful feeling. I couldn't change a carburetor or build a stone wall or raise tomatoes, but I knew the mind of God. This is pridefulness, a powerful liquor. Other writers were assailed by self-doubt. Not me. Not even now.

15

The Guntzels

O maiden, young maiden, I worry for you.
To marry a writer, you should not do.
He will put on a suit and kneel down in church
But for him marriage is only research.
He will write a novel that's set in your home
And all your best lines he'll take for his own.

I MET MARY GUNTZEL AT the Guntzel family cabin on Cross Lake the summer after I quit the paper. I was twenty and living at home that spring, writing poems and dark allegories and was in emotional turmoil over my place in the world, if there was such a thing and whether I was a writer or a bus driver with pretensions, and for solace I walked every evening over to Corinne's house and sat on the porch with Helen and poured out my heart for an hour or two and she listened. She invited me to spend a couple weeks at the lake with her and Hilmar and Corinne, and of course I said yes. Corinne's boyfriend, Leeds Cutter, had died in February in the horrible car crash and I had visited her several times at Carleton College, where she was practicing stoicism but in deep mourning. Leeds was on a clear track and meant for great things in the world, we knew that, but we didn't talk about him, anything you could say was a cliché, it was all so much beyond words. We listened to Tchaikovsky's *Symphonie Pathétique* on a turntable in her dorm room. She was reading Rilke and found comfort in German and tried to translate for me—"It's impossible," she said, "like trying to describe stones."

She and Leeds had been necking in his car in her parents' driveway and her dad discovered them and forbade them to see each other for a few months, and their courtship became more passionate by telephone and letter. He and she talked about marriage, making a family, and buying a farm. He sent her a lamb as a birthday gift. A beautiful plan was forming in the near distance and then the phone rang and she went to the hospital where he died.

I wrote her long letters that spring—*"When the burden of life's problems can no longer be borne, I escape into the healing darkness of a rainy night—rain pelts my face, rivulets of water run down my cheeks, mingled with my tears"*—that sort of letter. Once I asked her straight out: *"What do you think will become of me? I am twenty. I need to do something that shows direction and purpose. I drifted into the U, into radio . . . then to the newspaper. Now I need to get serious."* Corinne wrote back that she was no judge of my writing but that she did like the poem I sent her.

> *Come to me in your dark green dress,*
> *Open your arms, be impetuous.*
> *Rest awhile. Let peacefulness*
> *Immerse you as our fingers touch*
> *Nobody's hand on the steering wheel,*
> *Nobody's feet on brake or clutch,*
> *Each one following what we feel.*

A love poem. I wrote it for her but didn't say so. Nowhere in the raindrop-spattered letters did I ever say, "I am in love with you, Corinne." She was in mourning and I was in distress and kept my distance, but I loved her family and went north to Cross Lake. Corinne's cousin Mary was there with her parents, Marjorie and Gene. It was a simple one-room frame cabin built by Hilmer and his dad, Hugo, back in the Twenties, four double bunkbeds separated by canvas curtains strung on wires, a back door leading out to the outhouse, an old yellow kitchen table and wood stove in the middle, a refrigerator and stove and sink on one side, wicker chairs, a flowery green linoleum floor, a screened front porch looking at the great blue lake, a swinging couch on the porch, a hammock in the trees, a dock down below. A breeze blew through the cabin, from screened porch in front to screen door in rear, and we seven sat around the old yellow kitchen table and played Hearts, each with our drinks, Marj and her Rob Roy, Gene and his Manhattan, Hilmer with a bourbon and soda, and the rest of us drinking white wine. Smatterings of conversation. Whoever held the queen of spades tried to hold her till the dramatic last moment, then lay her down in a trick taken by whoever was ahead.

The Guntzel family was my first look at adult life in which grown children and their parents are free to be themselves in each other's company. The younger can think aloud and not be dismissed and the elder are offered due respect. This easy tolerance was unknown in Brethrendom, where your doctrinal shoelaces had to be tied properly and the bows knotted. The cabin was very chummy. I loved that. Corinne the socialist declaiming against corporate greed to her father the Republican plumber, afternoons swimming off the dock, card games and Scrabble, drinks on the porch, family gossip, world affairs, curling up with books, and Mary, a piano major at the University, very shy, lying on an upper bunk observing the rest of us from above. Hardly a word passed between her and me, but I called her a few weeks later and asked her to a movie.

Corinne told me to do it: "You should call Mary. I think she's in love with you." So I did. We went to a jazz concert and a week later to an organ recital. We were two awkward outsiders with many inexpressible feelings about music and poetry. She told me she'd gone on a date once and the boy had tried to take her blouse off and she'd jumped out of the car and walked two miles home. I was twenty and had never dated. I admired girls, I loved their company, I couldn't imagine one being attracted to my hangdog face and long silences. Mary was the first girl to show serious interest in me. Naturally, I was stunned.

We went to the movie *Splendor in the Grass*, and afterward, in the parking lot, discussing Natalie Wood who declined to have sex with Warren Beatty and thereby wound up in a mental ward, Mary said, "When are we going to make love?" There it was, on the third date. A card laid on the table. I said something wordless, like *Mmmmmm*. I was a twenty-year-old virgin and I decided not to become a twenty-one-year-old one. A week later, we went to dinner and afterward to her apartment, and her roommate took one look at us and decided to go study at the library and we sat in the dark and necked. A few weeks later, my brother Philip asked me to babysit his little kids while he and Ann-Britt visited friends in Duluth overnight. He said to bring Mary if I wished. She was eager to come. The children went to bed early. She led me into the guest bedroom. I had never been naked with a woman before. I was astonished at how easy it was. So simple, my body knew what to do. I withdrew at the crucial moment—*how did I know to do this?*—and seed gushed out of me and she laughed to see it. If she'd been disgusted, everything would be different. Life is full of these small but crucial intersections. I had done as she wished me to do.

I think she saw romance as a simple transaction, like what her parents had accomplished, two odd individuals forming a gentle pact to be partners and make a life with its own limits and comforts. Gene was a premature baby, not expected to live. His mother swabbed him with oil and set him in a cigar box on an open oven door at low heat and he survived. He grew up shrimpy, unathletic, injury-prone. Marjorie was a North Dakota farm girl in the Dirty Thirties, her father a dedicated drinker, her brother likewise. Money was scarce; the mother had to fight for the money to put food on the table. When the dust blew, it sifted through the cracks and covered the furniture. Marj had no sweet memories of childhood. She and Gene made a gracious and pleasant home with good china, wall-to-wall carpeting, tasteful furniture, pictures on the walls, a piano, and she was a good cook, standing over the stove, stirring gravy, a Winston in one hand, a drink in the other, keeping an ear out for the conversation in the living room. She had a kind face, a boisterous laugh, and if Mary sat down at the piano and played Chopin, Marj was transported by the loveliness of the home she had created, it brought tears to her eyes, the clean house, the smell of chicken and gravy, the Chopin, and I meshed into the picture as the boyfriend. She escaped from the Dust Bowl through gracious living. I saw this. She had banished the dust, the drunken men, the Depression by her hard work and her good taste, and her buoyant hospitality. As a writer, I felt obliged to scorn suburbia but that ended at Marj's doorstep: I was welcome in her home and I admired her spirit.

Having grown up among alcoholics, Marj dreaded harsh words and bad feelings. She ran a tight ship, a contradiction of my dark sophomoric writing: the ball game on TV, sound off. A relish tray on the coffee table. Each of us holding a drink, a smoke. It was very convivial, miles away from the rigid conventions of Brethren table talk. A classic middle-class suburban Sunday held together by the good-natured matriarch, a Republican Methodist reader of Reader's Digest Condensed Books, and I enjoyed their company even as their style was what I'd set out to avoid. I was a junior at the U, an editor at the *Ivory Tower,* trying to be talented, hanging out with artists who used the word "bourgeois" for everything shallow and insipid, and I liked Marj and Gene, bourgeois though they were, more than what I'd seen of bohemian life, the squalor and carelessness and self-infatuation of hippie friends. Eventually, I put Marj into the Lake Wobegon saga as the unflappable Marjorie Krebsbach, and she liked that. She wrote me a kind letter thanking me for "immortalizing" her, a few years after Mary and I broke up.

I was living on the West Bank near Seven Corners, in a neighborhood of hippies and dissidents and musicians, everyone living in shifting romantic arrangements, and I hung out at the Mixers bar with cranky old lefties and would-be writers, men bitching about academia, the government, the decline of journalism, ripping into the manager of the Twins, the abject emptiness of corporate life, the deficits of famous writers. It was the Critics Corner and I admired their ferocity. The military was idiocy in action, the English Department was dedicated to the hatred of literature, the Democratic Party was the dull leading the ignorant, the Holy Mother Church was full of pedophiles. It was classic saloon talk, nihilistic but all about personal style. I sat and listened, enjoyed the chatter. They had no money, no great prospects, but plenty of attitude.

They would've regarded the Guntzels of Hopkins with a degree of contempt, so I kept the two worlds apart. I enjoyed Hopkins, mowing their lawn, mixing their drinks, staying for supper, even as I maintained a big beard, aimed to be a writer and escape the regimented life, enjoy the company of musicians, artists, iconoclasts of a similar stripe. But sometimes I experienced bolts of lucidity. A poem of mine was published in a literary quarterly, which was nice until I looked at it on the page across from a poem by a real poet, Donald Justice, and saw mine clearly for the fake that it was. I admired his poem: *Lights are burning in quiet rooms where lives go on resembling ours.* Mine was a rummage drawer of images, nothing more. It was edifying to see what a shitty poem I'd written, and so was the experience of studying in the periodicals room of

Walter Library. Prestigious literary magazines were kept there on shelves, and I sat under fine old chandeliers and noticed that nobody ever walked in and picked up those magazines that I longed to be published in. I thought, *If that's prestige, then the ultimate honor is to be embalmed.* But plenty of people picked up *The New Yorker* and looked at the cartoons. There was a lesson here: *People will come for the dessert who may then stay and eat the spinach.*

I was leading two lives, the life of literary ambition and the life of family comfort, and then I was yanked away when Grandma Dora was felled by a stroke in July 1964. I was back at the U, in summer school, working at KUOM, and I went straight to the Catholic hospital in Onamia and sat at her deathbed for two days, stroking her arm, holding an ice pack to her brow. She had collapsed while vacuuming at Eleanor's and never recovered consciousness. Her daughters tended to her, Eleanor taking charge. My uncles dropped in the next day and sat at the other end of the room, uneasy, uncertain what to do with themselves. They each came to the bedside, looked at her, then retreated to the other end of the room and sat in awkward silence, having no words, and talked about cars. I was disgusted that they weren't paying homage to Grandma and reminiscing about her. It was all about cars. They couldn't bring themselves to express grief. As Brethren, they believed that death transports us into God's presence so we should rejoice in it, but they didn't do that either. They talked about the superiority of Ford to General Motors, then they talked about their gardens and building projects. Eleanor told me I should go back to class, but I stayed, holding Grandma's hand, stroking her hair, pressing a cold cloth to her forehead, moistening her lips with ice chips. Eleanor said, "You have a job. Mother would want you to go to work in the morning." In this family, tending the dying was women's work, and I respected that. They pulled the bedclothes off her and they lovingly bathed her, my naked grandmother, the gray clump of hair where each of them had once descended into the world, and I left then, but with a heavy heart, knowing that now the door was closed to the story of Grandpa Keillor and his sister Mary and Grandma's job as a railroad telegrapher, why her dad John Wesley Powell had moved to Anoka from Iowa—a hundred questions in my mind—that door was now locked forever.

A few days later, when her coffin was carried through the cemetery gate, I stood in the back of the crowd and sobbed and didn't try to hide it. The men of the family believed in strict adherence to rules, but Grandma admired spunk and ambition. She liked having a writer in the family. She said so. She is ever in my heart. And I still have her farm firmly in my head and the Model T where my cousins and I sat singing mournful songs and at night, lying awake in a strange hotel somewhere, sometimes I imagine myself back to Grandma's, washing my face in cold water from the hand pump on the back step and coming in for Post Toasties and a cup of Postum. Grandma and I will kneel on the parlor floor as Uncle Jim prays and I'll go out and collect eggs in the machine shed where the hens have laid them. Uncle Jim hitches up Prince and Ned and lifts me aboard Prince, and I put my arms around his neck as the harness jingles and the wagon creaks, and I smell the new-mown hay and fall asleep on the way to the meadow.

16

Settling In

I GAVE MARY A DIAMOND engagement ring in 1965, which made Marj happy, but no date was set since my prospects were vague. I graduated from the U in 1966 and sold my car to pay for a trip by Greyhound to New York to interview for a job at *The New Yorker*—Mr. Lindsay had written them a splendid letter of recommendation and they said, "Send him out" so I went—and if I were hired, I imagined maybe I could disappear into the city and let the wedding be canceled. Disappearing into New York seemed like an excellent way of simplifying my life. And Mary could find a better man than I—of that I was certain.

A few nights before I left town, I went out to Metropolitan Stadium to watch the Twins play, maybe for the last time, with my friend Arnie Goldman, who was on his way to a teaching job in Australia. We bought steak sandwiches and a couple Grain Belts and sat in the second deck behind home, two birds on a wire. Out beyond right, Holsteins grazed in a pasture, and behind us in the press box sat Herb Carneal announcing play-by-play in his Virginia drawl to Minnesotans sitting on porches from here to Gull Lake as his cohort Halsey Hall puffed on a cigar and did commentary in a voice like gravel sliding down a washboard. Arnie was an Army vet, married with three kids, a cheerful guy, a good friend, and it was sad to think we'd drift apart. "I'm in the wrong line of work. I'm no scholar, I'm a bullshitter. Teaching is okay but I should've been a shoe salesman," he said. "You're different. You'll do okay. You're a loner. You come in a tight package." We sat and smoked, and he said, "I'm a happy man in a sad life, and you're a sad man in a happy life."

When the Met was torn down in 1982, I went out to look at the demolition. I walked around the mountains of wreckage where the grandstand had stood and slipped through the security fence and onto the field, which was in good shape except for bulldozer tracks in the infield. The left field stands and bullpen and scoreboard were intact and the flagpole. I walked across the outfield. There wasn't another soul on the premises, just me and the grackles. I felt like an archaeologist at the ruins of an ancient temple. And his line came back to me, *You're a sad man in a happy life,* and I'm still not sure what to make of it.

I rode the bus to New York thirty hours in a stupor, rolling through the Lincoln Tunnel around midnight, and I walked out with my duffel bag into Times Square where Broadway slices across 44th and Seventh Avenue to make six different canyons hundreds of feet high, flashing signs, rivers of people, and I hiked south on Broadway and found a cheap hotel crowded with welfare families, their kids roaming the halls at 2 a.m. When I opened the door to my room, there was skritching and skittering and a crowd of cockroaches broke for the closet. I left the light on and lay on the bed, fully dressed, shoes on—it was a 10-watt bulb so it didn't keep me awake—I was awakened by the sun shining through the dusty window. I washed my face and shouldered the duffel and headed for Chelsea and into a Hispanic neighborhood, looking for a boarding house I'd seen in the want ads and found it on West 19th next door to a convent, a four-story brownstone. I walked through the door and into a big dayroom and met the manager, a social worker named Libby Lyon. She said it was a salon for struggling artists and writers and rented me a little room slightly below sidewalk level, with toilet down the hall, for $55 a week including breakfast and dinner. There was one window in my room, through which I could see the shoes of people passing by on the sidewalk. Some residents sat in the sunny courtyard under an ailanthus tree, looking at a twelve-foot wall, painted pink. They may have been artists and writers, but clearly this was a halfway house for the mentally ill, newly released from hospitals; they were doped up on Thorazine, listening to nuns in the convent garden chanting in Spanish. An old man, hearing I was interviewing at *The New Yorker*, said he was an old friend of Dorothy Parker. "I used to see a lot of Dottie, I don't anymore," he said. He also told me that Marion Tanner, who cooked in the kitchen, was the aunt of Patrick Dennis and the model for his character Auntie Mame, which turned out to be true. She was not the comic grande dame of the novel, though: she had her hands full, cooking and keeping an eye on a foster daughter who kept trying to light fires. Life was a banquet for other people, but she was working to put lunch on the table and keep the house from burning down.

The next morning, I walked uptown toward 25 West 43rd, an address I knew by heart, having sent a dozen stories there with stamped, self-addressed envelopes. I thought of the greats as I walked along 44th, the Algonquin where George S. Kaufman, Robert Benchley, Dorothy Parker, and Marc Connelly gathered to mock the pieties of the day and resist sobriety, where Harold Ross conceived his humor magazine that against his better judgment became *The New Yorker*, which Frayne Anderson handed me a copy of when I was young and impressionable.

It was high drama, walking the street A. J. Liebling had walked to the Paramount Theater to interview Pola Negri, lying in a white peignoir on a white chaise longue like a crumpled gardenia petal, and to the Hotel Dixie, home of Colonel John R. Stingo, the horse racing columnist for the *National Enquirer*, who said, "I sit up there in my room at the Dixie, and I feel the city calling to me. It winks at me with its myriad eyes, and I go out and get stiff as a board. I seek out companionship, and if I do not find friends, I make them. A wonderful, grand old Babylon." I doubt that Colonel Stingo ever said exactly that, but I forgive Liebling everything. Walking around his city, I regret that he died before I got to meet him. He was the rare writer to confess to enjoying writing, unlike E. B. White and others who considered it a sort of internal hemorrhaging. Liebling simply said he wrote better than anyone who wrote faster and wrote faster than those who wrote better. He said of Marcel Proust, "The man ate a cookie, the taste evoked memories, he wrote a book about them. Imagine if he had had a real appetite, he might have written a masterpiece."

I crossed Sixth Avenue with its cold gray office buildings like thirty-story filing cabinets. A man wrapped in a blanket lay in the doorway, his possessions in a shopping bag. Around the corner, Times Square, Neon National Park. I looked up at the Royalton Hotel where Robert Benchley had sobered up when he needed to and I crossed the street to No. 25 over the door—NATIONAL ASSOCIATION BUILDING. I walked into the long narrow thru-lobby and stopped for ten minutes at the deli for a large coffee and a kaiser, buttered, working up the nerve to ascend to the sacred offices, and finally made myself board the elevator.

My interview was with Patricia Nosher, who suggested I write some tryout pieces for "The Talk of the Town," and so I set out to do that. A Black evangelist in a cheap blue nylon suit pacing the corner of 43rd and Eighth Avenue, a big Bible in one hand, thundering at the river of passersby, who shrank from him. "Do you know where you will spend Eternity?" he cries. He is of a vanishing tribe of the Lord's foot soldiers— maybe he had a story to tell me, but I didn't ask. Women in tiny skirts and low-cut blouses tried to converse with me: I ignored them. A string quartet in a doorway, playing Mozart's "Eine Kleine Nachtmusik."

I walked around all afternoon, taking notes. An exciting city where something was always happening, most of which you wouldn't want to be involved with personally. No alleys in Manhattan, so it's all happening out on the street. A man peeing against a storefront. Hustlers grabbing at you. Down the block, flashing lights, a water main broken, water bubbling up from the pavement. Men sitting on front steps, talking machine-gun Spanish, listening to Latin dance music. A man dancing on the sidewalk. Cars with the windows busted out, smoke in the air, a building on fire and people throwing stuff out the windows onto the street. Late at night, people walking down the street in their pajamas and then I realized it was people getting out of bed to move their cars to a new parking space. NO PARKING signs were complicated, like eye charts, and 4 a.m. seemed to be a deadline in that part of town.

Meanwhile I ignored the story that was right under my nose, Auntie Mame working in the kitchen and trying to discipline an unruly daughter. She was busy and I didn't want to bother her. I tried to write a story about a guy named Irwin Klein, who drove a taxi by night and walked the streets by day, shooting portraits of the lonely and destitute, photographs in the style of Robert Frank, black-and-white, on the fly, nothing posed. This became my tryout piece for *The New Yorker*. He lived in a tiny apartment with his wife and two little girls, a maelstrom of clothing and debris, his wife seemed distraught. I think he let me follow him around, supposing that if I sold the story to the magazine he'd get some good publicity, but in the week we spent together, I could see how bad off he was, broke, desperate, doing a lot of LSD. I didn't know how to write the story. A few years later, he jumped from a rooftop and died.

I got on an overnight bus to Boston and washed my face and changed my shirt at the Boston bus station and went over to *The Atlantic* in an old red-brick mansion near the Public Garden, and had a polite interview with an editor who said they didn't have an opening for me at the present time but to keep them in mind in the future. I thought of staying in Boston, finding work as a dishwasher, changing my name, writing a novel, writing a letter to Mary—*I don't think we are right for each other. It's my fault. You should find someone who is steady and can give you the life you deserve.*—and yet, marriage seemed plausible, we were both lonely, we both liked classical music. And hockey. Mary got very excited at Gopher hockey games, lost her self-consciousness, stood, whooped and yelled. And the thought of disappointing Marj was too painful, so the next day I boarded the bus back to Minnesota.

Mary still wanted to marry me, so I married her. She wore her pale blue wedding dress at the Methodist church with her bridesmaids in their pastel gowns, including Corinne. Mary had been the Talented Girl in her high school class, who played the Tchaikovsky Piano Concerto with a youth orchestra, was made much of, and arrived at the University to find out there were others more gifted, and that's when she and I met, she feeling defeated, I feeling full of myself, striding across campus, backpack in hand. Every time she sat at a keyboard, she felt more inadequate, meanwhile I was editing the *Ivory Tower* and sending stories to New York. Now, in a tuxedo, feeling far from confident, I promised to love her for the rest of my life.

We moved into two rented rooms in an old mansion on Lowry Hill. I wrote stories and she and I fell into silence. We believed that marriage would make us friends, but we had little to say to each other. We languished for three years, separated, and a month later she told me she was pregnant. So we moved back together. On May 1, 1969, the boy was born after twenty hours of labor, delivered by a young resident whom I saw in the hall poring over an obstetrics textbook. I told him that Mary was frightened, that her aunt had lost a baby in childbirth, and it was 2 a.m. and we should get started. Three hours later, my son emerged, handsome, bright-eyed, a little bruised from the forceps, a Dixie cup taped to the top of his head to protect the IV needle inserted into his soft skull tissue. He was born at University Hospital, a stone's throw from where I'd done my first newscast at WMMR, and in the early dawn light I walked up the Mall toward Northrop and over to Al's Breakfast in Din-kytown and ordered steak and eggs. I told Al that my wife had just given birth to a son and he wished me well in Swedish.

Walking through campus, I realized that that chapter of my life was now over. No more messing around. I looked on them as wasted years—and I still do—the courses in How to Write Brilliant Obtusity about Moldy Work by Dead Men Who Deserved It—and then I think of the friends I met who changed my life, Jon and Marcia, my closest writer pal Patricia Hampl, Bob Lindsay, Barry Halper, Roland Flint, Arnie Goldman, Maury Bernstein the folklorist and curmudgeon. Maury was a compulsive lecturer who'd grab your elbow and expound upon Sephar-dic music and cowboy ballads and the Hardanger fiddle, and days would pass as you stood on the corner of 15th and Fourth Street listening to him. In a just world, he'd've had an endowed chair at the U and authored definitive books, but a lack of social grace doomed him to obscurity. He knew everything, and he knew it and he didn't tolerate interruption. He never got a driver's license, was allergic to everything, lived in tiny rented rooms, picking up a few bucks playing accordion at birthday parties and bar mitzvahs, organizing an annual Scandinavian music festival. I once saw him and a friend, both down on their luck, pull an old Laurel & Hardy gag at Gray's lunch counter. Maury sat down and ordered the giant breakfast platter and when it arrived the pal sat down next to him and they got into a pretend argument, yelling at each other, and the pal grabbed the platter and tore out the door, Maury chasing him, and they ran around the corner and sat down and shared the free meal. It was a comedy routine that traveled from one lunch counter to another.

Maury introduced me to Koerner, Ray and Glover, the Sorry Muthas with Bill Hinkley and Judy Larson, Little Stevie Beck the Queen of the Autoharp, Peter Ostroushko and Dakota Dave Hull, Sean Blackburn, the Middle Spunk Creek Boys, musicians who all knew each other and con-stituted a small town in the midst of the big city, and that small town was where *A Prairie Home Companion* began. Maury never forgave me for the success of the show, and whenever I ran into him on Cedar Avenue or the

Riverside Café, he told me what a dreadfully ignorant show it was and I thanked him for listening. That success rightfully belonged to him, he knew, and the injustice was clear to him and clearly anti-Semitism was behind it. As the show grew and thrived, he enjoyed loathing it. I was his enemy, a nobody, he was a *wunderkind* from the age of ten on, playing his accordion for Lubavitcher weddings and I was a schnook from a small town who knew from nothing. I felt bad for him. He deserved better. He thought so and so did I. I still do. He died of Parkinson's, still lecturing whoever'd listen. I think of him as an old friend, even though I never got a word in edgewise.

17

Radio Days

THAT FALL, I DROVE UP to St. John's University in Stearns County and applied for a job at their new radio station KSJR. The manager, Bill Kling, was my age, twenty-seven, but dressed like a manager in a dark blue suit and white shirt, narrow tie, and he looked at me and saw a proto-hippie in a flowery shirt and fringed vest, leather boots and bell-bottoms, chain-smoking, bearded, longish hair, who claimed to be a writer. Mr. Kling and I had one thing in common: we'd grown up in the Forties before TV and we liked the old radio shows, especially the comedians. I got on a long spiel about audio being memorable and video self-erasing, that the ear, not the eye, is the door to the brain, and I kept yakking, and eventually it dawned on me that I was the only applicant and he needed me to do the 6 a.m. shift and to start soon. So I was hired. I was his sixth full-time employee.

Mary and I and the baby drove up to Freeport with a trailer of beat-up furniture and ate lunch at Charlie's on Main Street. Freeport was a rail-road town, the tracks running along Main Street, beside the Swany White Flour Mill, a handsome yellow-brick structure on a stone base, five beau-tiful old enameled maroon rolling machines humming along. We set up housekeeping in a rented farmhouse a mile south of town. Rent was $80 a month for a four-bedroom brick house with a porch that looked out on a well-kept farmyard, a granary and machine sheds and corncribs and silo and windmill, and a classic red barn and feedlot where Norbert, the farmer I rented from, kept his whiteface beef cattle. This was the farm his wife had grown up on, her family now gone, the Hoppe farm. Beyond the windbreak of red oak and spruce to the west and north lay 160 acres of his corn and oats. Our long two-rut driveway ran due north through the woods to where the gravel road made an L, where our mailbox stood, where you could stand and see for a couple miles in all directions, the green fields, the thick groves around the farm sites. We walked west on the straight road toward town, the baby on my back, and took a picture of our farm site, the grove of trees, the barn rising, the windmill. We awoke the next morning to church bells. It was Sunday. We had missed church. Our first mistake. If we intended to know people in Freeport, church would be the place to start. Dress up, take a seat, wait for people to introduce themselves.

One Monday morning, 4:30 a.m., I drove east to St. John's to do the show. KSJR was a classical music station, but I ignored that in favor of free-form entertainment. On Sunday I had sat at a turntable all afternoon listening to LPs, picking music for the show, fugues, études, blues, Jew's harp-tuba duets, Jussi Björling, the Fruit Jar Drinkers, *King Porter Stomp*, Sousa played on a kazoo. My theme song was the Mills Brothers singing "Bugle Call Rag" with a jazzy vocal reveille—*You're bound to fall for the bugle call; you're gonna brag 'bout the Bugle Call Rag.* I ran through medleys and sequences of things, minimal talk, some remarks on the weather, offered to play requests and got a few, wished a woman named Rhonda a happy birthday and played the Beach Boys' "Help Me, Rhonda," an inspiration. The phone lit up. A couple complaints, but they were more astonished than complaining. It was a good morning—no paper-pushing, no staff meeting. We were too understaffed for that. Rhonda called and said I had brightened her morning and that was good. A couple people whose mornings I didn't brighten spoke to Mr. Kling and he comforted them.

I felt good about the 6 a.m. show from the get-go. Taking requests gives you a feel for the audience—a diverse bunch: rural intelligentsia, librarians, Unitarians, sexagenarians, birdwatchers, Lutheran dissidents, nuns and Catholic lefties, office workers with an unfinished novel in a desk drawer, teenage nerds of a humorous persuasion, potters and artists but also farmers and truck drivers, prisoners at St. Cloud Reformatory. I put Bix Beiderbecke on the turntable and Gid Tanner and the Skillet Lickers, and it was like David said in the psalms, serving the Lord with gladness, and I let the Georgia Sea Island Singers shout for joy and the

Golden Gate Quartet sing praises to the Most High with a glad heart as a bridegroom coming out of his chamber. I drove to work through the darkened houses in Avon and Albany and thought, "That's my flock, they need to be uplifted," and I got to the studio fully enthused and hauled the stack of vinyl into the control room and sat down and did the show.

My home life was dark. Mary's depression, the silence between us, the little boy playing alone in the big house. My workroom upstairs, the Underwood typewriter, the stack of manuscripts in the works. The silent meals. This dark life moved me to do a show of gaiety and exuberant transitions from the Marine Corps Band to a steam calliope and spoon player and a tuba trio playing the "Ode to Joy" with scraps of poetry and items from the local police reports and commercials for Jack's Auto Repair and Ralph's Pretty Good Grocery. I just wanted to make people feel buoyant in the morning, including myself. If other people were sitting down to a glum breakfast with a silent partner, then maybe I could jiggle them out of it.

"Help Me, Rhonda" became a running joke, the awful song you're addicted to. I'd play it, then swear off it, go for days Rhonda-less, then weaken. In the middle of the forecast at the mention of six inches of snow and high winds, I'd softly sing the refrain. *Help, help me, Rhonda. Help me, Rhonda, yeah, get her out of my heart.* Something galvanized for me in that studio. *Keep it light. Make it new. Keep changing the subject:* A skip-rope rhyme, *Mother called the doctor. Doctor called the nurse. The nurse she called the lady with the alligator purse*—into a Bach gigue, a surf band, whales singing, a Welsh chorus, "Bells of Rhymney," the Pachelbel *Canon,* a twenty-one-gun salute, and Gus Cannon's Jug Stompers playing "Walk Right In." *A man walks into a bar that's crowded with dogs. The bartender is a dog and the waitress. She says, "What can I get you?" The man says, "I'm off alcohol, how about water?" She says, "The toilet's down the hall, help yourself."*

There were plenty of listeners who didn't care for it. They had donated money to support a classical music station and didn't feel they needed to hear medieval and Renaissance dances mixed in with ragtime and bluegrass and they were not amused by the chatter. I don't blame them. I go to a ball game, I go for baseball, I don't care about video close-ups of couples kissing. The dissenters protested to Mr. Kling, and he never breathed a word about it to me. Some of them were major donors. I sat in the control room in my fringed leather vest and jeans, and he sat in his office in his suit and tie and dealt with people on the phone.

Long ago, I met a man in a remote village in Alaska, who'd escaped there from Minnesota where he'd been a hell-raiser in a small town and caused damage and was marked as a cheater and liar. He fled to Alaska to escape his notoriety. One night he drove his pickup through twenty-seven miles of blizzard to take a young woman in the throes of childbirth to a hospital, and on the basis of that good deed on a treacherous night, he became a town cop, and a good one. He was redeemed by the simple fact of making himself necessary. And that's what radio did for me. As a poet, I was a mild nuisance, and on radio, I was useful, at least to some people, entertaining them at 6 a.m. on a winter morning when they really needed it. Useful work: the antidote to self-pity.

The radio show changed my life. And so did the death of the poet John Berryman, which hit me like a hammer. He was a hero of mine, he taught at the U, I admired his formal verse:

Master of beauty, craftsman of the snowflake,
inimitable contriver,
endower of Earth so gorgeous & different from the boring Moon,
thank you for such as it is my gift.

I cared less for his famous *Dream Songs,* but I went to his readings: a brilliant man blind drunk, hanging onto the podium, ranting his poetry in a crazy unintelligible voice for an hour and then sitting down to a standing ovation. Insanity was considered a symptom of genius back then. But one cold winter morning in 1972, Mr. Berryman climbed up on the railing of the Washington Avenue Bridge, paused, waved goodbye, and leaped to his death in the coal yard below, joining the select society of Hemingway, Hart Crane, Virginia Woolf, Sylvia Plath. He'd tried AA, had written a novel about recovery, had written a series of beautiful "Addresses to the Lord" (*Whatever your end may be, accept my amazement. May I stand until death forever at attention for any your least instruction or enlightenment.*), but in the end, his death came as no surprise to those who knew him. It seemed to have been his goal all along. I took a hard look at my own poems with their impressive display of despair, and I said to myself: *You*

*are not headed for the bridge, so it makes no sense to stand by the railing.
Where is the nobility in lamenting stupid things you did to yourself?* I had
tried to think life is absurd, and now I decided to try comedy. The basis
of comedy is the great question: *If people saw us as we really are, one foot in
pretense, the other in vulgarity, would they still like us?* We look at the stars
and worry about our hair. I had adopted a heroic tone:

> *What the elders know in their Sunday clothes*
> *I feel: lonely and old, faraway, poor,*
> *Driving by day and night in the car*
> *That the moon has turned to rust.*

But what in heaven's name is that about? It's about a guy with a headache.
Get over yourself. I did. I wrote Mr. Berryman a poem.

> *There was a dark poet named John*
> *Who jumped from a bridge, landing on*
> *A yard full of coal.*
> *God rest his soul.*
> *He made a small hole, now he's gone.*

I made a swift, sharp turn, and I accepted the idea of working within narrow boundaries. I was thirty, and my job was to entertain people, some
of whom knew more about loneliness than I ever would. *Do your job.* I
wrote about cats, fireworks, the prairie, sweet corn, socks. Mary recorded
a piano track of "Ain't Misbehavin'," and I sang,

> *The theology's easy, the liturgy too.*
> *Just stand up and kneel down and do as the others do.*
> *Episcopalian, saving my love for you.*
> *At St. Michael's, we recycle.*
> *At St. Clements, we suck lemons.*
> *Morning dawns on great white swans on the lawns of St. John's*
> *There's white folks and Black, and gay and morose,*
> *Some male Anglo-Saxons but we watch them pretty close.*
> *Episcopalian, saving my love for you.*

I read items on the show from local police blotters, such as the one about the dog who swam under the ice and caught a walleye and with fish in mouth, burst up through the hole in the fishing shack of Mr. Bauer who was intoxicated and in his panic knocked over the propane heater and the shack went up in flames and the dog disappeared before the firemen arrived, and will the owner of a black Lab please notify the sheriff's office. Some donors complained to Mr. Kling, who took them to dinner, listened to them, thanked them for their support. And the show gained a following.

Three weeks after I started at KSJR, I walked out to our mailbox and found a letter from *The New Yorker*, on creamy stationery, two pages, hand-typed with scrawled corrections, the fiction editor Roger Angell apologizing for turning down my story "The Life of Nixon" ("which was good in so many ways") but accepting my story "Local Family Makes Son Happy"—a short short story he said was "nearly perfect"—for which they would pay me $500. I sat down in a field of alfalfa and read it three times and thought to myself, *Now I have done something with my life. If I die now, they'll mention* The New Yorker *in the second graph of the obit.*

The night the letter from Roger came, we drove into Freeport to Charlie's Café to celebrate, our little boy asleep in the baby sack on my back. According to my diary, I had the ham dinner with baked potato, lettuce salad, dinner roll, and coffee, which cost $2.50. And a five-inch high lemon meringue pie was $1.10 extra. I felt flush. I never bothered to balance my checkbook after that.

My mother read the story, about a family who hires a call girl for their son, and asked, "Why can't you write something more positive?" I said, "I need to write what pays, I have a family." My pal Roland Flint wrote to me: "I was so happy when I saw your name in the Table of Contents that I forgot to be jealous for two, maybe three, minutes. The piece is damned good & funny. Nuts to modesty. Most modest people should be." I set about writing a batch of new stories for Roger, what they called "casuals" to distinguish them from serious fiction. I worked Monday through Friday at the station, 5 a.m. to 4 p.m., plus Saturday night. After supper, I sat in my workroom upstairs and wrote. *The New Yorker* had been my goal since eighth grade. I went into high production, no brooding, all business, filling a notebook with fragments of ideas, sketching outlines, newspaper clippings, aiming to complete three stories a month, and bat .333. That fall, a letter arrived from a New York literary agent, Ellen Levine, who'd seen a story of mine, "The Magic Telephone," in a literary magazine and wondered if I'd like to avail myself of her services. And soon she had wrangled a book contract with Atheneum, and I was in business. A show, a magazine, a book deal, all in a few months' time.

I worked in a small second-floor bedroom, my black Underwood on a slab of ¾-inch plywood atop two steel file cabinets, a stack of yellow copy paper by the typewriter, and *Webster's Unabridged*, Second Edition. Out the window behind my chair, the driveway curved through the windbreak toward the county road where I could see the mailman come cruising along in his green pickup, a cloud of dust behind, and stop, or not stop, at our big tin mailbox on its post, and leave, or not leave, an envelope from New York from Roger Angell. Some of them began "Sorry about your story *SUCH AND SO*, which came very close indeed but which seemed to us to fall somewhat short and to lack the sureness and inevitability of your writing at its best and though there was much to admire in it, there was also a faint sense of strain to the writing. I am terribly sorry to disappoint you and trust you won't let this discourage you or slow you up for an instant. This really came close, believe me." And others started off, "Good news! We are taking your story *YES INDEED*, which seemed to everyone here really funny and surprising and perfect in every way." The rejections were always soft, reluctant, "wonderful writing, but somehow it wasn't quite you at your best," and sometimes a "Perhaps we are all wrong about this" was tossed in. The acceptances were generous: "I've been passing it around the office and all of us here are in admiration of your latest." And now and then he'd write a beseeching letter: "People come up to me in the halls to ask when we're going to see another story by Keillor. Write, I beg of you." And I went straight to my typewriter and wrote and a week later: "Sorry about your latest, which came very close indeed. There was much to admire in it." Et cetera, et cetera. He was a great and compassionate editor, never dismissive. You were his author, and he was with you all the way. And he was pleased by my story "Don: The True Story of a Younger Person," which contains a quintuple interior quote, a quote of a quote of a quote of a quote of a quote, the deepest interior quote ever published there, so he said.

And then there were the envelopes that contained a check. It might be $700, or $1,200, or $1,500, a windfall, I'd throw a party on Saturday, buy bottles of Armagnac, friends drove up from the city, we built a bonfire in the woods, roasted steaks, drank a toast to the Pleiades and Orion. I knew I'd found my place in the world, the writerly life, the little room with the Underwood and the plywood desk, but I had a wounded wife, alone with our little boy all day, a wall between us. I took a long drag on a cigarette and snapped it, sparks flying, into the dark. I said, "A man can have a happy home life or a big career, but you can't have both." I was drunk, I said it to hear what it sounded like. "Go for the career," someone said. I already had.

Mary had been eager to have a family. Before we got married, she drew up a list of names for our children: Johann, Hugo, Eleanor, Elizabeth, Peter, and Katherine. But that year, as I sat upstairs and wrote stories, she became mournful and weepy and let her piano drift out of tune. I, the bustling industrious loner, was no help for a lonely woman. She went to bed early, and I worked late and arose at 5 and drove to the radio station. I came home for supper and went back to the typewriter. I knew we couldn't go on like this, but what could be done? She stands in my doorway, in her pajamas, waiting, waiting. "What is it?" I say and she shakes her head and walks away. Why can't we face each other and talk about this? Because I can't give up radio or my writing. A sensible life isn't possible. I know men who are good family men and I am not one. I had to burn the candle at both ends. She walks down the hall and closes the bedroom door.

An audience grew that liked the crazy-quilt show. Rev. Gary Davis into the Brandenburg No. 3 into "Hop Scop Blues" and "What Wondrous Love" by Southern shape-note singers, into "Hesitation Blues" and then a limerick for *Bernie up in Baudette where limericks are bawdy, you bet, and men smoke smokes and tell dirty jokes till everyone's trousers are wet.* His daughter called yesterday and said he's dying of lung cancer but still telling jokes and could I wish him a happy seventieth. Of course. Maybe I shouldn't have put "smokes" in but it rhymes.

I don't know how many people complained: Bill Kling fielded the complaints. He listened to anger and never got angry back. He was out to create a network uniting Lutheran and Catholic and state colleges in one enterprise, build a news operation, open the door to bold discussion of public issues, promote the arts. He believed in a community with a strong magnetic center rather than a scattering of fringe interests. We broadcast *La Traviata* from the Met because he believed everyone had a right to get the chance to enjoy it, not just opera nuts but your uncle Al and cousin Millie and the butcher at Red Owl. When I was down in the dumps, he told me that he knew a lot of people who loved my show, "including some who would surprise you." He never used the word "inclusivity" but he believed in it, the big tent, and if people came for the jug bands and the jokes and stuck around for the Met and the New York Phil and got a sense of how big the tent is, it was all to the good.

18

Joe

SOME OF THE LISTENERS BECAME friends, Father Hilary Thimmesh, Fred and Romy Petters, the writer Jim Harrison picked up the signal from Duluth in his cabin on the Upper Peninsula. Joe O'Connell was a sculptor, whose studio overlooked a meadow along the Great Northern tracks near St. Joseph, down the hill from KSJR. He invited me down one day after my show and I found him looking at a half-finished wooden Christ on the cross leaning against the wall, a tiny crack on the left cheek— Joe ran his fingers over the face, brushing away sawdust, squinting at the grain, worrying over it. He decided the nose was slightly off-kilter and needed reshaping; meanwhile, the church that commissioned the figure was hounding Joe for a delivery date so the dedication could be scheduled. The original date was three months ago. Joe was supposed to telephone the priest today—he groaned at the thought.

Joe had a wife and five children to support by carving and sculpting for Catholic churches, who paid modest commissions because how could you ask for more, knowing that churches could buy plaster statues that their congregations might even prefer to Joe's work? His sense of the absurd kept him afloat, it was all comedy to Joe. He paid me a compliment in his last sculpture, commissioned by a church in Las Vegas, a granite triptych showing Christ among the poor and oppressed: I am in it, a prisoner behind bars.

Joe pours us each a glass of brandy and we sit in his little loft, like the bridge of a ship, with a bunk, a work table, a file cabinet, and shelves holding his tape and record collection, New Orleans jazz, Jelly Roll, Bix,

Buddy, Ella, Benny, Fats, Duke, and postcards and clippings tacked to the walls. I sit on the bunk, and he brings out a few of his prints to show me: Peter strangling the cock that crowed when Peter, confronted by the mob, denied knowing the Lord, and Adam in the Garden waiting in abject boredom for Eve to finish doing her hair, her magnificent haunches visible through a window, and a print of a man in a suit grabbed by giant talons in the dark. Joe did not portray elation or contentment, his subject was the dignity of suffering. He'd been shipped to Okinawa in the closing days of World War II, had seen horrible bloodshed and destruction, and the one time he told me about it, tears ran down his face. He sticks a fresh log in the woodstove and turns down the volume of the Bix Beiderbecke tape and leans back in his swivel chair and lifts his glass.

Joe looked like an old boxer, a bantamweight. Wiry, with large sinewy hands, a hank of black hair falling over his forehead, black horn-rimmed glasses on a creased face, and a majestic grin. Joe knew how to bestow friendship. Through him, I met J. F. Powers, author of *Morte D'Urban*, a Catholic iconoclast, who attended Mass every week sitting in the balcony where the homily was unintelligible and nobody would try to shake his hand—he shunned the Exchange of Peace. If you google Powers, you find him bunched up with Flannery O'Connor, Evelyn Waugh, and James Joyce. Powers never googled anybody. The only Google he knew was Barney Google with the goo-goo-googly eyes. He loved baseball and old jazz and olives, despised Walt Whitman, disliked teaching creative writing at St. John's and discouraged as many students as he could, and he was good company, though he never could accept the idea of grown men going around in jeans. He stared at mine as if I were wearing leotards.

One fall morning, Jim Powers and I sat in the studio and Joe told us about the circus that came to the ballpark in St. Joseph in July. "It was one of those little tent circuses where the woman who sells you your ticket is also the bareback rider and has a dog act, and maybe sells cotton candy on the side. But my kids thought this was the last word in entertainment, to sit on the top row of the bleachers under the canvas and jump down to the ground and run around. So we went, and the next day we drove to town in our old VW to get groceries. It was like a clown car with four of them in it and the back seat full of groceries. They were still talking about the circus when we drove by the ballpark and there, staked in the middle of the field, was the elephant, Mazumbo. This was a one-elephant circus and she was it. The kids wanted to go feed her. They begged me. 'Please oh please, please, please, can we? This would be the neatest thing. We've got peanuts!'

"Well, we did have peanuts. Two big bags of them. I said, 'All right, but you stay in the car. Nobody gets out of the car.' And I drove onto the ballfield and up to the elephant. And Eric rolled down the window and stuck out a handful of peanuts and Mazumbo swung her trunk over and picked them up and put them in her mouth. Then it was Brian's turn to feed her. And Laurie, and Duke. By the time they got through a bag of peanuts, Mazumbo had quite a bit of her trunk inside the car, feeling around for provisions. It made me nervous, this gigantic long bristly thing snaking around inside the VW and brushing the back of my neck and snuffling around the kids, especially since the tip of Mazumbo's trunk looked like Mazumbo had a bad cold. But the kids, of course, were delighted. Utterly beside themselves. They were squealing and sticking fistfuls of peanuts in her trunk, of which almost the whole trunk seemed to be in the car. And when we ran out of peanuts, we opened up a pack of Oreos and some candy bars and potato chips. I was trying to keep calm, and then I felt the car lift slightly and then this large cold thing on my face and I jumped and banged my head on the ceiling and slipped the car into reverse and backed up, slowly, because Mazumbo was reluctant to let go of us. We inched back and I could hear the ridges on the trunk slide across the window frame, *bonk, bonk, bonk, bonk, bonk*, and the kids were laughing all the way home, and I was imagining the story in the newspaper, FAMILY OF 5 PERISH IN CIRCUS MISHAP; FATHER PARKED CAR NEXT TO ELEPHANT."

Jim turned to me and said, "That'd be a good one for your show." He said he wouldn't dare write a story like that because if he did, someone might die. That's the sort of writer he is. Irish.

Years later, I stole the story and put it into Lake Wobegon and sent Joe an $82 bottle of Armagnac, which he didn't drink, on grounds that it would only make him dissatisfied with his usual brand, the $10 brandy at the municipal liquor store in St. Joseph.

When Joe died in 1995, Jim read one Scripture passage at the funeral

Mass and I read another. At Joe's instruction, there was no eulogy. I had written one in which I said he was an Italian artist of the Renaissance, a friend of Ghirlandaio, who was dropped into Stearns County in the mid-twentieth century, one of God's better jokes. He was a fine artist who looked like a prizefighter and talked like a carpenter, and he was a Christian who lived by his faith, which included selflessness and so my eulogy got dropped, and they cut to the postlude, a jazz band playing "Please Don't Talk about Me When I'm Gone," led by Joe's son Brian playing clarinet, and here I've gone and done exactly that.

The radio network grew. Father Colman Barry, the president of St. John's University, was behind it all the way, and Dan Rieder, our chief engineer, was a dedicated problem solver, who knew about radio from his Navy days working with submarine radar. He assembled the KSJR transmitter and tower and ran the electric line out to it, and when we boosted power from 40,000 to 150,000 watts, it created so much heat it had to be water-cooled, so he built a giant radiator to run water through and a big fan to cool it. He devised ingenious gizmos to make the thing work. He was a bachelor married to his job, traveling around Minnesota to build transmitters and towers. He and Kling built the network, piece by piece. One looked like a successful insurance salesman, the other like an auto mechanic—one moved easily among the well-to-do, the other mainly talked to bartenders and waitresses—and together they created Minnesota Public Radio. I was a bit player, playing music, having a good time.

Mary was in severe distress, so we left the idyllic (for me) farm and moved back to Minneapolis, and I did the 6 a.m. show out of a jerry-built plywood studio in downtown St. Paul and the show happened to catch the ear of the two coolest people in town. Minneapolis *Tribune* columnist Will Jones gave it a glowing write-up, and Suzanne Weil asked me to do a poetry reading at the planetarium. She ran the performing arts program at Walker Art Center, the HQ of cool. She sponsored Merce Cunningham and Waylon Jennings both, Twyla Tharp, Philip Glass, B. B. King, and the Beach Boys too. She liked what she liked. There is nothing so buoying to a writer like having the right friends. Will and Weil: I was a made man. Another local columnist had dismissed me as "vanilla," but he probably only knew vanilla from McDonald's, which is artificial flavoring. Genuine vanilla has richness and complexity. To him, vanilla represented emptiness, but he was full of horseshit. Which itself is rich and complex and not without value. Though it's no substitute for vanilla.

That fall, I got invited to introduce my hero S. J. Perelman at his reading in Minneapolis. I met him at dinner at Murray's restaurant, at a narrow table in the corner; our knees kept touching, and I was worried about keeping up my end of the conversation, but he carried the ball. Once he learned that I wrote for *The New Yorker*, he complained bitterly about the editing, the miserly pay, the punitive first-reading contract, and then he looked at me and asked, "Who's your editor?" "Roger Angell," I said. "What's that like?" he said. "He's great, he writes very kind rejections," I said. Mr. Perelman harrumphed. He tossed in a few disparaging remarks about the Marx Brothers and his regret that he ever agreed to write for the bastards, and then it was time to go do the show. I picked up the check. I felt honored, stunned, dazzled, that the great Perelman regarded me as a fellow professional. No monkey talk about subtexts and motifs, it was all about earning the dough and keeping editors' clumsy mitts off your work. I was in his club. I called him *Mister* Perelman but I thought of him as Sid. I don't remember the reading, just my dazzlement.

19

A Prairie Home Companion

I WAS CURIOUS ABOUT THE invisible radio audience who listened at 6 a.m. I wanted them to be friends, so one morning I announced try-outs for the Jack's Auto Repair softball team and the next Saturday a big crowd showed up at a ballfield in south Minneapolis, and we chose up sides and played a dozen innings, drank a case of Grain Belt, and went home. But the idea took hold. A team of strangers spontaneously formed. John and Ann Reay took down names and phone numbers, and we held a practice and played against the St. Paul Chamber Orchestra team, their conductor Dennis Russell Davies pitching. We took the game seriously, regardless of ability. Lots of infield chatter, throwing the ball around the horn. Serious attitude. Remorse at your errors, no joking around until later. The Minnesota Orchestra sent over a team, the Walker Art Center, the Guthrie, serious play, a case of beer afterward. Friendships formed. When *Prairie Home* got big-time, touring, Sunday afternoon softball disappeared but some friendships remained. Russ Ringsak, an architect, a Harley and blues guy, wound up becoming a friend. He once built a long twisting snow slide on a hillside behind his house with banked curves designed for maximum thrills: you jumped on a plastic saucer and the slide threw you around for a couple minutes. He told a joke every time he met me. He got fed up with architecture and came to work for *Prairie Home* as our truck driver for the last twenty years or so, drove the big red Peterbilt cross-country and wrote up pages of notes on each broadcast city and, when he got sick and needed to retire, he played electric guitar and sang "Six Days on the Road" at our last broadcast at the Ryman Auditorium in Nashville. The loyalty of good people like Russ and Tom Keith and Kate Gustafson—I took it for granted at the time and now I'm astonished.

In the summer of 1973, thinking this was something a radio guy should do someday, I rode the train to Nashville with my friend Don McNeil from the softball team to see the Saturday night broadcast of *The Grand Ole Opry* at the Ryman Auditorium, which was completely sold out that night so we stood in the parking lot behind the hall and listened to it on WSM from the radios in nearby pickup trucks. There was a whole crowd of us out there. We got to see Loretta Lynn's tour bus pull up in the alley and she herself step out and walk by in glittering white gown, long black hair, and the crowd parted for her, nobody asked for an autograph, a few people said quietly "Hey, Loretta," and she smiled and picked up her skirts and went around back to the stage door. The Ryman wasn't air-conditioned and the windows were wide open, and when we ducked down behind a low stone wall we could see the lower halves of performers on stage, Dolly Parton and Roy Acuff and Bashful Brother Oswald, and almost all of Stonewall Jackson. My hero Marty Robbins sat mugging at the piano and sang "Love Me," grinning on the falsetto part in the chorus, and then jumped up and did "El Paso," strumming a little Spanish guitar up on his shoulder. Listening to the music from car radios in the parking lot surrounded by reverent fans on a hot summer night, I felt happy, excited, even exalted. I thought, "I'd like to do that someday."

The next spring I went back to Nashville and wrote a piece about the Opry for *The New Yorker*. Roger Angell handed me over to a fact editor, Bill Whitworth, knowing Bill is from Little Rock and knows country music, and Bill at the time was the trusted deputy of William Shawn, the editor, and so the assignment was made, though Mr. Shawn's interest in country music was slight at best. On this daisy chain of connections my whole career hangs. If Roger had handed me to an editor from Connecticut, or if Whitworth had fallen out of favor with Shawn, or if Shawn had mentioned the Opry to Lillian Ross and she said, "You're out of your mind," I'd be wearing a TSA badge and patting down men with suspicious pants at the airport.

I went to the Friday night show and skipped the Saturday night because Richard M. Nixon would be there, trying to slip the bonds of

Watergate, and I didn't care to write about him. I sat in the balcony of the Ryman and watched the sequined ladies with big hair, men in gaudy suits, commercials for chewing tobacco and pork sausage and self-rising Martha White flour and Goo Goo Clusters, Cousin Minnie Pearl (*I'm just so proud to be here!*), the red-barn backdrop, the haze of cigarette smoke, the fans and their flash cameras, the announcer in his funeral suit, and I resolved to go home and start up a Saturday night show of my own. I wrote the piece, Bill Whitworth shepherded it into print between ads for Chanel No. 5 and Cartier diamonds and Cricketeer yacht wear, and I went up the stairs to Bill Kling's office at KSJN to talk.

Kling kept meetings short. He had a low tolerance for the prefaces and digressions by which people show they have a liberal arts education. He was a true believer in radio, listened to it religiously, and in public radio, surrounded by malcontents, he got excited by good ideas. I proposed the show and he told me to go right ahead. Saturday at 5 p.m., between the Met Opera and the New York Philharmonic broadcasts. He called in Margaret Moos, who worked upstairs in publicity, and asked her to produce it. "Have fun," he said. It was a ten-minute conversation. Saturday evening was a dead zone in radio, but I was in a sinking marriage and had nothing to lose.

A few years later, I invited Mr. Shawn to come to Minnesota and play piano on the show, and he wrote back: "Unfortunately, I don't travel and in my opinion I don't play well enough, so I must decline." A perfect Shawn sentence, not one unnecessary word in it.

Twenty years later, when the Ryman Auditorium reopened after renovation, *Prairie Home* was the first show back in, a classic show with Chet and the Everlys, Robin and Linda Williams, Buddy Emmons, Vince Gill, and Mary Chapin Carpenter, and I just stood off to the side and waved them on, one after the other.

The name *A Prairie Home Companion* came from a Norwegian cemetery in Moorhead, opened in 1875 by a man named Oscar Elmer who planned to make his bundle and head back East, leaving this godforsaken treeless plain behind, but then his brother John died, apparently a suicide, and the tragedy made up Oscar's mind to bury his brother in Moorhead and call the cemetery Our Prairie Home. And Oscar wound up staying. The story appealed to me—Norwegians establishing a graveyard as a sign of loyalty—so I took the name and stuck "Companion" on it as a dark joke. I felt about radio as Mr. Elmer felt about North Dakota. Radio was a temporary job until I could finish my novel about a small town in Minnesota, but then I lost the manuscript in the train station in Portland, left it in a briefcase in the men's toilet, went back and it was gone. The story of Oscar and his cemetery spoke to me. *Here we are. Life has its sorrows. Make something beautiful out of it.*

I wanted an ecumenical show and Kling wanted a live broadcast, which eliminates the tedium of editing. I'd grown up with commercial radio so I invented sponsors, the Café Boeuf, the Fearmonger's Shop (*serving all your phobia needs*), Guy's Shoes, and Powdermilk Biscuits. (*If your family's tried 'em, you know you've satisfied 'em, they're the real hot item, Powdermilk . . . Heavens, they're tasty and expeditious.*) I had musician friends who were game—Butch Thompson was a classmate at the U and I met Bill Hinkley and Judy Larson busking on the West Bank. And Robin and Linda Williams playing a college coffeehouse, singing to fifteen people with pinball machines dinging and cash register ringing. I knew Philip Brunelle, Vern Sutton, and Janis Hardy from the Center Opera Company. Vern and Janis had big voices and could improvise if I wrote a script about singing furniture, plus which they could do speaking

GK and Bill Kling, KSJN studio, 1975.

roles. Vern did weaselish characters, con men, card sharps; Janis could sing precisely a quarter-tone sharp or flat and convulse the audience. One week she brought her dog Freckles and they did "Indian Love Call," Freckles howling when Janis hit a certain note. Philip at the keyboard could sight-read or play by ear or both. The three of them could set any words to music in any style, on the spot, a pork chop recipe à la Chopin, a list of cocktails à la Philip Glass.

The music was sociable, old jazz, love duets, bluegrass, ballads, nothing that took itself too seriously. No Dylan. His *"Half-wracked prejudice leaped forth, 'rip down all hate,' I screamed. Lies that life is black and white spoke from my skull I dreamed"* was like stuff I wrote in my sophomore year at the U. Why repeat it? Go for the visceral, skip the gaseous emanations of sensibility.

I was the writer with the idea, but the musicians were the ones who made it real, as I very well knew. Bill and Judy did "Barnyard Dance" (*It was late last night in the pale moonlight, All the vegetables gave a spree. They put out a sign that said, 'The dancing's at nine' And all the admission was free.*). Soupy Schindler played jug, did a steam locomotive on his mouth harp. Vern Sutton sang "Curfew Must Not Ring Tonight" about Nellie hanging on to the clapper of the church bell as the hangman waited to hear it so he could execute her daddy. Butch played "How Long Blues." And so we proceeded down the road, not knowing what a fine education it would turn out to be. It went on the air on July 6, 1974, admission $1, 50 cents for kids. Margaret Moos sold tickets and her sisters Martha and Becky ushered, and Margaret quickly became boss because she knew what to do and we didn't. I was the doubter. I thought it might last the summer. I wore a white suit and a big white hat to make myself look authoritative, but I was in over my head, which you could see if you went to the show, which luckily not many people did. Attendance at the first show was thirty-six, half of whom left at intermission. On the radio, it sounded better than it was; on stage, there was a grim-faced man in a white suit struggling to have a good time. And the next week I got the first fan letter, from a listener in St. Cloud.

We enjoyed the show Saturday night and hope you were happy with it all because it seemed to work out real good. You might want to try that sort of thing again. I heard most of the show while getting my file cabinet organized, the appliance guarantees, unpaid bills, vacation brochures, and all such. I don't really believe it will work, but it is good to purge oneself on occasion and feel you have done good. People need this sort of thing. After the show Romy and I went downtown for dinner.

Tell those people to have it quit raining.
Fred

It was a folk music show that went on week by week, live, unedited, four microphones, no rehearsal, no stage monitors, songs thrown together on the fly and mixed on an 8-channel mixer. I tried to sound friendly because that's what Bob DeHaven of "Good Neighbor Time" sounded like, so I tried to chuckle as I introduced the acts and promoted Jack's Auto Repair (*All tracks lead to Jack's*) and the Chatterbox Café (*Where the elite meet to eat*), Ralph's Pretty Good Grocery (*If you can't find it at Ralph's, you can probably get along without it*), the American Duct Tape Council (*It's almost all you need sometimes*) and the Federated Organization of Associations (which became the Associated Federation of Organizations and then the Official Federated Organization of Associations), Bertha's Kitty Boutique (*For persons who care about cats*), and the Catchup Advisory Board (*These are the good times, strong and sure and steady. Life is flowing like catchup on spaghetti*). Commercials freed us from the academic formality of public radio and let us talk about indigestion and sore feet, cat hair, bad breath, and the need for adhesives. Sponsors such as Bebopareebop Rhubarb Pie, Thompson Tooth Tinsel, the Coffee Advisory Board (*Smells so lovely when you pour it, you will want to drink a quart . . . Keeps the Swedes and the Germans awake through the sermons*).

Ray Marklund, an electrician for Northern Pacific railroad, was our lone stagehand (unpaid, at his own insistence; he said, "I don't want to have to take orders from people who've got no idea what they're doing"). He carried a toolbox and could solder wires and unlock doors, and once he unlocked a piano. He liked jazz more than bluegrass, but he stuck with us because he could see that we needed him. We played little theaters—one hundred or so capacity—and I learned that Minnesota audiences are thoughtful and cautious and don't laugh unless people near them laugh. I learned to get their attention by speaking softly. I took no pay at the start because I felt unnecessary; the acts got $50 or $75 each—without them, there'd be no show. We finished our first year of shows, and I popped a cork in a real champagne bottle and it flew sixty feet to the back row and struck a four-year-old boy named Ben Ellingson, who cried out in surprise. I took the microphone up the aisle to apologize to him. (The family attended our twenty-fifth anniversary show; Ben was fine and had graduated from grad school.) For several summers, we played in a downtown park a block from the main fire station, across from the Church of St. Louis. Bells rang at 5 p.m. and now and then fire trucks came screaming past and we made ourselves ignore them. Once, an old drunk with a harmonica wandered in and tried to join the show and had to be restrained. Our audience, mostly Minnesota liberals, liked him because he looked like a Dust Bowl refugee, but he was a lousy harpist and a worse singer. Much to the liberals' displeasure, we ushered him out. Some of them protested, but we were a radio show, not a treatment program, and the guy couldn't play harmonica.

Our first engineer was a former Marine sergeant, Tom Keith, who mixed the sound until we added him to the cast doing sound effects, heart-rending loon calls, gunshots, talking dogs and hysterical chickens, and various varieties of flatulence. He did silly things with great dignity. I was a self-conscious English major and he made me a storyteller who could have a Chinese

Mr. Ray Marklund, stagehand, seated at GK's desk, 1984.

Tom Keith at the SFX table.

ICBM cross the Pacific heading for a Scout camp in Aspen where loons sing "Kumbaya," but breeding dolphins east of Oahu emit high-pitched euphoric cries that confuse the rocket's guidance system and it lands amid nougat storage tanks in a series of splats and splorts, and thousands of aspen release a cloud of aspen gases that are ignited by a Scoutmaster lighting an exploding cigar as a glockenspiel plays Bach. That sort of thing.

We rehearsed in my living room, Bill and Judy on the couch, Cal Hand playing dobro, Rudy Darling fiddling in the archway of the dining room, sometimes Mary at the piano, my little boy sitting enrapt in the middle of the floor, buoyant music in a sad household. I kept writing for *The New Yorker,* shipping the stories off, waiting for Roger's response— his gentle rejection letters—*didn't seem entirely successful* was as harsh as he got—and his acceptance letters: *FRIENDLY NEIGHBOR is awfully good, and we are delighted to take it, of course. It grows gently but strongly as one goes along, and it's like nothing else I have ever read.* And Mr. Shawn wrote soon thereafter, saying, "This is the sort of deadpan humor one doesn't see much of anymore. The more you write for us, the better."

Lavish praise on a *New Yorker* letterhead and then a generous check and we were rich for a month or two, and then went back to oatmeal, hot dogs, and spaghetti. We lived in St. Anthony Park, a Lutheran neigh-borhood, and I could let my little boy wander out through the backyards and find his playmates and a few hours later a mom would call and ask if it was okay if he stayed for lunch. No need to hire child care, with

Lutherans around. I sat at my Underwood with a faint *O* and off-kilter *F* and *P* and wrote the show.

I broke up with Mary in 1976. There was no anger, only silence, which we each misinterpreted as rejection. A simple language barrier, the inability to say what you feel. We had some good times in our little house with the gazebo on the hill where friends came for bratwurst and beer and played sweet old songs. She gave piano lessons to the children of friends. She took up guitar. We plotted the first broadcast of *A Prairie Home Companion* and she picked out "Hello, Love" as the theme song. We never made such a cheerful home as her parents had. I married for happiness of course and the mystery of love, and what I found was loneliness, which made me think there something wrong with me, and then I found someone who wanted to be with me, and so I left one mystery and walked into another. I packed up my clothes and papers. Our son said, "Couldn't you and Mom take turns being right?" Mary said something about counseling. But we had had so little to say to each other for so long, each of us burdened with remorse; where does one start? I drove away with no words of farewell and we hardly ever spoke again.

The show hit the road in a Winnebago motor home for twelve shows in twelve towns in twelve days, in Minnesota, Iowa, Wisconsin, pitching a tent each night—the Powdermilk Biscuit Band and I, and did fifty live broadcasts that year, with a shifting cast of Bill and Judy, Dakota Dave Hull and Sean Blackburn, Rudy Darling, Peter Ostroushko, Robin and Linda, and Stevie Beck, the Queen of the Autoharp. Eventually we settled on a house band of Bob Douglas, Mary DuShane, Adam Granger, and Dick Rees, a classic mando/fiddle/guitar/bass string band that, thanks to my ignorance of music, enjoyed a lot of freedom, covering gospel, swing, and old-time fiddle tunes. They started out at $40 apiece per show and got up to $150, not bad for freelance folkies.

Bob knew dozens of gospel songs, like "Prayer Bells of Heaven (oh how sweetly they ring)" and "Anchored in Love" (*The tempest is o'er, I'm safe evermore, what gladness what rapture is mine. The danger is past, I'm anchored at last. I'm anchored in love divine*). Tom Keith mixed sound and drove. I sang bass on the gospel stuff, and now and then sang something of my own. Once a boy in the first row threw up as I sang, *The old radio, the old radio that held a place of honor in our home of long ago. The folks are dead and gone and I am moving on, sitting all alone by our family radio.* He had the flu, his mother explained later. I stood and talked to give the band a chance to retune, look at the chord chart, get a drink of water, use the toilet, so I said: *I am from Minnesota, a state that ranks forty-seventh in the use of irony, a serious state where every year, nature makes serious attempts to kill us, and then it's summer and time for giant carnivorous mosquitoes, who no bug repellent even discourages. A crucifix helps but you have to hit them really hard with it. Why do I tell you this? Because our sponsor, Powdermilk Biscuits, is the only baked product that gives shy persons the strength to get up and do what needs to be done. . . . Heavens, they're tasty! And expeditious.* And so on.

In Duluth, we played the train depot, using baggage carts for a stage. We played a Lutheran church in Sioux Falls, for which I wrote a Lutheran anthem:

Episcopalians are proud of their faith,
You ought to hear 'em talk.
Who they got? They got Henry the 8th
And we got J. S. Bach.
Henry the 8th'd marry a woman
And then her head would drop.
J. S. Bach had twenty-three kids
'Cause his organ had no stop.

I was raised to keep a lid on it,
Guard what you say or do.
A Mighty Fortress is our God
So he must be Lutheran too.

That night we got snowed in, slept on the floor of the Sunday School wing with the Good Shepherd looking down from the wall. We made it through on snow-drifted roads to Worthington and Mankato. When the audience had had enough songs about the lonesome whistle's wail and *When I'm dead, let your teardrops kiss the flowers on my grave,* Tom Keith jumped up on stage with me and we did a story about dogs, engines with piston problems, a mammoth catapult, giant condors, demented elephants, stuttering butlers, exploding beer bottles, Alpine horns, fast trains—he was game for anything. I was merely the narrator, the enabler, winging it toward a big finish (a ship departing, seagulls, surf). People loved Tom. He had been a mere engineer and we made him a star. People asked for his autograph, so we had 8 x 10 glossies printed up.

Judy Larson, Bill Hinkley, GK, Bob Douglas, Rudy Darling—Worthington, MN, 1975.

We lived in close quarters on the road and had to endure Bob Douglas's incessant practicing of Irish hornpipes and jigs on the mandolin and, to distract him, we worked up a Sons of the Pioneers number, "Blue Shadows on the Trail," in five-part harmony with some tricky passing chords in it, and we got it almost to perfection so we sang it in Moorhead, or started to sing it, and hit a chord so awful we all collapsed in helpless laughter right around the line "a plaintive wail in the distance." It wasn't plaintive, it was putrid. Rudy fell on the floor and could not get up. The audience had never seen professional musicians fall apart physically like this before. To restore sobriety, we swung into *On Jordan's stormy banks I stand and cast a wishful eye to Canaan's fair and happy land, where my possessions lie.* A song about death always settled us down. We never ventured into "Blue Shadows" again. We knew that if we did, we'd see the plaintive wail approaching and we'd crash into it.

We traveled by motor home mostly, but once a small corporate jet was put at our service to fly up to do a tent show in Bayfield, Wisconsin. We did two shows and were driven to the airport for the flight home. The airport manager said, "Frank is on his way." We asked who Frank was and he said, "He has to drive a truck ahead of the plane to scare the deer off the runway." We boarded the plane and Frank raced down the runway and we followed, the plane took off, and Adam took a deep breath. I asked him what he was thinking. He said, "I was thinking I might be the answer to a trivia question: who was the guitarist on the plane that crashed and killed Garrison Keillor."

I doubted the show would last but we drew capacity crowds and I was curious to know what the appeal might be, so I kept going. It sure wasn't my personality. I was a tall sourpuss with a big beard and a white suit, looking like a Confederate general on trial for his life. But in 1976, the News from Lake Wobegon came along, and soon made the jump from one-page letter to fifteen-minute monologue—*Well, it's been a quiet week in Lake Wobegon*—based on the four seasons, the school year, the national holidays, and the liturgical year—starting with a word about the weather, then the news of the Norwegian bachelor farmers, the Thanatopsis Society, the Sons of Knute lodge singing: *Sons of Knute we are, sons of the prairie, with our heads held high in January, hauling our carcass around in big parkas, wearing boots the size of tree stumps.* And with the arrival of Lake Wobegon, the show took on a clear identity.

I was out to play with the familiar, talking about a place where you could count on others in time of need as Mother had during the war. Religious and ethnic differences aside, it was tightly knit and had little tolerance for pretense. Satire was a sign of good health. Mutual benefit was fundamental, and industry and loyalty and a decent reverence for the natural world, while waste was abhorrent and cruelty not tolerated. Midwestern modesty prevailed. Children were brought up to be deferential and self-effacing and behave appropriately, which, it was assumed, you knew without being told. Nobody encouraged you to follow your dream. Spiritual longing was a private matter, as were grief and regret.

The town motto: *Sumus quod sumus* (We are what we are). Grace was the town librarian, Gary and Leroy the town constables, and Bud ran the snowplow. Dr. DeHaven was the physician, though he was seldom mentioned; he took a "Let's wait and see what develops" approach to disease. A central figure was Father Emil of Our Lady of Perpetual Responsibility church, and to offset his sternness, I placed a nun in the church,

Sister Arvonne, in honor of my friend Arvonne Fraser, a cheerful liberal and optimist despite personal tragedies, still canoeing, still smoking, into her late eighties. Her adversary, Father Emil, is strict and brusque: to the weeping girl who found out she was pregnant, he said, "If you didn't want to go to Chicago, why'd you get on the train?" To the German Catholics I added, for dramatic interest, an equal number of Norwegian Lutherans led by Pastor Ingqvist. The Norwegians, ever status-conscious, vote Republican, and the Germans vote Democratic because the Norwegians don't. The car dealers are Bunsen Ford and Krebsbach Chev, which means that Lutherans drive Fords and Catholics drive Chevies, and if you drive something else, people watch you very closely. Dorothy ran the café and Wally the Sidetrack Tap, and the Mercantile belonged to Cliff with his amazing comb-over, a piece of hair architecture. And it ended: *And that's the news from Lake Wobegon, where the women are strong, the men are good-looking, and all the children are above average.* Like most of the best lines, it came out of nowhere. I woke up one morning and it was in my head.

I put Lake Wobegon in central Minnesota because my city audience knew the scenic parts of Minnesota, the North Shore, the Boundary Waters, the Mississippi Valley, and nothing about the midsection with all the hog and dairy farms. The town was founded by Father Pierre Plaisir who named it Lac Malheur for the pestilence of mosquitoes. It was later settled by Unitarian missionaries. The town was not on the map, having been left off by surveyors in the 1860s who had surveyed more of Minnesota than there was room for between the borders, so about fifty square miles had to be folded under. I said that Lake Wobegon took its name from the Ojibway word that means "the place where we waited all day for you in the rain," and somehow people believed this and other historic details. I said that, in 1938, Babe Ruth appeared in an exhibition game with the Sorbitol All-Stars barnstorming team and hit a home run that cleared the center field fence and was never found. Near the ballpark stands the statue of the Unknown Norwegian with the stalk of quack grass growing out of his left ear, from a seed implanted there by the tornado of 1965, which no herbicide has been able to kill off. The Unknown was so famous in the 1890s that nobody bothered to put an inscription on the base, and now nobody can remember if he was a Swanberg or Swenson.

Because I assumed the show would end in a year or two, I didn't keep orderly notes on the town; it was all in my head. The ball club was the Schroeders, then it became the Whippets. The town barber began as Jim, then became Bob. The town clerk was Viola Tors, though before she'd been a Tordahl. I had a hard time keeping the Tordoffs straight from the Tommerdahls, Thorvaldsons, Tollefsons, and Tolleruds, and sometimes characters migrated from one family to another. Val Tollefson was married to Charlotte and later turned up married to Florence. I had the same problem with Krebsbachs and Kreugers: Wally, the owner of the Sidetrack Tap, was sometimes a Krebsbach, other times a Kreuger. Carl Krebsbach is the town handyman, married to Marjie though once he was married to Betty. The Ingqvist family is complicated, sometimes appearing as Ingquist or Inkvist or Ingebretson, and the relationships are not clear. Roger Hedlund is married to Marilyn except for a while she was Cindy.

I made a crucial decision from the get-go that, instead of Cool, I was going for Sweet. I was clear on this. I was cool in college. Now that was over. One day, a security woman checking IDs at an airport lounge saw me coming and said, "Good morning, sunshine," though she didn't know me from Adam. She glanced at my driver's license and said, "Have a good flight, darling." This was in the South, of course. That woman's "sunshine" shone on me for the rest of the day. On the flight that day, I sat next to a Black woman my age from Alabama, who was in a chatty mood. I said, "You've seen a lot of history in Alabama." She said, "And it isn't over yet." We got to talking about Dr. King and his family, and she blurted out, "I just cannot forgive those children of his for never giving their mother a grandbaby. Four healthy children. I don't know their sexual orientation, but you would think that one of them could've produced one baby for Mrs. King to hold. She died without ever getting those babies to hold in her arms. Do you have grandbabies?" I said, No. "I've got two," she said, "and every time I look at them, that's me." She patted my hand. "I am going to pray for you to get grandchildren." When the plane pulled up to the gate in Chicago, she touched my knee and said, "It was good talking with you, darling."

In Minnesota, we don't address each other as "darling." I went to a big dinner of diehard liberals in Texas and was *darlinged* left and right and *sweetied* and even occasionally *precioused*, but if you were among

Democrats in Minnesota, it feels like a meeting of insurance actuaries, a cold handshake and a thin smile and that's all you get. We are wary of affectionate banter with strangers for fear we'll end up with a truckload of aluminum siding or a set of encyclopedias. We're burdened by the need to be cool. I decided early to do a Southern show up north. So I avoided the sardonic and ventured into sweetness. I wrote a song about the town.

> *Oh little town, I love the sound*
> *Of water sprinklers in the evening,*
> *The siren tune at 12 o'clock noon, or 12:04 if Bud is late.*

> *And when you walk down Oak or Main,*
> *Everybody knows your name,*
> *They ask you how you are, you say, "Not bad, all right, I guess about*
>   *the same."*

> *Wobegon, I remember O so well how peacefully among the woods*
>   *and fields you lie—*
> *My Wobegon, I close my eyes and I can see you just as clearly as in*
>   *days gone by.*

As the Sons of Knute say, "There's no place like home when you're not feeling well." Or, as Clarence Bunsen says, "When you're from here, you don't notice it so much."

The monologue took its place after intermission, and when I walked downstage and said, "It's been a quiet week in Lake Wobegon," the audience let out a soft sigh, as if an old uncle had returned. The key to the story was to maintain a modest tone, avoid smart and uppity language, stay in the background, as a Wobegonian would do. Every spring, a monologue about the sadness of leaving school behind. Every October, the glory of autumn days. In January, a long tale about heroic Minnesota winters, keeping warm by the exertion of wearing heavy clothing while shoveling the walk and throwing the snow up on the snowbank fifteen feet overhead, clothesline tied to our belts so that in case of avalanche, they could pull us out in time, watching for enormous icicles falling like daggers and also for coyotes who would take on a boy immobilized by heavy clothing.

Every week I felt their pleasure at the familiar. It was not an accurate story—for one thing, there was no profanity—I grew up among people for whom "Oh shoot" or "Fiddle" passed for curses, and so I don't have an ear for it either. And death was rare. The hermit Jack died in his hunting shack in the woods, and a Norwegian bachelor farmer too, and my aunt Evelyn died in her sleep, but no main characters, and they tended not to get older either. Some of them remained in their late fifties for thirty years. There was genuine feeling and occasional tenderness among taciturn people, a man weeping for pride as his daughter makes a crucial jump shot in a game, old couples dancing at the Sweethearts Ball in an unmistakable embrace, the hush of Christmas Eve, the Catholics weeping as they sing "Stille Nacht" in their grandparents' German. Myrtle and Florian Krebsbach drove toward Minneapolis to visit their son and fell into squabbling, and when he stopped at a truck stop for gas and bought a Snickers bar and came back to the car, he didn't look in the back seat where she'd been napping and so he drove away, leaving her in the ladies' john. Her anguish and his shame led to a joyful reunion, whereupon the battle resumed.

Lake Wobegon was a departure for me, I who once imitated Kafka and Lorca, and it led to sentimental songs that, ten years before, never would've occurred to me.

> *Look in every smiling face,*
> *Keep the memory of this place,*
> *And before we must depart,*
> *Sing one chorus from the heart.*

> *From this prairie, from this home,*
> *We shall fly to realms unknown,*
> *Carrying no souvenirs,*
> *Just our memories and our tears.*

We were amateurs, made no attempt to hide the fact. And we were proudly provincial. Chauvinism begins at home.

> *Minnesota is the best*
> *University in the West.*

Harvard University is pleased
To be called the Minnesota of the East.

Other songwriters sought the universal, and I embraced the ordinary. People came to the show and wrote greetings on slips of paper and passed
them down front and I said hello to Jody in St. Joe and Benny in Nowthen
and Will and Sonya in Minneapolis and I wished Rachel well on her graduation from St. Ben's. And I wrote songs—not the best, but good enough.

M is for the falls of Minnehaha
I, of course, for Irving Avenue S.
N for Nicollet Mall and Nicollet Island
The second N is anybody's guess.
E is for the street they call East Hennepin.
A is Aldrich Avenue Southwest.
Polis is a Greek word meaning city
And Minneapolis is the best.
It's a bower of bliss on the Miss- issippi
And when all is said and done,
Now I see there's one ZIP code for me,
And that is 5-5-4-0-1.

A small town was the lodestar. The show was never about peace and harmony, never about Daring to Be Me. It was always about loyalty. Be True
to Your School.

We toured to the Fox River Valley and I wrote a song for Appleton. *It*
was the Garden of Eden back when time begun. Eve took a bite of the apple
for fun and said, let's settle here in Appleton. A columnist the next week
called it "shameless pandering," but I thought it was funny. I was not out
to deepen or broaden. I was a man at play.

I went dancing one night in East Lansing
We sowed wild grains across the Great Plains
Spent a wild youth in Duluth
Found euphoria and joy in Peoria, Illinois,
And my all in St. Paul—It's you—that's the truth.

In the early years, musicians doubled as actors and I walked around backstage, scripts in hand, and asked for volunteers. Some musicians were eager, others dreaded the thought. Bluegrass musicians preferred to stay in safe territory and not have to shout, "Allons, camarades!" and cross swords with a guy named Pierre who turned out to be a woman, but singers were always game, and so were bass players. Still, there was an awkward self-consciousness about it—and when I found out that George Muschamp and Molly Atwood, who lived across the street from me in St. Paul, were actors in the Children's Theatre Company, I grabbed them and they were great and we never looked back.

I turned a *New Yorker* story of mine, "Lonesome Shorty," into "The Lives of the Cowboys" about Dusty and Lefty and it went on for decades. Tom Keith did horse snorts and whinnies, the pouring of whiskey in the glass, the shuffling of cards, the slow tread of the big boots of the bully Big Messer as he approached, the cocking of his pistol, the slow leakage of gas from him despite his attempts to tighten his sphincter, the lighting of a match, the explosion that sends him crashing into the aspidistra, and all I had to do was write dialogue.

LEFTY: I got a confession to make, pardner. Whilst I was making that soup, I dropped a bar of soap in it by accident and by the time I fished it out, it was a fraction of its former size.

DUSTY: So that's why you didn't have any soup yourself.

LEFTY: I wasn't hungry.

DUSTY: I wouldn't've been either if I'd known there was soap in it.

LEFTY: Well, you ate two helpings of it.

DUSTY: Didn't know it was soap soup.

LEFTY: You couldn't taste it?

DUSTY: Tasted about as good as anything else you ever cooked.

LEFTY: Well, maybe I should make it more often then.

DUSTY: I guess you didn't notice that there was more bourbon in the bottle last night than there was yesterday morning when it was practically empty.

LEFTY: What are you saying?

DUSTY: Take a wild guess.

LEFTY: Are you saying you pissed in the whiskey?

DUSTY: Nope. It's horse piss. You drank three glasses of it, evidently you've
forgotten what good whiskey tastes like.
LEFTY: Why in the world would you go and do a thing like that?
DUSTY: I'm trying to stop drinking.
LEFTY: So that's why you didn't have any.
DUSTY: It works!

Writing for *The New Yorker* was an uphill climb—shadows of Perelman and Frazier and Woody Allen on the wall—but with radio, the coast
was clear: the greats were long gone—we had no competitors, nobody
else did scripted comedy on radio. It was a walk in the park compared to
my dad's hard labors—working on the train, building our house, doing
carpentry for others, raising a garden. I was the boss, so my work was
never rejected except by me. Nobody said, "I'm sorry, but this is not you
at your best." Maybe it wasn't, but we had a show to do and *better* and
best don't mean all that much when you're the only café in town. Shut up
and enjoy your pancakes.

I played the title role in *Dr. Brad Triplett, Wildlife Urologist*, performing a prostatectomy on a white-tailed deer and explaining to my adoring
nurse Sharon that urine is how wild animals mark territory and so a
urinary dysfunction also affects social standing and the ability to mate,
which is why I gave up my lucrative practice in Winnetka to work the
woods of northern Wisconsin—"Yes, the deer are overpopulated," I said.
"But a doctor can't play God. We're here to help, not to judge the worth
of a life. A man has to follow his heart, and this is my mission. Urine is
in my blood somehow."

I wrote the sketch after a visit to Mayo and a consultation about my
prostate. Real life fed the imagination, just like the Mississippi turned the
wheels that ran the mills of Minneapolis. There was no agony involved, I
just sat and wrote sketches, monologues, songs for the pleasure of it. E.g.,
the childish pleasure of rhyme:

Long distance information, give me South St. Paul,
Someone down at FedEx just gave me a call.
The wedding's in an hour when she and I'll be hitched.
It's a package from my dentist, and it's my lower bridge.

I bought her the big diamond and a fancy bridal wreath,
But I don't think she'll marry me if I don't get my teeth.
I'll be in the parking lot, so tell them, hurry please,
My car's the one with tin cans and the windows smeared with cheese.

A simple story straight from me to you. So simple. Everyone else in public radio lived with the burden of high standards, shades of the BBC—the ambition to do investigative stories on the moisture of oysters farmed in Worcester. Not I. Parody was my beat, and my generation had a wealth of big shots to beat up on—Bob Dylan, for one.

May you grow up to be beautiful
And very rich and slim.
May God give you what you want
Though you don't believe in Him.
May you stick your finger in the pie
And always find the plum
May you stay forever dumb.

And once, for a show at Bethel Bible College, we sang "Catch a Wave" (*If you're saved, you'll be sitting on top of the world*). And a wedding sketch in which the bride sang (to the bridal march from Wagner's *Lohengrin*: *Why am I here? Who is this man? Why is he dressed up and holding my hand?*) and the groom (*Why does she cry? I wish she'd stop. I'm not bad looking and I have a job. I don't smell bad. I am not gay. I'm in good shape and I floss twice a day.*) and the minister (*It's not so bad. It could be worse. It's better than coming to church in a hearse. Just say the words that must be said and then you can undress and go off to bed.*).

20

An Essay on Cowardice

In *Foxe's Book of Martyrs*, I found a Keillor who was burned at the stake by Catholics for reading his Bible, and I made a note to avoid martyrdom and so far have succeeded. If ordered at swordpoint not to read the Bible, I would be okay, I have enough of it memorized to last me for a while.

The one time martyrdom was offered was in the summer of 1968 when I was ordered by Local Selective Service Board No. 51, Hennepin County, to report for induction into the Army on a specified Tuesday at 7:30 a.m. I wrote back to say I would not report because the war in Vietnam was immoral—mindless carnage, the weekly body count, B-52s bombing rice paddies, Marines in choppers barreling down into villages, all in defense of a corrupt regime, a war irreconcilable with our values, etc., etc.—it was a long letter, about four pages in ballpoint on lined yellow paper, and I did not show up to board the bus for boot camp on that Tuesday. I expected an FBI guy in a shiny gray suit and aviator shades to knock at my door with a warrant for my arrest.

The day I was ordered to report, I went to visit my Uncle Don and Aunt Elsie, who still were fond of me though I'd left the Brethren. My sweet-tempered aunt, who kept her girlish enthusiasm all of her life, and my plain-spoken uncle, who was bigger than anyone else and also more boyish and loved games and sports. We sat on their porch and talked about old times. I recalled the tremendous line drive he hit in a softball game at the 1956 Grace & Truth Bible Conference at Lake Minnetonka, Married Men vs. Single. It was in the middle innings, the score close, the game in the balance, I was playing third base for the Single Men, and he came up to bat and took a big cut at an inside pitch and hit a scorcher down the third-base line that had double written all over it. It bounced just inside the line and took off from the topspin, and I stabbed the glove to my right, backhanded the ball, planted my right foot, saw Uncle Don steaming toward first, and threw him out by a stride. I told him that this play was a highlight of my entire life. He said: "The reason you remember that play so well is that it was the only time you ever threw anyone out from third base."

I kept expecting the knock right up to when I started *A Prairie Home Companion* in 1974 and so I never used my name on the air lest I wind up at Sandstone prison, and the knock on the door never came. Probably it was a bureaucratic glitch, papers misplaced, the discrepancy of the two names, Gary had been ordered to report, Garrison wrote the letter saying no, though I liked to imagine a savior at the draft board, a clerk who was moved by my letter and at great risk to herself stuck my file in the Inactive drawer. Being a draft dodger makes Memorial Day more meaningful to me. The Light Brigade rode into the valley of death on the orders of an arrogant fool, and men have been riding off to death in behalf of arrogant fools ever since. Vietnam was a lost cause, and anyway it didn't matter to the security of the United States. Saigon fell and now cruise ships stop at Ho Chi Minh City and life goes on except for the dead. They died for their own sense of honor and nothing more. You walk along the Vietnam Memorial wall and you know that many of those honored dead were dissenters but went anyway. I hope the man who was called in my place got assigned to the Army Post Office in New York City, like my dad, and spent two years in the city and developed a taste for Japanese cuisine and Broadway musicals and returned, safe and sound, to Minneapolis. I wish I could meet him so I could honor him for his service.

I escaped the draft, and my ancestor Elder John Crandall escaped the Puritans of Massachusetts, who drowned young girls accused of witchcraft. He was once arrested in Boston for preaching Christian charity toward the Algonquin people, and some men who were arrested with him that day were publicly whipped, one of them whipped to death, but Elder John got to Rhode Island to join Roger Williams and the Baptists and founded the town of Westerly. I don't know if he'd want me as a descendant but I'm proud to have him, and the fact that our connection also connects me to Katharine Hepburn and Lucille Ball is no problem whatsoever. But in his place, I wouldn't have preached to men who were holding whips, I would've bit my tongue and headed west and found a nice Quaker settlement somewhere.

In 1776, a number of Crandalls loyal to the Crown fled to Canada to escape the Revolution. They didn't find ease and comfort up there, and the nineteenth century was as grim for them as for everyone else. Aunt Ruth had a little piece of hand stitching:

> *Susanne Crandall is my name & Canada is my nation.*
> *Amherst is my home & Christ is my salvation.*
> *I am a girl of ten years old. When I am lying dead and cold*
> *& all my bones are rotten,*
> *If this you see, remember me. When I am quite forgotten. 1841*

A girl of ten meditating on death and ignominy, sewing a little monument for herself—and I know nothing about her except that she had the same morbid streak I had at that age.

I know more about my distant ancestor Prudence Crandall, who opened a school for young women in Canterbury, Connecticut, in 1831. When several young women of color applied for admission, Prudence accepted them, whereupon the town turned against her. She was jailed, a mob attacked the school and broke the windows, and Prudence closed up shop and lit out for Illinois and then Kansas Territory and took up the cause of women's suffrage. She did not live to see it come to pass, but she knew what was right. Had it been my school, I would've asked the young women of color to wait while I formed a committee of educators to study the matter, solicit community input, and find a solution that everyone could live with. I also would've upped my property insurance.

My grandfather James, whose middle name was Crandall, left New Brunswick to rescue his sister Mary on the verge of widowhood and her three little children. Our relatives who took our family in during the war were cut from the same cloth. My brother Philip was a good father and grandfather, worthy of esteem. I am a hanger-on in this line of worthies, but I do hang on.

Years later, I was hung out to dry for a mutual email flirtation and my career came to a screeching halt, which I felt was unjust, and then I came to believe it was justice for my cowardice of 1976 when I ended the marriage to Mary. Justice deferred, and all the more painful for it.

We had a quiet marriage that became silent and unbearable. I'm a person who maneuvers out of difficult situations by subterfuge—I evaded the Darwins, I skipped out on swim class and then persuaded my mother I could swim, I slipped away from the Brethren without confrontation or explanation. And I broke up with Mary without ever facing her and saying why. I needed to depart swiftly in silence by the cowardly device of a love affair with someone else. I have revisited those scenes many times over the years. How a gentle, evasive man, aware he is doing a dishonest thing, will hurry up and try to dismiss it from his mind. I know that man and I could find excuses for his behavior—I could argue that self-righteousness does not teach ethics, that the invisible middle child learns how to get away with deceit—but it doesn't alleviate the damage I caused. I could argue that I was single-minded in my vocation and cut corners on honesty. I could argue that humor is itself an act of evasion. Give me five minutes, I can come up with other explanations. But really, it's cowardice.

My wife, Mary, had stood by me through hard times when I worked eighteen-hour days and we were isolated in a farmhouse far from her people, and in 1976 I left her behind, simply walked away. Her mother, Marjorie, and I reconciled ten years later, but I failed to make amends with Mary and that lies heavy on my conscience. The inability to forgive and to reconcile and resume decent friendly relations with people you care about whom you broke away from. This is a heavy weight forty years later.

Soon after I left her, she found her vocation as a social worker, advocating for the elderly and impoverished in their complicated dealings with weary bureaucrats. Where the clients were sheepish and confused, she was forceful and direct on their behalf and, if necessary, spoke with faintly concealed cold fury. She'd had a habit of timidity with me, but for clients in desperate circumstances, she looked authority in the eye and demanded attention and mercy. We saw little of each other except at funerals, and at our son Jason's graduation we sat together. The sight of her made me forlorn. A man would like his former wife to remarry and be happy with someone else, but that didn't happen.

Over the years, I heard stories of her good work defending hopeless cases, and every year around her birthday, March 8, I thought of calling her and wishing her well but didn't, not sure she wanted to hear from me. She died the Friday before Palm Sunday, 1998, in Fairview Hospital in Minneapolis, of a massive infection after a hip replacement. Jason had spent days at the hospital, talking to her though she was in a coma, and spent the last night at the hospital, holding her hand, talking. She was 53. I had sent her gifts of money over the years but I should've asked for her forgiveness.

Her death hit me like a hammer. It was the Friday before our annual Talent Show at Town Hall in New York. People said it was a good show, but people always say that. I flew back to Minnesota and helped Jason clean out his mother's apartment. A grim afternoon. So many mementos of our married life. A photograph of the white frame cabin where we'd met when she was nineteen. At her funeral, I sat in the back row next to Judy Larson and I wept a bucket of useless tears, thinking of that girl's wistfulness, longing for a life, lying on a dock at the lake in northern Minnesota or sitting at a piano in a practice room in Scott Hall, playing the Bach *French Suite No. 6*. We longed together, the fragile man and the fearful woman, he waiting for her to affirm her love, she mistaking his silence for anger, when all either had to do was to reach over and embrace the other. The music at her funeral was a Gillian Welch song:

> *There's a mile of blacktop*
> *Where the road begins,*
> *It takes a time or two to recognize.*
> *Growing at the roadside,*
> *Scattered by the wind,*
> *Are everybody's unsaid sad goodbyes.*
> *But there's only one and only*
> *Who could go and leave me lonely.*

Tears poured out of me, at those words "only one who could go and leave me lonely." I never cry at funerals, but I'd never attended the funeral of one whom I had so badly disappointed. The funeral ended, I edged through the crowd, people reached over to pat my shoulder, but there was no comfort, no words, and there still are not.

I disappointed several women badly. I was too restless to be a good father or a true friend. I found it terribly hard to set aside hard feelings and make peace. I'm not a good person, but I did a radio show for forty years that attracted a great many good people—teachers, social workers, nurses, musicians, skilled workers—and I did my best to amuse them for a couple hours. My own life was tangled and ragged, but when I walk down the street, sometimes a person sees me and smiles, remembering a show I did, and that counts for something.

By all reasonable standards, I was rather unemployable in this world, which turned out to be an advantage. The smart guys went off to become serfs in tall buildings, and I, at the lower end of mediocre, was well-positioned to be wildly lucky. As my friend Sydney Goldstein said, "That you could make work for yourself that suits you and has ended up giving you and other people a lot of pleasure—what more could you ask for?" She lived in San Francisco, ran City Arts & Lectures, which she'd invented, was smart and elegant and loyal, and every year she invited me to come out and do a show in her theater on Nob Hill and enjoy the trolleys rumbling along Market Street, the Mediterranean buildings, the river of fog in the Golden Gate, and the beautiful faces of young people, with their Asian eyes, Hispanic cheekbones, Creole skin. One friend as good as Sydney is enough, and I had her *plus* Bill Kling, and my artist friend Joe O'Connell, and my old J-school professor Bob Lindsay with the dent in his head. Bob was a Marine, sparing with praise, but when he said, "Last week's show was pretty damn good," to me, it was the Peabody Award. He sent the note on Sunday and I read it on Monday, and it was all the encouragement I needed.

21

Coast to Coast

In May 1980, the show went coast-to-coast, uplinked live by satellite. Bill Kling had pushed for that and I was the defeatist—the show was local—but he said, "You'll never know unless you try, and if you don't try, you will someday wish you had." So he pushed us out of our comfortable nest and he was right. New York turned out to be a hot spot for the show, along with Seattle, San Francisco, and Washington, DC, and big names were glad to come on the radio, the Everly Brothers, Renée Fleming, James Taylor, Marilyn Horne, Taj Mahal, Yo-Yo Ma, John Sebastian, just as Kling said they would. I grew up, as Minnesotans do, with a keen sense of inferiority, and Kling was a skier and said, "If you stay on the beginners' slope, you'll never get better."

He'd campaigned for the national satellite system but public TV was in the driver's seat, radio being considered an antique, like the Victrola. Public TV was riding high on the basis of BBC costume dramas and a puppet show called *Sesame Street* and a soft-spoken guy in a cardigan sweater named Mister Rogers. Parents could park their kids in front of the PBS screen and they'd never see violence except for sword duels. A retired Navy admiral was in charge of the satellite project, no mention of radio, until Bill Kling stepped in. He formed a consortium of radio stations that demanded thirteen regional uplinks rather than the one uplink that NPR wanted for itself in Washington. The admiral, after vigorously denying the need for radio, gave him a twenty-four-hour deadline to name the thirteen uplink sites, knowing that in public radio, due to the Eeyore tendency to form task forces to consider worst possible scenarios, decisions take years, not hours, but Mr. Kling promptly delivered the list of thirteen, one in St. Paul, and that put us in business. Mr. Kling was an entrepreneur who believed in the power of a good idea to win out over cliques and claques, inertia and neurosis, and he prevailed.

The show went up on the satellite May 3, 1980. Same show, staff of four plus the stage crew, now available to listeners in New York, LA, and all stops in between. I wrote the show. Same drill. Friday rehearsal. Extensive rewrites. Sound check on Saturday: once through each script, more rewrites, and then I jiggered the order of the show and typed it up and passed it around.

Tom Keith (and, later, Fred Newman) was the key to the kingdom of comic surrealism, which had never been my ambition but the audience loved it, a bloodhound reciting "To be or not to be, that is the question," Bach played by a duck pecking a glockenspiel, that sort of thing. Writing prose fiction, I never came up to the high plateau of Thurber or Perelman or Charles Portis, but writing the show was child's play. NPR was high-church solemnity, and we were the kids who saw the butt crack of the man knelt in prayer. The beauty of nonsense became clear: in our jittery times, with the winds of correctness blowing through public radio, playing to a crowd that was somewhat leftist and feministic and sensitive to stereotyping or biases or unfair generalizations, nonetheless the crowd liked to be teased and toyed with, as once, for Father's Day, a poem with the lines:

Sperm beneath their shiny domes
Contain important chromosomes
And their tails can kick just like a leg.
O nothing could be fina
Than to swim up a vagina
In search of a rendezvous with an egg.

The laughter at the word "vagina" was gender-balanced, as many trebles as baritones, and so was the laughter at my limerick about the girl from St. Olaf, an Ole, who spread herself with guacamole and two theologians put on their Trojans and had her completely and wholly. The pun, "wholly" was not lost.

I'd loved limericks since the eighth grade, and now I had a reason to write more of them.

There was an old man of Nantucket
Who died. He just kicked the bucket.
And when he was dead
We found that instead
Of Nantucket he came from Barnstable.

The crowd got excited at "Nantucket" though they knew they shouldn't, it was bad, and then "Barnstable" came along as pure innocence.

GK at Lake Harriet Band Shell show, August 4, 1979. A huge crowd, thanks to free admission and good weather. A first indication of Prairie Home's *appeal, and that is puzzlement on his face.*

I was happy to tread the boards of low comedy on the air, just as Chaucer and Shakespeare had, but what I loved most about the show were the great singers who sat in a dressing room sipping tea and then came out on stage and sang from their heels and made the room levitate, singers like Hazel Dickens, Dave Van Ronk, Cathal McConnell, Aoife O'Donovan, Joel Grey, Renée Fleming, Jearlyn Steele, Soupy Schindler, Odetta. Each one singular, indelible, nobody else like them—between Hazel's haunted, evangelical voice and Joel's Yiddish patter song learned from his dad, Mickey Katz, and Jearlyn's soul and Renée's soul and Soupy's R&B honk, each one carrying the full force of distinguished ancestry, a whole world on their shoulders. I loved them all. Soupy was master of the harmonica and the jug, sang in a blues growl, whooped and cried, and whatever he did, the audience wanted more, so I had to step on his applause. Soupy had the raw passionate voice I wished for myself: there was nothing soupy about it, it was all muscle, all heart. He'd grown up singing in synagogue in north Minneapolis, the son of Fanny and Julius, two Holocaust survivors, and he took up blues during a hitch in the Air Force, won everyone's heart with his big personality. A Jew singing Black music, one oppressed people adopting another to make something beautiful out of pain. Soupy was funnier than I was and he could have taken over the show but for one thing: Soupy laughed hard at his own jokes. I never laughed at mine. In radio, cool trumps hot. Soupy's spirit was strong, but he couldn't earn a living in music and he worked as a men's clothing salesman, drove cab, became a public schoolteacher, a fine one, and one day he dropped dead of a heart attack at 57. A great man in a difficult life.

Soupy.

I was so engrossed in writing the show, I couldn't see what a beautiful thing it was, a loose variety show with gallant musicians playing hot numbers interspersed with the comedy of loon calls and glass breakage and French double-talk, and a slow sweet story in the middle—a homely miracle but I couldn't tell, I was too busy. We did good shows, the band shell at Lake Harriet and a ballfield on Nicollet Island, the Guthrie Theater, and in 1978 we rented the World Theater, an old rundown picture house whose owner, Bob Dworsky, was weighing a developer's offer to tear it down and put up a McDonald's. The World was a second-run theater, where if you had an afternoon to kill, you could sit in the dark and see the double feature for a couple bucks. Bob had four kids, a singer, a violinist, a drummer, and a pianist (Rich, who in due course, became our musical director), and in honor of his kids, Bob rented the place to us for $80/show. A gang of volunteers came in to scrape gum off the seats, and a crew of feminists whited out the "Ladies Toilet" sign in the lobby and painted "Women" over it. Our home. We renamed it the Fitzgerald in 1994.

In 1982, I boxed up a batch of stories ("Jack Schmidt, Arts Administrator," "After a Fall," "Don: The True Story of a Young Person," "U.S. Still on Top, Says Rest of World") to make my first book, *Happy to Be Here*, and thanks to the radio show it sold pretty well. I cut off my beard, an immense one that made me look like a man eating a sweater, and I did a publicity tour and as the book crept up the best-seller list, my accommodations upgraded from Holiday Inns to hotels with heated towel racks and rosemary-scented soap. At the end of the book tour, in Utah, I was put up in a private lodge at Sundance with high windows and views of snowy peaks and tall pines, where, alone on a chill March afternoon, I took off my clothes and went out to the hot tub and the door closed behind me and clicked. A solid click. It was locked. I had no key. Naked men often don't. (Where would you put it?)

I sat in the tub, hoping a cleaning lady might drop in, or St. Jude, or a Saint Bernard, and when nobody did, I wrapped myself in a blue plastic tarp I took off the woodpile and trudged barefoot down the gravel road and knocked on the door of another lodge to ask for help. I learned that a naked man wrapped in blue plastic does not win friends easily. I knocked on the doors of five lodges with lights on and cars in the driveway and nobody showed their faces though I did see curtains move slightly. I waved in an urgent way to three men driving by in a pickup and their heads swiveled left and they drove on. The blue plastic was cold. My feet hurt from the sharp rocks. I considered dropping the tarp and being arrested for public indecency and getting warm in the back seat of a squad car. At the sixth house, a woman came to the door and opened it a crack. She agreed to call the resort office. She didn't invite me in, so I walked back to the hot tub and was rescued an hour later by a security man, and that was the parable of the naked author in the blue plastic. Moral: *A best-selling author is somebody and a naked best-selling author is nobody. You may be a big success, but be sure to put on pants.*

GK at his Selectric in a rental apartment on Lincoln Avenue, St. Paul, 1981. A pack of smokes by the typewriter, old radio scripts on the floor. On the table behind, he's assembling his collection, HAPPY TO BE HERE. Bachelor décor, a beer sign.

An old poet friend wrote to me: "My advice: work as little as you can for as much money as they'll pay. Get the rent money and depend on your pen for the rest. Be a writer, not a comedian. The show is okay short-term but you have better things to do." But he was wrong: I had found a vocation. My good intentions had found a road and a car to drive down it. The show was my education. Had *The New Yorker* hired me, I might've spent six years living in a basement in Brooklyn and trying to be E. B. White. Instead, I'd found an old abandoned house—the radio variety show—and put a new roof on it and moved in with my friends and made a house party every Saturday and learned to step up to the microphone and talk to the people. I learned to write compact sketches that delivered jokes, do a meandering monologue about minor issues, and as a reward for good service I got to sing a duet now and then, but mostly I talked. After Jearlyn and Jevetta Steele came juking onstage to do "R-E-S-P-E-C-T," my story about Clarence and Arlene Bunsen's miserable Florida vacation fit very nicely, like after the high-wire act it's nice to bring out the man who juggles cats. It was not hard labor. Any third-grade teacher worked harder than I. Once a week, two hours at 5 p.m. Central, a lazy man's dream.

With the proceeds from *Happy to Be Here*, I went to Murray's and ordered the Silver Butter Knife Steak, and then I bought a big frame house on the corner of Goodrich and Dale in St. Paul, a hospitable house with four bedrooms, a fenced-in backyard, a commodious screened porch in front. Guests moved in when they played the show and stayed, sometimes for a week—Jean Redpath was a perfect houseguest and could remain for two or three weeks, no problem. Cereal and fruit were set out in the morning, the coffee was on. Help yourself to the refrigerator. She stayed in her room and wrote letters and read, and every day she sang for a half hour or so, songs in Scottish Gaelic that maybe she wouldn't have sung to an American audience but my God they were magnificent—her voice came down the back stairway and I listened. In the evening, we met for a meal and I never told her how I admired her singing for fear she might prefer privacy.

Robin and Linda Williams were regular houseguests and Kate MacKenzie came over one day and we formed the Hopeful Gospel Quartet. We sat in the garden behind the board fence and sang, *Come thou*

The Hopeful Gospel Quartet, Robin, Linda, Kate, GK.

fount of every blessing, tune my heart to sing thy praise, and *Sheep, sheep, don't you know the road—yes, Lord, I know the road* and when Jean Redpath heard us in the yard, she came down to join us, her Scots soprano filling out, *You're drifting too far from the shore* and *He may not come when you want Him but He's right on time.* I sang bass. Finally I was a member of a band, a big jump in status from hostship. Gospel music was unknown on public radio, except in a documentary about the civil rights movement or an Aaron Copland arrangement, but I'd grown up with it and loved the sonorities: the descending bass part on "Now the Day Is Over," singing, *Shadows of the evening steal across the sky.* We sang "Softly and Tenderly Jesus Is Calling" and sensed that, for most of our audience, songs of repentance were not what they'd come to hear, but what the hell, a little guilt never hurt anybody. And our "Calling My Children Home" actually made people cry, especially parents of teenagers: *I'm lonesome for my precious children, they live so far away. Oh may they hear my calling—calling—and come back home someday.* We did a couple of national tours and even played Carnegie Hall, and we sang my dad's favorite poem, *Twilight and evening bell, and after that the dark! And may there be no sadness of farewell when I embark.* Helen Schneyer was another houseguest who joined us in singing, she of the flowing white dresses and pounds of turquoise jewelry on fingers and wrists and hair and neck, singing spirituals and ballads about mining disasters in her rich baritone, playing gospel stride piano. Hazel Dickens sat in the living room and sang "West Virginia"—*In the dead of the night, in the still and the quiet I slip away like a bird in flight. Back to those hills, the place that I call home.*—her voice, rough and tender, a country voice of someone who's handled horses and beheaded chickens. I loved the powerful singing of mature women, and it was satisfying to find out that others loved it too. Our producer, Margaret Moos, took a big chance and booked the enormous Orpheum in downtown Minneapolis for a Big Lady weekend—Jean and Helen and Lisa Neustadt—and sold out three shows. When the three of them sang, "Dwelling in Beulah Land" or "Palms of Victory," it was Baptist revival time, the crowd standing to shout the choruses, led by two Jewish ladies and an agnostic Scot. Truly God works in mysterious ways His wonders to perform.

I loved my house on Goodrich and wish I had held on to it. Minnie Pearl came up from Nashville with her husband, Henry Cannon, and did her act on the show (*Brother went in and applied for a job and the man said, "We can start you at thirty dollars a week and in five years you can be earning five hundred." And Brother, he says, "I'll be back in five years."*) and she sat on that front porch with a bunch of us and reminisced about her friend Hank Williams, the saddest man she ever knew, drunk, dosed with morphine, dead at 29 in the back seat of a car heading for Canton, Ohio, and she recalled when Red Foley sang "Old Shep" and then introduced his guitarist Mr. Chester Atkins, who played "Maggie," and afterward

Miss Jean Redpath.

Minnie walked up and kissed him and said, "You're a wonderful musician, you're just what we've been needing around here." Her face shone as she told stories. She was a shining presence. Comedy was only part of it: she loved people with her whole heart, and that was the heart of her act—she was the happiest person on stage that you ever saw in your life, and she told those jokes so well you almost forgot how old they were, and nobody ever looked at you with so much joy as Minnie did, except maybe your grandma if you were lucky.

Chet Atkins walked into the picture around 1983, and that pretty much brought the Amateur Hour Era to an end. After the friends and neighbors have heard Chet Atkins, they're no longer content to hear "Go Tell Aunt Rhody" strummed on a dulcimer, the bar has been raised.

Chet called Margaret Moos and said he was a fan of the show and would be happy to come up north and play on it sometime. He was the most famous guitarist in the world, a soft-spoken, stoop-shouldered gentleman in a pale green sport coat and tan pants who walked into the theater one Friday afternoon and set his guitar case down and shook my hand. He said he admired the show. He had no entourage, just him and his wife, Leona, and his sideman, Paul Yandell. We sat backstage and talked. He was a real storyteller. He grew up dirt poor in a broken family in east Tennessee, suffering from asthma, painfully shy, and he

Mr. Chester Atkins, (CGP) Certified Guitar Player.

made himself a banjo with strings pulled from a screen door. Got a Sears Silvertone guitar and played it morning and night, trying to sound like Les Paul and Merle Travis and Django Reinhardt, whom he heard on the radio. He knew that if you could play guitar as they did, you would join a natural aristocracy of artists in which white or Black, Southern or Northern, shy or charming were accepted equally. Anybody with an ounce of taste would respect you for it, and to hell with the others.

Every time Chet came on the show, he'd sit backstage and jam with Paul and whoever wanted to join in, Johnny Gimble, Bill Hinkley, Howard Levy with a harmonica, Peter Ostroushko, and the tunes would flow along from old-time to swing, one tune emerging into another, "Just as I Am" into "Stardust," Stephen Foster, George Harrison, "Seeing Nellie Home," "Banks of the Ohio," and maybe *Recuerdos de la Alhambra*, Boudleaux Bryant, "Freight Train," one sparkling stream, it was all music to him. He held his guitar like a father holds a child, he was happy, the genuine article. He loved jamming backstage, where he wasn't obligated to be Chet Atkins and could be a man in a crowd of friends. He had made his way in the country music business though his real love was jazz, and when he sat backstage with the others, a sweet equality prevailed in which strangers were old friends—the music made it so. I envied that and asked Chet once if I should learn to play guitar and he said, "The world does not need another mediocre guitarist. Stick with the monologue. Nobody else does what you do." So I did.

Chet gave me good advice: "Never read anything anybody writes about you. No matter what they write, you won't learn anything from it, and you'll probably read something that'll be a stone in your shoe for months to come." I could see the reasoning, which was the same as what LaVona Person told me in the eighth grade: *It's not about you. It's about the material. Don't make it be about you.*

My front porch looked across Goodrich at the house Scott and Zelda lived in when he wrote "Winter Dreams," after they returned briefly to St. Paul in 1921 for the birth of their daughter. His parents' row house, where he wrote *This Side of Paradise* when he was 24 and broke, is a few blocks away on Summit, and Mrs. Porterfield's boardinghouse porch where he sat with his friends and talked about the great life he would live. He was a romantic. His parents, Mollie and Edward, had lost two little girls to influenza the year before he was born, and so the boy's feet were not allowed to touch the ground. He grew up believing the world would smile on him. He had little fondness for St. Paul: his city was New York, and he and Zelda left town after a few months and never returned.

I started to get a whiff of success now and then myself. I'd walk to the drugstore on Grand and someone'd stop me and say they liked the story about the Gospel Birds or the one about the truck stop. They didn't gush, they just mentioned it like you'd say, "I like your shirt."

Success felt precarious. Around the corner on Lincoln Avenue was the little walk-up apartment where I'd lived before, a daily reminder of what might befall me if I should take up bad habits and go fallow. I worked hard to avoid that. I sat in the garden by the high board fence, drank my coffee, smoked, scribbled on a yellow legal pad, writing epic verse for the shows—"Cat, You Better Come Home" and "The Old Man Who Loved Cheese." And "Casey at the Bat" from the perspective of the opposing fans overjoyed at his downfall:

Ten thousand people booed him when he stepped into the box,
And they made a vulgar sound when he bent to fix his socks.
He knocked the dirt from off his spikes, reached down and eased his pants—
"What's the matter? Did ya lose 'em?" cried a lady in the stands.

I'd given up my 6 a.m. daily show, but I arose in the dark and went to work, writing, a pack of Pall Malls nearby, and in February 1982, tired of worrying about it, I quit smoking. I was a three-pack-a-day man and Butch Thompson and I made a compact that we'd phone the other before lighting another cigarette, and that slight social pressure, the reluctance to admit defeat, did the trick. Smoking and writing were inextricably linked, and I spent about three days in the public library and other No Smoking zones and ate buckets of popcorn, and then I was done with it, the inextricable was extricated, a long-running comfort gone, no regrets, a knapsack of rocks lifted from my shoulder. It simply needed to be done.

The show was doing well, though I was oblivious. One day, the station's music director, Michael Barone, walked up to me at a staff lunch and thanked me for bringing so much money into the operation. And I was surprised to learn that *PHC* was in the black. Way in. I did not think to ask for a raise, but Bill Kling gave me one anyway. Around 1982, the show had taken a mercantile turn—Powdermilk Biscuit posters, LPs, the four-cassette "butter box" of Lake Wobegon monologues sold enough units to start a new catalog company.

And then another phenomenon, very charming and also bewildering: I noticed women taking an interest in me. Normally this should happen around the age of fifteen, not in your forties, but the road life and the warmth of audiences loosened me up, the beard came off, maybe I switched to a deodorant with aloe and rosemary in it, and I started to encounter women who made it clear they enjoyed my company and wished to spend some time in it. This was an astonishment. I was tall, not bad looking, sort of professorial but not overbearing, and they made their feelings clear, standing close, speaking low, placing a hand on the small of my back, laughing at what I said, maybe their forehead to my shoulder—women have ways to indicate interest. The first time was at a party after a Valentine's Day show. A woman took me in hand and danced me around, though I'm not a dancer. None of the girls at Anoka High School had done this, so I was grateful. We stood outside in the yard and kissed with some conviction and she asked if I'd like to continue the evening at her apartment. I said, "I'm a little drunk," and she said, "We'll just make the best love we can." So we did.

I met a woman at a party who asked me to sing Everly Brothers songs with her and we did "Devoted to You" and "All I Have to Do Is Dream"—she sang lead, I sang harmony, and our voices fit well together and later so did we. It was a beautiful romance and she wanted to marry, but I was afraid of disappointing her and then I was unfaithful to her with another romance and we parted, sweetly, and I was happy when she found a good husband. They were Lutherans and made love at least once a week, as Luther recommended, which I was glad to know. A man wants his old lover to be loved well.

There was an old classmate who flirted with me and we became lovers and then gracefully eased back into friendship where we were content to remain. This struck me as so civilized, friendship turning passionate and then returning to kindness and attentiveness. It was a series of pleasant fantasies, to not go looking for love but see love come looking for me. I had gone into radio for purer, finer reasons, but I did not mind being suddenly attractive to women. I'd been the nerd holed up in the library scribbling in a notebook: women glanced at me and kept walking. Radio made me appealing somehow.

One day I flew out to Santa Barbara to do a show and afterward went around the corner to a café. I'd found a note in the dressing room when I arrived:

Mr. Keillor,

I am coming to your reading tonight because I find your stories ridiculously delightful and if you feel like having company afterward, I will be in the café on the corner. I've never done this before, I swear to God, but it would rock my world to meet you.

Cheers,
Marty (Martha)

She was 21, tall, lean, a grad student. We ate chicken quesadillas and had a beer and afterward we sat in my rental car in the parking lot and I asked, "What do you want from life?" She said, "Adventure." She asked what I wanted and I said, "Impetuosity. Courage." "To do what?" she said. "To kiss you."

She smiled and looked away. "I'd play hard to get but I'm leaving on a peace mission to Bolivia in two weeks." And we kissed. She said, "Where can we go to be alone?" I drove us to my hotel. I turned on the gas fireplace. We sat on the couch, kissing. We went into the bedroom. I pulled the sheet up over us. It was all so easy. We made love and lay together for a while. She said, "Either I am going to go home now or I am going to stay the night." I said nothing. She arose and got dressed. I kissed her goodbye.

It was stunning a woman had gone out of her way to seduce me—and not a crazy woman but a smart one, off on a mission to South America.

She wrote to me a week later:

Our evening together was wonderful and for me very much an indulging of fantasy and part of me wishes there would be more but I've talked to a trusted friend about this and she says, "Leave it at one night. Don't be fascinated by celebrity. Too complicated." So that is the way it shall be. But I love you and want all the best for you. Marty

I didn't think of myself as "celebrity"—I'm from Anoka, Minnesota. But she had come upstairs with me because she liked my show and I enjoyed being seduced. I am not a strong man, my ego is made of butterscotch pudding, to think that admiration of my writing makes a woman want to take her clothes off strikes me as irresistible. She found a good husband and they started a family and every five years or so she drops me a line. I am an episode in her wild youth. When she is old, if she thinks of me, she'll shake her head and laugh.

After *Happy to Be Here,* I sat in my big house and worked on a Lake Wobegon book. No plot, no crisis to resolve, a set of merged stories arranged by seasons for a semblance of structure. With some history of Lake Wobegon, the early Unitarian missionaries who sought to convert the Dakotah through interpretive dance, the immigrants who settled here because the land reminded them of home, forgetting they had left home because the land was so poor. As I worked, I thought about the draft board order I'd ignored sixteen years before, imagined the FBI at the door, the book rejected, the show canceled, a rented room over Gray's Drug in Dinkytown, a job in a parking lot, sitting in Al's Breakfast, a sad old man of forty. "I used to be on the radio on Saturday night," I'd say to Crazy Phil, and he says, "I know, I was your biggest fan."

No such luck. My editor at Viking, Kathryn Court, came out for a week and then another week to work on the book I was patching together, trying to make a novel out of a set of stories. She was crisp and British and set up shop on the dining room table and we glued pages and paragraphs together into chapters and hung them on the walls in long yellow banners. Somehow, she believed that *Lake Wobegon Days* might be a big seller so I kept rewriting it, revising the rewrite, editing the re-rewritten, repairing the edits. If so many people were going to read it, I wanted my book to be good enough. My girlfriend at the time resented this intrusion and sniped at it and said it was a big mistake. She'd never lived with a writer who was engrossed in making a book. I forgot to watch TV and never went out at night. I wrote some for *The New Yorker*, wrote the show, worked on the book. I could feel it coming along.

I shipped the manuscript off to New York and the girlfriend and I broke up in the spring. She said that I couldn't get along without her. There was only one way to find out. As it turned out, I could.

Work, not domesticity, was what kept me on an even keel. I woke up in the morning and worked. Sometimes I woke up in the middle of the night and got out of bed and wrote things down. Work was therapeutic: I talked to a shrink once because I felt depressed, and she was very nice, but I needed to write myself out of depression, which made me feel good and sometimes produced good work that maybe even earned money, so why pay her?

The girlfriend disappeared in May 1985. *Lake Wobegon Days* came out in August, and the *Times Book Review* printed a front-page review of it by Veronica Geng, ranking it alongside Thurber and Lardner, setting my (small) marble bust on the shelf alongside the masters. I should've written her a thank-you note and did not lest I be thought a greenhorn, and the book shot up to No. 1 on the *Times* list and stuck there. It was hard to look my writer friends in the eye that year. A journeyman novel

A published author, feeling good about himself. One book out, another on the way, the beard is gone, he's quit smoking, and for the first time in his life, certain women seem to take an interest in him. But still a nerd at heart, and still wearing the work boots he wore in college.

sold by the carload, while masters and innovators went scarcely noticed. If you'd written a novel about someone like me, a Brethren Boy, suddenly become Mr. Wonderful, it'd be turned down and sent back, *Sorry, better luck next time.*

For years, I had looked down on best-selling books and then one of them was mine and it turned me upside down on a roller coaster of confusion. In hindsight, I see I should've stayed home, locked the doors, turned off the phone, stuck to business, and not strayed from the sensible and self-sufficient, but looking back, I see that that would've made for a much less interesting memoir.

22

I Found a Great Sorrow

ONE BLAZING HOT AUGUST DAY in 1985, the same week my face appeared on the cover of *Time,* I drove up to the Guntzels' house on the river, where some classmates were gathering in advance of our twenty-fifth high school class reunion and out of the house came running a woman with strawberry hair who threw her arms around me and kissed me. She was terribly attractive to me, with a melodic voice, and was delighted to see me. I was delighted by her delight: I had had a secret crush on Ulla in high school, the day I climbed into Will Peterson's VW one spring day in 1960 and he told her, our Danish exchange student, to sit on my lap, and she did, her slender rear on my thighs, my arms around her waist, the smell of her hair in my nostrils. I was not a popular boy, didn't dance or drink, wasn't invited to parties, so a girl sitting on my lap was a momentous event to me, on the order of physical levitation. Time had not dimmed that memory. She was divorced now, with three teenage kids, living in Copenhagen, and she had taken out a loan to pay for this trip. She showed me her copy of our yearbook, the *Anokan,* where I had written that I'd marry her as soon as I had written a best-seller. And here I was.

She and Corinne and I went hiking through the woods along the river shore. I took her hand to help her over the rocky places. It was a perfect summer day, old friends, all of us curious about the others. Jack was there, Christine, Elaine, Thatcher. We had all settled into adulthood. Thatcher, a lawyer in Oshkosh, and Corinne an economics professor out East. Ulla, a social worker in a state employment office. Me, a writer. Ulla and I stood in the kitchen, doing dishes, talking. We were back in old times, I was Gary to her, not Garrison. We were our young selves. We never mentioned our teenage children, since we were teenagers ourselves. Ulla and I stood close together and Corinne noticed and whispered to me, "Ulla always attracted the boys." And when I drove back to St. Paul, I was looking forward to seeing her again. I'd been working hard for a couple years, writing stories, and a romance with an old friend seemed like the perfect reward. I needed to get caught up in a good story of my own. And so, without looking, I leaped.

When I think back to that August afternoon, I see the man drive up the long dirt driveway under the poplar trees. He is 43, an odd loner in the Class of 1960, now unaccountably a public figure, and being a Minnesotan he is embarrassed by the attention. He pulls his red Mustang onto the grass and climbs out. I wait to see if the woman will still run across the lawn and throw her arms around him or maybe she is engrossed with Corinne and Christine so he will have a drink with Hilmer and hear about the plumbing business—but no, the red-haired woman keeps running out of the house and he keeps tumbling into a love story with her.

She was in town for only one week, so I had to step lively. I found an album of Danish songs and memorized one about lost love phonetically, and the next evening, at the Guntzels' for dinner, washing dishes at the sink, when she picked up a dishtowel to dry them, I casually sang it to her, as if it were something I'd always known.

> *Jeg fik en sorg saa stor*
> *I mine ungdoms dage,*
> *den aldrig fra mig gaar*
> *saa lange som jeg leve.*
> *Den største sorg forvist*
> *at man kan overgaa,*
> *det er at elske en*
> *som man kan aldrig faa.*

I found a great sorrow in my youth that I will never get over as long as I live, the greatest sorrow that one can endure, which is to love a person whom one can never have. (It's better in Danish.) Corinne saw what was up. She tried to caution me. "It's none of my business what you do," she said, "but I have to tell you, as an old friend, that Ulla had a big romance with a classmate of ours and she came to America, thinking she might marry him, and she decided it wouldn't work, that America was too different." I thanked her for the advice, but it was a golden summer, I was in love with a love story and I didn't care to hear a second opinion.

It was a mistake, born of a best-selling novel that earned enough money to finance a fairy tale that wound around the magical forest and across the sea and ended on the stone pavement of cold reality. He had stuck to business, building an odd little traveling show made of rein-vented parts of antique shows, and it was intoxicating to be recklessly in love. It felt destined.

I marched forward on a nonstop book tour, flying around doing readings nightly to big auditoriums packed with hushed crowds. The publisher sent a footman and coat-holder along to ease my way. People lined up around the block night after night, sometimes two blocks, and I walked along the line apologizing for the wait, which only made the wait longer. Book signings went five and six hours. Bookstores hired security men. I adopted, for convenience, a policy of indomitable agree-ableness, a smile, no request denied—Personalize sixty copies? *Certainly.* Sign photographs? *No problem.* I bought dozens of roller-ball pens, black. A tailor came to the hotel in Seattle and fitted me for three suits, I had lost twenty pounds. Local TV news crews at every reading: Report-ers rode with me in limos: "How does it feel?" I was ever cheerful and charming. I was moving so fast, my front didn't know where my back was. I took so many flights, the C Concourse at MSP felt like my own backyard. There were specific urinals where I thought, "Hey, I peed here a week ago."

I did Studs Terkel's interview show in Chicago, and he took me to a two-martini lunch at his favorite bar where his friends, ipso facto, became my friends on the spot. I called Ulla every night and wrote her a letter every day. I proposed marriage like you'd propose a weekend at the lake. I was a Midwesterner, bred for caution, and I threw caution aside. It was impossible, I was wedded to my work, the weekly routine, the Selectric typewriter at the rolltop desk, the congenial staff that made the good life possible. Why the sudden wrongheaded detour? It was just as the Brethren had taught: success is perilous. The rich man built his house upon the sand. Good fortune was my downfall. If the *Times* had assigned the book to a vicious critic who'd dismissed it as a shapeless goulash of refried nostalgia, if *Time* had ignored me and put Nancy Reagan on the cover instead, the book would've sunk into the remainder bin, I'd have waved goodbye to Ulla and gone back to my needlework. Beware of what you wish for. Those whom God loves, He chastises. Because what is the alternative? Stupidity.

I flew to Copenhagen in October and landed early in the morning at Kastrup Airport and rode a taxi alongside a stream of bicyclists in brightly colored rain gear, past gold stucco houses with red tile roofs and a green and gold church steeple with intertwined crocodiles on it. I landed at her apartment, we flung ourselves into bed, I awoke hours later, jet-lagged on a golden autumn afternoon. She lived with her daughter, Malene, fifteen, whose name I liked to pronounce, *Ma-LEAN-e(r)*, and her cat, Pjok, in a two-bedroom apartment on Jagtvej, up the street from the big cemetery where H. C. Andersen is buried. The cat was able to cross two busy streets and make her way to the cemetery where she could wander freely. The girl attended *gymnasium* and studied hard and arose at 4:30 a.m. Saturday and Sunday to work at a nearby bakery. I was exhausted from book touring, but we three went out to dinner at a pavilion by a lake. We walked through town, down avenues of five-story brick houses shoulder to shoulder, along the walking street, Strøget, passersby speaking their sweet, chirpy language. It was a dreamy few days in a handsome storybook city, a city of socialists fond of royalist grandeur, a world apart from what I knew. We ate herring on rye bread with a shot of aquavit, a salad, a slice of roast pork with a glass of beer, a slice of blue cheese, and coffee, and the next day in her kitchen, we talked about marriage, not about *whether* but *when*: two 43-year-old teenagers. I met her teenage sons, Morten and Mattias, her friends Jens and Lis, and her mother, Elly. We had dinner at the home of my Danish translator, Mogens Boisen, and there on his walls were enormous photographs of a naked woman, every part of her, who turned out to be the woman sitting across from me at dinner, his wife. Nobody remarked on this. Mr. Boisen explained that his translation of my book was considerably shorter than the original because Danish readers are not so interested in rural America and also, the pay for translation is so meager, he couldn't afford to spend more time on it. I thanked him for his forthrightness.

The romance got in the papers, a sweet story: AUTHOR COURTS HIS FOREIGN EXCHANGE STUDENT SWEETHEART.

I wrote her a poem.

I believe in impulse, in all that is green,
Believe in the foolish vision that comes true,
Believe that all that is essential is unseen,
And for this lifetime I believe in you.

Love that shines in every star
Love reflected in the silver moon.
It is not here, but it's not far.
Not yet, but it will be here soon.

"I believe in impulse, in all that is green" is a nice thought but "all that is essential is unseen"?? What exactly does that *mean*? "Not yet but it will be here soon"? There was nothing tangible, it was all perfume and candy wrappers. But it was a lovely time. We both craved intimacy, and we didn't know each other at all, and it didn't matter. It was liberation from common sense, a crazy story we could make up as we went along.

In November, she flew to Minneapolis and we boarded a bus with the show people and did a live broadcast from a Lutheran church in western Minnesota in the midst of genuine blizzard. The next day she and I walked through deep drifts to look at a big red-brick manse with a walled backyard in St. Paul and bought it on the spot for the asking price. Flagrant spendthrift behavior. The book was selling like crazy. In December, we bought a flat in Copenhagen, on Trondhjemsgade, a big echoey flat with majestic fourteen-foot ceilings and elaborate plaster molding that made you feel you were about to sign the Treaty of Ghent. I went to Copenhagen for Christmas and met her former husband, Paul-Verner, a theologian. It was impressive, so civil, so Danish, friendship between the ex and his successor, celebrating *Jul* together. I liked him immediately. He and I had come from righteous fundamentalists—we sympathized. He knew about the Rapture, the Tribulation, the Last Judgment, all of that. Ulla had come from Danish humanists, Lutheran on paper but secular at heart. He and I were brothers, brought up on the literal Word. When you feel a bond with your lover's ex-husband that you don't feel with her, this should tell you something. But I was not in the mood for doubt, I was in love.

Ulla and I married on December 28 in Copenhagen, in a snowstorm, our four teenage kids as witnesses, the boys in tuxedos, Malene in a blue dress like her mother's. A dark time in Denmark: the sun rises during the first coffee break and sets soon after lunch, but we were a festive bunch. A formal dinner afterward, at which eleven Danes stood one by one and gave speeches in excellent English, graceful, humorous, *written* speeches, each about three minutes long consisting of a witty opening, a telling anecdote, and an affectionate toast, and my brother Philip stood up and spoke off the cuff about his happy marriage to a Swede. We packed up. Malene would come with us to America, and she gave her beloved Pjok to two children and said goodbye to her classmates who came to the airport to wave goodbye, along with Ulla's mother, who wept as we went up the escalator.

In St. Paul, I invited old friends over for dinner and they were charmed by Malene, who was eager to see America, having been fascinated by it since childhood, her parents both exchange students in America, so Malene grew up fond of Levi jeans, Coke, MTV, *Little House on the Prairie*, Michael Jackson, Madonna, and old Hollywood movies. She worked late into the night on homework, enjoyed parties though she understood only fragments of what was said to her. She plied us with questions about Midwestern manners, the frequent use of "Excuse me" and what should you say when someone asks, "How are you?" Tell the truth? No, we said. Unless you are bleeding from an open wound and need medical attention, you say, "Fine. How are you?"

She adopted America enthusiastically, and Ulla wrote long letters home about how sad and provincial life in St. Paul was. She felt out of place among women talking about their children rather than politics. There was poverty in America, inequality, poor education, so clearly evident: why did people not talk about this rather than their child's basketball team? Minnesotans seemed fearful of disagreement and tried to keep conversation focused on trivialities, whereas Danes loved a good debate.

American women deferred to men: why? She met women who spent their days volunteering, a frivolity of aristocracy. She missed her job. Then, *voilà*, she found a job in a Jewish agency as a social worker among Russian émigrés, which she liked; she could empathize with them, appreciate how mysterious America was, how hard it was to get their feet on the ground. But then she felt trapped by the job: in Denmark, you get five weeks of vacation a year; this job provided one week, not enough time to get back to Trondhjemsgade and keep in touch with friends. So she quit. "I have never wept so much as I have the past six months," she told me that spring. I was baffled. When school let out, we got on a plane and flew to Copenhagen. We lived well, we were passionate with each other, so why was she so mournful?

> *She told me the old story*
> *Of the mermaid from the sea*
> *Who comes ashore to wed her love*
> *And suffers cruelly,*
> *And this became our story,*
> *We couldn't be as one.*
> *I had found my happiness*
> *Whose pain had just begun.*

It was a hard winter, and then a worse spring. We were in love and we were miserable. St. Paul was provincial, American furniture clunky, the women oppressed. I was happy at a computer in a 15 x 15 room with a woodstove, snow falling in the yard, the kitchen nearby, a show to write, work to do, Ulla was not. She tried to hold me to regular work hours, close up shop at 5 p.m. but I was not an assembly-line worker. Work was my calling, and inspiration did not go by the clock, but to her, a man who worked until 5:30 showed callous disregard for his family. We never got this worked out between us.

She could not abide my reading the morning paper at the breakfast table. A lifelong ritual for me, and to her a personal insult. Promptness was for her a prime virtue: to keep someone waiting even five minutes was to say they didn't matter. To me, a person unable to amuse herself for five minutes is lacking imagination. But Danes are a compliant race: they wait for the green light even when the streets are deserted. They don't like to jaywalk. And then there was the issue of planning: Danes plan their summer vacations two and three years in advance. I live by improvisation. Marriage to a Dane involved many footnotes. *Why do Americans work so many hours a week? Why don't more people ride bicycles? Why is Johnny Carson considered funny?* I took her to a Twins game, and after I had explained baseball for twenty minutes, we agreed not to talk about it anymore. I took Danish lessons twice a week: acquired a good accent, modest vocabulary, could manage simple declarative sentences but couldn't understand Danish spoken to me. I was like an eight-year-old deaf child.

Corinne came to visit in February. She'd been hit hard by asthma, was ashen, looked unwell, spoke with hesitation. She was on a powerful steroid, she said, that made her feel weird. She was not teaching this semester. She said, "I feel like my life is a cruel joke." She had been happy a year ago, working to establish the Women's Rights National Park in Seneca Falls, site of the 1848 convention where Elizabeth Cady Stanton read her declaration that "all men *and women* are created equal." The chapel where they met had become a laundromat, and Corinne and her cohorts had raised money to save the building. Now she felt adrift. She felt like a failure as an economist, wanted to quit teaching and come live with her parents for a year and write a book about the family plumbing business that her father was about to sell. She said, "Theory makes no sense to me anymore. Time to write about microeconomics. Individual enterprise. You had the guts to leave academia and write your homely little stories about Anoka. I should write the story of Guntzel Plumbing."

What I should've done, wish I had done, and didn't do was tell her it was a great idea. *Come home. You can live with us. I'll be your editor. When it comes right down to it, it's all about plumbing. People can skip church, not vote, turn off the TV, but they do not give up water or sewer. The fact that we don't have to shit outdoors is a basic part of human dignity. Let's write that book.*

I didn't say it. I was flummoxed by her anguished manic talk, it was so un-Corinne of her. She was a debater, adept at rebuttal: you told her what you thought and she took it apart and handed it back to you, rearranged. She being an articulate intellectual, I assumed she was rational. It was befuddling to find her feeling defeated by invisible dark forces.

I felt terrible for her. I felt guilty. My show was booming along, my book on the best-seller list, Ulla and I ensconced in a lively household with her daughter and my son Jason, both 15; meanwhile my old friend was scraping bottom. The next night Ulla and I went to the Guntzel house where we'd met in August, where I had sung her the song in Danish. We sat in the lofty living room, the tropical fish drifting around the bubbler in the big tank, the picture window overlooking the frozen Mississippi, the piano where Corinne used to play "On the Road to Mandalay," and we watched her, manic, opening a bottle of wine and fixing hors d'oeuvres, chattering, trying to be upbeat, though her mom was in the hospital for dialysis and her dad was dazed and confused. Hilmer, standing in the middle of the room, lost control of his bladder and stood, stock still, in alarm, as a pool of liquid spread around his feet, and Corinne, talking a mile a minute about the book she'd write about Guntzel Plumbing, tossed a bath towel on the floor and tried to mop up the urine with her left foot, smiling at me as if nothing odd were happening. She put the best china and crystal on the table, set up a tape recorder to record, she said, our "witty repartee" for her mom to enjoy later, which pretty well killed the conversation. She scorched a pot roast and potatoes, put out a salad, served blueberry pie and ice cream, kept pouring wine. It was an eerie dinner. We left as soon as we could. I owed it to my old pal to break through this craziness and wrap her up and take her into our custody. I did not know how to do it, but that is no excuse. The way to do it is to do it and keep doing it until it's done.

And two months later I was back in this living room, listening to Hilmer weeping, making funeral arrangements, telling someone on the phone, "My daughter committed suicide out in New York, and her body is being flown back here on Friday." Helen sat in a big chair and murmured, "We were lucky to have her as long as we did." Two stoics in mute grief, facing their own deaths approaching, their old neighbor boy the famous radio host and magazine cover boy standing helpless nearby. Corinne had left a note for them. She begged their forgiveness, said she loved them dearly, said she couldn't go on another week in such despair. Hilmer looked at me, tears in his eyes, and said, "Why? Why? We had no idea. We loved her." Then he choked up and went in the bathroom and shut the door.

I flew to upstate New York where Corinne had taught at Wells College in Aurora and walked into a memorial assembly, an auditorium of young women weeping, unbelieving, a colleague speaking through her tears. Corinne was staunch, indomitable, someone her friends turned to in their darker hours, she was energetic, positive, charismatic, and yet one dark rainy night, April 7, 1986, the night of a new moon, she hit a rock of despair. She was subletting a colleague's apartment near the lake while he was on sabbatical. She sat down and wrote notes to colleagues about students whose theses she was supervising, and she left instructions for her cleaning lady about what to do with her cats and plants, and then she put rocks in the pockets of her leather jacket and walked to the end of a dock and climbed into a canoe and paddled out to the middle of Cayuga Lake and tipped the canoe and sank and drowned. The next day was sunny. Her body was spotted by a helicopter, washed up in a gully on shore. News spread around campus, and people who knew her gathered and tried to understand her death. She had visited friends in Seneca Falls the night before who were worried about her in her anguished state and tried to get her to spend the night with them, and she would not hear of it. She who had been a caregiver could not accept being cared for. She drove home and called one friend, then another, weeping on the phone, and now they saw what they should've done, which was: *get in the car and drive over to Corinne's and sit with her and don't leave.* I said the usual things, "You're not to blame. She chose this. You can't save someone who doesn't want to be saved." But I felt responsible too. Back home in February, she found her parents in terrible shape, in decline, trying to maintain their lives, and she felt incapacitated herself, and there I was, Mr. Moneypants, my gaudy life a mockery of her own. Two of her friends took me to her small, dim apartment and showed me her diary. It began with Leeds Cutter's death in 1962 and ended with her plans to take her life in 1986.

She worried about a house she'd bought, that she couldn't make the payments. She was worried about her cat, who had a urinary infection. She went down the list of her friends including Ulla and me, and decided none of us would miss her. On April 6, she had tried to paddle out in the canoe but the wind was too strong. She wrote, *My basic affinity for caution and pleasure are standing in the way of resolution. If I could just snap my fingers and end consciousness and life—okay. But to work out a method that will work is harder.* The next day she wrote, *Some panic allayed primarily because self-destruction in a physical sense is not easy.* And then at 2:30 a.m. *But the impossibility of my position just awakened me again. I cannot even get through the bills for this month, let alone this summer's. There is no way out.*

She was buried in Crystal Lake Cemetery in north Minneapolis, where, a few months later, Helen joined her. She was at Hennepin County Medical Center for dialysis, and one day I stopped by to visit her and the nurse looked surprised and said, "I guess you didn't get the message. Helen died about an hour ago. If you want to see her, she's in that room there," she said. I went in and there was Helen, wrapped in a white sheet, looking peaceful, a strip of cloth tied around her jaw to hold her mouth closed. My old friend who, the summer I was twenty and besieged by misgivings, welcomed me onto her porch and sat and listened as I poured out my troubles. And now she was gone. Hilmer died a couple years later and was laid in the cave with his wife and daughter. I grieve for them still. Dark depression was a place Corinne had not visited before. Perhaps her resolute nature kept it at bay, her disdain for self-pity, her duty to be, like Helen, a cheerful, steady presence. And then that resolution failed her. She sat down that cold rainy April night and wrote in her journal and went out in the canoe and sank it.

In my imagination, her phone rings as she is heading for the door, rocks in her pockets, and she picks it up and it's me. We talk. I talk about the Guntzel living room with the piano and the fish tank bubbling and the steep hill by the old stone water tank. I remember when she and I were eight and stood on that hill beside the toboggan and she was excited, her hands fluttering at her sides, and she knelt in front and I behind her and shoved off and down the steep hill we flew toward the river and flew off the last hummock and slid across the ice almost out to the middle and stood up and towed it back up the hill and did it again. I describe this and she takes the rocks out of her pockets and tears up her suicide note. She comes home, and we become fast friends and the dark April night is just an interesting story. She comes and lives in our spare bedroom and life goes on.

I was supposed to rescue her from the canoe on Cayuga Lake. The horrible dinner was my cue to save her life and I ignored my cue. It's unbearable to think about and so I don't, a peculiar talent I have, to box up a dreadful memory and throw it downstairs, and move on to something else, as I am doing right now.

23

Climbing Out of the Soup

I liked Denmark, the loose elegance, the scrupulous honesty, the timely trains, the stout cheese, the hash they call *biksemad,* the fried herring, the streets of the beautiful city. I enjoyed hiking through Ørsteds Park and the great earthen walls of Kastellet to the Gefion Fountain with the immense bare-breasted goddess, her whip raised, lashing her oxen as water gushes up from the blade of her plow and sprays from their flared nostrils, and through the streets to Gråbrødretorv—the loveliest square in Copenhagen and the hardest to pronounce, with four separate *r*'s to swallow, and down to the sea to look at the lights of Sweden across the water. I loved the absence of chauvinism. Danes never said how proud they were to be Danish; they made fun of its insignificance, the guttural language, the high taxes. The sort of bombast required of an American politician—you couldn't *say* those things in Danish. I liked the frankness of Danes. You could talk about death, God, sex, politics, how boring Denmark is, how thin the literature is, and the Dane is not offended. You can say anything you like so long as you do not speak badly of the Queen or comment on the peculiarity of her husband. Be an anarchist, if you wish. But even an anarchist must remember to send his mother-in-law a nice card on her birthday and attend her birthday lunch and arrive exactly at the designated time. I liked Ulla's friends, serious people, well-read, who loved the back-and-forth of conversation, give-and-take, no harangues, no monologues.

In this small country of seagoing people, children start learning English in the fourth grade along with their multiplication tables; everyone is bilingual, even tri- or quadri-, and English is their language for travel. So it makes little sense for an American of 45 to try to learn Danish. Nonetheless, I tried. We went to dinner at a Dane's apartment, his shelves packed with American and British literature, and he said, "Shall we speak English?" and I said, "Nej, nej, vi er i Danmark, så skal vi taler dansk naturligvis." I enjoyed the feel of Danish on the tongue, the musicality, the comfort of the many cognates: a table is *bord,* cup is *kop* and glass is *glas,* a knife is *kniv* (pronounced k-NEE-oo), so with English (*Engelsk*) under your belt (*baelte*) you've got a good start (*starten*). But the real reason was pride. I didn't want to be an Ugly American so I became a Half-Witted One.

I took my elegant mother-in-law Elly out to lunch, champagne and oysters—"This is what Karen Blixen loved to eat," she said. She told me about her train trip to Moscow in August 1939 with her lover Jacob, a sailor who had no interest in traveling for pleasure, but he consented to going overland to Russia and they traveled through peaceful countryside and arrived back in Denmark on September 1, the day Germany invaded Poland and the war broke out. She told me about Victor Borge, who played in a jazz club back then and how she danced with him a few nights before he fled to Amsterdam and then New York. She wept as she described the war years, the stringencies, the shame of the German occupation, her brother Harry active in the Danish Resistance helping to smuggle the Jews over to Sweden. Then she brightened up and showed me the picture of our wedding in the newspaper *Aftenbladet,* the smiling bride and groom standing in a garden. I didn't tell her how unhappy the bride was only a few months into the marriage.

We came back to St. Paul to try to make a Danish Yule and we roasted a goose. We put it in the oven and put candles on our Christmas tree. I got the goose out of the oven in its glass baking dish and hot goose grease spilled on my wrist and I dropped the dish and it shattered, and the carcass skidded across the floor collecting cat hair, dust balls, and glass fragments. We scraped it clean as my family arrived. I opened an expensive white wine, which was too dry for them, and they stood holding their glasses politely as my stepson Morten lit the candles in the next room and when he came out, I threw open the door and there was the storybook tree, ten feet tall, candles burning on every bough, and my mother smothered a scream—her lifelong nightmare there before her eyes, what looked like a Christmas tree fire. We trooped around the tree, singing carols, Mother still quaking, and then we started to open gifts. My family was reluctant to open my gifts—they sensed lavishness, but they had to unwrap them, and indeed, everything was much too much, imported glassware, art work, exotic woolens, wondrous picture books, an atlas the size of a coffee table, and afterward the goose was greasy and the sweet potatoes overcooked and the pie was boughten pie from a bakery, and when finally my family extracted themselves and escaped into the night, I went upstairs and lay on the bed and wept. What I thought was generosity was bullying and boastfulness. Ulla wept because she missed Denmark. We lay in bed, grief-stricken, on the joyfullest day of the year, and after a while, I said, "Det kunne vaer vaerre (It could be worse)." And she said, "How?"

I took a break from the radio show in June 1987, flew back to Denmark for Midsummer's Night and took the train to Svendborg, to our friends Ole and Hanne's farm, and sat with thirty guests at two long tables in the garden behind their 300-year-old farmhouse looking down a slope of hay meadow toward the fjord. A festive three-hour dinner of shrimp and salmon and salad and lamb and seven songs and six speeches. The lady next to me said, "Skal vi taler Engelsk?"—*Nej, nej*, I said, but it turned out she was a Brit, a Cambridge grad, the author of a monograph on Milton, and so we spoke English, and made fun of what obsessive planners Danes are, their lives locked into itineraries and agendas. And the after-dinner speeches that night. Very clever, well-crafted, and rather lacking in feeling. She agreed: "It's a nation of dentists. Everything clean and well-done. No poetry." She leaned toward me and spoke softly: "Their dirty little secret is how well they got along with the Nazi occupation. They like to talk about how they helped the Jews escape to Sweden, but they leave out the fact that the German commandant told them when the Jews would be rounded up. So the Danes took the Jews across the Storbaelt to Malmo. Big deal. You didn't see a Danish Resistance like the French. Basically, they put salt in the Germans' pepper shakers. It was a very comfortable occupation." We all strolled down to the shore where Ole lit the bonfire and the children came bearing the effigy of a witch on a broom, a black dress stuffed with straw, and threw her on the fire as we sang hymns to

Denmark and St. Hans. In the dark, you could see bonfires along the shore for miles. At 2 a.m., we adjourned to the house for coffee and cake. A Dane tried to engage me in a discussion of the American bombing of Vietnam and I told him, politely, to go fuck himself.

I was working on a novel, *Love Me*, in which I was the *New Yorker* writer Larry Wyler, whom Mr. William Shawn fires after Wyler's piece on backpacking in Alaska ("Our Far-flung Correspondents: Humping the Chilkoot Pass") is found to contain dozens of sexual euphemisms ("parallel parking," "the man in the stocking cap rowing the boat," "warming the bratwurst") that escaped the eyes of the fact-checkers. I sat in the maid's room, laughing at my own wit, and when Ulla looked in, I read her the passage and she didn't think it was funny. A problem a man doesn't anticipate when he marries into another language. It made me miserable to not be funny at home. We lived in a magnificent apartment, but I was out of place in Denmark. I missed Lake Wobegon. I missed baseball. I do not consider soccer an organized sport; it is only recreational milling. I can manage herring, but I don't eat fried eel. I missed English in which you know dollars from doughnuts, open and shut, rain or shine. I attended a little Anglican church, and one Sunday when the opening hymn was "All hail the power of Jesus' name, let angels prostrate fall," I got teary-eyed.

We decided to get away and talk, so we rented a stone cottage on a hill on the island of Patmos and spent a month there, reading, biking, lying on the beach, eating in little cafés in town. The month was supposed to draw us together, and it only made us uneasy together. It was a waste of time, two people trying to have a vacation and not face up to the obvious. It is not possible to talk another person out of their unhappiness. She had been lonely before she met me, and now she missed her loneliness. We were impersonating a marriage. One night we had dinner with her father, Jacob, the sailor who had seen the world but always from the same ship, a joyful man who made everyone around him happy, Jacob with whom Elly had taken the lovely train trip to Russia, arriving back home the day Germany invaded Poland. Elly conceived Ulla by him and left him soon after for an optician, Otto. In Jacob, I was sure I saw the man Ulla wished I were, not the diligent farmer of comedy, haunted by Brethren ghosts, but a man who loved to laugh. She was his long-lost daughter, kept from him for almost thirty years, and the sight of her made him very happy. I loved Jacob. Other Danes might be rule-bound, punctilious, but he overflowed with kindness and good humor. There was no language barrier, language didn't matter, when Jacob laughed we all laughed with him. And between dinner and dessert, he thought of a song and sang it and jumped up and took Ulla in his arms and danced her around the table and she was delighted. She got a look of transport on her face. Sheer happiness. My wife who'd been so disheartened in Minnesota, all she needed was a dance, some lightness and gaiety.

I decided to be frank and admit that the marriage made no sense and had nowhere to go but down. She and I were a contradiction. I was a provincial from Anoka, an earnest striver from the potato fields who flew away to an exorbitant fairy tale to discover that he is not a sailor, not a dancer, he is a patient assembler of sentences, a repairer of paragraphs, capable of an obit, a limerick, a radio sketch, but unable to delight my wife. Money led me astray and now I must give up my illusions and resume my life. One day I packed a suitcase and called a taxi to take me to Kastrup Airport. I carried my suitcase out the ornate front entrance on Trondhjemsgade and did not look back. I felt no hesitation: I boarded a flight to New York and walked into the terminal at JFK and was delighted. I could overhear dozens of conversations at once—I didn't need to study someone's mouth in order to grasp what they were saying—I was surrounded by symphonic English and could hear every instrument.

My great experiment was over, the attempt to become bilingual, European, tolerant, community-minded, secular, egalitarian, rule-following, turn-waiting, a lover of order, and I went back to being my own confused and disorderly self. And New York was the right place to land. Minnesota is my home and family, and New York is colleagues and fellow travelers. I saw it with my dad when I was eleven and then when I was twenty-four and looking for a job. When Malene enrolled at Bryn Mawr College, Ulla and I had bought an apartment on the Upper West Side, and that's what I came back to—she got the majestic Treaty of Ghent flat on Trondhjemsgade, and I took a cab to my building and up the elevator to the apartment and out on the terrace that looked out over the roofs of brownstones like the deck of a ship anchored in the city, a sea of lights below, cliffs of lighted facades around.

High in the tower above the terrace, Sinclair Lewis had lived in his last years before he went to Italy to die in 1951. I read *Main Street* and *Babbitt* when I was in seventh grade because he was a Minnesota writer and I wanted to be one, too. He fell out of favor, crushed under the weight of a Nobel Prize and his own alcoholism and irascibility, and sat in his tower, awaiting death, aware that he'd been eclipsed by Mailer and Bellow and a new generation and that his own ambition had led him to write a stream of potboilers as his star sank lower and lower. His presence up above was a cautionary reminder: *Your time is short, your successors are waiting in the wings, you're not invincible, so be sensible, and above all, avoid winning prizes.*

I stood on the terrace and I called Bill Kling and told him my sabbatical was done. Ulla remained in Copenhagen. Each of us had a fax machine, and some days we'd exchange twenty letters across the Atlantic, accusing, pleading, protesting our love, alternately sentimental and bitter, hopeless, grieving, until there was simply nothing more to say. We were a wonderful romance but we never got to be friends.

The sabbatical from the show wasn't a real one: we'd been doing Farewell Shows steadily, even a Farewell Tour, kept saying goodbye until I came back in 1989. But it accomplished what a sabbatical is meant to do: it gave me a break from business and a chance to be a nobody again. The show had burst into phenomenal success in 1985 and landed me in the craziness of fame that America bestows now and then, like a typhoon, flattering offers and invitations, requests for interviews that promise to be flattering, everybody admires you, there is no bad news anywhere, people want you to write something about anything at all, sign your name, answer questions, endorse something—it was unreal and had nothing to do with me. I still thought now and then of the FBI knocking on the door and asking if I was the Gary E. Keillor who failed to report for induction, and I thought how quickly all of this admiration would dry up when the news came out, PRAIRIE HOME HOST INDICTED FOR DRAFT DODGING. Nobody would speak my name kindly in public again, I'd be in the paper, head down, handcuffed, on the steps of the federal courthouse, a common criminal.

Denmark was a break from all that. The deck was cleared. I resumed the show at the Brooklyn Academy of Music under the name *The American*

Radio Company with New York actors and a sixteen-piece band, The Coffee Club Orchestra, led by Rob Fisher, a botanist from Norfolk who, America being the land where people can change their minds, became a Broadway conductor (*Chicago, Wonderful Town, Anything Goes, An American in Paris*), and we nabbed him in between engagements. He loved that band, designed to play rags, stomps, swing, boogie, B'way, bop, himself bouncing at the keyboard.

We hired a St. Paulite working at the Academy of Music, Christine Tschida, as our producer, who brought her showbiz fervor (she was a tap dancer) to radio. She had several qualities that I lack: one was business sense and another was glee—when she saw a performance she loved, she jumped up and down. And she had gumption. I am unable to bring myself to ask a favor of a stranger. She didn't hesitate. She got Allen Ginsberg to come and read from Walt Whitman's "Song of Myself." He was uneasy about whether I'd be interviewing him, relieved when she said, "No, it's only the Whitman and you choose the passages." She talked the New York Public Library into allowing a live broadcast from the Rose Reading Room, the audience sitting at long oak tables with study lamps. A historic first for the library, a day's work for her. A doo-wop group sang "Book of Love," Dave Barry sang "Proofreading Woman," and we did a version of "John Henry" in which he's a writer and is challenged to race against a steam-powered computer.

Once, a few days before Christmas, I thought I'd like to close down West 43rd Street so the audience could stand in the street and sing "Silent Night." The NYPD was slightly incredulous when she called them—"Close what? When? Is this a joke?"—but she got them to send over six cops and they closed two lanes and a thousand people stood and sang "Silent Night." I still run into people who were there, and they get choked up remembering it, singing *Radiant beams from Thy holy face with the dawn of redeeming grace* and looking west toward Times Square. They recalled that snow was falling. There was no snow, it was too warm. But in their memory it was snowing. In my memory, it is a beautiful three minutes of pure childlike sincerity a block away from Yowza Yowza USA. It was moving.

I created the private eye Guy Noir, muttering out of the corner of his mouth in Brooklynese, complaining about the landlord and other lowlifes, dealing with Mafiosi, gun molls, con men, shysters, chantoozies, footloose dance-hall tootsies, bozos, bimbos, demented duchesses, tycoons, Lutheran galoots, whatever. Walter Bobbie played Pete, who walked into Guy's office and they got into an argument over some triviality such as "Was it Sal Maglie or Tom Magliozzi who lost Game 5 of the 1956 Series to the Yankees, Don Larsen's perfect game?" and they shot each other and died after an extended death scene during which the argument continued.

Guy was anti-Midwest: he minced no words, tolerated no fools unless they were paying clients. He paced his office in the Acme Building, hoping to foil the insidious schemes of the Bogus Brothers (*XXX-Large, solid muscle, legs like tree stumps, shaved heads, eyebrows the size of fruit bats, scar tissue from breaking down doors with their foreheads . . . they were known for knocking off irksome guys and making them part of construction projects*) and the poet-turned-con man Larry B. Larry, a convicted plagiarist who liked to leave a poem at the scene of the crime, his calling card.

THIS IS JUST TO SAY

> *I have taken the body*
> *that was in the icebox*
> *and which you were*
> *probably saving for evidence.*
> *Forgive me it smelled bad*
> *So pale and so cold.*

Every week, the urban *misterioso* theme song, a smoky-voiced woman sang, "He's smooth and he's cool and quick with a gun, a master in the boudoir. A guy in a trench coat who gets the job done. Guy . . . Guy Noir." *It was one of those grim January days when the sun sets around five and people go around bundled up so you can't tell men from women and when it's this cold it doesn't even matter—gender is no more important than shoe size. Your face won't smile, your heart is a lump of anthracite, your manhood has shrunk to the size of a peanut. This is why October birthdays are so rare.* Walter Bobbie also played my mom. *You have such a lovely voice, Honey. You sound so professional. It's a shame you can't find a job. A two-*

hour show on Saturdays—I don't call that a job. The problem is: you sound so Minnesota. It's that long O. People hear you talk and they know you were raised on meatloaf and potatoes and your best friend was a Leghorn chicken. Otherwise, you'd have an office with a big walnut credenza and a secretary named Megan. Walter could do it all, hitman, Mom, the prophet Jeremiah, he sang a walloping "Sit Down, You're Rockin' the Boat," and he sang, from his childhood, a Polish carol, "Gdy się Chrystus rodzi, I na świat przychodzi," that made us all misty-eyed.

And then the world turned and Walter directed the musical *Chicago* on Broadway, which ran for years and bumped Walter into a higher tax bracket, but if I met him today outside of Gray's Papaya on 72nd, he'd be the same Walter and give me the same big grin, and that's a sweet thing about New York. Underneath the churn of business, friendship is what counts. I still see Rob Fisher once in a blue moon, the most positive man in show business, and it's like old times. Our old violinist Andy Stein, who played swing with a little megaphone wired to his fiddle, is the same free spirit he always was.

I got back to New York as Mr. Shawn was leaving *The New Yorker* and I had lunch with him at the Oak Room. I had a hamburger and fries, he had dry toast and a cup of hot water. It was an awkward lunch, since we weren't friends and he wasn't an editor anymore, so what was the point? It was to thank him for what he did for my life by publishing the story in 1974 about the Grand Ole Opry. No doubt about it, the prestige of the magazine was what got me the chance to do *A Prairie Home Companion* on hyper-status-conscious public radio and gave me decades of pleasure. But he was having none of it. He said, "I take no credit for that. That was Mr. Whitworth's story." Closed subject. I tried to be cheery and suggested he start on a memoir. He said, "I wouldn't know how to begin writing about myself. I'm not a showman like you," and he said "showman" with no admiration intended. I asked him about Liebling, and that cheered him up. "Joe was the exception," he said. "He enjoyed his own work. You could hear him laughing down the hall in his office. He'd take the paper out of the typewriter and look for someone to read it to."

"So he was a showman then."

"You could say that," said Mr. Shawn.

"I could write your memoir—'*as told to me*,' " I said. He said he wouldn't care to read it, so why would anyone else?

"You lived a life that nobody will ever live again. You edited a magazine that was loved like no other. You were responsible for publishing 'In Cold Blood' and Hersey's 'Hiroshima' and 'Silent Spring' and Edmund Wilson's stuff on the Dead Sea scrolls—" He interrupted me: "Any editor who saw those manuscripts would've published them." It dawned on me that Shawn didn't know about the adoration of thousands of small-town Midwesterners like me who pored over the magazine every week, their badge of membership, proof that they were not provincials. He, the captain, had been so engrossed in his work, he was ignorant of its import and reach. He was the isolated provincial, not us. I picked up the check. There had been plenty of books about the magazine and he declined to add another to the pile.

Roger Angell wangled me an office at *The New Yorker*, and I rode the B train to work, standing in the front of the first car as we came through the tunnel, past rows of beams, the sharp curve below 59th to the Seventh Avenue station and then down Sixth Avenue to 42nd. I wrote unsigned "Talk of the Town" pieces for the front of the magazine, the gray matter around the cartoons, the real stars of the magazine. I'd been writing for *The New Yorker* since I was fourteen, though they weren't aware of it at the time, so I knew the breezy tone of "Talk" and loved the anonymity, writing about the statuary at Woodlawn Cemetery, the different styles of pedestrians jumping over large puddles, National Frozen Food Month, restlessness, the meaning of life in Midtown, whatever came to mind. I was befriended by Mark Singer and Ian Frazier, Calvin Trillin, and the legendary copy editor Eleanor Gould, who, as her eyesight dimmed, had become a fan of my radio show.

I liked to write in the Rose Reading Room at the Public Library and eat lunch in Bryant Park among plantings of tulips and irises, beside a plane of lush grass, looking around at a box canyon of handsome buildings, my face turned up to the sun. I ate egg salad sandwiches with Veronica Geng there, and she and I planned a performance for an Authors Guild dinner, an exchange of love letters between S. J. Perelman and Flannery O'Connor that we had written. Perelman was easy, I just used a thesaurus, but her O'Connor was a piece of genius.

I'm only a tourist in New York, and I'm dazzled by the knowingness, the competence, the pride of waiters who take waiting seriously, cabdrivers who study the city. I admired the editing to be found at *The New Yorker*, diligent people balancing clarity and comedy and idiom, Mr. Shawn's penciled comments in the margins of galley proofs gently suggesting "among" replace "between" since there were three people involved, writing, "Isn't this too confusing even if the confusion is intentional?" I love the fact that, on any given night in New York, you might go to a show that knocks your socks off—maybe *A View from the Bridge* at the Met or Vince Giordano and His Nighthawks at a little club in Midtown or *Sweeney Todd* with Patti LuPone strutting on stage and playing the tuba or *Fiddler on the Roof* in Yiddish, and as you get older and your socks get tighter, this is more and more exciting. You hear the Berlin Philharmonic play Brahms at Carnegie and you head for the subway, walking on air. You descend into the station packed with people and feel relieved that some of the job of waiting has been done by others—and along comes the train. You sandwich yourself into the crowd, avoiding eye contact, reading the ads for teeth whitener and bunion removal, and feel united with humanity.

It was good to be back with work to do, maneuvering in English. I started a novel about a radio station in Minneapolis, WLT, with a crippled songstress, Lily Dale, and a radio preacher, the Rev. Irving James Knox, and a gospel quartet, the Shepherd Boys, who liked to light the newscaster's script on fire. I was back where I belonged. I assembled a collection of stories, *We Are Still Married*, which was published as the divorce from Ulla went through.

The marriage to Denmark started to feel like a beautiful piece of foolishness, a necessary mistake. It brought a bountiful benefit: a daughter, Malene, who managed very well to love two antagonists, as only a Dane can; it is a nation of amiable mediators. She was happy at Bryn Mawr College, and one spring she went to LA with me to interview Ronald Reagan for the *Times*. The editor made it clear that I was to be humorous at the old man's expense. When we saw Mr. Reagan at his office in Century City, a shadowy version of himself, with a young woman minder to prompt him, it put a whole different light on things. He was not himself. And then my daughter, a fan of 1940s Hollywood, asked about the Warner Brothers Studio days, and the old man's eyes lit up. She mentioned her favorite movies, and they all starred old pals of his. He was delighted that a college girl liked the old Hollywood. It was a sweet afternoon: I came with cruel intention and she made an old man happy who needed that. I never wrote the story and the *Times* never asked me to write again. Malene went off to London and there, having dinner with the ex-girlfriend of a friend of mine, she met Peter Sheppard, a violinist, and he became my son-in-law and they produced Marius, a grandson. So it was an unhappy marriage with an extravagant bonus. They settled in London, so now I have a reason to go there and a guide who knows all the Wren churches and aspects of English history omitted from history books, such as the square where his ancestor the famous highwayman Jack Sheppard was hanged in 1724 before a crowd of 200,000.

And in due course, I happened to find my own life, which was a short walk away, up on 102nd Street.

24

A Good Life

I CALLED HER IN THE fall of 1991 on the advice of her older sister, who was a classmate of my younger sister at Anoka High School. She and her sister were violinists, one with the orchestra in St. Paul, one a freelancer in New York. She lived on 102nd, a ten-minute walk away, and I asked her if she'd like to have lunch with me and she said she wished she could but was about to leave on an orchestra tour in Southeast Asia. "Okay, some other time, good luck with the tour," I said.

I asked no questions, where in Southeast Asia, what orchestra, what repertoire?—if "Southeast Asia" was the best excuse she could come up with for not meeting a stranger for lunch, okay, but I did think I would call again in a few months when she returned, if indeed she were going away. She sounded lively on the phone, funny, unguarded. I didn't know her family except that her dad, Ray Nilsson, was clerk of district court in Anoka, an elective office, and I'd seen his campaign signs on the road to my Aunt Jo's. Jenny knew me, at least she'd been to a show of mine with a friend, she said. "Oh," I said. I thought, "A friend." She could've said, "My boyfriend," but had not so if it had been with a boyfriend, perhaps he was one no longer.

My mind did not go down that path, nor did I tell her that I had a girlfriend, a Dane named Dorrit, a singer and teacher and tennis partner, who wanted a decision from me, and I had decided that, though we were good together, I could not be responsible for the happiness of another Danish woman in America. It was complicated. She went back to Denmark, taught at a *gymnasium,* married Thorkild. I still loved her. A few months went by, thoughts were thought, I looked out from the terrace across the rooftops, spring came around. In May 1992, I had lunch with Jenny Lind Nilsson at Docks seafood restaurant on 90th and Broadway, at a table by the window. I ordered scallops, she got a lobster roll. There was wine. I liked her smile, the wit of her thrust and parry, her dedication

Jenny.

to music. She was thirty-five, had lived in New York since she was seven-teen, making her way playing on City Opera tours and at Glimmerglass Opera and whatever else presented itself. She was quick and never at a loss for a comeback.

She told me how, on tour in Asia, she had hiked up into the hills above Kuala Lumpur to see a Hindu temple and saw dozens of wild mon-keys who were adept at picking tourists' pockets. She talked about Japan and Brunei and Malaysia. I'd never been to Asia. She talked about the eccentrics in her family, which included everyone, so it was centricity, not eccentricity. Her great-grandfather John emigrated from Sweden to become a streetcar conductor in Minneapolis, and her grandfather Ragnar taught violin at his music school on Lake Street and played in pit orches-tras in theaters. Her parents were pianists, and her two sisters and brother were violinists, too. She loved the freelance life—from opera tour to pop show to Broadway pit to church gig; she'd played for Leonard Bernstein and also for the Lipizzaner horses—and though she lived on the edge of poverty, she had no complaints, living with roommates, sometimes their dogs, in tiny apartments in buildings where you might step over junkies asleep in the foyer and the oven is used for a closet and cockroaches pass without comment, and you learn to cure bouts of discouragement by tak-ing long walks. A slight young blond woman, she knew what it felt like to be two steps removed from homelessness. I did not. I had offered myself up to New York back in the summer of 1966, looking for a job, and wasn't offered one: I couldn't have endured living on the edge in New York. Jenny did it and thrived on it. Lunch lasted three hours.

I fell in love with her out of admiration. No money, loved music, no complaints, no regrets. She loved going out at night, and I took her to the Rainbow Room and we danced on a revolving floor to a big orches-tra. Alone, I was lost in New York, but as Jenny's escort, I had a plan and a purpose. She loved to be going places, seeing things. Saturday night, after the show at Town Hall, we strolled across Times Square and up to Picholine restaurant, me in a tux with a classy woman on my arm, an Anokan from Rice Street who'd become a real New Yorker. We went to a manic *Fiddler on the Roof* and the Brahms Fourth at Carnegie. As a child, she'd been taken by her dad to see *Carmen* and stood through the whole opera, dazzled by Grace Bumbry, so I took her to see Renée Fleming in

Der Rosenkavalier singing to the young lover Octavian and proclaiming her erotic fervor for him and at the same time setting him free—and I, the middle-aged man with the young woman up in the cheap seats, was moved to tears. Opera is the impossible art, an outpost of melodrama in an age of irony, sung in foreign languages by abnormal voices, and it can take you by the shoulders and shake you. And in *Rosenkavalier,* Octavian is my love Jenny Nilsson and I am the Marschallin warning her not to fall in love with an old man, it will only lead to heartache, but I hope she won't listen.

I'd been married twice, and that surely raised questions in her mind. I was the past imperfect, and she was the present indicative, but we were good together and she accepted me. I took her to supper at Café des Artistes, with murals of naked ladies gamboling in the woods, and that night she told me she lived with a guy in a walk-up and went to the trouble of explaining that he was a *roommate* roommate, nothing more, so now I knew she was interested in me and we eased into a life together. I had a big sunny apartment on 90th, she had a futon in an alcove of a dim room on 102nd. I was brought up to share, so we packed her up and she moved twelve blocks south. No reason for delay. I wrote to my friend Thatcher: *She's a violinist, slight and athletic, cheerful by disposition, passionate about music and opera and art, close to everyone in her family, eminently adaptable after years of touring in foreign places, a woman of simple needs after years of supporting herself as a New York freelance musician, and we love each other.*

It was a big year, 1992. She came to my fiftieth birthday party in St. Paul, though I didn't introduce her as my love. I wanted her to observe my friends and family and not be inspected critically. I got us a big room in the St. Paul Hotel. She took me to Anoka to meet her parents, Ray and Orrell, who were warm and welcoming and generously so, considering their youngest daughter had an older twice-divorced boyfriend who made his living in radio comedy featuring horn honks and glass breakage and seal courtship. They loved classical music and I was a writer of limericks. As clerk of district court, Ray knew that Keillors were not criminals so far as authorities were aware, and he knew my uncle Lawrence was president of the First National Bank, but still. Their warmth was touching. Literally. They were huggers, unlike us Keillors.

I started writing sonnets that summer and fall, and a few years later *PHC* conducted a sonnet contest for St. Valentine's Day and received piles of them. I was not eligible to win a prize, but I did enter one under the name Gary Johnson.

Up in the sky we lovers lie in bed
Naked, face to face and hip to thigh,
Your leg between mine, my arm beneath your head,
Our hands clasped together, up in the sky.
In the dark, Manhattan lay at our feet,
A blanket of glittering stars thrown down.
Beyond your bare shoulder, 90th Street,
Your elegant leg lit by the lamps of Midtown.
We came to the city for romance, as people do,
And with each other we scaled the heights
And now, united, we lie at rest, we two,
The bed gently rocking in the sea of lights.
Are you asleep? I think you are. So silently
I promise, my love, this is how it ever shall be.

That fall, the name *American Radio Company* was dropped and we resumed being *A Prairie Home Companion,* since it was really the same show, and we moved back to our old theater on Exchange Street between the Methodists and the Scientologists, looking up the hill at the great dome of Cass Gilbert's state Capitol, and the Coffee Club was replaced by the Guy's All-Star Shoe Band, or GAS band, with Pat Donohue and Peter Ostroushko, but mostly Jenny and I lived in New York. She went on another Asian tour. She returned to me.

The actor Sue Scott came aboard in 1992 to play all the female parts, smothering mom, Edith Piaf, witch, weary waitress, whispery New Age herbalist, and a year or two later, Tim Russell, a radio veteran, took over all the male roles, hipster, cowboy, punk, various pretentious gasbags, Winston Churchill (*We will fight on the beaches and in the fields, we will hide behind the trees and sneak up on them from behind and we will poke them with big sticks*), and when I wrote *Unintelligible voice* in the script, he did an amazing echoey voice of male authority so perfectly unintelli-

Tim Russell, Sue Scott, Walter Bobbie, 2008.

gible it reduced the audience to rubble. Rich Dworsky at the keyboard improvised the music cues on the script—*Urban Hustle*—*Big Western Horizon at Dawn*—*Aztec Liturgy*—*Parental Alarm*—and Fred Newman at the sound-effects table with the bells and buzzers, coconut shells, gravel box did his vocal effects, the singing dolphins and bullet ricochets, deadly snakes, bagpipes, talking horses, jet flyovers, Southern evangelists, p.a. feedback, operatic loons, and growling stomachs.

The three of them covered the waterfront, though we brought in Erica Rhodes, thirteen, to play the daughter in "Raised By Psychologists," the story of a child whose parents know too much. She came home sobbing, having been pushed by a boy and spit at, and her mother the Ph.D. said, "And how did that make you feel?" and talked about passive aggression that invites pushing and spitting. Erica also played an 85-year-old woman who, tired of being around elderly people and their incessant complaining, got a fabulous surgeon to pull her skin taut and do a larynx makeover and now she could pass for eighteen and enjoy being hit on by young men, but she said, "They can redo the face and the boobs, but it's hard to pretend you don't know what you know. You know? Just once I'd like to sit down and have lunch with people who remember Clark Gable and were around for V-J Day. August 14, 1945. Remember? Remember that?" And she sang, "Happy days are here again, the skies above are clear again," except it wasn't Erica, it was Sue Scott doing a cracked old-lady voice. I said, "Are you okay?" and the old lady voice said, "I need to take a deep breath and let the vocal cords relax." I said, "You still look great." The old lady excused herself to go lie down. The sketch wouldn't have worked on TV, but it was good on radio.

We were America's Last Live Radio Variety Show and, as if that weren't enough, we became America's Only Live Outdoor Broadcast From Unlikely Places. There was a thunderstorm show in an outdoor arena in Oklahoma, the audience holding garbage bags over their heads. At the Starlight outdoor theater in Kansas City, we did the show in 105-degree heat and 78 percent humidity as stagehands sprayed the audience with a cold mist. There were blizzard shows, like the one in Birmingham, Alabama, with thirteen inches of snow by showtime. I stood on the stage of the Alabama Theater with the Shoe Band looking at an audience of a hundred who'd managed to make their way downtown. No guests had arrived, the soundman's mother and girlfriend were working the lights. The audience kept straggling in and a gust of wind blew in as the stage door opened and Emmylou Harris came in, just off her bus, and she and I sang "From Boulder to Birmingham," no rehearsal. A gospel group, the Birmingham Sunlights, made it in by the end of the monologue and finished the show. A fine show backed up by sheer heroism, and it gave Minnesotans a chance to admire Alabamans. At the Kansas State Fair, on a stage on a dirt track, a mighty wind came up during the Guy Noir sketch, featuring Governor Kathleen Sebelius, and blew the scripts out of everyone's hands and we had to improvise while blinded by a cloud of dust that made your hair stand straight up. At a country ballroom in Gibbon, Minnesota, we did a polka show with four bands and hefty couples in bright matching outfits twirling on the dance floor, and there was dissension between spectators who'd come to see and dancers who'd come to dance and twirl, and so that was the last polka show we ever did. Couples in matching outfits are not shy about defending the right to polka. At a tent show in Wyoming, the lights went out and a dozen men ran to get their pickups and park them around the front of the tent, and we did the show by headlights. At Yellowstone, a buffalo lay down by the satellite uplink dish, and a stagehand asked a park ranger how to move the animal and the ranger said, "We don't try to tell them what to do." In Juneau, I did the News from Lake Wobegon in which someone's aunt went to Alaska and found gold and I got tangled up in storylines and could not extricate myself, and I could hear the Inuit dance troupe behind the curtain, getting warmed up for the closing number, as I kept talking and finally the stage manager came out and pointed to the clock and said, "Just say goodnight," and I did and the ON THE AIR light went dark. One could mention the Walker Art Center rooftop broadcast, which went dead at 6 p.m. when a museum guard turned off the power at the usual closing time: it took five minutes to dash down three flights and find the circuit box and flip the switch on.

There are several reasons why you'd rather record a show and edit it rather than perform live. (I'd rather you read what you're reading now than the first draft of three years ago.) But the audience loves liveness, and so you take a deep breath and do it live, which makes the show extraordinary, which means you can do a show about ordinary things. You can sing about coffee: *Coffee helps you do your duty in pursuit of truth and beauty. No reason to debate it, just be sure it's caffeinated black coffee.* You can pay homage to sweet corn and egg salad, the pleasure of sitting beside a river, the beauty of snowy mornings, the joy of friendship. I sang:

> *Friendship is a beautiful blessing as through life we are progressing.*
> *Be kind to strangers, high or low—you were a stranger once, you know.*
> *Life is just a brief rehearsal, then we go to the universal.*
> *And there, my friend, you will find out:*
> *Love is what it's all about.*

Outsiders assumed it was stressful to do a weekly show, and I let them assume that because to me, a flatlander, it is unbecoming to show personal pleasure lest you cause pain to the sorrowful. But it was mostly a great pleasure. We had a few unhappy employees who wanted the show with its big audience to advocate for noble causes, but every time I did that, it felt creepy whereas when the audience got happy it felt right as rain. I did 1,557 performances and walked downstage without a script—who needs a script to talk about your family—and told Lake Wobegon stories, and because I was so nearsighted, I never felt stage fright. There wasn't another show like it. It was like owning the only root beer stand in town: if people liked root beer, they came to us. For a sermon or a discussion about parenting or a gin martini, you went elsewhere.

Public radio kept a lectern between it and the audience. *Prairie Home* removed the lectern. Public radio wanted to sound *literary*, and *Prairie Home* spoke in a Minnesota voice and people remember when they are spoken to. Sometimes, people walked up to me weeks, months, later and repeated an elaborate Lake Wobegon episode involving multiple characters and transactions and misunderstandings and it astonished me. With *New Yorker* stories, people might say, "I liked that story about the midlife crisis of Dionysus," and that was all, but with radio, they remembered the story itself. Once I talked about Pastor Charles Ingqvist, and a hundred people reminded me that he is David, not Charles. Also, that Roger Hedlund's wife is Cindy, not Elizabeth. "Or did he dump Cindy?" someone wrote. Nope. My mistake. People told the Tomato Butt story back to me and the truck stop and the twenty-four Lutheran pastors on the pontoon boat for the weenie roast and their ecclesiastical dignity as the boat sank slowly under their weight—it showed me that I was in the right line of work. Literary prizes look nice on your bio, the Booker, the Hooker, the Pullet Surprise, but what matters is saying what you have to say to people who hear it and hold onto it. I've been in *The Atlantic* and *Harper's* and *The New Yorker* to be glanced at by people in neurologists' waiting rooms, and I prefer to stand on a stage in Worthington, Minnesota, and tell stories to 700 people to whom this will mean something.

A Prairie Home Companion was the result of purely fortuitous timing: the satellite uplink system made it a national broadcast in 1980, and twelve years later public radio still had an amateur spirit and people who loved radio were still in charge, people like Bill Kling. Eventually he retired and the coroners took over, but Bill was a man who got excited about what he admired and wasn't afraid to show it. His successor would've been happier as the CEO of a dry-cleaning chain. Kling loved a good time. He encouraged our annual season-opening street dance with meatloaf and mashed potato dinner, a series of contests (loon-calling, Bob Dylan impressions, Minnesota accent, Beautiful Baby, a joke-telling contest for kids, a dance contest, an overacting contest) and then the street dance and the host got to sing "Great Balls of

Street dance on Exchange Street, 2007.

Fire," which once almost came true when the piano player's coat caught on fire from a space heater on stage. It was festive and friendly and it was free. People looked forward to it year after year. We did it because *we enjoyed being around our listeners*—the sheer variety of them, including a great many who *don't look at all like public radio listeners* but they were. The coroners felt insecure out in the open and preferred to work behind closed doors among familiar male faces and nobody speaking out of turn.

The show's success gave us the luxury to ignore management and all we needed to do was to have fun. The show observed all the major holidays. On Labor Day weekend, we honored working people, especially those unlikely to listen to public radio:

> *O the plumber is the man, the plumber is the man.*
> *Down into the cellar he must crawl.*
> *He is not sleek and slim but we don't look down on him*
> *For the plumber is the man who saves us all.*
>
> *When the toilet will not flush and the odor makes you blush*
> *And you cannot use the sink or shower stall,*
> *Then your learning and your art slowly start to fall apart*
> *But the plumber is the man who saves us all.*

We celebrated Halloween with a menagerie of monsters, demented dentists, psychotic school bus drivers, evil evangelists, and "Her Blood-Crusted Fingers Tore at His Throat," in which a lady director auditioned actors for a horror movie, had them do blood-curdling screams and blood-chilling gasps and evil chortles, and when they failed the audition they were hurled into a vat of boiling oil or eaten by rabid banshees, their choice. It was thespianism at its best. A month later we did Thanksgiving with Brunelle and Sutton and Janis Hardy improvising a gratitude cantata from slips of paper collected from the crowd, which was so much better than your standard cantata about love and peace, etc.—ours got into favorite recipes, useful skills, new appliances, specific behavioral traits. We moved to New York City for December, with a version of "Hush, Little Baby" with new verses about Papa taking Baby to see the sights, and new rhymes (*hayseeds/ Macy's, oysters/Cloisters, solemn muse/St. Bartholomew's, blue cheese/Balducci's*, etc.). We did the annual Talent from Towns Under Two Thousand show with an array of giddy performers thrilled to stand on the Town Hall stage in front of a New York crowd unafraid to show wild enthusiasm. We did a Christmas show in which we ridiculed holiday songs we hate: *I sure hate this song, pa rum pum pum pum. I hear it all day long, pa rum pum pum pum. I think it's awfully dumb, goes on ad nauseam, I'd like to kill the bum who plays the drum. Let's break his thumbs.* And it ended with the audience singing "Silent Night" a cappella, four verses, which made everyone mist up; I got tears in my eyes and could hardly sing the words about radiant beams and redeeming grace. I couldn't talk afterward, so we hummed a verse and I said, "Merry Christmas, everybody," and the band struck up "Joy to the World" as a fiddle hoedown and we clapped ourselves off the air. We came back to St. Paul in January to earn the right to talk about winter, which our Southern audience was eager to hear. We did a Joke Show, the radio audience our main research resource, skirting the danger zones of humor but Unitarian and Norwegian jokes went over well. And a medley of sung jokes, all of them dark:

> *My daughter brought home a boyfriend*
> *With great big ugly tattoos*
> *And long black greasy hair*
> *And Lord how he hit the booze.*

I said, "Darling, I'm sure he's nice,
But something makes me nervous."
She said, "He's extremely nice.
He's doing 500 hours of community service."

For Valentine's Day, we wrote new love songs:

I've got you under my skin.
You are some kind of a skin disease.
I've taken drugs and other remedies
And now you're in my heart,
And I may need surgery—
I've got you under my skin.

We did a couple shows down South, took a break in March, during which I generally came down with the flu, and then back to Minnesota for the spring run, broadcasts from Moorhead, St. Cloud, Bemidji, or Duluth. And thereafter, a June Picnic Tour of big outdoor venues, the old amphitheater in Chautauqua, New York, Wolf Trap on Memorial Day weekend, Ravinia near Chicago, Marymoor Park in Seattle, the Greek Theater in LA, Red Rocks in Denver, and we wound up at Tanglewood in the Berkshires. When you play to 3,000 or 6,000 or 8,000 persons outdoors, you must focus on Clarity, do joke jokes, lean on the SFX man for buzzard shrieks and elephant cries, but keep an opening for sheer beauty—the crowd sits holding their breath as the soprano sings "Ave Maria"—so familiar, so brave, so perfect—or a guitarist plays the Don McLean tune "Vincent"— or a solo cello plays a Bach adagio and nobody talks and no dogs bark. At Tanglewood, the crowd spread their blankets on the sward of grass beyond the Shed and after the broadcast they pushed down front as the swells headed home and we stood around singing old campfire songs for an hour or so. It was pure pleasure. We sang *Amazing grace, how sweet the sound* and I saw a young woman with a crooked arm in a wheelchair, her mother leaning close and singing into her daughter's face, looking into her daughter's eyes. There were several families with young adult children with severe disabilities, their parents' arms around them. It felt like a healing service, which I don't offer, but music works in its own mysterious ways.

In the course of time I learned that *people like to be paid attention to* so I tried to write a song about every city we performed in. Baltimore, for example:

John Waters, Pimlico
Little houses in a row
Mencken, Tyler, Mister Poe.
Oyster buffet on the Bay
Crabs fried or sautéed
Fifty different combinations
In the city of crustaceans,
Baltimore.

Many people have written songs about Milwaukee, but when I sang mine in Milwaukee to Milwaukeeans, they felt warm inside.

Down on Polish Flats,
Near the brewery where they made Blatz,
And there is a bar on every block.
So you'd never drink and drive, you'd walk.
You could make some stops
At Leon's or Kopp's
For brats with mustard
And frozen custard
And deep-fried cheese curds,
Maybe seconds or thirds.
Which is why people in Milwaukee
Tend to be stocky,
Not delicate like me the poet,
But when Milwaukeeans put their arms around you, you're going to know it.

No city got off song-free: I sang,

I could sing about the glory that was Greece, or Rome, or Florence in the
   time of Lucrezia Borgia
Or the glory that is Columbus, Georgia.

A good life, flying around, doing shows hither and yon, talking about my hometown on the edge of the prairie—"Not the end of the world, but you can see it from there." A big tent with a circus of musical talent, and we prized old songs (*The little boy stood in the barroom door and he cried, "Oh Papa, come home. Benny is sick and the fire has gone out and Mother is waiting alone. We've sent for the doctor and he cannot come, the fever's a hundred and two. Benny is worse and is likely to die and, Papa, he's calling for you."*) and it ventured into the near-bawdy (*There was a young girl of Madras who had a remarkable ass—not soft, round, and pink, as you probably think—but the kind with long ears that eats grass.*) and gospel songs (*There'll be joy, joy, joy, up in my Father's house*) for an audience that included a goodly portion of ungodly. Gospel is what I grew up with, and I am moved by *His Eye Is on the Sparrow* and *He Wipes the Tear from Every Eye.* I don't feel the same for Gershwin as I feel for *How Great Thou Art* because Gershwin wrote for the handsome and prosperous and gospel is for people who know distress up close. The comedy didn't require that you be a Democrat or a college grad or under forty. So we rolled along broad avenues with the redoubtable Tim Russell, the sterling Sue Scott, fearless Fred Newman, and dependable Rich Dworsky, and mostly it was clean but then I'd toss a verse into "Deep Blue Sea"—

Lucy, she was very deep
Lucy, she was very deep
Lucy, she was very deep
It was Willie what got drownded in the deep Lucy.

Juvenile, yes, and them what got it, grinned, and the others went on, unmolested. Meanwhile, Dusty and Lefty rode the arid plains in search of a woman who wanted a pair of boots under her bed and Guy Noir searched for the answers to life's persistent questions. *Word had gotten around in the rodent population at the Acme that I was not a killer but a conscientious objector. The one time I set a mousetrap it caught a mouse by the ankle and he walked with a limp after that. I took care of him. Fed him. He became very fond of imported bleu cheese so I named him Mister Bleu. We became close. I made him a wheelchair out of a child's roller skate. I found a vet willing to care for a rodent. He was on dialysis for a year. What can I say? I have his ashes in a little medicine bottle on my bookshelf.* When the show was over, the crew loaded it into the semitrailer and Russ Ringsak headed for the next town.

Parody was a staple of the show, as it was back in my high school years, and now I used it to remind my generation that it was aging, using the Stones' "Honky-Tonk Women":

I found a long tall woman in New York City
She stood behind the chair that I sat on
I said I want my hair to come down on my shoulders
She looked at me and said, Those days are gone.
It's the long tall hair salon woman
Gimme, gimme, gimme a very hard time

I took the delicate sensitive "Teach Your Children" of the law firm Crosby, Stills, Nash & Young, and made it more relevant:

You who recall this song
It's been a long time since the Sixties
Your hair is thin up there
Your memory's very dim and misty

Hear your children say,
It's moving day, today we're giving
Orders to you, today you move,
You're going to assisted living.
You can argue, you can cry, but the Sixties have gone by,
It's a sharp stick in your eye, but we love you.

We played to an audience of parents and we did our best to play on their anxieties.

I met you on the Internet
A chat room called EZ2Get
It was lowercase and phonetically spelled
We talked for hrs and we LOLed

You offered me a JPG
I said I don't have one of me
You sent me yr entire file
Yr blu blu eyes, your HD smile

Someday when I'm out of jail
Done doing time for stealing mail
When I get out and back on the street
Maybe you and I can meet.

In my late fifties, I set out to write love sonnets, seventy-seven of them. Helen Story required me to memorize for English class Shakespeare's "When in disgrace with fortune and men's eyes" and the cadence sticks in the mind. My sonnets were pretty good but when I recited them to a crowd, the response was muted, but a poem that began

O what a luxury it be,
What pleasure, O what perfect bliss,
How ordinary and yet chic,
To pee, to piss, to take a leak.

and people fell apart. I submitted it to *The New Yorker* and the poetry editor, Alice Quinn, said, "Oh, Garrison, you know we can't print that!" but so sweetly that a friendship bloomed. She suggested I do poetry on the radio, which led eventually to *The Writer's Almanac*, a five-minute summary of *This day in history* followed by a poem and a blessing ("Be well, do good work, keep in touch"), which led to poets like Maxine Kumin, Ron Padgett, Billy Collins, Rita Dove, Robert Bly, Donald Hall performing on *Prairie Home Companion*. I was a good reader of poems thanks to my lack of theater training. I read them as one would read Scripture and every poem I read could be clearly understood even by listeners scrambling eggs for unruly children. I chose the poems for clarity. And if the poem is not clear, then it needs to be fascinating. I did the *Almanac* daily for almost twenty-five years on public radio, then continued it as a podcast. It was the best good deed I ever did, putting poets out in public view, and it was all about clarity, the idea of poetry as powerful speech. Read Mary Oliver's "Wild Geese" or "A Summer Day" and you'll see what I mean. She said, "Whoever you are, no matter how lonely, the world offers itself to your imagination." She said, "Tell me, what is it you plan to do with your one wild and precious life?" No poet ever asked me that before and meant it. I plan to create written work that gets wilder and that some people will value, perhaps one or two hundred.

And I wrote to Jenny:

My dearest Jenny—I'm not myself without you, and it isn't my life I'm living when you're not here, it's a refugee life. We belong together. Otherwise my feelings don't work right unless we're together. You and I have a conversation that goes on and on. Will you marry me? We could marry in September in New York. I'm in love with you. You are extraordinary and beautiful and I feel sad without you, even when I'm having a good time. We have come through all of our awkward times without any ill feeling whatsoever and we have come to love each other more and more. I am crazy about you. You need to play music, and I need to sit in a quiet room and write but I can't endure that quiet unless you're near. Well, sweetheart, that is all for tonight. I will see you tomorrow after your show. I am so much in love with you.

In the spring of 1995, I wrote a letter to my mother, telling her I would marry Jenny in the fall. In my family, third marriages are unknown, and it helped matters that Jenny was from Anoka and her sister knew mine. Her people were within our constellation though not in the same orbit. Some of my teachers went to their church. One of Jenny's childhood friends had been a Brethren girl whose aunt was married to my Uncle Jim. Jenny's mother was behind the Great Books program in Anoka and knew Catherine Jacobson, mother of my classmate Christine. We had connections. We had been brought into the world by the same Dr. Mork. Marrying her was to marry Anoka to Manhattan, to belong on 90th Street and still hold Minnesota in my heart. And when I took her to meet John and Grace in Minnesota, Jenny threw out her arms and held the old lady close and then the old man, and that was that, no more needed to be said. They had not been huggers, except with grandkids, but they were delighted to feel her affection. Jenny stayed a Nilsson, didn't take my name, but she was accepted as a Keillor from the moment she met them.

We merged into marriage on November 21, 1995, in a side chapel at St. Michael's, Amsterdam at 99th, the bride elegant and jittery, kneeling under pre-Raphaelite apostles on the Tiffany windows, and we were blessed by a West Indian priest and heard Jenny's sister Elsa play Elgar's *Salut d'amour* on violin and Jenny's mother read, from Colossians, "You are the people of God; He loved you and chose you for His own. Therefore, you must put on compassion, kindness, humility, gentleness, and patience." We said our vows and Philip Brunelle played a rousing Bach postlude that incorporated the Anoka High School fight song, and we hiked down Broadway, Jenny in her lacy ivory dress carrying a bouquet of freesia, and passersby smiled and we got good wishes from numerous panhandlers. The wedding lunch was at La Mirabelle on 86th, about forty of us, grilled sole, with wine, and Roy Blount made a speech in which he told the joke about the man who described to his wife her two main faults and she said, "Those are why I couldn't get a better husband." Roland Flint recited the poem about love as "an ever-fixed mark that looks on tempests and is never shaken; it is the star to every wand'ring bark, whose worth's unknown, although his height be taken." And the waitress, Danielle, serenaded us with "La vie en rose," with rich Piafian vibrato. We ate the cake and hung around for coffee and lingered and talked and walked home.

We spent a week in Rome on our honeymoon, and the grandeur of it, the narrow twisty streets and the magnificence rising on both sides, was perfect: when you're in love, why would you want to be anywhere else? Thanks to our friend John Thavis, we met Father Reginald, the Pope's Latinist, who gave us a little Vatican tour, including the world's only ATM in Latin. We came home to do an open-air *Prairie Home* at Interlochen Arts Academy in Michigan, Jenny's old school where she was inspired to make music her life and where bats nesting in the trees got excited by the music and flew in big dramatic loops over the stage. I looked at the audience during the monologue, and they were looking up with sheer dread, thinking of vampires. We flew home in a small jet through a storm front, lightning to the north and south, around high cumulus clouds, a full moon above, and into Minneapolis between two layers of cirrus clouds, sunset to the west. We started writing a novel together about a small-town girl, Rachel Green, who loves to play violin. We hired Norzin, an undocumented immigrant from Tibet, and suddenly our apartment had flowers, and her cooking was like my mother's, noodles and meat. We paid her well and she saved her money and she and her husband brought their children over, hired a lawyer, they all became legal, and they moved to California. When she left, she took our hands in hers and cried louder than anybody I had ever said goodbye to. She left a long white silk scarf tied to the door handle, a Buddhist prayer scarf, and ever since then, I've had good fortune.

Our marriage was happy. Jenny was never at a loss for words; everything I said got a quick comeback. She made me laugh. I missed her when she went out for a long run, training for a marathon. I edited James Thurber's collected works for the Library of America and talked them out of doing it unabridged. Everyone, even Thurber, needs abridgment. We, however, set out to expand and become parents. There were lab tests of my sperm's motility. A man assumes his sperm are good swimmers, but I'm not and neither were they. To compensate for my defective sperm, I had to inject progesterone in her thigh, I sang, *Close your eyes, pretend I'm a Beatle as I stick you with this needle so that our seed'll create something fetal.* And finally, a lab guy named Ron injected my sperm into her egg under a powerful microscope. And in due course science worked.

I was driving home from a speech in St. Cloud when the car phone rang and Jenny told me she was indeed pregnant and the baby would be born in December. I was delighted, also shaken, as a man should be, and turned off the highway in a daze, and spent a while being lost on county roads, rolling this mystery around in my mind, fatherhood at 55, a stunning fact, a clutch in the heart. Friends of mine were parents and they'd set out to be beloved and wound up as parole officers, listening to angry offspring listening to a band called Degenerate Thrombosis. Others produced daughters devoted to mathematics and practicing Chopin. Hard to know where the apple would drop. I got home and we sat on the side of the bed, arms around each other, not saying a word. I knew she wanted this child, and I knew I wanted to bring the child up in Minnesota among relatives.

We were in New York in December 1997, as her due date approached. The baby was moving around, and I put my hand on the bulge and made contact. A nurse told us the fetus looked like a girl, nice and compact, no dangly parts, which was fine by me. We didn't need any Christmas gifts except the Infanta herself. We lit a few candles and sat in the dusk and looked at each other, two characters in an ancient drama. Christmas dinner was a light lunch, the little tree sat on the coffee table. She arrived on the 29th at 9:06 p.m. at New York–Presbyterian Hospital on 68th and York. The obstetrician examined the mother and gave her a pep talk and the nurses did the delivery, comforting the mother, easing the child's descent, and she emerged, took a breath, turned pink, aced the Apgar test, was loosely swaddled in a receiving blanket, and at 9:11 was handed to me, her arms and legs swimming, her dark eyes shining, her mouth prim, her long slender fingers grasping my finger, a kind of luminosity about her. Her heartbeat appeared as spikes on a graph on a TV monitor. It was a religious moment. I have hiked the Grand Canyon, seen Pavarotti in "Pagliacci," dined with S. J. Perelman, sung with Emmylou Harris, and once, on national television, I tossed a basketball over my left shoulder without looking and hit a swisher at twenty feet, but none of those compared to holding a five-minute-old daughter in my hands. I was struck by dumb wonder, the thought that this is how everybody comes into the world, just this way, and turned to my wife, who did not have the same sense of wonder I had. She looked like the victim of an assault.

We named her Maia, after Jenny's Swedish grandmother, and Grace, after my mother. I walked out of the hospital, thinking dumb profound thoughts, and walked a couple miles in a daze before I saw I was going the wrong way and I jumped into a cab at 14th and rode home. Carlos the elevator man said, "How's it going?" I said, "It's a beautiful little girl." I reached to shake his hand and then he hugged me. Carlos is Mexican; he knows that you shake hands on a real estate transaction, a new father needs an embrace.

She was a remarkable little girl, not a hobby baby you could shoehorn into your busy schedule. She lived on Australian Standard Time, ate like a wolverine, stored up pockets of gas not easily jiggled out of her. Sometimes she pooped while feeding, the entire digestive tract engaged at once. She fought off sleep, not wanting to miss out on anything. When her tiny head touched the pillow, her eyes flew open, she keened and wailed. She had no midrange; she was louder than anyone else in the family. When it was my turn, I slung the spit rag over my shoulder and walked the floor with her, a foot soldier in the old campaign, an exhausted, poorly informed man nobody would ever hire to look after a child.

We brought the little girl home to Minnesota to meet her ancestors. A flock of them came one afternoon to view her, and the sleeping child was passed from one elder to another, Ina and Louie, Joan, Elsie and Don, Jean, each holding her in their arms, the Last Niece. All the other nieces were having children of their own. It was a poignant visit, old aunts and uncles, knowing they would not see this tiny girl reach maturity, which made her all the more precious to them. They held her tenderly, murmuring primeval comforting sounds though she was sound asleep. They also spoke some to me and Jenny, though Maia was the beautiful mystery. Me they could read about in the newspaper. A few months later, Father Bill Teska came to the house in a magnificent black robe and baptized her with great ceremony and snatches of Latin, my old Brethren parents watching in silence as he anointed the infant with oil and water and salt and made her Roman Anglican, her aunt Linda and cousin Dan and friend Gretchen, godparents.

We lived in a cabin in the Wisconsin woods for less than a year. Seclusion was not what we needed; the new mother craved company and support, especially with the father often on the road. One day, heading out the long treacherous driveway, she collided with an incoming garbage truck and broke a finger. Another day, on her way home, a suicidal deer leaped into her car on the county road and cracked the windshield. Obviously for our own safety we needed to move to town so we bought the Doty house on Portland Avenue next door to the Hooleys and their four small children. The New York *Times* was thrown onto our front steps by 6 a.m. every day, and friends were apt to drop in. The house was designed by the French architect who did the St. Paul Cathedral down the street and looks very French, with a winding staircase and a slate roof. Years before, the house had been owned by the head of Northwest Orient Airline, a Mr. Hunter, and one winter, Mrs. Eleanor Roosevelt, stranded during a big blizzard, had spent two nights in his guest bedroom, a small room with bathroom across the hall. Surely the First Lady could've commandeered something grander downtown, but it was wartime and she was a Democrat and duty-bound to set a good example. We spent ten years in that house, had a hundred houseguests, and every one was told about their predecessor, Eleanor. When my mother was fifteen, she lived a few blocks away with Aunt Jean and Uncle Les, and after school she went door to door selling homemade peanut butter cookies to help pay her way in the world, and she remembered going to this big house. "Were they nice?" I asked. "It was the Depression," she said. "Everyone was nice. Everybody helped each other. People getting off a streetcar would take a transfer and if they didn't need it, they'd stick it into a crack in a building by the streetcar stop for someone else to use. Little slips of paper stuck in a wall. Free rides."

My workroom was next door to my little girl's bedroom. She grieved to be put to bed at night and always woke up early feeling exuberant, and toddled in to where I sat at a computer, a grin on her face. We padded downstairs for breakfast, and she savored each berry and chunk of melon and spoonful of cereal. We shared a love of peanut butter, Dairy Queen cones, cheese curds, and popcorn. We sat in the dining room, by the grandfather clock like the one my dad sang about, that went *tick-tock tick-tock* until it stopped short, never to go again, when the old man died. I read the prayer painted above the fireplace, *O Lord we thank Thee for the food, for every blessing, every good, for earthly sustenance and love bestowed on us from heaven above.* All was well for a time, and then we started to worry about our girl not hitting her developmental deadlines, the first utterance of *Mama*, standing up, walking, the first use of the past participle, etc. There were meetings with the pediatrician when I held my breath, I was listening so hard. And the slow suspicion that maybe we had not gotten the precocious neurotic child we were expecting. We had a sweet girl who adored her nannies Suzanne, Katja, Kaja, and Emily: they were the Sun and the Stars. She lived in the moment, every one. She could amuse herself with a bowl of water on the sidewalk. She got laughing fits easily—at loud belches and pretend stumbles and cries of alarm. She was not a finicky eater: she licked her chops the moment the bib was tied. She laughed as we put her tiny feet into wet concrete when we laid a new driveway. When she was two, I took her around the State Fair, and she touched a newly shorn sheep and looked into the faces of hogs and goats. We slid down the Giant Slide together on a burlap bag, and she laughed the whole way down. She ate part of a corn dog that I pre-chewed for her, and we rode through the Tunnel of Love and she was delighted by her own echo.

One spring we were visited by Diana Cummings, the daughter of Paul Doty, indomitable at ninety, born the year our house was built, who grew up in it. Maia's bedroom had been her room. She remembered every family who lived on our block in her childhood and remembered hearing people gossip about Scott and Zelda Fitzgerald when they returned to St. Paul for the birth of their daughter in 1921. Diana and my little girl sat together on the couch, holding hands, communing, and the lady said, simply, "I have only happy memories of this house."

Maia was a fish in water, strong arms, steady kick, little pink goggles rising and plunging. A dog jumped on her when she was three and terrified her, and thus we were spared the burdens of dog ownership. An aunt took her horseback riding, and I worried that the virus of horse-womanship might get in her blood, but no. We kept her away from sports and saved ourselves a lot of trouble. What she loved was to be in a roomful of people talking. She also loved musicals. She loved the Radio City Christmas show in which one Rockette kicked off a shoe and kept dancing though off-kilter; our girl was delighted. She grew up backstage at my show, called me "Show Boy," adored the women singers, Heather, Aoife, Sara, Jearlyn and Jevetta, her sisters. She showed no interest in performing but was proud of her sisters. We bonded over jokes, musicals, trains, water fights. "Make me laugh," she said, and I did my best. The best way is to reach for a glass of water and pretend to throw it at her, except if we are in the backyard, I actually do and she goes to pieces. She has a vigilant mother, so she didn't watch television (except for approved videos) or eat fast food or drink soda pop or use foul language. She was taken to kiddie concerts of classical music and to children's theater. At bedtime, with a little prompting, she bowed her head and prayed for people. But she loves to laugh, and I have a video of her on a raft ride at the State Fair, watching waves of water wash over the side and onto her father's pants, and she is convulsed, howling, weeping, like me when I was twelve and read the limerick about the young man of Madras.

One morning I heard a shriek from upstairs, a long primeval wail, and there was Jenny on the landing, holding the stiff body of our little girl. I dashed up and took Maia in my arms while Jenny called 911. The child was unconscious, her breathing shallow. She went into convulsions in my arms and her body stiffened, her mouth clamped shut. I thought she was dying. And in about three minutes the St. Paul fire department paramedics arrived at the door.

In those three minutes, the heart of the father got scorched with dread. We were back in the Middle Ages, a peasant family, a dying child. The paramedics came in, four of them, and lifted her out of my arms. They laid her on the floor and tended to her, took her temperature (she was running a fever), put an oxygen mask on her face. One of them began explaining to me about febrile seizures, how common they are in small children, which Jenny knew about but I didn't. We had bought a dozen books on child-rearing, and Jenny had read them and I hadn't. And then one of the paramedics pointed out that I was still in my underwear. I pulled on a pair of trousers and we rode off to the hospital and hustled in the door and there was a pediatrician, a short man with a bow tie, like most pediatricians. I don't remember what he did. We were there for less than an hour,

GK and Maia, 7.

and then we came home with a very tired little girl. For the first time in years, she took a nap and I sat by her bed and watched her breathe.

And there was the day we found my heart pills scattered on the floor and didn't know if she had ingested some, and if so, how many, so she had to have her stomach pumped, three nurses holding her tight while a fourth pumped charcoal down her throat, my daughter writhing in terror. Still vivid to me, years later. And her tonsillectomy. I was the one who wheeled her into the OR and held her head while the anesthetist put the mask on her. As she was wheeled out afterward, she saw me, the Judas, and stuck out her tongue.

In a rash moment, against Jenny's better judgment, I sold the Doty house and bought a house overlooking the Mississippi, with wild turkeys and raccoons and a red fox living in the woods behind. As the movers emptied the place, I took a last walk around, remembering my son Jason's and Tiffany's wedding on the staircase, January 1, 2000, and my little girl crawling under the dining table during dinner, and the garden with the board fence where I spent my luxurious recuperation after heart surgery, reclining on a chaise, coffee in hand, writing on a yellow legal pad:

The secret of a long career is to keep going and not fade
And not think about your reputation for one minute.
It's like becoming Tallest Boy In The Sixth Grade,
Stick around and you're bound to win it.
So do your work, keep going straight ahead,
And you can be a genius someday after you are dead.

The new house was built in 1919 for a family who had a cook and a housemaid who lived on the third floor, short women from undernourished countries, so the back stairway had low clearances and I banged my head often. Maia took an upstairs bedroom and sat at an old desk where, twenty years before, I banged out *Lake Wobegon Days*, which changed my life though not to the extent that she has. We put her in preschool, then into a church school, because the thing we feared most was bullying, and a teacher told us, "Sitting in a class of twenty kids, she isn't going to learn anything. She needs individual attention." We searched for the right school desperately as our girl sank into the academic slough and found one that came as a miracle, a school designed for kids with learning challenges, where everyone is an oddball in some way or other and a spirit of acceptance prevails, no bullying. She was not going to become an English major and write term papers about Joyce, but she was joyful and jokey and affectionate. For her, the right place turned out to be a boarding school in New York state, a thousand miles away, and Jenny and I did the painful necessary thing and packed her suitcase and one September day took our girl to her new school and left her, weeping, in the arms of a kind teacher, and walked to the car and drove away in silence, brokenhearted, a day burned into my memory, the day we abandoned our own. She was fourteen. A long quiet ride into the city. She didn't change her clothes for days because those were the clothes she was wearing when Jenny hugged her goodbye. We had given her a wonderful month of August, and it only made saying goodbye harder.

The next day the school emailed us pictures of Maia, bravely trying to smile. We'd done the right thing, which became clearer and clearer as time went by, but there was little pleasure in it. We missed our girl. Every time I walked past her bedroom door and looked in and saw her stuffed animals, I felt hollow inside. Her sociability got her through the hard times, and she made friends with KK and Nora and Marisa and charmed her teachers and she came to love schedules and look forward to weekend outings, and Jenny and I woke up every morning and saw that door to the empty room. I missed her. The school became her family and we became distant relatives. Sometimes I thought about the brilliant neurotic daughter I'd been expecting, the one who'd stay up late at night writing angry poems. And then I missed the heroic humorous girl away at school, the girl who loved to come up and hug me and who said, "Make me laugh," and I did.

I went to a dance at her school a year ago, the gym crowded with boys in suits and ties, girls in prom dresses, some with an odd gait, some quirk or twitchiness, a speech abnormality. My heart clutches, remembering what outcasts they would've been in the gym of my youth, how cruelly we treated the disabled and gimpy, and now the band strikes up "My baby's so doggone fine, she sends chills up and down my spine"—the band is five old guys my age, the lead guitarist is going bald with a white ponytail down to his butt, playing "Brown-Eyed Girl"—and I see my daughter's friend who was injured as an infant and now, at sixteen, is blind in one eye and walks with a lurch, one arm semi-paralyzed, and she is dancing to Van Morrison, utterly transported, dancing like mad, laughing and a-running, skipping and a-jumping, and singing "sha la la la la la la la la de dah," not the least bit self-conscious. And then a slow waltz and I sing the words to my daughter, "I hear babies cry, I watch them grow; they'll learn much more than I'll ever know. And I think to myself, What a Wonderful World." And it's true. The world has come a long way in my time, and it looks wonderful to me with her in it.

25

Friendship and Fame

THE DOTY HOUSE ON PORTLAND and the big white manse on Summit, the houses Maia grew up in, were a couple blocks from my pal Patricia Hampl, a St. Paulite born and bred, raised by the nuns, and she'd written genius memoirs about the neighborhood, *A Romantic Education* and *The Florist's Daughter,* and owned it literarily. I was Protestant, a visitor. Back in college days I used to walk the streets that Fitzgerald had walked and look at the old Commodore Hotel where he had a few drinks and his parents' row house where he finished writing *This Side of Paradise* and where he ran out into Summit Avenue and stopped cars to tell people that Scribner had accepted it for publication. Down the street was the Empire Builder James J. Hill's enormous stone castle, looking like a Victorian train station or an insane asylum, take your pick. Mr. Hill built a railroad and is also known for having died from an infected hemorrhoid. Across the street, Archbishop Ireland's cathedral designed by the French architect Masqueray, whom the archbishop worked to death building majestic edifices, fifteen of them. He died of a stroke at age 56 while riding a streetcar down Selby Avenue and was carried off and laid on the grass and died looking up at the cathedral dome. Downtown is Wabasha Street, named for the Mdewakanton Dakota chief who ceded all this land to white men in 1837, adopted Western dress, became Episcopalian, supported the government during the Dakota Uprising of 1862, did his best to knuckle under, and for his loyalty the government shipped him in iron shackles to Nebraska along with his people, where he died and was buried in a little grove of trees on the open prairie. Down the hill is Kellogg Boulevard, named for Frank B. Kellogg, a St. Paul lawyer and Calvin Coolidge's Secretary of State, who negotiated a treaty, signed in Paris by all the major powers, men in morning coats and top hats, renouncing warfare as a means of settling disputes, which won him the Nobel Peace Prize, after which Kellogg retired to a big house on the hill and watched the world fall apart: Japan invaded Manchuria, Italy invaded Ethiopia, Russia invaded Finland, and Hitler invaded Poland. Kellogg would've contributed more to the world had he invented Grape-Nuts. He intended to be a savior and instead he became a boulevard.

Frank Kellogg drew up a pact
Outlawing war—that's a fact.
It was quickly signed
By the deaf and the blind,
And the powerful promptly attacked.

And then there was Fitzgerald, who said, "Show me a hero and I'll write you a tragedy." He was thinking of himself, as he generally did. He didn't like St. Paul, so he left in his twenties and never returned. He was a literary sensation at the age of 24, the Handsome Schoolboy of the Jazz Age, and wound up burned out at 44, an invalid in Hollywood, worrying about his daughter at Vassar, in debt to his agent, watching his old pal Hemingway coming out with *For Whom the Bell Tolls* as Fitzgerald wrote stories about a hack writer, based on himself, and a few days before Christmas, he jumped up from his chair and fell down dead from a coronary.

It's a neighborhood of cautionary tales about the perils of prominence, nonetheless I persevered, since I was enjoying myself. Fame is a role and some people play it very well, such as George Plimpton, who crashed a party at my apartment in New York one night. I hadn't invited him because I didn't know him, he was too famous for me to know, but he wanted to be friends so he came around midnight and sat at the dining room table, jiggling a glass of Scotch and holding court, talking about Hemingway at the Café de Tournon and the bar at the Ritz and E. M. Forster whom he interviewed for the *Paris Review* and Ezra Pound. George invited me to lunch at the New York Racquet Club and showed me the tennis court modeled after the one Henry the Eighth played on, an actual courtyard with walls and a roof to play the ball off. He explained the arcane rules of court tennis and took me down to the library where we sat in leather chairs and he told about the book he'd found in which an Old Member had hidden his correspondence with his mistress, describing her breasts as "gleaming rosy-tipped orbs." My Midwestern bias against clubbiness runs deep, but George was a real writer, his *Paper Lion* and *Out of My League* part of the literature of sports. And his great adventure was founding the *Paris Review* in Paris when he was 26 years old, living in a toolshed, sleeping on an army cot, dropping in at the Hôtel Plaza Athénée to write letters on hotel stationery to his parents assuring them that he was having a fine time and wasn't ready to get a job on Wall Street yet. He remained 26 on into his seventies. He was a tireless encourager, and generosity, not cleanliness, is what is next to godliness. That night at my apartment, he left around 4 a.m. "I miss staying up all night," he said. "That gray light in the morning. You think your time is up and then you get a second wind." We stood out on Columbus Avenue, cabs passing by. He said, "I envy you getting to talk to all those people on the radio. People hear my voice and they get their backs up, they hear Harvard snob. I tell you, friendship is what it's all about. It's all it's ever been about. All my deepest regrets are about people I missed my chance to get to know, and it's always for the dumbest reasons." And then a cab stopped and he got in, waved, and was gone.

Friendship is what it's all about, all it's ever been about. I think of my disapproving father whom I never knew and how happy he was with his sister Eleanor. He never was at ease with Mother's family; with Eleanor, he was completely happy. I sat in the next room and listened to them, talking and laughing, he was someone I didn't recognize at all. I was in the business of impersonating friendship on the radio, and one day I got a friendly letter from Maggie Forbes, my Latin teacher at the U, for whom I wrote clumsy translations of Horace, who wrote from Texas to say she loved the show, and I stared at her letter in happy disbelief. The woman had seen a dense dull side of me and now we were friends. My doorbell on Portland Avenue dinged one morning and there was Charles Faust, my old history teacher and now he wanted to be friends. Helen Story came to a party at my house and said she admired *Pontoon* and admired *Love Me* even more. She was on her way to the Stratford Festival, flying to New York and London, planning a trip to Machu Picchu, not a word about her years of servitude at Anoka High, only about her love of theater. LaVona Person asked me to speak at her retirement dinner; she was proud of having been my teacher—this thrilled me more than any prize could, that I'd won the regard of the woman who showed me that if I took off my glasses, the audience became a Renoir hillside.

I acquired a friendship with the writer Carol Bly, who wrote me weekly about her anger at oppressive Lutheranism and the need for boldness and honesty in all things artistic and the need for comedy that doesn't jeer at people but facilitates self-confidence and psychological growth, and why, instead of teaching critical reading in English classes, they should require kids to memorize stories from age seven on up through college, so you can tell *Moby-Dick* to someone or *Lord Jim* or *David Copperfield*—she kept trying to enlist me in good causes to open all systems wide and let the sun shine in. When she read that I was going to speak at the dinner of the White House Correspondents Association and the Clintons would be there, Carol badgered me to not tell jokes but call the administration to battle.

I wrote a funny speech and went to the dinner and sat next to Mrs. Clinton, who was good to talk with. I'd just attended a Supreme Court session, and I talked about how inspiring it was to see them at work and suggested she visit sometime. She laughed and said, "I don't think it'd be a good idea for me to show up in a courtroom where a member of my family might be a defendant." It was the year before the impeachment of her husband. And then she turned and bestowed her attention on the old Republican bull sitting on the other side of her, Speaker Dennis Hastert, whom nobody was talking to. It was her duty to be civil to him, not to amuse me, and she focused on him and even made him chuckle a few times, no easy task.

Out of nowhere came a friendship with the jurist Harry Blackmun. It was his idea, not mine. I don't aspire to be on a first-name basis with the US Supreme Court, but Harry grew up on Dayton's Bluff in St. Paul, a blue-collar Republican, and he listened to the show regularly, or so he said. We wrote back and forth. I met him years later at the Court and we took a walk around the block, he in a blue cardigan frayed at the sleeves, an old blue raincoat, and, coming back, he stopped to listen to the picketers on the Court plaza, protesting the decision he wrote in *Roe v. Wade* that struck down state restrictions of abortion. They paid no attention to me or the slight bespectacled gray-haired man next to me. He said, "Maybe they take you for my security," but it was his own humility that shielded him. "They still write me a lot of letters," he said, "and I try to read them." Then he walked up the steps under the Equal Justice Under Law inscription and went in to his office where he kept, in a frame, a chunk of his apartment wall with a bullet hole in it where some anonymous sniper had fired at him and missed. He was still miffed at the insurance company that did not fully compensate him for the upholstered chair that the bullet had passed through.

I sang at his funeral a few years later. His daughter Nancy had asked for the two songs he'd sung to his girls when they were little and he came home late from a long day at work and found them already in bed, the "Whiffenpoof Song" and "Toora-loora-loora," so I did those at the church. It was a big Methodist church, downtown Washington, and his colleagues were there in their black robes, sequestered in a library with two glass walls, to protect them from fawning. I'd seen them in session, on a high dais in their magnificent Cass Gilbert courtroom, like the Nine Grand Masters of the Ancient Order of Woodmen, hearing candidates for apprenticeship, and now they trooped into the sanctuary and sat in the front pew. When the minister nodded to me, I walked up front and said that at the family's request we were going to sing the lullabies Harry sang to his girls when they were little and launched into "Toora-loora-loora," and the congregation joined in but not one of the Justices. Not even the liberals would so much as move their lips. (Had they taken a vote on this? Had they examined the text and found a *loora* that was inconsistent? Or lurid?) President and Mrs. Clinton sang, and so did Al Gore and numerous senators, Bill singing with a big grin:

> We will serenade our Louie while heart and voice shall last
> Then we'll pass and be forgotten with the rest.

Maybe it was the "We are little black sheep who have gone astray, Baa-baa-baa" that made the Justices uneasy, fearing it would undermine their authority, but they sat mute, unmoved, resolute bad behavior in a crowd of singers. I thought about it all the way back to the train station. A hardworking jurist loved his little girls and wanted to have a few sweet minutes with them at the end of a long day. He'd stayed late at the office doing his duty, untangling the deliberate obfuscations of highly paid attorneys, and now he allowed himself to sing *Toora-loora-loora toora-loora-li* to his little Whiffenpoofs in recognition of his true purpose in life. Bill Clinton got that and sang, and the judiciary declined. A court that cannot comprehend a father's love is weak on fundamentals, I say. Lord have mercy.

One night in New York, a guy in an NY baseball cap sidled up to me on 86th Street where I was waiting for the light to change and he said, "The writing on the show has been really good lately." It was a very famous comedian, I forget his name but I knew it at the time and so did everyone else in America. This is a beauty of fame, the ability to bestow a blessing. I once sat in the NBC Green Room waiting to go on the *Letterman* show and suddenly Al Franken was there, leaning down, to give me good advice. He said, "Just remember: this isn't a conversation, it's a performance, you can't go out there and just sit back and get comfortable." Of course, that's exactly what I went out and did. Dave said, "So what've you been up to lately?" cueing me for a routine, which I hadn't worked up, and I said, "Oh, not much. How about you?" I died a slow death. But Al had given me his blessing. He's from Minnesota, some of his best friends are Protestants, he knows our problem: *we do not want to be seen trying too hard to look good. We prefer to be casually offhandedly humorous, not determinedly funny.*

I went to the 1996 Grammys in New York, expecting to win one for my recording of *Huckleberry Finn*, and I saw heavy security at the Garden and heard police helicopters and realized that Hillary Clinton was in attendance and the fix was in. The First Lady had not come all this way just to watch me accept the Spoken Word trophy. Mark Twain had lost to her warmed-over Unitarian sermonette on interdependence, *It Takes a Village*. So I turned around and got back on the C train and she got the prize and rode to the airport in a motorcade that tied up traffic for a couple hours. *Huck Finn* was a better piece of work but I'd already won a Grammy in 1987 for *Lake Wobegon Days*, which I listened to a few days later and decided was a phoned-in job. So you win with a piece of crap, you lose with a masterpiece. Anyway the subway is a better place for a writer than a motorcade, and when you're wearing a tuxedo, as I was, you're a person of interest. Your fellow passengers take long looks at you and see no instrument case so you must be a waiter but why is a waiter on the uptown train at 8 p.m., was he fired? But he's so unperturbed. And then they get it: he quit, he was insulted and walked off the job. And you stand up at your stop and there is silent applause in the air. I felt admirable. A waiter who refuses to accept insult is the equal of a Grammy nominee. I'd been nominated sixteen times and so what? The real prize was the line in the dark from the famous guy in the NY cap.

The radio show was on cable TV for a while and I was camera-shy like my grandma—in every snapshot of her she looks irked, and so did I on TV. Self-deprecation is the Midwestern default mode. On the screen I look like somebody's brother-in-law looking for his car keys. The TV director didn't dare direct me but Jenny told me a dozen times: *Do not turn your back on the audience. Do not try to be inconspicuous. It doesn't look good.* But I kept turning my back. In the act of concentration, talking or singing, I'd wheel around, stare at the floor, wander down to Dworsky at the piano, stare into the wings, the host of the show trying to avoid drawing attention to himself, which was absurd.

I was slightly famous in a transitory off-center way, but I saw the real thing back in 1989 when I had a small part in a 100th birthday salute to Irving Berlin at Carnegie Hall. He wasn't there, but everyone else was. It was the Show Biz Hall of Fame, but the statues were living, breathing people. I shook hands backstage with Tony Bennett, Rosemary Clooney, Marilyn Horne, Shirley MacLaine, Willie Nelson, and Ray Charles, who reached for my hand before I could get up the nerve to reach for his. Tommy Tune walked over in tap shoes before his big number, "Puttin' on the Ritz." Walter Cronkite was there and a rather low-key Bob Hope. Isaac Stern. Joe Williams. One household name after another and also me. I got to see Leonard Bernstein walk up to Frank Sinatra and say hello, two men whose like will never be seen again. Bernstein wore a boa and was all bonhomie. Sinatra seemed uneasy. Bernstein said, "Love your stuff." Sinatra sang "Always" on the show and muffed a few notes and the stage manager had to walk out onstage and say, "Mr. Sinatra, one camera was out of position, the director would like you to do it again." Mr. Sinatra said, "Of course." It was very comfortable. They were all phenomenally famous and very good at playing themselves. I was the walk-on. I got to stand on stage and recite "What'll I Do?" as a poem, all eighty-eight words. From memory. It was good enough. But I could not bring myself to walk up to the gods and make small talk. Frank Sinatra— my one chance to say hello to Frank Sinatra and admire the toupee and the tan, and in the interest of being cool, I stood off to the side with my hands in my pockets and looked at the wall above his head, pretending to be unamazed.

The people at the Berlin tribute were world-famous. I was famous in downtown St Paul. I walked up Wabasha Street to Candyland for buttered popcorn one day and was stopped by a grizzled old guy who said, "You're Garrison Keillor, aren't you? I haven't read your books, but I saw your picture in the paper. How about a few bucks for an old bum down on his luck?" And I reached into my pocket and pulled out a twenty. I handed it over. "You wouldn't happen to have another one of those, would you? It'd sure help me out." I gave him another. I felt that I was buying good luck. I wished him well and he walked away.

To me, fame was like having a bright pink convertible parked in your driveway that isn't yours but people think it is. I enjoyed the silliness of it. One fall, the Minnesota North Stars invited me to drop the first puck and open their hockey season. I asked John Mariucci, a Stars exec, why I was chosen, and he put his hand on the back of my neck and squeezed it. "We've had our eye on you," he said in his Lucky Luciano voice. "We've seen you drop quite a few things over the years, and we like your style. You have a good release." So I went shuffle-sliding out to mid-ice, the two opposing centers posed, I dropped the puck, they feinted toward it, we shook hands, I shuffled off. A moment of public meaninglessness, but a pleasure still, and I got to keep the puck and stay for the whole game.

I used my platform to honor my heroes. I had the power to do it so I did. Roger Miller came on the show, Wynton Marsalis, the jazz violinist Svend Asmussen, Victor Borge, Jim Jordan who played "Fibber McGee," the great Paula Poundstone.

I did an eighteen-city tour one summer with Chet Atkins and his band, and in every show I recited James Wright's poems "An Offering for

GK and Jason Keillor, 1986.

Mr. Bluehart" and "A Blessing" (*Just off the highway to Rochester, Minnesota, twilight bounds softly forth in the grass, and the eyes of those two Indian ponies darken with kindness*) as my son Jason played a guitar underscore. James was a courageous man who wrote transcendent verse in the face of serious trouble and could be wildly funny at the same time. I was inspired one day to talk to the state Department of Transportation about putting James's "A Blessing" on a plaque at a highway rest stop near Rochester— and an engineer named Kermit McRae got it done. It's a great poem and the DOT can be justly proud of it—for years, "A Blessing" appeared in the State Fair crop art exhibit, the words spelled out in seeds glued to a sheet of plywood, a singular honor for a contemporary poet—and now it was written on stone. Celebrity is capable of good deeds. People asked me to do benefits, so I did, though the celeb aspect of it—my name in big letters on the poster associated with historic restoration or a cure for MS or a good woman's run for Congress—felt unseemly and piggish. But how could I say no to a benefit in Rochester for a residence for transplant patients run by two Franciscan nuns? I sat with a ten-year-old girl named Chris, who had undergone months of chemo and now was waiting for a bone marrow transplant to try to cure a kidney tumor, a long shot, I was told. The will to live was palpable in that place. She wore a face mask. She sat next to me and leaned against me and we talked. She was a skater and she wrote poetry. So I wrote her:

My friend the ten-year-old Chris
Is a poet who writes about bliss
And as she waits
For a poem, she skates
And each LINE is a STRIDE just like THIS.

I was happy to meet her. What was hard was the much-too-extravagant gratitude of the sponsors. I wanted to tell them: "I'm not really a good person. I'm incredibly selfish. I drink very expensive whiskey and I fly first class. If only you knew."

We honored Studs Terkel on his 86th birthday. I put him in a Guy Noir script, playing a gangster just as he'd done fifty years before on *Ma Perkins* and *The Romance of Helen Trent*. He wore a blue blazer, red checked shirt, red sweater, red socks, gray slacks, gray Hush Puppies. The audience sang, in honor of the old lefty, to the tune of the Battle Hymn:

It's time for working people to rise up and defeat
The brokers and the bankers and the media elite
And all the educated bums in paneled office suites
And throw them in the street.

Let's reverse the social order—oh wouldn't it be cool?
Down with management and let the secretaries rule.
Let the cleaning ladies sit around the swimming pool,
Send the bosses back to school.

And a bathing beauty wheeled out a cake with eighty-six candles, the frosting melting from the heat. She wore a tiny top, her left breast bursting out of it, and when she adjusted herself for modesty's sake, she almost popped out. The old man blushed. He reached over to assist her, then thought better of it.

I put together a committee to celebrate F. Scott's centenary in St. Paul in 1996. Somebody else would've done it if I hadn't, but I did a good job along with Page Cowles and Paul Verret and Patricia Hampl's help.

Carol Bly considered FSF a "racist alcoholic social climber who stole his wife's writing," and she argued for a Thorstein Veblen celebration honoring the Wisconsin author of *The Theory of the Leisure Class*, a favorite of hers, published in 1899—I said we could hold a Veblen festival around my dining room table. Fitzgerald still had a large readership because he still sounded contemporary and he created a great narrator, Nick Carraway. The writers who pitied Scott and wrote his eulogies—Glenway Wescott, John Dos Passos, John Peale Bishop—all of them unread today except by a few graduate students, and Dorothy Parker, who looked down at his body in the coffin and said, "The poor son of a bitch"—Dorothy Parker is more quoted than read. The centenary was lovely, the University of Minnesota Marching Band and Fitzgerald's granddaughters and great-grandchildren in an open car and Gene McCarthy and J. F. Powers in another, an Irish piper and a Bookmobile, the parade wending to the old World Theater, where Scott and Zelda's descendants took buckets of Mississippi River water and threw it at the building and it was christened the Fitzgerald Theater. His old secretary Frances Kroll Ring was there, eighty, hearty and rambunctious, her memories of him vivid. He'd hired her via a Los Angeles employment agency when she was 22 and she typed up his last work and intervened with his friends and dealt with Zelda and daughter Scotty and disposed of the empty bottles, and then he arose from his chair, clutched his heart, and died, 44, a famous American failure, and she defended him as a conscientious gentleman and man of letters working hard in the face of addiction and financial distress. She was a peach. It was amazing to be in the same room with her, his last and best heroine.

The statue committee decided not to put Fitzgerald on a pedestal, so he stands on the ground, coat over his arm, as if waiting for his ride to come. He was 5'9" in real life, which seems shrimpy today, so the sculptor gave him two more inches. There was a reading of *The Great Gatsby* at the Fitzgerald Theater, a packed house, the entire novel, with one intermission. The book reads well, a tribute to the author who survived the small mean anecdotes told about him. Survival: who can explain it? Fitzgerald survives.

26

John and Grace

AFTER DAD FELL OFF THE barn roof and cracked his head and developed
spinal meningitis, it affected his sense of balance and he had to give up sorting mail on the train and take a job in the post office. He also suffered sinus
problems that made a Minnesota winter less and less bearable, so, much to
Mother's sorrow, they flew off to Florida when he retired and spent their
twilight years in a double-wide near Orlando, returning every summer—
family meant everything to Mother, her sisters, nieces, in-laws—and she
was overjoyed when they came back for good in 1991, just in time for the
Halloween blizzard. They settled back into our old house north of Minneapolis, the house Dad built in a cornfield in 1947, and they gently relaxed
their grip on things. They forgave their children for leaving the Brethren.
Dad gave up driving and Mother gave up cooking big meals and served up
sandwich meats and potato salad from a deli. The days got lighter. They
were cheerful and kept their worries to themselves.

I was on the road more or less constantly in the Nineties when one
by one my beloved aunts went down the long road to the graveyard.
Our noble Aunt Josephine died. Aunt Eleanor collapsed and died in her
kitchen while preparing Thanksgiving dinner. She was a kindred spirit,
and her death was a grievous loss. She often told me, "Your father loves
you, you know," trying to make up for his disapproval of me. I saw
Uncle Lawrence at her funeral; he looked stricken. He said, "You won't
have me or your dad around much longer." Elsie died at home, tended
by Uncle Don. That generation passed into silence as I flew around the
country telling stories about Lake Wobegon, the town where I tried to

keep them alive. In the winter of 2001, my father took his leave of the world in a bedroom that had been mine when I was eighteen, where I looked at the red light of a distant water tower and read *A Farewell to Arms* while smoking a cigarette and blowing the smoke out of the window and seeing it blow back in. He had chronic pneumonia that antibiotics didn't clear up and he'd made it clear that he didn't wish to return to the hospital for more of the dreaded suctioning procedures, so he was brought home and put on hospice care. His morning nurse Ramona played her guitar and sang, "When Johnny Comes Marching Home," and he smiled.

Dying at home is labor-intensive, and it helps to have six children who can take turns on night duty, administering the nutrients and Tylenol, adjusting the oxygen. It is an up-and-down business. At various times, he seemed to be at death's door, and then one day he saw my three-year-old daughter standing at his bedside, poking his foot as it moved under the blanket, and this got his interest. He wriggled his toes. She tried to grab them. He wriggled, she giggled. She tossed a ball to him, and he threw it back. She kissed his hand.

The hospice people gave us a handbook on dying that advises you to forgive the dying person, and express your love, and your gratitude, and to say goodbye. It doesn't explain how to do this with someone who, even when he could hear, never went in for such intimate declarations. And what about all those things you're not sure whether to forgive or feel grateful for? When I was eighteen, he told me he wouldn't pay a penny for my college education, and I was grateful for his disapproval: it meant I was on my own. I worked my way through school and never needed his permission. When my little daughter grabbed for his toes and kissed his hand and he grinned at her, that was the best gift I could give him. "All I do is nap all day," he said to me. "They keeping you busy?"

I was keeping myself busy. It was February 2001. Shows in Berlin and Dublin, and off I went. Nobody suggested I not go.

From my diary:

Feb. 27. Flew Minneapolis to Amsterdam in a window seat on a 747, wrapped the blanket around me, swallowed the Dramamine, put on the sleep mask, inserted the earplugs, eased

*the seat back, visualized a beach and surf and birds and was
gone. Woke briefly over the Atlantic, dozed off, then the flight
attendant told me to raise my seat back and the wheels hit the
pavement. I raised the shade and was blinded by sunlight.*

*Feb. 28. In Schiphol, ran into a choir from South Dakota head-
ing for Venice, touring Italy with a program of Negro spirituals.
White kids, whose director wanted them to sing in dialect. And
a guy from Butte heading for Syria where he works in the oil
business. Thirty days in Syria, thirty off in Montana. Norwegian ancestry, about my age. The beauty of being a minor celeb:
people walk up and introduce themselves. Friends wherever you
go. Met Charlie Cutter, Leeds's sister, heading for Kathmandu.
Why? I didn't ask. She's a French chef, lives on the West Coast.
I wanted to tell her how much I admired him and just couldn't
find the words. There was a clarity to Leeds at eighteen that
nobody else had. He knew where he was headed and what for.*

*Took a KLM flight to Berlin, same drill, blanket, mask,
beach, sleep. The beach that works for me is Stinson Beach
north of San Francisco. Tall grass, big surf.*

*In Berlin, taxi to the hotel Adlon, built on the rubble of the
old Adlon, a Nazi watering hole from the Twenties and Thirties, a stone's throw from the Brandenburg Gate, not far from
the Reichstag. Came here with my Danish stepkids in '87 when
it was still East Berlin and the Wall was up and you waited
hours to cross. I remember my stepson Morten leaning across a
konditorei table and saying, "These people are so much like us."
Which is true though Danes didn't want to think so. The show
is in Charlottenberg, in a theater just off the Kurfürstendamm.
Breakfast arrived, scrambled eggs and coffee, and I ate it sitting
at the laptop. pecking away at Guy Noir. Time to start writing
that term paper.*

*Mar. 1. The American embassy gave a big party for us. Ger-
mans, Americans, Brits, Irish, Midwesterners in the Foreign
Service, military attachés, spouses, their German tutors. A*

wonderful array of festive people. I was pushed onto a dais and told to speak and so I did. Introduced the crew and led the crowd in a few verses of "Home on the Range," the one about the air is so pure, and how often at night, and the graceful white swan, then we mingled for a while. A German asked me if I was going to talk about the war on the show. I said no. He offered to show me where Hitler's bunker had been. I declined. I didn't come here to put on a show of righteousness.

Called home later. Mother said, "He's losing ground." She was managing the feeding tube with liquid nutrients. My older brother said he had a long conversation with Dad and asked if he had anything on his conscience that he needed to make peace with—Dad said he didn't. Philip was the only one in the family who could've asked Dad that question. In 1947, Dad wrote dozens of letters to the Ames Brethren begging them not to split away from the Booths, so he didn't have that on his conscience. He was a loving father even if he couldn't express it. I had nothing to forgive him for, only regret that we were strangers.

At 11 p.m. Saturday, we did a live broadcast back to America from the Neues Berliner Kabarett-Theater in Charlottenberg, just off Bismarckstrasse. I sang the opening theme and said, "How good of the Germans to name a street after the capital of North Dakota." I brought on a German crooner, Max Raabe, and the Comedian Harmonists and "The Lives of the Cowboys" with "I Ride an Old Paint" in English and German. A rhubarb pie commercial: *Pflaumen Torte*. A good show and the crowd was like a rural Minnesota crowd, rather quiet, then a standing O at the end. We took a group bow and the crowd started clapping in rhythm, and brought us back for an encore, and another and another. And afterward the German crew and musicians and I went across the street for beer. The Germans who yesterday had been stiff and correct now were downright affectionate, and it was very *gemütlich*, candlelit faces leaning forward over mugs of beer and in the spirit of the evening, I sang a verse of *Hier in des Abends traulich ernster Stille*, which I still remembered from high school choir, and then a song from an old Pete Seeger album:

Die Heimat ist Weit
Doch wir sind bereit.
Wir kämpfen und siegen für dich.
Freiheit!

And a verse about how we shall not be afraid of Franco's fascists, even though the bullets fall like sleet. One of the women said, "We learned that as children in school. In East Berlin. It's a communist song." She was mildly amazed.

I called home. Mother sounded flat, running on empty. The hospice nurse was there, explaining what happens when a person dies. I am a coward. I was glad to be thousands of miles away.

I flew to Dublin, cold and rainy, and the seedy old Shelbourne Hotel, creaky floors, heavy drapes, musty carpets. My room faced an airshaft. I went for a walk down Nassau Street, old men walking by in worn tweed jackets and black sweaters and nicely shined shoes, men with craggy faces like Joe O'Connell's and Jim Powers's. I walked into Merrion Square, all lush and green, daffodils and daisies, with the statue of Oscar Wilde lounging on a rock, and off in a corner a couple engaged in heavy necking, his hand up under her shirt.

I called home. The hospice nurse had gotten them started giving him morphine to ease his breathing, and my niece Kristina had gotten Mother to lie down. Dad was sleeping all the time, the morphine making him less restless, and in brief wakeful moments he seemed unaware of his surroundings.

From the diary:

> *Went to dinner at 7 after a lousy day of writing, got back to the hotel room and found messages on my phone from home, my father is sinking fast. Called home and my sister answered, on the verge of tears, to say that his morphine dosage is up and the hospice nurse says he probably won't make it beyond tomorrow. Spoke to my mother who is tired and distressed and who then had to go to his bedside. My sister came on the phone and said, "I think he's going."*
>
> *And now I sit here weeping in Dublin, weeping for my*

daddy whom I will never know. I gained so much freedom when I was thirteen and more in college, then he moved to Florida, and we didn't have the wherewithal to make each other's acquaintance. Keillor men are somewhat fortresslike. They sat by their dying mother and discussed cars and it wasn't from coldness of heart, quite the opposite: overflowing feeling and the fear that if it's expressed, what comes out will be awkward and sound stupid. My dad was friendly with the Prairie Home *staff and he'd introduce himself backstage ("I'm his father") and there seemed to be pride in that, but of course he couldn't express it to me for fear of what it'd sound like. I am sure he's dead. And a little later comes a call that he died, about 4 p.m. Very peacefully, with children around, and people singing hymns, and my mother holding his hand, he floated away. Johnny, whom she met on July 4, 1931, at a picnic at the Keillor farm, in a crowd of young people, their eyes caught each other's and held on and that was it, that's where I come from.*

He drove the car when I was a little kid in the back seat, he ran the power saw and built our house from the basement up, he planted the garden, he raised the car on jacks and put on snow tires, he said the same blessing over every meal. He was handsome and capable, and loved his nieces, and liked being silly with them. He favored girls over boys and should've had more daughters. He was so close to his kinfolk that as they got old, they could sit together silently and communicate by pure proximity. He loved long car trips and was an expert packer of luggage in the trunk.

His granddaughters knew him best. They knew him in his sixties and seventies, his prime. But I remember him as an elegant 34-year-old guy in a fedora and topcoat, walking with me along Bloomington Avenue in Minneapolis in 1947. I am riding a trike alongside and I am proud to be identified with him. And I feel the same today. It's good to cry, but I want to do a funny show on Saturday, not a word about Dad, not a word. And now I really have to get to work.

I wrote in the diary, and then I sat in my hotel room and wrote Guy Noir:

> *It was March, and warm out, and I assumed that with no more heat-*
> *ing costs, my cash flow would stabilize, but then I got hit with a bill*
> *from my long-distance provider for $3,358. I had been carrying my*
> *phone in my back pocket and every time I sat down it called a number*
> *in Dublin. The one in Ireland.*
>
> *GUY: I don't know anybody there. This is an outrage.*
> *PHONE REP: Oh my. Let me write that down. "This is an outrage."*
> *Oh, that is priceless.*
> *GUY: I'll fight you people to the death. I'll write my congressman.*
> *I'll write letters to the editor. I'll organize marches.*
> *PHONE REP: Oh, you are the highlight of my day. A march! Make*
> *sure there are bagpipes!*

I wrote a Mournful Oatmeal and Dusty and Lefty and decided to quote Yeats in the monologue, "Had I the heavens' embroidered cloths." I took a cab to the Vicar Street club, a smallish venue, seating about 600. It dawned on me as I entered that a live 6 p.m. broadcast to the States starts at an hour when Dubliners are well into the whiskey and feeling free and easy. I sat on a stool to do the News from Lake Wobegon, it was like talking with friends after dinner except these friends were well-soused and not afraid to interrupt and when the host clutched the microphone close and tried to ignore them, they spoke louder and used language we don't accept in American broadcasting, but thank goodness they mispronounced the words, *fook* and *fookin'*, so I just plowed ahead and when the music resumed, the fookers shut the fook up. The singer Frank Harte sang a couple ballads and was tickled to be cast in "Guy Noir" as Father Paddy O'Furniture, and two sisters sang beautifully in Gaelic and we closed with "The Parting Glass":

> *Oh and all the money that e'er I had,*
> *I spent it in good company,*
> *And all the harm that e'er I've done,*
> *Alas it fell on none but me.*

And all I've done for lack of wit,
To memory I can't recall.
So fill to me the parting glass,
Good night and joy be with you all.

And that was the end of it. My dad died, and I did a show and it was good enough. Were I an Irishman, I would've talked about him on the show and the fookers would've been ashamed of themselves, or maybe not. Maybe they'd have wanted to talk about their own poor dead dads and the good deeds they did. But I was done with it: my first interactive show with drunks. I headed for the exit and walked fast back to the hotel and threw myself on the bed and lay there for a long time.

Dad mellowed with age. His children had all fled the Brethren, and he accepted that with equanimity. He loved his Catholic daughter-in-law and vice versa. I was grateful for him and for my siblings who gave him a good death. I wept for all of us. Rare for me. And I was glad for that visit to his bedside with my daughter grabbing at his foot under the blanket and laughing, the dying man with a grin on his face. She was my parting gift to him.

His life had integrity, built on the principle of Self-Reliance. He taught himself to play hymns on the piano by ear, chord by chord. I can see him, thirtyish, building our house, sawdust in his dark hair, running a two-by-four through a circular saw, trimming it, holding it up to the studs, pulling a nail out from between his front teeth, taking the hammer from the loop on his pants where it hung, and pounding in the nail, five whacks, and a tap for good luck. His hammering was as distinctive as John Hancock's signature. Every few weeks, he cut his boys' hair, sat us each in turn on a sawhorse in the garage, bedsheet around the customer, trimmed the top to a short clump with a shaved arc around the ears. The haircut was as intimate as he and I ever got, and I wished he'd talk to me and tell stories, and now I think, *He'd put in a long day of work and now he had four heads to trim and you expect him to be Andy Griffith? Give the man a break.*

There was a cadence to his life. He was a gentle man: anger is not useful when dealing with power tools. When he raised the axe and chopped off the chicken's head, he did it cleanly. He was a sure-handed barber.

Once he carved a boomerang for me, and I threw it and it flew and rose in the air and curved back toward me. His prayer before a meal had a set rhythm—he bowed his head and said, "Our God and heavenly Father, we do come before Thee this day with grateful hearts to thank Thee for these temporal blessings. We think of our loved ones wherever they may be, that Thy good hand of mercy might be over them throughout the day. So we ask it all in our Savior's precious and worthy name. Amen." He was never bewildered until the very end and even then not so much, he had no time for skepticism, there was no bluster to him. He died at home, surrounded by family, as his father had and a long line of Keillors before him. He made my little girl giggle, he drove the nail into the pine, he killed the chicken, he said the prayer over the food, and he rode the train across North Dakota sorting mail in the mail car, a .38 pistol strapped to his waist.

> *Daddy was a carpenter,*
> *He loved to cut and trim.*
> *Whenever I hear a power saw*
> *I always think of him,*
> *Nails in his mouth, hammer in hand*
> *Way up high on a ladder he'd stand.*
> *I think of him in his coveralls*
> *Packing up the tools as evening falls.*
> *The living leave, they move away,*
> *But the dead are with us every day.*
> *My old dad.*
> *My friends have drifted far apart*
> *But the dead are living in our heart*
> *My old dad.*

Mother languished in the big empty house for a while, a lonely widow with her memories, but family gathered around her, Linda and Stan and grandkids and nieces, and she rallied. Family meant everything to her. I bring my little girl to visit and she puts her cheek up to Grandma's ancient cheek, and the old lady murmurs with pleasure and the girl hugs Grandma, careful not to squeeze too tight, and the old lady says,

Ohhhhhh, I love you, and I stand a distance away. My girl is a hugger and I am not. Because my mother was not one when I was little. But she is now. A few years ago, she and Dad went to hear a Christian psychologist speak and it struck her hard when he said, "Do you ever tell your children that you love them?" and Mother realized to her horror that she did not and never had. It didn't bother us children—we could see perfectly well that she did—but it horrified her. I suppose her parents did not: with thirteen children, the expression of affection might be crowded out by sheer weariness. And besides, they were Scots, a tribe better known for murder ballads than for lullabies. But after the psychologist, whenever Mother talked to one of us, especially on the phone, she tossed in an "I love you, you know." I never heard Dad say it but I'm sure she spoke for him in the matter.

I am a man of many regrets, a multitude, and visiting her, I remembered the show I did years before at the Edinburgh Festival when I had invited my parents and Uncle Don and Aunt Elsie to fly over to Scotland for a couple weeks. I flew them first class, got them hotel rooms, a rental car, and when they showed up at my hotel in Charlotte Square to come to the show, I could not bear the thought of having Dad sit and listen to me tell stories about Lake Wobegon. It was too intimate. I had developed a conversational style on stage that I could not perform for my father. It was irrational, but I panicked at the thought of him seeing the show, he'd be twenty feet tall in the audience. I told them, "It's too cold and rainy. The show is under a tent. You'll catch cold." My mother said, "Do you not want us to come?" Finally, disappointed, confused, they went away. I saw them for breakfast in the morning: they were still confused and hurt. I still feel bad about it. They had forgiven me for leaving the Brethren and wanted to see the show, but I felt unable to perform in front of them—I was comfortable talking to strangers and not to family, particularly my father. Suddenly, in my mid-fifties, I was twelve years old.

I decided to atone for that and I offered her a trip to Scotland, which she declined ("I'm too old. It's too expensive."), a ritual decline, a habit in our family—we say "No, thank you" to all generous offers at least twice, sometimes three times, and thus we miss out on some wonderful things in this world that are only offered once—but I pushed the matter and told her she could take six people with her, and that caught her interest.

That gave her a stronger motive than the chance to see Scotland: the chance to be generous to family. And she agreed to go, in the company of my sister and her husband and a niece and her husband, and another niece, five of Mother's favorite people whom she felt easy and comfortable with. I told Camille, the travel agent, to make it deluxe and I, of course, stayed home. (To have the donor along would've meant a daily litany of gratitude and guilt.) My goal was to give a beautiful trip to a woman who'd been a lifelong scrimper, to enjoy in the company of her near and dear without worrying about extravagance. We wheeled her to the airport gate and she boarded in a festive mood, and was pleased to be in first class and didn't ask how much it cost, and according to my sister, she flew across the Atlantic in style, ate a hearty meal, and drank a glass of red wine. This was my small payment for two divorces, some unsavory jokes on the radio, and general neglect. The six of them stayed at the Ritz in London and rode the *Scotsman* to Edinburgh and then traveled around the Highlands in comfy bedrooms on a private train. I told Camille not to tell me how much it cost, and a week later she asked, "Are you sure?" and I said I was sure. Mother & Company visited the old family home in Redding and ate hearty breakfasts and enjoyed the Scottish tongue, the voice of her childhood, and the streets of Glasgow. She ate haggis. She made more trips in her nineties. Boarding a plane lifted her spirits: she, the old worrier who insisted we go to the southwest corner of the basement at the least tornado alert—she got happier as the plane rolled down the runway and rose into the air. She sometimes demurred ("It's too expensive") but only briefly and then she went off, wide-eyed as a teenager: Alaska, Florida, Paris, New York, Nova Scotia. And so the prodigal son tried to serve up fatted calf to his faithful mother and alleviate his regret. I gained independence early and as an adult never got to know John and Grace, and I regret that I didn't reach across the gap, though perhaps it was beyond my reach. But at least I could give her trips that made her eyes light up.

When Mother was 96, she told me in a lucid moment, "There's so much I'd still like to know, but there's nobody left to ask." A poignant line. She missed Elsie and Jean and other contemporaries whom she could talk to and stimulate her memory of Longfellow Avenue, weekends at the Hummel farm, the trolley to Anoka, the Keillor farm. To amuse her, I told a story on the radio about her career in the Denham Brothers, Canner & Campbell Circus, a tightrope walker and sharpshooter, Grace the Great, and Dad was a clown, standing blindfolded on the trunk of an elephant, a lit cigarette in his mouth, which Mother shoots with a pistol aimed over her left shoulder using a hand mirror. The hot coal explodes in a cloud of sparks, the elephant tosses Dad into a double backflip, landing on the elephant's back as his pants fall off, and the elephant steps forward on a switch that fires a midget out of a cannon who lands on Dad's shoulders, and the crowd goes crazy. I told this story and the next week she said, "That was nice what you said about me on the radio, but it's not true, you know." And she smiled. And then, for Mother's Day, I made her a star of Senior Women's Hockey known for playing rough. As she says, "Old age is not for the timid. I didn't get to be ninety-six by baking sugar cookies." I created my bad brother, Larry, who is awaiting trial for mail fraud. He sells Powerball Bibles with winning lottery numbers hidden in the first chapter of Leviticus and brokers enormous loans to evangelicals persuaded that the Lord will return before the due date. She said, "I am not going to let your brother rot in jail," and one day she got the drop on three US marshals and freed Larry at gunpoint and drove him to a grass landing strip south of Minneapolis and they took off in a small jet and made it to Venezuela, and there they are today, my little mom and her son the felon. She enjoyed hearing this; she told her caregiver, "He likes to make things up."

So much yet to know, but nobody's left. Her confidantes were all gone. An epoch, vanished. She was the last survivor on the island. Mother sits in the kitchen of the house Dad built and she murmurs to herself, audible but unintelligible, the cadence is that of conversation, and then she laughs. A very cheerful dementia. I guess she is reminiscing with her lost siblings, Elsie and Ina and George. A strategic dementia. Everyone's gone, so Mother has taken leave of the rational world, the comings and goings of family, the daily business of life, shopping and cooking and laundry—and she has gone to live in her imagination.

There she sits, creating a novel before our eyes, which can't be put in writing because that would destroy the perfection of it. Thus she escapes from a life in which she has nothing to do but sit and nobody to talk to who remembers the Fourth of July picnic in 1933 and the handsome farm boy and his crippled father whose arm Grace took, and she assisted him down the steps and into a chair on the lawn and held an umbrella over his head. She is very tender, living in her girlhood. One day she looks up and tells me to kiss her, which she never told me before. So I do. An old, old lady with snow-white hair brushed back, almost blind, her skin papery, reaching out to put her old hand on my hand—she sits, murmuring to herself, and her caregiver Ramona says, "She's praying for you."

And then alertness returns. She sits in the sunlight in the living room, a picture window with two full-length side windows forming a sunny alcove facing south. She tells us that Dad wanted to take a shortcut and omit the side windows, and Mother insisted he follow the plan. Now in her nineties, she sits in the alcove and feels the sun on her back, and she knows exactly where she is. She is at a historic site, where she won an important concession.

She listens to the show every week. Once I had the Lutherans of Lake Wobegon sing an old Brethren hymn, *How good is the God we adore, our faithful unchangeable Friend, whose love is as great as His power, and knows neither measure nor end. 'Tis Jesus, the First and the Last, Whose Spirit shall guide us safe home. We'll praise Him for all that is past and trust Him for all that's to come.*—and Ramona said Mother perked up and moved her lips to the words.

She lived her last days in the bedroom where Dad had died, my old bedroom, where I smoked Luckies and read Hemingway and imagined a literary career, where now I sit with my siblings, holding her hand, and we sing "Sweet hour of prayer" and "Blest be the tie that binds our hearts in Christian love" as she lies unconscious, breathing her last. She is fifteen feet from the kitchen where we stewed tomatoes in the pressure cooker every summer, forty quarts in Ball jars with Kerr lids. I'm so glad the folks came home to spend their last days in familiar rooms rather than in an anonymous death motel in Florida. Down below is the laundry room smelling of Hi-lex bleach, where she scrubbed clothes on a washboard and rinsed them in tubs and wrung them out by hand and hung them outside on the line. Beyond the bedroom window is the driveway where Dad worked on his car and the garage where he cut my hair. Across the hall is the closet where the Hoover vacuum stood, its handle the microphone into which I told jokes on "The Gary Keillor Show." We talked to her and held her hands, and then she was gone and I left the house and never went back. It remains in my mind exactly as it was in the mid-Fifties, a Sunday in summer, the comics pages spread on the living room floor, I'm in my Meeting clothes, pot roast in the oven, and Dad and the uncles sit and discuss cars as I read Skeezix and Dagwood and Little Iodine and Dick Tracy, and then Mother tells me to go out and pick a bagful of corn for dinner, the water is coming to a boil.

I broke away from John and Grace and caused them grief in the process but now we're at peace. She is very much alive for me whenever I stand on a stage and speak and hear people laugh and I feel close to him when I'm on a train. He dreaded the thought of spending his life milking cows and when he got a job sorting mail on the train he knew he was free. I like to ride his old run, St. Paul to Jamestown, but even more I feel his company when the Lake Shore Limited pulls out of Penn Station and into the tunnel under Park Avenue to emerge eventually along the shore of the mighty Hudson. A train heading north along water bound for the sea and he's there. When I'm in my eighties, I might start up a conversation with him.

I want to go back to the fall night in 1936 when John drove the Model A from Anoka down to Minneapolis to pick up Grace and take her away to lie on a blanket in the grass in a cemetery, their arms around each other, fumbling with each other's clothing. I want to stand at the gate and protect them from interruption. Two good Brethren young people, brought up with impossible standards, shamed for even slight dereliction of duty, ever aware of God's unwavering gaze, had spent five years thinking about each other over family opposition and the realities of the Great Depression and now they made love under the starry sky and conceived a child. After five years of uncertainty, this carnal sin finally joined them together. They faced the music and embarked on a life together, and what they didn't realize was that the sin freed them from the legalism of the Brethren, the judgmentalism, the arrogance, and made them loving and forgiving Christians. I guard the gate so nobody can call the cops. My life depends on those two lying in the grass behind the stone monuments. Thank you, Lord, and thank you, Uncle Bob, for lending John the car.

27

Mitral Valve

THAT SPRING OF 2001 I was inducted into the Academy of Arts and
Letters up on 155th Street, nominated by John Updike and Edward
Hoagland, a fine honor for Anoka High School and my teachers and
a shock to me. Standing in front of the Artists and Lettrists was nice,
but the people who should've been there, Mr. Buehler, Warren Feist,
LaVona, didn't get invited. They would've been astounded. As for me,
a humorist needs to avoid distinguishment because comedy is not
about triumph, it's about shame and defeat. A humorist has a moment
of passion in a VW with a tall dark beauty and to avoid the stick shift
they get into the back seat, which is too tight for him to remove her
pantyhose, and he bangs his head on the ceiling and she has a laughing
fit and Erectile Disillusion occurs and of course he is disappointed but
he also thinks, "This is good, I can write about this," which I just now
did.

The Academy had always been hospitable to humorists: Mark Twain
was a charter member, George Ade got in, Finley Peter Dunne, the great
Don Marquis, Art Buchwald, Peter DeVries, Calvin Trillin, Ian Frazier,
and David Sedaris, so it was not like entering the Academy of Irish Setters
or Veterinary Aromatherapists. The ceremony did not make me dizzy,
I know who I am, a hardworking writer, one of thousands, a deadline
man, a monologist who occasionally wanders onto the high plateau of
novelisticism and the greenhouse of sonnetry. It was a shock to go in and
stand between Philip Roth and Harold Bloom at the urinal. Of course,
it would've been even more shocking to stand between Ann Beattie and
Joan Didion.

Being admitted into an august Academy is exciting for one in the amusement business as I am. The citation about me used the word "hilarity," which was kind of them and made me think of the young woman I saw in a vaudeville show in London, who played a very sexy "America" on the kazoo, fluttering and fiddling with her décolletage, and then very demurely dropped her drawers, pulled a second kazoo out of her bosom and stuck it up under her long skirt into a private place and proceeded to give us (we imagined, we dared to hope) a two-part rendition of "America," the alto part from her nether region, a very accomplished orifice duet, all with the innocence of a 4-H'er performing at the county fair. It was musically flawless, it bent the borders of decency, and it made some of us laugh our heads off.

A lady performed on kazoo,
And then she played music on two,
One in her kisser
And one in her pisser,
My country, America, 'tis of you.

I envied the elegance of her joke, the kazoo up the wazoo, and didn't want the induction into the Academy to tempt me to be distinguished and a couple weeks later, I did a beautiful vulgar parody of Paul Simon's "Sounds of Silence" with gagging and retching and farting that moved millions of listeners with visceral intestinal distress. (Fred Newman did the sounds, I was only the writer and singer.)

Hello darkness, my old friend
I have gone to bed again
Because a virus came in to me
And I'm feeling tired and gloomy
And my head hurts and I'm achy and I'm hot
And full of snot
I hear the sound of sickness.

A modest start but it went on to thrill every thirteen-year-old boy in the audience:

I came home and went to bed
And felt a throbbing in my head
And I'm getting the idea
I will soon have diarrhea.

What Fred did at this point can't be represented in print, but it was vivid and meaningful and made the room spin.

Why am I the one who's fated
To be so awfully nauseated
And something like silent raindrops fell
And what a smell
I hear the sounds of sickness

It was the only time public radio presented a man at the brink of regurgitation. "Sounds of Sickness" as done by Mr. Newman was absolutely in the "America" kazoo duet class.

It was quite a year, 2001. My father died, I got Academicized, I entertained thousands of thirteen-year-old boys with a song about vomiting, I began to notice my own dizziness and shortness of breath onstage, and then I flew down to Nashville to speak at Chet Atkins's funeral at the Ryman Auditorium, his designated eulogist. He died at 77, after a brain tumor and a stroke. He wrote me after the tumor that he was having to relearn the guitar and he sort of did—he played on the show after the stroke, though he could barely make chords. "I'm getting better," he said, "but I'm no Chet Atkins." We wheeled him out onstage, guitar in hand, to a big ovation, and we turned off his mike as Pat Donohue sat directly behind him and played Chet's part so well that nobody noticed. I visited him in Nashville after that and reminisced about our touring days—the flight on the charter plane that ran into heavy weather over the Rockies, and Paul Yandell said, "I can see the headline, *Chet Atkins and Garrison Keillor and Five Others Disappear in Storm*, and I'll be one of the Others"—Chet sat slumped down and never looked at me and didn't say much. I'm sure he felt wretched and he didn't want to be seen like that, old and sad, wrapped in an overcoat, holding a guitar on his lap, unable to play it. He wanted to be alone with Leona and his daughter, Merle.

So I slipped quietly away. There was no consolation, only family. In the eulogy, I quoted from his letters. He was a natural writer. He wrote: "I am old and still don't know anything about life or what will come after I am gone. I figure there will be eternity and nothing much else and I will probably wind up in Minnesota and it'll be January. What I do know is that Leona has stayed with me through four percolators. We counted it up yesterday. She is mine and she is a winner." I said, "Let us commend his spirit to the Everlasting, and may the angels bear him up, and eternal light shine upon him, and if he should wind up in Minnesota, we will do our best to take care of him until the rest of you come along."

The season continued, shows in Norfolk, Seattle, Memphis, Tanglewood, and Wolf Trap, I kept writing. *Once again we take you to the hushed reading room of the Herndon County Library for the adventures of Ruth Harrison, Reference Librarian.* A woman who loves classical literature but longs for illicit love. And then *Roy Bradley, Boy Broadcaster.* "Even hard words like *sagacious* and *hermaphrymnotic* flowed from his tongue like cream from a pitcher, thanks to his having grown up in the town of Piscacadawadaquoddymoggin." I felt wheezy on stage and to avoid panting on the air, I parked myself onstage behind the piano next to the drummer. Jenny mentioned the wheeziness to our cousin, Dr. Dan Johnson, who directed me to the Mayo Clinic where Dr. Rodysill listened to my heart for a minute or so and gave me the lowdown: mitral valve prolapse, the very defect that kept me off the Anoka football team and turned me toward newspapering. The defect that killed off several Keillors, including two uncles my age. A surgeon was summoned, Dr. Thomas Orszulak, who looked like the tenor Jussi Björling, was from Pittsburgh, the son of immigrants, the first in his family to go to college, a Harley enthusiast and a fly fisherman who tied his own flies. It was Monday. He had an opening on Wednesday morning. I'd planned to fly to Europe, and instead I went up to the cardiac unit. It all felt very straightforward, tremendously competent people around me. "Open-heart surgery," which was front-page news in my childhood, now a well-traveled road. I signed up for an early morning slot, July 25, 2001.

Tuesday afternoon, I drank a gallon of liquid laxative to empty my bowels, and a burly man came in to shave my groin. Father Nick came in and prayed with Jenny and me, and we took Communion. I slept well and took a shower at 5 a.m. and was anointed with antiseptic and given muscle relaxants and wheeled out on a gurney with my wife beside me, her hand on my shoulder, she kissed me twice and then into the chilly OR I went and was slid onto the glass operating table. A moment of pleasant chitchat with the anesthesiologist and then I was in a small boat in a deep fog, bumping up onto a sandy shore in the dark, surrounded by angelic beings with Minnesota accents, Erin and Erin and Cliff, who removed the tube from my mouth, a simple breathing tube but it felt like the tailpipe of my old Mercury, and they assured me that I was alive, and I've been grateful for that ever since. I was in the ICU and it was five hours later, and then Jenny was there to say hi and they wheeled me back to my room.

The first big test was urination: could I do it? The catheter was removed and—*he shoots, he scores!* I took a shower. I took a walk down the hall, holding a nurse's arm. The surgeon's assistant inspected the scar, the cardiologist took my blood pressure (*Excellent!*), Dr. Rodysill came by to explain the sewing of the mitral valve, the angelic beings dropped in, Jenny returned and sat on the bed, holding my hand.

I was glad to be surrounded by brisk Minnesota women in blue uniforms who sized up the situation when they walked into the room and went right to work. "So how are we doing then?" they said. They made small talk to put the patient at ease. They cared and their caring was not generic, they'd been brought up to care. And when I was released and went home, every sense was heightened, every day beautiful, to rise early and smell coffee and pick up the *Times* and be alive. I lay on the chaise in the backyard feeling the luxury of ordinary life and did the crossword and watched my daughter as she wrote *Daddy* in green chalk on the driveway. One afternoon, I saw her swinging high into the air on the Hooleys' rope swing, laughing on the backswing up into the branches of the apple tree and a gasp of delight in the moment of weightlessness, and then she put her feet down and skidded to a stop and toppled over in the grass, laughing. My girl.

She was delighted with her speech therapist, Amy, and her physical therapist, Kim, and her nanny, Katja, all of them working on her speech and agility deficits. She'd been diagnosed with verbal apraxia, which turned out to be only one aspect of the problem, and clearly, she *wanted* to be with people, she loved company, and wanted to take part in things. She sat with her Czech nanny Katja, and later Kaja, arms entwined, imitating how they crossed their legs and brushed back their hair, kissing their hands, praying to be in their club. Sometimes I'd say, "It's been a quiet week in Lake Wobegon, baby," and she recognized the line and laughed. Eventually she was diagnosed as having Angelman syndrome, a genetic slipup that can be catastrophic, but in her case, thanks to her mother's determination and the help of dedicated therapists and the grace of God, she grew up articulate and humorous and good-hearted, and whatever her deficits may be, she makes up for with a sense of comedy.

Maia and GK, 2001.

Once we visited Prague with Kaja and sat near the Vltava, below the Castle, a stone's throw from the tourist mob on the Charles Bridge, near the Church of St. Nicholas, a big whoop of High Baroque with cherubs like glazed doughnuts and a marble bishop throttling Satan, near Franz Kafka's house on Celetná Street. He dreaded noise, footsteps, the gramophones of neighbors, his sisters' canaries, the bonging of church bells, the jangling town hall clock—he felt like he was living in a bowling alley. Now the town square is packed with tourists videotaping the clock, which has apostles instead of cuckoos, and drinking beer and listening to jazz bands. Kafka's problem was the lack of a daughter. He should've gotten his fiancée Felice pregnant and today the word *Kafkaesque* wouldn't mean "nightmarish" or "weird," it'd mean *funny.* "What do you name a guy with no feet? Neil." "Very Kafkaesque."

A month later, I was on the move. *Lake Wobegon Summer 1956* came out, and I did the usual book tour, two cities a day, two readings in two theaters. The book did well enough, and Viking signed me to write three more. The tour took me to New York for a reading September 10 at a bookstore in Union Square. A good crowd for a Monday evening. I talked about parts I had omitted from the book I was promoting, then stood around and signed copies. It was almost midnight when the last dog was hung. Holly and Dina from Viking were still there and Anne (Dusty) Mortimer-Maddox, a friend from *New Yorker* days, and we four crossed the square to a seafood restaurant on the south side of 14th. The place was packed and the maître d' led us to a table on a narrow balcony, and we camped there for two hours over martinis, oysters, scallops and linguini, some not-bad wine, and talked. Dusty and I gossiped about the old crowd at the magazine. She talked about the filthy barroom language that Pauline Kael liked to put in her movie reviews to get Shawn's goat. Kael once referred to an actress as "a walking advertisement for cunnilingus" and Mr. Shawn wrote in the margin: *Why does she do this? Why?* It was a splendid fall night, festivity in the air and New York magnificence. We could see the lights of the World Trade towers downtown. Holly said that 1 a.m. in Manhattan made her feel as if she were twenty-four again and just arriving in the city. Dusty announced that she was seventy but felt thirty-seven. "Aging is the opportunity of a lifetime," I said. We were all feeling oddly ecstatic, sitting up there above the canyons of lights, working people who've allowed themselves to stay up late on a warm September night, and seven hours later, two airliners crashed into the towers and fire and smoke billowed up and office workers leaped to their deaths and valiant firefighters hauled hose up the stairways and an hour later the buildings collapsed.

I was in my kitchen on 90th Street that morning, and heard a big plane flying low over the Hudson, and half an hour later a friend called and said, "Turn on your TV." I didn't have one so I went over to Docks, where a crowd was clustered in the bar, watching a news clip of people falling, arms outstretched, from high floors. It was too painful to watch. Men and women who walked these streets with us had, on a Tuesday morning, found themselves engulfed in horror and death. We read in the *Times* how many of them stifled their panic and looked out for the others on their floor and many of them, seeing that death was inescapable, called home on their cellphones to say, "I love you. Take care of the children. Have a good life." They called in the midst of smoke and panic to give a benediction. Weeks later, the city released some of the 911 calls from the Trade Center, the woman on the 83rd floor, overwhelmed by smoke, crying, "I'm going to die, aren't I? I'm going to die." A man on the 105th floor, gasping for breath, who screamed, "Oh my God" as the building started to collapse. They were people whom we might have sat near in a theater or restaurant, who suddenly found themselves facing the abyss, and firemen ran into the building to save them and died in the collapse, and it was all on TV. And then the politicians came out of hiding to seize the day, and Mr. Giuliani put on his public face and Mr. Bush mounted the wreckage with bullhorn in hand and vowed vengeance. The cops and firemen who climbed the stairs represented New York at its most courageous and caring, and the self-aggrandizing Giuliani was New York at its money-grubbing worst. He went around giving speeches on leadership for a hundred grand a shot, getting standing ovations as a stand-in for the police and firemen who died because police helicopters who looked down at the inferno and saw that the buildings would collapse couldn't get word to the fire chiefs on the ground who sent their men up the stairs to die. Giuliani had known about the radio problem for years and failed to get it fixed, and in the patriotic fervor post-9/11 escaped blame. Meanwhile, Bush, who had ignored earlier intelligence warning of terrorists flying planes into tall buildings, claimed Iraq had weapons it didn't have and sent 4,000 American men and women to die in an evil mess with no clear purpose and no end. It was a wretched time in American history. Those lives were not given for their country, they were taken, stupidly and carelessly. Politicians sacrificed them.

Two nights later, my neighbors Ellie and Ira and I went down to the

Village for dinner. Smoke in the air, trucks of debris roaring past, and yet New Yorkers were eating supper in outdoor cafés, resuming normal life as an act of resistance. *You tried to blow us up: we'll show you, we'll go out to eat.* It was an Italian restaurant, we talked for two hours, and not a word was said about the death and destruction. We talked about everything ordinary because we had no right to comment on the horror. We had read about the heroism of firemen who dashed into the burning towers, dragging hose up the stairways, who felt deep down the direness of the situation, a hundred-story tower with a huge gaping hole in the mid-dle—dashing into the building went against basic human instinct. But there were people trapped above so up they went. Nobody cared to be the first to turn tail and head for safety. We thought about them in silence, eating our linguini in clam sauce. Heroism on such a scale demands you revise your views of your fellow man.

The next Friday evening, a spontaneous event: thousands of residents stood outside their apartment buildings, holding lit candles, singing about the spacious skies and the land of the pilgrims' pride. I walked around the Upper West Side listening to it, a wholly other New York than anything I'd seen before. At LaGuardia, when I resumed the book tour, I met a young man who'd been on the 61st floor of the south tower, taking a training program. He said, "It was the worst day of my life, and the best." He looked radiant. I didn't ask how he escaped, and he didn't say. I talked to Jenny back in Minnesota: musician friends of hers went to a church near Ground Zero to play music for salvage workers on their rest breaks. They went day after day to play Mozart and Haydn.

September 11 was a tragedy, and the tragedy was George W. Bush standing on the smoking ruins and promising revenge and promoting the fiction that war in Iraq and Afghanistan was to defend the country against terrorism. Congress, which once spent an entire year investigat-ing a married man's attempt to cover up an illicit act of oral sex, showed little curiosity about a war waged on false premises that killed hundreds of thousands and led our own people to commit war crimes and squan-dered hundreds of billions of dollars.

I loved the road, doing solo shows after 9/11. Ann Arbor, Tulsa, Fort Pierce, East Lansing, Santa Cruz. Five nights in five cities, then the Saturday broadcast. I worked on a new book on the plane, arrived in a town, got to the hotel, took a nap. Walked to the theater, walked in the stage door, said hello to the crew, paced for ten or fifteen minutes, then took my place behind the curtain and made my mind go blank. The stagehands relax by the rope rigging, an easy night for them, accustomed to loading in massive sets and flies, and tonight, it's one microphone and one wooden stool. The house lights dim to half, the recorded announcement about turning off your cellphone, and the crowd waits, whispery— then I drift out into the spotlight, into the applause falling like warm rain. I stop and bow. And I sing:

> *Here I am, O Lord, and here is my prayer:*
> *Please be there.*
> *When I die like other folks,*
> *Don't want to find out you're a hoax.*
> *I would sure be pissed*
> *If I should've been an atheist.*
> *Lord, please exist.*

And then segue into "My country, 'tis of thee," and the audience sings, and "God Bless America," and that takes care of September 11th, no need for comment, and I walk back and forth, talking, picking out faces in the crowd, talking about Lake Wobegon, about my classmate Julie who liked to wrestle with me in sixth grade, the Boy Scout winter camping trip when I left the tent to pee and my extreme modesty made me wander far into the woods and almost freeze to death. The Uncle Jack story, in which his old wooden rowboat springs a leak in the middle of the lake and I try to stop the leak with my bare foot and he cries out *O Captain! my Captain! our fearful trip is done, the ship has weathered every rack, the prize we sought is won.* And the story about the pontoon boat carrying the Lutheran pastors that capsized in the wake of the speedboat and the great dignity with which they toppled overboard. There are good laughers in the crowd, a cackler, a whooper, and a guy who sounds like an old truck engine turning over. People laughing at the stories and also at the laughter. At the end, the audience and I sing "Good Night, Ladies," "Goodnight, Sweetheart," "Happy Trails," "Red River Valley," and I bow and exit to applause and stand behind the curtain, counting to ten. In theaters of a couple thousand seats all full of people, the audience is excited by its own applause, so you don't take it too personally. You count to ten and if you hear diminution, you walk away, but if it's holding steady, you walk out for another bow. My friend, the conductor Dennis Russell Davies, showed me how to bow years ago, and I try to do it right: stop, hold out your hands to the crowd, smile a genuine smile, bend, look at your fly for a count of five, stand, smile, march off. After the encore bow, the applause fades quickly—the show was two hours long and the audience is older and aware of its bladders so I walk backstage, where the stagehands sit around a table, eating the last of their supper, an awkward moment since they have no idea who I am or what it was I did out on stage—they're jazz guys, maybe C&W, but I always stop to say thank you, and then out the stage door I go and down the alley and cross the street and slip in the side door of the hotel and ride the elevator to the sixth floor and my room. Take off the suit and shirt and tie. Take my meds. Crawl into bed, feeling good—I gave good value to a couple thousand people and enjoyed doing it—and fall asleep. Up at 5. Make coffee. Three precious hours before I leave for the airport, the best time for work, so I go to it. There is always more to do. A writer's job never ends. This is a good life, an easy life. I hope it never ends, knowing it will.

28

You've the Top

I was set out on the writing road at the age of fourteen, handing a story to Red at the Linotype, reading the galley, watching the flatbed press slap out the *Herald*s and bundle them up and stayed on it, reading the *New Yorker* Mr. Anderson gave me, and reading Roger Angell's letter accepting "Local Family Makes Son Happy," and five years later the radio show appeared and gradually the work got to be fun. You start out with ambition and perseverance and with good luck and a boost from friends you get some outlandish good breaks and eventually, Lord willing, you may find yourself in the land of delight. "Sounds of Sickness" was a delight: to vandalize an anthem of idealism with lavatory humor and reduce the audience (most of them) to a puddle was a joy.

Writing "Guy Noir, Private Eye" was easy work but work nevertheless. What gave me joy was songwriting, which had never been my ambition—I wasn't a singer by trade, didn't play guitar, had no urge to write a song that moves a crowd into standing with arms waving back and forth in the air and weeping and thereby making the world a better place—songwriting was purely for recreation. I like to write rhymed verse, limericks, sonnets, song lyrics, it's all the same. It wasn't about creativity, I stole freely. I wrote new words for Jacques Offenbach's lovely "Barcarolle."

I once learned to play melodies
Even the difficult parts
By bending down and gently releasing
Lovely melodic farts.

I was a promising baritone
Off on an opera career,
But many more people wanted to hear
Music come out of my rear.

I did a show from Rochester, home of the Mayo Clinic, and wrote new words to "The Glory of Love"—*I'd give you my blood, give you my kidney, 'cause God told me to take care of you, didney, so I'm sticking with you everywhere, I'll manage your meds and push your wheelchair. No matter what, you're my story, whether or not you are ambulatory. That's not theory, it's the reality, dearie, of love.* It was the childish pleasure of rhyming "kidney" with "didn't he" and "theory" and "dearie." A child could do it. Children do do it. So did I.

Unlike other songwriters who had to wait months for their work to see the light of airplay, I wrote mine on Friday and sang them on Saturday. Sang them once and never again.

And then I rediscovered Cole Porter's "You're the Top," the raggedy 1934 hit with the sweet backbeat in which he rhymed "symphony by Strauss" with "Mickey Mouse," and "summer night in Spain" with "cellophane," the first person ever to think of that. The tune kept going through my head so I wrote new words to it.

You're the top
You're Honolulu
You're the whop
Bop a be bop a lula
You're so terrific, you're a South Pacific home
You're Barack Obama, you're the Dalai Lama, you're the pope in Rome.
You're Bill Gates,
You're Laurel and Hardy,
The candidates
Of the Republican Party
I'm a tragedy, a schlump from the Midwest
But if, baby, I'm the bottom, you're the best.

The Porter rhythm was irresistible, and I was hooked on it and did a version for Nashville:

You're Earl Scruggs
You're Jerry Douglas.
You're some hugs
When I've been hugless.
You're a pecan pie with a satisfying belch
You're an opera house, you're Alison Krauss, you're Gillian Welch.

I could not stop myself. I was addicted. And the Cole Porter Estate did nothing to stop me either. For a show at Goshen College, I did "You're the Top" for Mennonites, surely a first, and they sat and listened in awe-struck wonder:

You're the top
You're Anabaptist
You're the whop
When the truth just slapped us
You're pacifists, who persist in seeking peace
You're in the business, of forgiveness, may your tribe increase
God has promised
You will rise like eagles
You're like Amish
But with motor vehicles
I'm a fallen sinner utterly contrite
But if, baby, I have fallen, you're upright.

It was so much fun rewriting Porter (*You're the FBI, Guy Noir, and Scotland Yard. You're Giuseppe Verdi, the Bach concerti, you're the National Guard*) and people loved hearing it so I kept at it (*You're the cloth on my down pillow. You're Philip Roth, you're Don DeLillo.*) and nobody suggested I stop so I didn't (*Goodness knows, you're worth knowin', like Francine Prose or Leonard Cohen*) because if the great Cole Porter could get delicious delight from rhyming in metrical timing, then why shouldn't I?

This sense of delight I trace to a decision I made in 2002 when I was with my family on a cruise to Alaska and after a year of worrying about it I simply stopped drinking. Moderation didn't work for me, and I didn't want to join a group and sit in a circle of folding chairs in a church

basement and talk about my emotionally distant father. I had an enormous capacity for wine and liquor and could do two stiff martinis and
half a bottle of Barolo and a snifter of brandy and still talk in sentences
and walk without holding on. I didn't want to keep going down this
path and become a debauched nobody and cause anguish to my wife
and embarrass my little girl and be pitied by friends, and in my mind,
an alcoholic is someone who can't stop, so I decided to stop and not be
one and not have to go into a 12-step program. Fear of therapy led me to
change bad behavior. I'd been wayward long enough, time to straighten
out. And I did. I made no announcement. My mantra was *It's easy to quit
drinking so long as you don't drink.* Jenny noticed, and it came as a relief
to her. I got back my good mornings when I woke up clearheaded with
good ideas and could edit with a bold hand. A good early start leads to
cheerfulness that lasts the day.

I'd drunk whiskey to loosen myself up, but actually it made me
gloomy. Sobriety made me giddy. I started writing funny songs. It was a
sweet mystery.

*When God created Woman
He gave her not two breasts but three
But the middle one got in the way
So God performed surgery.
And Woman stood in front of God
With the middle breast in her hand
She said, "What can we do with the useless boob?"
And God created Man.*

In my giddy sobriety, I became enamored of the name *Piscacadawadaquoddymoggin* and started sticking it in scripts every week. We worked
our guests into the scripts, if they were willing, and most were, and we
made a running joke of putting *Piscacadawadaquoddymoggin* into the
guest's lines, which made some of them blanch during the sound check
but we assured them that it would draw a big laugh, which it did. And so
Jack Lemmon, Martin Sheen, John Lithgow, Meryl Streep, John Cleese,
Kelli O'Hara, Cokie Roberts, Walter Bobbie, Elvis Costello, Ira Glass,
all found the P-word staring up at them—and it focused their minds

but good. The fans in the audience knew the word was coming when the illustrious thespian approached the mike, paper in hand. Of course, he or she had been coached—the stress is on the third syllable and also the *quod*—and nobody fluffed utterly, but the anticipation of fluffage was fun to watch. Renée Fleming did it, as Renata Flambée, and Allison Janney as Carol Toledo of San Diego, and Emanuel Ax as Max Sanders, and maybe the line was *Piscacadawadaquoddymoggin on the Penobscot peninsula* and maybe they'd try to sell me a preparation made from pumpkin, peppers, peapods, peach pits, poppy seeds, purple peppers, and papyrus protoplasm that could cure priapism, pimples, impropriety, palpitations of the pupil, perspiration due to plumpness, and a propensity for pomposity. The guest who traversed all the pops and whistles got plenty of applause.

I was sober and flying high and the show was doing well, I bought a black Armani suit and a seersucker one for outdoor shows. I bought a bigger laptop. I had too much money, which gave me the chance to be stupid about real estate. Real estate ads were my pornography—I came close to buying a stone house on the Isle of Harris, it was insanity. I bought eighty acres of Wisconsin farmland and built on it, then realized I was a city guy and rural quiet made me uneasy. I grew up rural and rode my bike into the city and now I belonged there. By rights, I should have a legal guardian in real estate matters. I opened a bookstore, Common Good Books, a good deed that turned into a cash drain. It opened in a cellar under a coffee shop at Selby and Western in St. Paul: hundreds of people who walked by never noticed the tiny OPEN sign. I painted quotations from old heroes on the walls: *Where you come from is gone, where you thought you were going to was never there, and where you are is no good unless you can get away from it. —Flannery O'Connor.* But she and Updike and Roth, who painted recognizable American landscapes, were gone and the customers wanted novels about growing up abused and ostracized: ostracization was very big. The humor shelf was untouched, people preferred memoirs by widows, orphans, the mortally ill, mentally unstable, recovering fundamentalists, drug-dependent dental hygienists, that sort of thing. I was selling apples and people wanted zucchini. I lost a fortune. I was an absentee owner and when I walked in, the employees were shocked. The day I signed over the store to a new owner was a day of liberation. Someday I'll earn back the money with a memoir about bookstore ownership and how the loss of quality fiction led me to drug addiction.

My prosperity was the fault of Sally Pope who back in the Eighties came up with the idea of offering a Powdermilk Biscuit poster to listeners, and the show became a financial boon to MPR. The tidal wave of orders gave the station a fine mailing list to which they sent a catalog of PHC products, which became a for-profit business. A young secretary named Donna Avery was put in charge, and it turned into one of those inspiring success stories in which the nicest person is picked out of the chorus and becomes a star. She became the Goddess of Commerce, built Rivertown Trading, which began with Powdermilk posters, into an enormous success, and when it was sold, it contributed mightily to the MPR endowment. I visited the shipping center once and was astonished— acres of merch on pallets, conveyor belts, assembly line packing, trucks at the loading docks. Mountains of CDs, DVDs, T-shirts, caps. The radio station earned millions from it.

This financial boom stimulated the creation of a commissariat of vice presidents whom I didn't recognize because I was working all the time. They were like buzzards in a tree, defending their branch against other buzzards, feeding off the wounded below. They avoided me in the halls because clearly they found the show an embarrassment, the commercials, Piscacadawadaquoddymoggin, the gospel music, the joke shows. When you're the Executive Vice President for Interactive Synergy and you fly away to a public radio conference in Santa Barbara and the other attendees look at your name badge and ask you about a show with rhubarb pie commercials and stories about Norwegian bachelor farmers, you feel not just insulted but also degraded.

In 2002, I was, as I was in 1974, a man at a keyboard—from an Underwood typewriter to a Selectric, then a CPT word processor, a Toshiba laptop, finally a MacBook—trying to keep the balloon aloft. I'd had my illusions and taken wrong turns, but the show was real and the music authentic and the comedy sketches and stories rode on the back of the wagon, and its being a live broadcast saved us from perfectionism. We took short views. I don't remember what happened in 1991 or 2008 or 2012, but I remember what Thursdays were like, when the rubber hit the road, and the alarming rehearsal on Friday, and Saturday at 5 p.m. Central the show spread its wings and flew. And I remember the coroners moving onto the management floor and their resentment of the show's success. I don't remember the year it happened, just the chill.

In 2002, *Prairie Home* packed its bags and left the MPR building, an amicable disconnect under a new contract, and moved to an old one-story frame office building by the Soo Line tracks near the river, our home for the next fourteen years, which we called "The Fort." Everyone had an office with a window and a door; Kate had the big one because she ran the place. There was no time clock, people worked as needed to get the job done. There was a big lunchroom, and once a month a catered meal, sometimes a masseuse came in, and if you wanted to work from home, you did. This staff accomplished more than any other twelve people since the apostles. Weekly shows, tours, the annual Holland America cruise, a summer tour, books, CDs—it proved that friendly working conditions are conducive to good work.

It was a relief to make a home at the Fort. MPR had gone corporate during my years on the road and spoke a technometromatic language unintelligible to us civilians, and though Bill Kling still protected the show from people who talked about "content" and "metrics," he was loosening his grip, looking ahead to retirement, and I could feel the wolves watching from deep in the pines. The newsroom was enemy territory. Forty people working in tiny cubicles whose job was to fill small holes in *Morning Edition* and *All Things Considered.* There was no investigative journalism, not even a nod in that direction though everyone knew that public schools were in trouble, the Minneapolis Police Department was corrupt and beyond anyone's control, and the state legislature was a medieval fiefdom of powerful lords. The newspeople focused on the arts, authors, academics, the nonprofit world, the comfort zone of the liberal intelligentsia. It was the sleepiest newsroom in town. Whenever I walked past it, I could feel the chill. PHC had earned millions for MPR and what's more, we had a lot of fun doing it, and we were deeply resented by staff who, because they read the news in a college-educated voice, felt superior to the audience, and here was a tacky show with ketchup commercials and the damn *hymns*—what in hell is "Softly and Tenderly" doing on the same station that brings you the BBC News? And it was playing Tanglewood and Ravinia and Wolf Trap and selling all the seats, so it was beyond criticism. At the old KSJN, housed in cramped quarters, we rubbed elbows with news-people and classical music announcers, ate lunch together, knew each other's families, and now, having contributed to the company's bottom line, we lived among stone-faced people who wished we would die in a plane crash so they could write it up. As they say, *No good deed goes unpunished.*

I was teaching a class at the University, Composition of Comedy, and one week I flew back from New York for class and neglected to get back on Central Standard Time. I walked into the classroom, took off my coat, set my briefcase on the table, took out my notes about the importance of structure in comic writing, and smiled at the students and didn't recognize any faces. I leaned down and said to a girl in the front row, "This isn't composition, is it." She said, "No, it's trigonome-try." "Good," I said. "That's what I thought." And picked up my brief-case and coat and headed for the exit as a young man with a crew cut and clear-rimmed glasses arrived and set his briefcase on the table. He was the trigonometry guy. Not me. I was in the wrong place. That's how I felt about MPR. It was the home of the disgruntled, and I loved my job.

It was a happy time. I had a daughter who sat backstage and loved the women singers. I was sober. I ventured into philanthropy. I donated a saltwater swimming pool to a school and named it for my wife, who is a fearful swimmer. The audience was always lovely to behold. At a show at Tanglewood, a little girl in the front row fell sound asleep as people around her hooted and slapped their knees. She leaned her head against her mom and dozed off. A boy wrote to say that he loved Lake Wobegon because when it came on, his parents stopped fighting. A man died at a show at a winery near Seattle; he had been very ill for a long time but wanted to see the show and his wife brought him, and toward the end of the first hour he leaned against her and slipped away. She held him and during intermission, she told an usher and the EMTs came and carried him off.

I wrote a thousand songs. I wrote songs like some people make pies, occasional songs, nothing ever to sing again. I wrote a song for every stop on the way. The song about the Berkshires for a show at Tanglewood:

> *Under the bright blue Berkshire sky,*
> *cars with kayak racks go by*
> *the bakery where two old aunts*
> *sit with coffee and croissants*
> *and a ham and spinach quiche,*
> *and a small dog on a leash.*
> *Tourists holding bright brochures*
> *describing the sightseeing tours.*
> *Cellphone service is poor, or worse,*
> *so people sit down and converse*
> *with people a few feet away,*
> *as Emily Dickinson did in her day.*
> *As I do now, in your ear:*
> *I am happy to be here.*

I was a song machine, and Rich Dworsky improvised accompaniment. For Bend, Oregon (*Life is sweet at 3,625 feet and many people relocate to a city named for not being straight*) and Milwaukee (*In a city with so many breweries, how do they find people to serve on grand juries? Where Oktoberfest is not limited to Oktober, how many judges are sober?*) and Nantucket (*I am simply delighted to be in a town about which limericks are recited*). I wrote one about Los Angeles, sang it once at the Bowl. *No orange groves in Orange County. And Manhattan Beach? No way. Not much adventure in Ventura but you can bake in Bakersfield all day. Nothing surprising in Eureka, and San Jose—what can I say? Not much holy in Sacramento though it's sandy in San Diego Bay. Nobody's modest in Modesto but I admit I love LA. I feel empty in Yosemite. Take me away to LA.*

And having written one for LA, I wrote one a few weeks later for SF.

> *I walked in San Francisco in the fog and the mist.*
> *I went out a Lutheran, came back a humanist.*
> *Got back to the hotel and my spirit rejoiced:*
> *This town may be cold but by God it is moist.*

Richard Dworsky, music director.

I loved to write parodies of Dylan, who wrote so many great parodies of himself.

> *If not for you, I'd have no revenue,*
> *Never would've got through the U,*
> *I'd screw up my job interview, he totally screwed,*
> *One sad dude living in solitude in the nude,*
> *No aptitude to pursue,*
> *Wouldn't know beef stew*
> *From chicken cordon bleu,*
> *Or conditioner from shampoo, if not for you.*

Satire is perishable, like lettuce. The few songs of mine that still appeal are straightforward love songs. *I don't care about your wine list. I'll just have a glass of beer. I don't need to hear the specials. I just wish that she were here.* I wrote it when I was alone in New York and Jenny was on the road with City Opera and the city felt empty. I wrote one for my grandsons.

In the valley here we be, sitting on your daddy's knee, Freddie and his brother Charlie eating chocolate candy. Summer days I was a kid, all the funny things we did. When grownups came, we ran and hid, back behind the lilacs. In the heat of summer sun, round and round the yard we run, chase the dog and just for fun we put him in the sprinkler. Summer days my pals and I lay and looked up at the sky, wondered how do airplanes fly over Minnesota.

In my twenties, I aimed to be a satirist because it was an acceptable outlet for arrogance, and now, looking back, my *New Yorker* stories seem very dated, locked in the leather harness of irony. I loved the emotional freedom of the radio show that let me sing a lullaby to my child: *Little girl lost in a forest of dreams. For a moment it seems something big and cold got ahold of you. But Daddy's arms will gather you in. I will take you home. Where we go, there will be birds to cheer you. Where we go, I'll be right here near you. I will take you home.* The audience takes a deep breath, they recognize the feeling, they've been there, they appreciate freedom from irony, they feel comforted. My dad never put his arms around me that I recall. It doesn't matter. I was wealthy with aunts, and twenty years ago the last of them left the world while I wasn't looking and I wrote:

Goodbye to my uncles, farewell to my aunts.
One after another, they went and lay down
In the green pastures beside the still waters
And make no sound.
Their arms that held me for so many years
Their beautiful voices no longer I'll hear
They're in Jesus' arms and He's talking to them
In the rapturous New Jerusalem,
And I know they're at peace in a land of delight,
But I miss them tonight.

It's a good song. I still sing it now and then. When it comes to love, we are all amateurs. A person can develop fine skills of mockery, and, God knows, love makes us vulnerable to satire. You embrace your wife and speak tenderly and you hear the snickers of your teenage children. Love between the elderly is hilarious to them. Nonetheless, I hold her tight and grasp her rear end and the satirists go *Ewwww* in disgust, and this gives an old satirist like me pleasure, having love and being mocked for it, and also holding the finest of all buttocks. I have a framed photograph of my wife, naked, and when I die, I want it to come along with me, in the event I am accidentally buried alive. And also a flashlight.

29

Altman

ONE DAY I GOT ON the downtown B train at 96th and Broadway in Manhattan across the aisle from a young Black woman in a gray herringbone pantsuit, who, I noticed, was reading *Love Me*. I sat, watching her, trying not to stare. Young Black professional women are not supposed to be reading old white male humorists. She was way out of her demographic. She didn't laugh, but she kept reading, turning the pages through Times Square and 34th Street and 14th Street, past my stop, and I watched her. And then she smiled. And she laughed, quietly. An invisible thread connected us. I dearly wanted her to like me. I had worked two years on that book, and for fifteen minutes, it was all up to her, she held my heart in her hands. I don't care if the *Times* thinks it is immature, I wanted her to laugh. New York women keep a serious face on the subway, the equivalent of a DO NOT DISTURB sign, but I made her laugh. I almost walked over and said, "That's my book" but she might've said, "Hell it is, I bought it, back off, mister."

My career peaked with the publication of *Love Me*, but I didn't know it and I kept marching. I wrote a Lake Wobegon screenplay and Tony Judge called George Sheanshang, who was Robert Altman's attorney, and we learned that Mrs. Altman, Kathryn, was a regular listener to the show. *Aha! Connections! It pays to know the right people.* So a meeting was arranged, and I went to Altman's office in New York with his movie posters on the wall, *M*A*S*H, Nashville, Popeye, McCabe and Mrs. Miller*. He was 78, moving slowly, gruff, speaking in short sentences. He said his wife liked the show, that he often sat in the next room watching basketball on

TV and heard her laugh and came into her room to find out what she was laughing at. He did not say that he laughed along with her and I doubted that he had. I don't think small-town Minnesota was his territory.

The screenplay I offered him was about John Tollefson returning to Lake Wobegon for the funeral of his father, Byron, who died of a heart attack coming up from the basement with a bag of frozen peas. John had been fired from his TV weatherman job in Boston for having said, while forecasting a thunderstorm, the limerick about lightning coming out of the ass of the young man of Madras as he clangs his brass balls together and plays "Stormy Weather." He comes home in disgrace for his dad's funeral and falls in love with his old high school sweetheart and they marry. There was a lesbian couple who fight like cats and a drunken wake and a pissing contest. The story takes place in January. That is what killed it for Mr. Altman. He said, "I don't know if you've ever done location shooting in winter, but I have, and I don't plan to do it again. It's an interesting story except for one thing. The death of an old man is not a tragedy. So I don't get the point." He said he wanted to make a movie, though he was being treated for cancer and he would consider making a movie about a radio show and shoot it entirely at the Fitzgerald Theater. So I wrote him a new script in about a week, urged on by his illness.

He appeared quite frail when I saw him a month later; he walked gingerly across the Fitzgerald stage, as if on a tightrope, an assistant walking close behind him. I said, "Are you sure you really want to do this?" He was sure. "I want to go out with my boots on," he said. "I don't want to sit around and wait for it. I want to be missing in action." The producers had secured a relief director, Paul Thomas Anderson, who stood at Altman's elbow and was prepared to come in from the bullpen if needed. But the *going out with my boots on* made me wonder if bravery had overcome his good judgment—had I given him an amateur contraption of a screenplay and the man was desperate for work to take his mind off his mortality? I wondered about that for the next year: was it good enough? Being a Minnesotan, my answer was: no.

I mentioned to Jim Harrison that Altman was on the case and Jim, a great poet who'd worked on six movies in the Nineties, wrote me a letter.

Screenwriting is a visual, not a verbal, talent. You have to "see" every-thing you write and avoid the fandangos of words that we love. You go directly from the image to the word, never vice versa. Movies have to move. Don't worry about getting people in and out of doors. Audiences have a greater visual intelligence than any other kind. Reading books about it doesn't work. It's helpful to watch your five favorite movies and figure out how the writer constructed the narrative. Write the kind of movie you yourself love to watch. You can't do better than that because you're not a hack. Despite your Christian background you should have at least one 4-H girl bent over a bale of hay. Take all your money up front. A writer's percentage points are as valuable as gum wrappers.

Good advice, but I had no time to study five movies. I cranked out a screenplay about two singing sisters, Yolanda and Rhonda Johnson, and Mr. Altman said, "I think you've got something there." He lined up Kevin Kline to play Guy Noir and Woody Harrelson and John C. Reilly to be Lefty and Dusty. ("Casting is nine-tenths of what I do," he said.) He talked Meryl Streep and Lily Tomlin into playing the sisters. "Meryl is a terrific singer," he said. "And Lily will learn." I read an interview with Lindsay Lohan in which she said she was going to be in the movie playing Meryl's daughter, so I created the daughter. I wrote in the angel of death. "Okay to put a supernatural being in?" I emailed Mr. Altman. "Okay, but no special lighting effects," he said. He cast Virginia Madsen in the part, and when shooting began, he took a great deal of time fussing with the lighting as the angel walked unseen in the balcony. She was a radiant blond angel, and he loved directing her as she descended the balcony aisle, glowing in the dark.

I kept rewriting as Mr. Altman and his crew moved into the St. Paul Hotel in June, and truckloads of camera and lighting gear got unloaded in the alley behind the Fitz. I wrote a wheelchair version of the script after Meryl Streep had knee surgery and then she called to say she was ready to dance, so I rewrote the rewrite to un-handicap her, and then Mr. Altman saw Mickey's, a classic railcar diner around the corner and wanted to shoot a noirish scene there, so I wrote two, one for the open and one for an epilogue, and meanwhile the crew was laying down tracks for the dolly cameras and getting ready to start shooting. Mr. Altman did not flinch when I told him that I still had revisions in mind. He was an improviser himself. He kept encouraging his actors to toss in bits of business. John C. Reilly improvised a cowboy fart, and Altman approved with enthusiasm.

I met Meryl and Lily at the Fitz the Sunday night before shooting started. They had been rehearsing songs, and they wanted me to hear them. Meryl wore a red skirt and poofy white blouse, and Lily was in jeans and denim jacket. They claimed to be nervous and flounced around and got all girlish and then launched in. Meryl sang lead, Lily alto, and the harmonies were perfect, sweet and sisterly, pitch perfect. It made me want to rewrite the whole script and make it about them and send everyone else home.

Altman and I went to lunch and I got him to talk about World War II, which Kathryn said he never did. I asked him if it was true, as I'd read, that he lied about his age to enlist and he said it was. "A lot of young men did," he said. "It was a very different time. We believed in good and evil." He got into the Army Air Forces and became a very young bomber pilot, flying B-17s against Japanese installations in the South Pacific. It was a roaring loud plane, freezing cold at high altitudes, no fun to fly, but he survived, and it occurred to me that maybe that was what made him a fearless independent. When you've wrestled with the controls of a roaring machine, freezing your ass off, as people below are shooting at you, why would you worry about last-minute rewrites and improvisation?

I reported for work in the morning. A trailer for makeup was parked on Exchange Street, and a commissary wagon where you could order an omelet and pour yourself a cup of coffee. And there, eating breakfast, were a dozen old pals from the early days who'd been signed up as extras, the Powdermilk Biscuit Band, the Brandy Snifters, Peter Ostroushko, Butch Thompson, about to make their Hollywood debuts. I walked into the theater and the lobby was a warehouse of lighting gear and props. Young production assistants were buzzing around, and one of them handed me three pages of script, the day's shoot, and there was my name. As an actor. I got to sing a duet with Meryl, which I saw later on video playback—she is luminous, startling, gives off waves of feeling, and I look like the liability guy from State Farm. I did a scene with Lindsay in which she walked over, her eyes brimming with tears, and accused me of being a heartless jerk. I had written her lines but nonetheless she made them sting. We did the scene six times, and each time her eyes brimmed and the lines stung.

I did a scene with Virginia Madsen in which I chewed an apple. Kevin Kline said my chewing was evocative. And almost every day, I reported to the theater with rewritten scenes in hand. "Are those for today?" a producer said, turning pale. "The actors already memorized the pages from yesterday." "Bob said it'd be okay," I said, which was a lie, but the changes got put in. In between scenes, Kevin sat and played the piano, so I wrote him a scene in which Guy Noir sits and noodles and sings a few lines from Robert Herrick, with a bust of F. Scott Fitzgerald on the piano. Why not? I wasn't going to make a career of this, so I might as well have a good time.

One day Lindsay handed me the shooting script for the next day and said, "You aren't going to make me say all that, are you?" She was right: I'd stuck her with a whole page of exposition, a big doughy lump of speech. So I rewrote it into a scene. They shot it. It went well. It was interesting to see that Miss Lohan, a hot item in gossip columns at the time, was so intelligent about her line of work. She knew crappy writing when she saw it and she said so.

Altman loved his work, loved being on the set in the hubbub with the crew, the extras, the people with headsets and clipboards—he'd yell, "What am I waiting for? Let's boogie!" He could bark at cameramen and producers, but he was tender with the talent. He studied Meryl and Lily on the set, sitting before a long mirror, Lindsay reclining on a couch—Meryl and Lily are the Johnson sisters, reminiscing about their glory days on the road, and Lindsay is Meryl's daughter, writing a poem about suicide—a gorgeous dressing-room set, all lamps and mirrors, festooned with photos and souvenirs, bejeweled gewgaws, jars of cosmetics, posters, showbiz memorabilia, which the designer Dina Goldman created in a bare basement. Altman sat in his high canvas chair in the shadows, having instructed his son Bobby on the timing of the dolly shot, and he says, "Let's do one." A distant warning buzzer. Vebe Borge, the assistant director, calls out, "Quiet on the set." Mr. Altman leans in and peers at his monitor, and here we go again. The scene ends, and he says, "That was beautiful. Let's do it again." It was a good scene. I wanted to redo the whole story, make it a three-character dressing-room movie, no radio show, but the shoot was in its fifth week. *Dang it.* On the last night, after Meryl did her last shot and was officially released—at

2 a.m., standing in the intersection of 7th and St. Peter in downtown St. Paul—she hugged everybody and grinned and said, "Don't have any fun without me." A true benediction. A bunch of us stood around that night watching Altman shoot his last scene, at Mickey's Diner, its interior like the Hopper painting *Nighthawks*, two patrons at the counter, a counterman in white, and then Kevin Kline as Guy Noir emerging, lighting a smoke, and crossing the rain-soaked street. There were six takes. Altman conferred with him after each take, discussing the angle of the scratch of the match alongside the door, the gesture of lighting, the exhalation, the path across the street. Both of them seemed completely absorbed in this simple wordless action.

And that was the end of it. Bob edited the movie that fall, and it opened at the Fitzgerald the following May. Meanwhile he had directed an Arthur Miller play and started production on a new movie. He died in action in November before shooting could start. A great man, and his last scene was the one he shot in St. Paul, about 5 a.m. He wanted to keep going, but the sun was coming up and you can't stop the sun. I went to his memorial service in LA and heard a number of standard eulogies (*How This Great Man Enabled Me to Become the Artist I Am*) and instead of that, I told about his war service, the teenager at the controls of a monster plane, freezing cold, anti-aircraft fire coming his way, on a bombing run in the South Pacific. It's good to have fresh material. People listened.

I truly wish I thought it was a good movie, but I don't. Some critics liked it, and I was thrilled unreasonably when *Rolling Stone* liked it. It's their obligation, in behalf of their Midwestern readership, to kick me in the shins.

> Prairie *goes down so easy that you probably won't notice at first how artfully it's done. . . . I don't know how this movie works, only that it does. For those, me included, who used to think of Keillor's radio program as tepid, self-indulgent, repetitive and flat, you might even call it a revelation. Take a swig of this moonshine. There's magic in it.*

I didn't mind the "tepid, self-indulgent, repetitive and flat" at all—I'd thought the same myself often enough—and I wish I agreed with the word "artfully" but don't. I saw the final cut twice, and that was more than enough: I could feel all the last-minute rewrites, the jumpy edits, the lines that made my head hurt. It made me admire J. D. Salinger for refusing to let anyone make a movie of *Catcher in the Rye* or *Franny & Zooey*. Salinger loved movies, and he also felt that some things belong on the printed page and nowhere else. It was fun working with Altman. I wish I'd given him something better.

A couple years later, I was having lunch at the Cafe Luxembourg in New York and Meryl Streep walked over and kissed me on the cheek.

Jenny Lind Nilsson and GK at the movies, New York, 2006.

Miss Streep is a radiant being who emits light, and all eyes are on her most of the time. She said, "I love long slow elegiac movies in which not much happens, and you wrote a good one," and planted two smackers on me. The café was full of show people and their agents and attorneys, and all of them saw it and I was momentarily very, very famous even if some people couldn't remember my name.

30

Ingenuity! Art! Good luck! Goodbye!

I FOUND MY WAY TO the Episcopal church after I married Jenny at St. Michael's and went to 10 a.m. Sunday Mass when I was in New York and knelt in the cramped pew, sometimes thought of the tall girl in the VW, sometimes thought of my old college classmate Denis Wadley, a staunch liberal and devout Catholic. I had some anti-Catholic prejudices from reading about thin-lipped celibate priests denying birth control to impoverished Irish families, but he and I became friends. He earned a doctorate from Oxford and taught high school English in Minneapolis, and he died of cancer in his mid-fifties. He wrote about his approaching death, saying that Christians "have the presence of mind to consecrate inevitable suffering as part of the mystery of the cross, and by allowing that to remain a mystery, everything else is clarified. Dismiss it, and everything becomes mysterious, because nothing is fully answered. The church provides structure in the form of sacraments and defense of this revelation; and no one is more free and content than one committed to an outlook that holds that, contrary to all appearances, the spirit is the substance and the material is transitory."

The cradle Episcopalians go down on one knee and genuflect *shoulder to shoulder, spectacles to testicles,* but I grew up evangelical and we don't do ballet. Still, it's good to be here, removed from the weight of ambition, the dread of old age, at peace with my life and grateful to God for

His steadfast love. We rise and sing praise to the Creator, we hear from Isaiah and David and St. Paul and we sing *Blest be the tie that binds* as the priest and a deacon and the acolytes process down the aisle, the teenagers so tall and solemn as they hold the candles high, I am moved by the solemnity of teenagers, and we hear the Word of Our Lord. The homily loses me, too literary, so I write a limerick in the bulletin instead.

The book that we call Revelations
Is full of tremendous sensations
Of fear and trembling
And legions assembling
And the devastation of nations.
It was written by John
In a hot marathon,
Who was on some strong medications.

We stand to recite the Creed and kneel to say the prayers together and I think prayerfully of friends and family, my elderly classmates passing from the world, and I give thanks for eagerness and avidity in my old age and for my lively wife who is sleeping late this morning, and then it's time to shake hands with all in my vicinity and declare the peace of the Lord, and then the offering. I go forward for Communion as we sing *I will raise them up on the last day* and I can't sing, I'm crying. I grew up among Tightly Closed Brethren and now in my old age I am accepted at the Lord's Table at last and this moves me. I listen to the benediction and the rackety postlude and then the priest in the back of the sanctuary calls out the charge to go forth and do that which we've been put here to do. I was put here to write. And I head home to do that.

It felt more urgent, what with my seventieth birthday ahead. I thought about the boy whose mother towed him up to me in the Minneapolis airport where I was waiting to board a plane to Seattle. I was waiting at the end of the line so my fellow Minnesotans wouldn't see that I was sitting in first class. The boy's name was Jared, he was eleven. His mother said, "He loves your poetry. He's memorized a lot of them." When she said "poetry," I thought she meant sonnets, but no—she poked him and Jared said in a bright clear voice:

A young fellow from Pocatello
Said, "Why is my urine bright yellow?
Was it something I ate
Or maybe it's Kate
Who I dated on Saturday—hello!"

And he knew:

A young Baptist lady of Aspen
Fell down groanin' and gaspin'.
She thought she'd been bit
By a snake on her tit
But it was her Sunday School class pin.

And:

The young fellow answered an ad
And was hired and cried, "I'm so glad
To be given this chance
I could pee in my pants"
And we looked and saw that he had.

An alarming moment. Suddenly, waiting to board a plane, you've been informed what your legacy will be. You were hoping for better, but the Jared generation will decide. You will have no say in the matter. You hoped to be a journalist and actually you are a urinologist.

My aunts and uncles were gone, my friends were dying. Tony Judge and I went to see Studs Terkel in Chicago in 2008 as he was dying, and he wasn't eager for visitors but he was defenseless, 96, sunk in a deep chair, his walker nearby, a bottle of J&B within reach, smoking a cigar and nibbling blueberries, newspapers strewn on the floor. Born 1912, shortly after the *Titanic* sank. Studs used to say, "The *Titanic* went down and I came up." But now he said, "Ninety-six is enough. I've had my share. I'd like to check out. Let me tell you, kid, ninety-six is no picnic."

I studied Studs because I'm thinking about hitting 96 myself and not stop along the way. It appeared that cigars and Scotch might be critical to success. His legs were gone, his bowels didn't work right, his old friends were in the ground, but he was still lively and he did most of the talking because he was nearly deaf. He recalled the days of con men like Kid Pharaoh and Titanic Thompson who in 1928 lifted a half-million bucks off the gambler Arnold Rothstein in a rigged card game at the Park Central Hotel, back when Capone and Bugs Moran ran the town and if you handed a cop a ten he wouldn't bother you. Back when Smith & Wesson was standard apparel. A poke in the snoot was the modus operandi. The old man loved to say "modus operandi." "Titanic Thompson was the leading card mechanic of his day," the old man said. "He knew how to shuffle a deck and change the weave." Rothstein was the guy who put the "organized" in organized crime and fixed the 1919 World Series. He was no novice. He realized he'd been snookered and refused to pay up, which was not sporting of him, so they shot him, and on his death bed he refused to rat on the killer. He told the cops, "My Mudder did it." Meeting the old man, I was shaking the hand that shook hands with the man who knew the man who beat Arnold Rothstein at cards. There is grandeur to that.

Studs was dying and he was worried about his hero Barack Obama. The election was approaching. Was America capable of electing a Black president? He doubted it. I told him Obama was a cinch, but Studs was wary of cinches. He got his education in the lobby of his mother's hotel where he listened to the unemployed railroad men and alcoholic typesetters and old Wobblies argue about capitalism after the Depression crashed down. He got a law degree, became a radio actor, and in 1948 went into TV, then in its infancy. He was the host of *Studs' Place* on NBC and was headed for New York and maybe stardom when an American Legion guy named Ed Clamage accused him of being a commie. He'd signed petitions against lynching, poll taxes, Jim Crow, and Studs was asked to sign a loyalty oath and on principle he declined and New York canceled him, and so, in his mid-thirties he was saved from premature success and found his long happy career as a populist historian (*Working, The Good War, Hard Times*) and radio talker on WFMT. As with me, failure had served to close the door to rooms he shouldn't have gone in anyway. Now death was closing in, he was puffing on his Roi-Tan, worrying about the election. But he declined sympathy. He had canned beef

and biscuits in the cupboard and some bottles of 1938 Margaux plus a
case of Scotch and a hundred-year-old cognac. He totters to the door and
bids farewell to the search party and gives his benediction:

> *Every night when the sun goes down*
> *I say a blessing on this town:*
> *"Whether we last the night or no,*
> *Life has always been touch and go.*
> *So stick with your modus operandi.*
> *Ingenuity! Art! Good luck. Goodbye."*

We did the Rhubarb Tour in August 2008, seventeen shows in twenty
days. Studs wanted to live long enough to see Obama win, but he
didn't want to see him defeated. He died on Halloween, five days
before Election Day. He was born as the *Titanic* went down and he
went out as Obama was coming in. He died hoping, which was a good
way to go. Had he lived five more days, Obama's election would've
made Studs feel obligated to stick around and postpone the dying, and
Obama in the White House would've made Studs question his own
agnosticism and perhaps come to the Lord and at his age it would've
been too much, having to learn Scripture and all. God in His mercy
allowed him to die in unbelief. His ashes were mixed with those of his
wife, Ida, and deposited in Bughouse Square, where the cranks and
Wobblies and soapbox preachers held forth back in his youth. Peace
to them all.

It was a beautiful Election Night the vast crowd waiting in Grant Park
in Chicago, and the young couple walking out on the big stage with the
two little girls holding hands alongside. Your heart went out to them,
the two young strivers from the South Side who took the high road and
somehow knew exactly what to do in every situation. In February, I went
to Washington and spoke at the annual luncheon of the US Senate wives
and there, sitting at my table, was the wife of the former junior senator
from Illinois, Michelle Obama, now the First Lady. I'd been asked to tell
stories about Lake Wobegon, and it was hard to make the leap from the
Little Town That Time Forgot to the astonishing historic event before
our eyes but I tried. I told about Miss LaVona Person standing in the

aisle smiling as the fourteen-year-old me climbed up on the stage and said that we each have an angel smiling at us from our past. I recited the unrhyming limerick and they laughed. I remember how gracefully Mrs. Obama endured everyone's awkwardness, I remember her warmth when she put an arm around me for a picture. She asked me for a limerick, and I wrote her one on a napkin:

> *The latest First Lady Michelle*
> *Rode down to this town on the El*
> *From the South Side*
> *And is quite qualified*
> *To do good and do it quite well.*

A tiny gesture at a large historic moment that demanded "Endymion" or "Helen in Egypt," but time was short and her security detail was eager to get going.

My brother died that winter, at 71, skating on a lake near his home in Madison, Wisconsin. He stepped onto the ice and slipped and fell backward, hitting the back of his head, and was taken to the hospital, unconscious. He seemed to recover and even walked with assistance down the hall, but there was bleeding on the brain stem and he died a few days later. He was a sailor and an engineer, a problem-solver, not cut out for the suit-and-tie corporate life, and found his way to the Sea Grant research program and had a happy career doing environmental projects on the Great Lakes, much of his time spent aboard boats. He was the captain of the twenty-three-foot *Brita Grace,* and his son, Douglas, was his first mate. Sailing and family and following Christ were the grandeur in his life and also skating. You stride out onto the ice and leave the motorized world behind, gliding in rhythmic strides into the nineteenth century. He needed grandeur to get free of the pietists and the regimentation and paperwork. He was a happy traveler, to the fjords of Norway and Alaska, Paris, London, Berlin, and that square in Cádiz where we sat under the great white awning stretched like a sail over the plaza. There was a statue of a great man, perhaps a king, in the middle. Drunks had pissed on him and passersby ignored him. Great men don't notice grandeur, they are too busy being admired. My brother lived for grandeur and found it on large bodies of water, and I lived in search of intimacy. He was close to Dad, was Dad's successor. He learned carpentry from Dad, absorbed the love of cars and machinery, admired competence. The incompetent stood and cursed the problem and kicked it and caused more problems; the engineer studied the problem, devised a solution and when it failed, made intelligent revisions. I imagine that as Philip fell on the ice, his brain had noted how he'd lost his footing and was planning a correction for the future.

At the funeral, his body lay in a closed coffin with a spray of lilies on top. He didn't want to be embalmed and thereby leach poisons into the earth or be cremated and pollute the air—he intended to decompose and enrich the earth and rise up through the roots into the foliage of the red oak and maples—and so his body, from which many organs had been harvested for donation, was simply refrigerated and put in a spruce box and not exhibited. There was a great deal of singing. My sister Linda spoke about how Philip loved nautical museums and if you went with him, you'd be done after forty-five minutes and he'd still have two hours to go, so bring a good book. My nephew Douglas spoke about what a good teacher his dad was and how he'd taught his children how to skate and especially how to fall without hurting themselves: Doug inherited Philip's sense of humor. My mother, 93, sat in the front row, weeping for her first child, her mainstay, taken cruelly from her. A Black minister friend of Philip's sat down to the piano and played "I'll Fly Away" and "I'm Going to the Kingdom" in jubilant stride-gospel style, the congregation clapping, and I remembered how blessedly happy Philip had been sailing along the coast of Norway and into the narrow Sognefjord, so narrow the ship had little clearance on either side, and he stood in the bow, looking side to side, exhilarated, as if coming home. We took him out to the cemetery in his plain wooden box, sang a few hymns, and then one of the gravediggers walked up and bent over, revealing his butt crack, and cranked the box down into the earth. It was perfect. Praise and reverence, grief, and low comedy, all at once.

And that summer, old age came knocking on my door. I was at a day spa in Minneapolis, as Peruvian flute music was playing, and the Jamaican masseuse was telling me how good her life had been since she turned it over to the Lord Jesus Christ, and suddenly my mouth was numb, my speech slurred, my brain melting. I hoisted up on my elbows and said I had to go now. I dressed. I paid her. A balloon was expanding inside my head. I careened out the door, listing slightly to port, and eased into my car and drove twelve miles to a hospital in St. Paul, walked into the ER waiting room, stood sixth in line at the admissions desk, and when it was my turn, I said in a clear voice, "I believe I am having a stroke." An orderly brought out a gurney and helped me aboard and took me to a curtained alcove and said to strip down to my shorts and put on a hospital gown. And a nurse asked, "Do you need help?" *No, I am fine,* I said. A Minnesota reflex. The gown was light cotton, flowery. I lay on the gurney, on my back, hands clasped over my abdomen. If I died on the spot, I would appear composed. I kept calm. In my mind, I was reciting the counties of Minnesota: *Aitkin, Anoka, Becker, Beltrami, Benton, Big Stone, Blue Earth, Brown, Carlton, Carver, Cass, Chippewa, Chisago,* and so on, to test brain function.

The nurse announced my numbers—Blood pressure: 139/72. Pulse: 59—as a young Chinese neurologist walked in, shook my hand, and examined me. She tapped me with her little silver hammer and scratched the sole of my foot and told me to watch her index finger as she moved it out there and up here and down there. She said that she listened to my show when she was in medical school. She wrote on a form in her clipboard, "Very pleasant 67 y.o. male, tall, well-developed, well-nourished, flat affect, awake, alert and appropriate." I've always had a flat affect: I'm a Minnesotan, I thought it was the appropriate way to be. Other people aim for excellence, I am comfortable with wakefulness.

She shipped me off to the MRI Space-Time Cyclotron, where they ran me up a rail and into the maw of the beast for fifty minutes of banging and whanging, buzzing and dinging, and claustrophobia on the verge of panic, the nurse's voice in the speaker by my ear saying, "How are we doing?" I said, "I'm perishing." She said, "You're doing great. We're almost finished."

It was a simple thromboembolic stroke likely due to atrial fibrillation. I stayed in the hospital for four days. I walked the Stroke Ward, towing my IV tower, passed a thirtyish woman with a pronounced limp, slip-sliding along, gripping a walker, her mother at her side. Heartbreaking to see a young woman so stricken, but the mother had a brisk, let's-get-it-done air about her, and what else can you do? Take the blow and get up and go. I tried not to peep through open doorways but couldn't not and did and saw elderly persons lying speechless, crumpled, like lobsters trying to claw their way out of the tank at the restaurant, or slumped in a chair, anguished, unspeaking, and what if rehab can't restore the eminence you once were and you get shunted into a warehouse like a turtle in a gravel box with a couple leaves of lettuce? I, a rotgut sinner, had escaped serious damage and was still ambulatory, like a veteran of Pickett's Last Charge who suffered a sprained ankle. The doctor showed me a map of my brain and pointed to a dark spot: "That's where your stroke hit." What she called a "silent" part of the brain. Sort of the Wyoming of the brain. And if it had hit the Chicago Loop, a couple millimeters away, I would've had significant motor and speech losses. Maybe become a cabbage or an artichoke. She had put me on a powerful blood thinner. I who had disdained chemistry in eleventh grade. (How many chemists had been saved by reading a novel?)

It did occur to me, lying in bed, that had I exercised strenuously every day as a person should do, my heart would've been stronger and it would've fired the blood clots harder and they'd have flown over Wyoming and landed in Chicago and today I'd be a gimp, a feeb, a crip, a wacko with big X's for eyeballs. Thanks to my sedentary habits, the bomb landed out on the lonesome prairie, no big deal, so be grateful for what you have. I did not share this thought with Jenny, who was terribly anxious about me. She brought Maia to visit, and she and I sang, "I want to hold your hand," and she checked my nose for boogers and I told her the one about the two penguins on the ice floe—"You look like you're wearing a tuxedo."—"What makes you think I'm not?" An old favorite. She'd heard it dozens of times. It's one of those rare jokes that improves with repetition until all you need is the first line: *These two penguins sat on an ice floe.*

A reporter called from the local paper to update my obituary, and she was very nice. "We just want to make sure everything's accurate," she said. "You're on your third marriage—is that correct?" *Yes, ma'am.* "Three children?" *Including my stepdaughter, correct.* "Are there any honors or awards we may not be aware of?" *None.* "How are you feeling, if you don't mind my asking?" *Never better.* "Do you plan to resume your show?" *I do, yes, indeed. Of course.*

I am fond of my brain, the elaborate dreams it stages at night, some-times a nightmare in which I'm proofreading a manuscript and nothing makes sense. I'm grateful for the ideas it offers on a silver plate in the morning. I once lived in a little house beside a waterfall in Marine on St. Croix and lay in bed listening to the low rumble of the creek falling over the stone ledge and twenty feet down to a pool and racing down the hill to the St. Croix River, and after three minutes fell asleep and awoke at 4 a.m. with a whole morning's work in my head. I miss that waterfall.

Lying in the stroke ward among the stricken, it seemed like a good idea to think about a funeral and spare Jenny the guesswork, so I scrib-bled a few notes (*Episcopal Low Mass, no eulogies, none—hire a choir—"Abide with Me" and "O Love That Will Not Let Me Go," and Mozart's* Ave Verum *and "The Blind Man Stood in the Road and Cried"*), and thinking about a funeral made me think about sex, of course—what else?—and I remembered making love upstairs in the farmhouse in Freeport, the Valentine's Night tryst of 1976, the apartment on Jagtvej in Copenha-gen, the waist-deep water off Oahu, the hanging bed in the log cabin in Wisconsin, the Ritz in Boston. I remember the lodge at the national park and Jenny and I stepping out on a balcony and there, in the moonlight, the vastness of the Grand Canyon. Memories of sensual delight, the bag of blood thinner attached to the needle in my forearm.

I revisited Anoka, Minnesota, in 1954, the swanky window of Col-burn-Hilliard men's clothiers and the gray wool sportcoat I coveted, Shadick's soda fountain, the front window of the Anoka *Herald* where I typed my sports stories, Anoka Dairy across the street. I remembered how it felt to ride a bike no-handed. I remembered Mrs. Moehlenbrock, who gave our fourth-grade class the essay topic "What would you do if you had one day left to live?" We had just read an inspiring story about the rich, full life Helen Keller led despite being blind, deaf, speechless, and rather homely, and Mrs. Moehlenbrock suggested we write some-thing inspiring about appreciating the ordinary things of life, but I wrote that I wanted to fly to Paris. She pointed out that it would take a day just to get to Paris. I thought that maybe I could get a good tailwind and glimpse it for an hour before I died. Maybe the prospect of seeing Paris would be good enough.

A tall dark-haired nurse named Sarah brought me a hypodermic to coach me on self-administered shots of heparin, and without hesitation I plunged it into my belly fat. No man is a coward in the presence of a young woman. I shuffled around in a faded cotton gown like Granma in *Grapes of Wrath* and peed into a plastic container under the supervision of Sarah, who made sure I didn't get dizzy and fall and bang my noggin. A social worker asked if I wished to see a counselor. I said, "My wife is the only counselor I need." "What about a chaplain?" she said. I said, "God forbid."

Doctors came to consult. An important neurologist arrived, judging by the retinue of disciples in his wake who observed as he tapped me and had me stand on one foot, arms extended, in my little gown, like Clara awaiting the Nutcracker. The disciples observed in silence. I imagined that, out in the hall, he had said, "This is the guy with the finicula of the esplanade, complicated by deviated nobiscus linguini in the odessa." They looked at me solemnly, folks who had aced all those math and science courses I avoided so that I could read the transcendentalists. And what had Henry Thoreau done for me anyway? "The mass of men lead lives of quiet desperation." *Thanks a lot. Exactly what I don't need to hear.* Thoreau had to transcend lousy medicine, whereas science was offering me a productive old age. I was grateful and I told them so.

The nurses were cheerful women who strode into my room, noted the urine flow chart, asked the questions, prepped me on upcoming events, took my blood pressure. Women with the caring gene that men don't get (or don't dare exhibit). To the male orderly, I was a body, but the nurses knew me as a brother. They drew blood gently with some small talk to ease the little blip of puncture, and I felt our common humanity, a great gift to one struck by a stroke. Injury and illness and death are all so ordinary, they come too soon and we're all in the same boat and your fine intellect does not prevail against it, but in the way she takes your blood pressure—a simple mechanical procedure, a robot could do it— she conveys by touch and the tone of her voice her recognition of your humanity.

And then she leaves and I do the crossword, pondering 24 Across, "Could turn into the next story" (spiralstaircase), and the phone rang, someone said, "So how are you doing?" and I said, "Doing great. Never felt better." Which is what you should say, unless your eyeballs have popped out of your head. There was an old airline clerk in Minneapolis who, whenever I asked, "How are you?" he said, "Living the dream." Me, too. My brain had dark blotches in it, but I could still write a limerick.

An old man suffered a stroke
And, grateful that he didn't croak,
He flew to Oaxaca
And a yellow mocca-
Sin bit him. He died. That's no joke.

I wrote a letter to Jim Harrison, who'd gotten his own close-up looks at mortality:

I went to church this a.m. and found myself on the prayer list. It was nice to be there though my faith is rather faint. But the church preaches gratitude and what else can one feel after one's brain took a shot without too much damage. Back at the hospital I left twenty or thirty people collapsed in wheelchairs and here I am walking to church and singing praise to the Lord and walking home (a little wearily). I feel like the amnesiac who got Alzheimer's and forgot he didn't know who he was.

I went back to work and my main guy, Dr. Rodysill, didn't tell me to find a sunny corner to sit in so I didn't. The show started up in the fall and I went gadding about as a speaker—graduations, lecture series, college convocations, book club luncheons, sometimes for money, often not. One week: Walnut Creek, CA, Austin, TX, Opelika, AL, Madisonville, KY; landed in Hot Springs, AR, on a Friday, did the broadcast Saturday, on Sunday flew to Greenville, NC, then DC for the Poetry Out Loud finals, then Albuquerque for an orchestra benefit, Milwaukee to do APHC, Boston Pops the next week, a speech at the Harvard *Lampoon*. No wonder I never got to know my neighbors. When the *Lampoon* invites you, you say yes, knowing that one day soon you'll be a nobody like everybody else.

Back in those days, I was in demand as a graduation speaker, and on numerous June afternoons found myself in a procession of the Board of Trustees, the faculty and me, the speaker, the noose around my neck, as the crowd looks eagerly beyond us for the graduates themselves and cameras flash, then a vague invocation is offered, retiring faculty are applauded (gratitude? relief?), and then I, the guest of honor, am given a big booming introduction as if I had brought the serum to a snowbound village by dogsled and en route rescued small children from the path of a speeding locomotive. I rise to tepid applause and realize that 89 percent of the crowd hopes I will speak for three minutes or less; I have 3,000 words in front of me and the crowd only wants 150 of them. So I skip the introductory self-mortification and launch in and after two paragraphs about the importance of rising to challenges, the audience is gone-gone-gone. Everyone is focused on a particular graduate, Madison, Hannah, Joshua, Jacob, their shining star, and I am merely a clothing rack. The honor of speaking turns out to be public shame.

I dressed up in a long black gown and gave the baccalaureate address at Princeton, climbing a long flight of stairs to the pulpit high on the chapel wall, so my speech began with labored breathing. The speech was funny, theoretically, but nobody laughed for the first few minutes because my voice was ricocheting around in the magnificence of the Gothic arches—I kept hearing what I'd said five seconds before, a distraction that slowed me down, which made it all worse. I finished the speech in fifteen minutes by cutting out pages four, five, and six, and descended from the mountaintop to grateful applause and went to the reception, where nobody mentioned the speech in specific terms. They said, "Good job," as you'd say to a child who'd delivered a large bowel movement.

St. Olaf College invited me to come speak at a convocation, assuming I would poke fun at them, but when I stood up in Boe Chapel I put the speech away. The title was "I Regret, You Regret, We Rejoice," and it was about the power of community and when I saw the chapel was packed to the rafters, the speech suddenly wasn't good enough, I needed something better so I punted. They were in the midst of midterm exams and needed to feel communal, so I walked down the aisle and sang, "My country 'tis of thee" and the whole room joined in "sweet land of liberty," and by the time we came to "where my fathers died" we were in spontaneous four-part harmony. No piano, no organ. It was powerful. And then "O beautiful for spacious skies" and "Amazing grace, how sweet the sound" and "Mine eyes have seen the glory of the coming of the Lord" and

"She was just seventeen if you know what I mean"—some students had to google that one on their phones. We sang "Children of the heavenly Father safely in His bosom gather," and we got tears in our eyes from the promise that God will not forsake us and also the harmony that promises we will not forsake each other. And then "O Lord my God, when I in awesome wonder consider all the worlds Thy hands have made." The sweet chariot swung low, we worked on the railroad, Old Man River rolled, there was a sweet hour of prayer in the amber waves of grain over the rainbow, and we sang good night to the ladies and the sweet acquaintance that should not be forgot and the Amen chorus. A solid hour of a cappella singing, and off they went to class. I declined the check and headed home feeling uplifted by youthful melodious fervor. Lutherans can break your heart with their singing. It was a genuine service, unlike the crappy speech I'd written. I guess St. Olaf saw it otherwise, though, because they never invited me back.

I was on the road, week after week, thirty-three *Prairie Home* shows, standing at the middle microphone in the path of powerful talents, The Iowa poet Greg Brown, the king of the bass sax Vince Giordano, the twelve-string guitar master John Koerner, big talents leaping upstream over the rapids. Vince stood in with the band, and the big honk of the bass sax was the engine that drove the bus, the piano steering, and John's twelve was a one-man threshing machine. The DiGiallonardo Sisters' three-part jazz vocals were right out of the Forties, an old b&w photograph come to life in full color.

Then Sunday at home and a week on the road, theaters in Buffalo, Kansas City, and Seattle, a Lutheran convention in Omaha, a college in Indiana, two-hour shows with a standing singing intermission, sometimes three hours, which is too long, but they didn't want to leave so I stayed. I loved the pontoon boat story with its interlocking parts, Aunt Evelyn, the disgusting Bruno the Fishing Dog, the canceled wedding of Debbie Detmer the successful veterinary aromatherapist, Evelyn's boyfriend Raoul, the visit of the twenty-four agnostic Danish Lutheran pastors, and Kyle's attempt to fly his parasail over the lake and drop Evelyn's ashes in—the parts all fit like a fine clockwork, and each could be extended if the audience wished—and it was all told in a rush and ended with Bruno sticking his nose up Kyle's butt and the line, "But as we say in Lake Wobegon, it could've been worse," whereupon the audience fell apart. A person never wearies of telling a story that good. I certainly didn't. I was living in a tunnel, waking up some mornings not sure what city I was in. Arise and step into the bathroom, but actually it's the hotel hallway, and the door clicks shut. It's 3 a.m. The hall is empty, just me in my underwear. I pick up a house phone and a pleasant security man comes along to unlock my door. He doesn't ask for identification, only my last name. He wishes me a good night. It's Dallas, dummy. I flew to Austin to speak at something and the columnist Molly Ivins picked me up at the airport in her pickup truck, and we stopped at a café for chili and everybody there knew her and I basked in virtue by association.

I taught a course at the U, "The Composition of Comedy," which was mostly about economy. *A man walked into the bar with a handful of dog turds and said, "Look what I almost stepped in."*—add one word to it, and you smother the joke. I had a hundred students, and the best of them got to stand up for five minutes and make the class laugh. Men and women who'd never done this before stood up and killed. I never let anyone stand up and die, I worked with them until they were good and homicidal. Comedy sets out to gain the crowd's attention and confidence in the first half-minute, to win over the sleepy and cynical, make it worthwhile for them and surprise them into laughter, a success shared by speaker and hearer equally. Most of what's said in this world goes unheard and is a waste of time. Comedy is the beautiful exception.

And in the midst of teaching it I flew to Las Vegas to speak at a breakfast at the tire dealers' convention, which I did as a favor to a cousin. Seven a.m. in Hangoverland and they want *joke* jokes, ripsnorters, not humorous recollections of small-town life, and after five minutes of me, they'd heard enough. I did six more minutes, got a faint trickle of laughter, cried, "You've been great!" and ran out through the kitchen, tore up the check, and went to the airport. It was the Worst Show of My Life and I was glad to get it out of the way and not have to wait for it anymore. It was done.

I arose at 5 a.m., worked hard, gave up reading novels and going to movies. I wrote on yellow legal pads, on planes, in hotel rooms. I got no exercise except for walking rapidly through airports, and my daily water intake was less than that of a garter snake. I was the lone writer of the show, though the credits listed Warren Peace, Xavier Onassis, Ben Dover, Rhoda Dendron, Ida Dunmore, Hugh Mungus, Barbara Seville, and sometimes John Calvin. I sat at the laptop on the long desk looking up at the big photograph of Grandma's schoolhouse where Grandpa had followed her around, cleaning blackboards, and finally kissing her, and it was clear to me: nature cares not about our golden years, nature wants turnover, so keep going while you can, your time won't last long. I wrote quiet weeks in Lake Wobegon, and I sent the cowboys in search of Lefty's love Evelyn Beebalo, and every week there was *A dark night in a city that knows how to keep its secrets but one man is still trying to find the answers to life's persistent questions. Me. Guy Noir.* Every episode began with a line about the weather. *It was a gorgeous September, bright blue skies, warm sun—the weather that makes a man want to buy an easel and a beret and paint landscapes that will sell for $12 million after you're dead for fifty years.* Guy told his girlfriend, Sugar, "Of course I love you. If I didn't love you, why would I have been dating you for the past thirteen years? It ain't for your fabulous gams, sweetheart." He fought off the criminal element and was drawn to interesting women. *She was tall, her hair was like melted caramel. Her jeans were so tight you could read the embroidery on her underwear. It said, Tuesday. And the T-shirt with a picture of Mount Rushmore on the front. Take it from me, Lincoln and Jefferson never looked so good.*

I wrote the sound-effects scripts with the singing caribou and rancid bagpipes and whooping cranes and helicopters dropping chimpanzees on parachutes. I wrote the story about the anonymous economist from Menomonie, Wisconsin, who drove a semi-load of salami to Miami for Naomi who danced Salome in a steamy pajama drama called "Mama-rama" and a minute later Guy Noir was scoping out a Girl Scout cook-ie-scalping scam run by scantily clad schoolteachers from Schenectady. The childish concatenation of alliteration. It amuses people.

I worked all the time because I was running away from death. It had knocked on my back door and I went out the front. Comedy is God's work. You see it in Ecclesiastes. *The thing that has been is the thing that shall be; and the thing that is done is that which shall be done: there is nothing new under the sun.* That's the essence of comedy. The Resurrection was a joke. The disciples came to the tomb and saw the tomb was empty. Jesus walks up and says, "Who you looking for?" You do God's work and He will grant you a little extra time. Studs was gone, my brother, Chet Atkins, who said, "Now that I am on the back nine, my passion for the guitar is slowly dying and it makes me sad. I never thought my love for the guitar would fade. There are a lot of reasons: as we get older the high frequencies go, music doesn't sound so good. And for some damn reason after hearing so many great players, I lose the competitive desire." The old Icelander Bill Holm died, collapsed in the Sioux Falls airport, having just visited Jim Harrison, who died a year later. My friend Carol Bly was gone, who loved a good contentious conversation, and I was brought up to defer to a woman and didn't stand up to her and provide the adversary she wanted. My classmate Margaret Keenan, who became a psychiatrist and psychoanalyst. She didn't claim to heal people but to lead them toward some sort of understanding. I never heard her speak with contempt or derision about anyone, not even Death, whom she saw coming a long way off and met with serenity. She contracted a cancer that stumped the specialists and finally accepted that the end was near. She called me one last time, to say that she'd been to a Hopi healing ceremony and didn't understand one bit of it but was moved and felt wonder, a highly educated woman transformed by religious mystery. She now felt at peace and asked me to sing a song for her on the show, one her father had loved, so I did, a duet with Sarah Jarosz: *When all is sad and dark within, and hope seems only born to die, He steals within the shadows dim and wipes the tear from every eye.* My cousin Olive Darby died, clear of mind at 104, the last living person to have known my grandfather James, and for years I meant to go visit her in Iowa and never did.

Tom Keith died in October 2011. He was 64. He had worked the show a week before, spent a quiet week at home, felt ill on a Sunday, collapsed in the evening, was put in an ambulance, regained consciousness briefly, and died of a pulmonary embolism. His friends put on a show at the Fitz in his memory with bagpipers and a magician, tango dancers, jokes, a video of Tom in a kilt singing "A Wee Deoch an Doris," and twice I came out on stage with paper in hand as if to give a eulogy and Vern Sutton came out of the wings and pied me. Banana cream pie. He did it well, you don't throw the pie, you push it. People loved it, both times. It was a eulogy I was incapable of delivering due to the fact that I owed so much to someone I barely knew. I met him in 1972 at KSJN in

St. Paul, where he was a studio engineer assigned to my morning show. I wanted to be my own engineer, so I made him a sportscaster and a laconic sidekick and then found out he was happy to do sound effects, animals, engines, explosions, gunshots, dramatic stuff, and that was what led me down the path of radio comedy. Otherwise I would've jumped ship, gotten a job in an MFA program teaching decorative writing, and lived a quiet bungalow life going to movies and playing golf in the low 90s. My mentor was this polite ex-Marine and former right fielder who had a secret ambition to personify chickens and follow in the footsteps of his parents Jim and Betty, who played Ma and Pa Wiggins on KSTP's *Sunset Valley Barn Dance*. The man changed my life, sent me down the comedy path, was a loyal colleague, did what needed to be done, stood on stage and did sound effects, and we never really knew each other.

31

Seventy

I CELEBRATED TURNING SEVENTY, SAILING on the *Queen Mary* out of New York harbor, a fireboat alongside shooting a fifty-foot plume in the air, the Staten Island Ferry bobbing in our wake, our funnel eased under the Verrazano Narrows Bridge with a few feet to spare, and we sailed along the coast of Brooklyn and out to sea. Jenny and Maia and I lay in deck chairs on the sun deck, behind the funnel, and of course I thought about the *Titanic* as any Brethren boy would. The gospel preachers of my youth loved the *Titanic*, the story of the rich and famous drinking and dancing as the ship sped through the field of icebergs toward its doom, wealth and privilege enjoying a high old godless time, and then the crash, the screams, the alarms, sinners ushered into eternity to stand before the Judgment Seat. We would pass over the ship's resting place two nights later. If God wished to provide the affluent with another object lesson, here we were.

I'd been off alcohol for ten years but it was my seventieth and so at dinner on the great day itself I splurged on a bottle of 1942 Bordeaux, the year of my birth. I didn't let Jenny see the wine menu; the price had risen somewhat since World War II to something like the price of a small used car. The figure made my brain go dark for a moment, but I nodded to the sommelier and he pried out the ancient cork in a few small pieces and some cork crumbs and poured a splash in my glass. It was not a bad wine, sort of magnificently ordinary. Bordeaux was under German occupation in 1942 and the patriotic French were not about to bring forth superior vintages to be enjoyed by Nazi butchers so there you are. Drink a glass, it's history, and next time order a 1948.

Maia attached herself to a troupe of British actors who were doing performances on the ship and she became a faithful fan, and Jenny lay in a chaise and read books and attended lectures, and I wandered around and thought my thoughts. I am not good at relaxation. I am very good at regret and remorse. I regret periods of *Prairie Home* when I was distracted by my own random ambitions and lost focus on what mattered. I left a long trail of failed attempts at screenplays, a couple fragments of plays, part of a musical, an unfinished novella, bits of essays: why would you go roaming through the woods pitching tents when you own a castle? I had a Saturday night show with millions of faithful listeners—why did I spend days and days laboring over a cowboy musical nobody would ever be interested in when a big audience was waiting to hear about Lake Wobegon? I walked around the ship kicking myself for that.

I hiked stern to bow and back as the site of the *Titanic* sinking approached and I plowed through my regrets. All the times I offered political views on the show, my little outbursts of piety. My lifelong resistance to the idea of *rehearsal*. I kept rewriting the show up to airtime and now and then was known to reach over an actor's shoulder and scratch out a few words. It was nuts, hanging onto amateurism and looking for spontaneity, throwing a show together on the fly. No production meeting: I abhorred meetings. Other people did vocal warmups, I never did. I did not want to be caught taking the show seriously.

Large regrets, small, all painful. Driving to Friday night rehearsal in St. Paul once, I was almost sideswiped by a driver cutting in front of me and I screeched at him some crazy homicidal stuff for a minute, forgetting that I had a colleague on the phone—I stopped yelling and said "Sorry" and no more was ever said about it but it's still vivid in my mind, the things I yelled at her that were intended for him. I have a vivid memory of the day I dropped in at Uncle Jim's farm and played chess with his little boy Jimmy who was a good chess player. This meant something to my uncle who said he hoped I'd come back and do it again but I never did. My beloved aunts faded away and a visit from the notorious nephew would've been welcome, I know, but in the fury of work and travel, they became strangers. I have a large ego and was unable to resist invitations to fly off and go be admired by somebody or other, the Duckburg DeMolay, the Wistful Vista Historical Society, the Loyal Order of Walleyes, the

Federated Association of Organizations. As a Minnesotan, I'm good at disguising my ego as public service or professional obligation but it was a 300-hp ego in those days and it kept me on the road, going from town to town, enjoying public attention. When you are an old man you can come clean about this. I loved standing in front of people and I resented the man who recited my accomplishments by way of introduction—he was stealing my limelight—and I grabbed the microphone out of the lectern (no need for that) and walked downstage so as to give them a better view and launched in to regale and amuse. Money had nothing to do with it, it was about admiration, a thousand heads bent forward, listening and laughing.

Forgiveness. This is what I go to church for. I can't forgive myself, but Sunday morning at church, in the midst of Black and Asian and white families and gay and morose and miscellaneous, we kneel and lay down our sins in a deep silence and we are absolved, and people ramble around the sanctuary shaking hands and hugging, a cheerful democratic moment, milling in the aisle, smiling, saying *Peace of the Lord. God be with us.* This is what I go to church for.

Meanwhile, the parade of losses continues. My cousin Bruce Bacon, an organic farmer who lived in a wreck of a house and kept a beautiful garden. He taught young people how to care for soil, working land that had been in the family for more than a century. He kept bees and whenever he visited, he brought a jar of honey. He was hopeful to a fault.

I lost track of Arnie Goldman when he was 78, alone in Sydney, planning a trip to New York, misquoting Thoreau ("As long as possible live free and uncommitted. It makes but little difference whether you are committed to a farm or the county jail or marriage or a retirement home."), promising he'd ride shotgun with me up to Tanglewood that summer, passing the red-eye, smoking dope, keeping an eye out for the *federales*, and I never saw him again.

The poet Louis Jenkins, author of *Nice Fish*, the world's only play about ice fishing, an independent observant man unencumbered by careerism. My stage manager, Albert Webster, who brought a happy spirit to backstage, had a great laugh, was never flummoxed, and though he was a big man, he could leap into action when necessary. My New York neighbor Ira Globerman, who, though his office was across the street from Yankee

Stadium, never went through the gates because he grew up in Brooklyn and was still loyal to the Dodgers, though they were long gone to LA. He brought the same fidelity to his judicial duties. I had dinner with him and his wife, Ellie, three days before he died. He roasted steaks. He was moving slowly and deliberately, but his mind was lively. He talked about his Brooklyn boyhood and not much about old age except a joke—a psychologist takes a survey on frequency of male sex: many men have sex once a week, others once a month, and then he meets an old man who has sex once every two years. "Oh, that's so sad," says the psychologist. The man smiles: "Yes, but tonight's the night!" Ira died that week in his sleep.

Meanwhile, this easy life fell to me while people I knew were dying, and I am standing on a stage and singing:

A man walked past the insane asylum:
They were shouting, "Twenty-one! Twenty-one!"
So he looked through a hole in the fence;
It sounded like they were having fun.
He put his eye to the hole in the fence
To see what crazy people do
And they poked him in the eye with a sharp stick
And yelled, "Twenty-two! Twenty-two!"

I told about Florian and Myrtle Krebsbach, their classic argument, which goes exactly like this:

MYRTLE: Why don't we ever go anywhere? I'm sick of staying at home.
FLORIAN: What do you mean, "never go anywhere"? We went to Rapid City in September.
MYRTLE: Rapid City, I don't call that somewhere.
FLORIAN: There's just no satisfying you. Fight, fight, fight, it's all we do. Why should I pay a fistful of money to travel and be miserable when I can sit and be miserable at home.

That's how the argument goes, but this time he didn't give her the line about Rapid City, he said, "Where do you want to go?" and she said,

"California," knowing how cheap he is, and he, to get back at her, said, "You got it. Deal." So they flew to La Jolla to visit their son Wesley. He was the quiet boy who did well in school and became a software engineer and what it is he does, they have no idea, only that he is very successful. Wesley and Donna and their three kids live in baronial splendor in La Jolla and go around in sweatpants and T-shirts and are always doing six things at once and apparently adhere to no religion other than physical exercise. The whole family is deeply involved with triathlon, running, swimming, biking. The weather was perfect, the grandkids remarkable but mostly busy elsewhere and both parents are mysterious and speak a language that is mostly English and partly something else. What the old folks realized after a week was: (1) they were eager to return home, and (2) their rascally son Donnie, with the whiskey habit and the roaming eye and the screwed-up kids, is the son they know very well and the successful son is a complete stranger. Donnie needs them, Wesley doesn't. La Jolla was full of wonders; Lake Wobegon is where their hearts are. Scripture says, *Be ye not conformed to this world but rather be ye transformed by the renewing of your mind that you may prove what is the good and acceptable and perfect will of God.* Stories are essential in the renewing of the mind. We must renew our minds to love what we truly love. I enjoy being in New York because I'm a visitor here and don't have a big stake in the outcome. Minnesota is my home, which I know because it can break my heart. I don't care what Wisconsin, Iowa, or the Dakotas do, but if Minnesota voted for Donald Trump, I would feel it my duty to jump off the Washington Avenue Bridge.

I rambled around doing shows and included more and more a cappella audience singing, which the audience loved, a singing intermission and an encore that lasted as long as they wanted, starting with *My country 'tis of thee.* I sang *O beautiful for* and they were all there with the *spacious skies.* Once in Little Rock, I got a crowd that was predominantly liberal Democrats, judging from their discomfort singing *I wish I was in the land of cotton, old times there are not forgotten,* but they sang it, in standard dialect, not minstrel, which was good for them, an exercise in history. Some sing it as *good times* are not forgotten, but it's old times, and why forget them? Of all the *Prairie Home* shows, one that moved me deeply was at the old Methodist tabernacle (capacity 7,000) at Ocean Grove, NJ, dating back to Civil War days when the Methodists pitched tents and held prayer meetings and revivals and enjoyed the fellowship of kindred believers. It was August, we were on a tour, I walked into the crowd, sang the first notes of "America" and 7,000 people joined me on "sweet land of liberty." I sang the line, "When peace like a river attendeth my way," and the crowd picked it right up—*And sorrows like sea billows roll, whatever my lot Thou hast taught me to say, "It is well, it is well with my soul"*—and there we were, Christians gathered, some fallen, some strays, some Jewish brethren, but they were all there on the chorus, *It is well—(It is well)— with my soul—(with my soul).* People were weeping, moved by the mass vocal symphony around them, surrounded by souls who knew the same words. *They had not come here for this; it was a revelation.* White hankies came out, men wiped their eyes on their shirtsleeves. We segued into the Doxology and two verses of "How Great Thou Art," also overwhelming, and I walked up the aisle and saw a slight fellow in brown leather jacket and recognized Bruce Springsteen. I nodded, he nodded. And then the Battle Hymn and a quiet *Glory, glory, Hallelujah* and an even quieter *In the beauty of the lilies Christ was born across the sea*, and you could feel the spirit of the crowd floating in the air. I hummed a G, or something close to it, and sang *O say can you see* and the crowd rose to its feet. The national anthem is nobody's favorite song, but once you get into it and hear the voices around you, you feel it take off, and when we hold the note on "free" and the sopranos go high, it's opera. I looked over and saw Mr. Springsteen standing, singing *home of the brave*, and I added an *Amen* chorus. It was twenty minutes of Methodist fervor on public radio, and then a Powdermilk Biscuit commercial. I was shaken. Schismatic politics have beset the beloved country, but here we were under one roof, 7,000 individuals united in singing the peace of our souls, a rock star anonymous in our midst. I was only the prompter, and the power was tangible to all, a vision of union triumphant.

In the grand sweep of *Prairie Home* history, the Fox and the Flynn and Ryman and Palace and Radio City, the hills of Tanglewood and Hollywood and Chautauqua and Ravinia and Blossom, the Starlight and Ocean Grove and Yellowstone, the Greek and the show from Mark Twain's house in Hartford, the ones I am fondest of were the twelve broadcasts from the Minnesota State Fair grandstand, the very stage where I'd seen the great Buster Keaton do his stepladder routine years before, his stooge holding the ladder horizontal and suddenly turning, knocking the old man on his keister. I had loved the Fair since I was a small child, and there I was with a microphone walking into the crowd as they all sang "Minnesota, Hail to Thee" on coast-to-coast radio. The Fair is the old Minnesota, which is disappearing and yet here it is and you can get corn on a cob and pork chops on a stick and admire pigs and chickens. And then there was the broadcast from Anoka High School in October 2015, when the school band played and a famous alumna, Metropolitan Opera soprano Ellie Dehn, sang, and my guests were two of my best teachers in whose classes I had done my worst, Stan Nelson and Lyle Bradley. Stan taught phys ed and that included chin-ups and the rope climb, which I couldn't do but he required me to try. Lyle taught biology. Both of them had served in World War II. Lyle served on a carrier in the Pacific, and his excellent bird-watching skills enabled him to spot kamikazes aimed at the ship, and he spotted forty of them in one day and they were duly shot down. Stan was also in the Navy, a lieutenant and deck officer on a landing craft in the first wave to hit the Normandy beaches on D-Day. Neither of them made a big thing of their military service, both were dedicated teachers, Stan coaching football, baseball, and golf. Both remembered me and my cool indifference; it was poetic justice for their worst student to come do them honor.

I was moved to update Dylan's "Times They Are A-Changin'" to remind his old fans how old they are getting to be:

Come gather round people wherever you roam
My daughter just called me up on the phone
And said she's been looking for a good nursing home
That I need help with bathin' and shavin'
She said that she doesn't dare leave me alone
And the times, they are a-changin'.

My house is a mess, and my stories are stale,
I buy all my clothes at the church rummage sale
I can't figure out how to answer email,
Despite her constant explaining.
I'm bald but I still have this long ponytail

And the times they are a-changing.
No, no, no, it ain't me, babe.
It ain't me who's getting old, babe.

Time was passing. In 2013, WNYC in New York made noises about maybe dropping the show; young staffers there thought the Lake Wobegon stories were "parochial," which, literally, they were, and I took that as a signal not to be ignored. On a book tour the next year, during the Q&A, inevitably people asked, "How long are you going to keep doing the show?" A question that can be taken as a suggestion. And then the National Association of Broadcasters tried to induct me into the Radio Hall of Fame. I declined but it felt like a death knell, the invitation to become a statuette. In the winter of 2015, I heard the Muse of Maturity suggest that the next season should be my last. "Your numbers are down, from four million to slightly below three. Don't wait too long," she said. "Don't wait until stations start dropping you. Stop when people regret that you're stopping." This made sense to me.

The show was still drawing a crowd, howbeit older and heavier, as we could tell from the applause, the claps sounded more like clops or clumps, the whooping got wheezy, the standing ovations became slow-rising, leaning ovations, people trying to restore blood circulation, and some customers headed for the exits early so as to avoid traffic. The fan mail was more and more about shows of long ago, the story of Myrtle Krebsbach being left at the truck stop or Bruno the Fishing Dog, "The Finn Who Would Not Take a Sauna," the pontoon boat story, and other historic items. I was happy to be in harness and still got the jitters as I sang, "O hear that old piano from down the avenue, I smell the onions, I look around for you." I wanted to keep going, wanted to do a show in Rome, maybe Copenhagen, on forever, I still felt capable at 72 and 73 and loved singing duets, loved the stunning young talents and the old reliables. The Muse said, "The time to go is while you're still having fun—just as you'd leave a party while everyone is still upright and not stay until the fights start."

I wasn't inclined toward Bob Altman's *Die in action* philosophy. I wanted to have a long retirement and disappear into the sunset and outlive everyone qualified to give my eulogy. I wanted people to read my

Front row: Maria Jette, Vern Sutton, Mary DuShane, Joe Newberry, David Rawlings, Gillian Welch, Prudence Johnson, GK, Iris DeMent, Heather Masse and The Wailin' Jennys (Nicky Mehta and Ruth Moody), Robin and Linda Williams, Jearlyn and Jevetta Steele. 2014, singing "Just a Little While to Stay Here."

obit on page B47 and have to google me to find out who I was. I wanted to drift into anonymity and spend years with Maia and Jenny and reconnect to friends and family I'd neglected out of over-scheduling.

On the other hand, the show sounded better than ever, though I couldn't say that, being a Minnesotan, but it was true. Kate Gustafson was the manager—whatever you needed to know, she knew—and the staff was tight, no wasted motions, and our tech guys were the best in the business. You can write a fine show and book all-star talent but if your mixing board melts or a squirrel chews the transmission line, you are six ways from nowhere. We'd started in 1974 with a mixer the size of a hatbox and now we had a souped-up Mercedes and two guys, Sam Hudson and Thomas Scheuzger, who could take it apart if necessary. They were the backbone of the show—I had known this for years. I think back to 2007 and the annual Rhubarb Festival in Lanesboro before 2,000 people on blankets and lawn chairs on the ballfield. The sky turns black and rain pours down just before

airtime and the power goes out, so I stroll into the crowd and we all sing the national anthem and "Take Me Out to the Ball Game" as I walk through the crowd of umbrellas, declining an umbrella; it is good showbiz for the host to get drenched, for some reason it makes everyone feel good. Our tech guys, Sam Hudson and Thomas Scheuzger, hook up a generator, the storm moves off to the east, and the show goes on, the crowd quite proud of themselves for having stuck it out, and the near-disaster casts a warm glow on all that follows. The theme "Tishomingo Blues" and the opening marquee, the Creation story in which Adam eats rhubarb instead of the apple, a conversation with Orval and Marie Amdahl who've been married sixty-five years and for whom Rich Dworsky has written a lovely waltz. A brief homily on bravery for a Powdermilk commercial. On "The Lives of the Cowboys," the cattle have been feeding on rhubarb and were feeling good and independent. A sixteen-year-old girl named Yvonne Freese sings (beautifully) an Italian aria, "Pur dicesti, O bocca bella" and knocks it out of the park. We learn that she sings in ten different choirs around the area. In Lake Wobegon, Florian Krebsbach is bitten by a walleye and infected with a fishy virus that causes gabbiness and restlessness for which rhubarb juice is the cure. The Rhubarb Sisters inform me that rhubarb is a metaphor for finding happiness in your own backyard. It's a good show, we honor young talent, old matrimony, a common vegetable (or is it a fruit?). Five million Americans get an impression of the town of Lanesboro as a place where people aren't afraid of being rained on, plus which the great Joe Ely from Texas sings four of his songs. Ten years later, people still recalled that Lanesboro show to me. It was memorable.

There were numerous shows where during the warm-up I noticed feverish activity around the mixing board, and I was glad nobody told me what was going on. Our guys are the best in the business, and they don't need an English major leaning over them and asking questions so I didn't. There was the Avon show on a ballfield where traffic was backed up for a couple miles on I-94 due to a lack of parking in town and the power generator was slacking off, which made the Hammond organ a half step flat. There were numerous shows before which Thomas was on the phone with the telephone company trying to get an installer to come to the site and hook up the lines we needed. We used high-tech ISDN (integrated services digital network) copper lines; fiber-optic lines were coming in but copper was more reliable at the time and offered the bandwidth you need to broadcast music with good fidelity. Ma Bell, however, is not interested in broadcast lines: she gets her wealth from your teenage children, not live radio. In Honolulu, for a New Year's Eve show, the phone company sent two installers on bicycles who were seriously stoned, and an hour's job took most of a day. In Town Hall, a few minutes before airtime, I once saw them working feverishly with screwdrivers—the stage manager, Albert Webster, said, "They're trying to reset the codec box." Which sounded like Kotex box to me, but wasn't. It got fixed. For a broadcast in San Francisco, the phone company sent six trucks, one after another, to set up the lines, and only one guy knew what to do with ISDN: the other five ate lunch.

Sam was our mixer, a man with a great ear who could make a live show sound as good as a studio recording—better, with audience added—and Thomas was the man who solved problems and dealt with the phone company, spent a lot of time on Hold and saw a great many basements of theaters. Sam made the show sound good; without the two of them, there wouldn't have been one.

At Tanglewood, after a rainstorm, the power went out shortly before

*Sam Hudson at the mixing board, Thomas Scheuzger at the broadcast rack,
monitoring the quality of the signal.*

airtime and the power company sent an electrician out who got a police
escort through the crowd and went up in a cherry picker to check the
power pole, and he tossed down a dead squirrel whose electrocution had
blown a fuse. We named him Sparky and he joined the Yellowstone bison,
the Interlochen bats, the coyotes who howled during the monologue at
the Greek in LA, the cicadas who maintained a steady throbbing during
a Wolf Trap show, Murray the sea lion, and Freckles the singing dog.

And then, as the 2015–16 season was about to launch, the Muse
spoke more clearly. One night I was awakened by bright lights—I had
been metamorphosized into a patient in a hospital bed, a bad dream with

Around the office, we were all business, intent on not letting the others down. Nobody told the tech guys how crucial they were; they already
knew. Nobody said, "That was a great idea, walking out in the crowd
when it poured and we lost power." I was only doing my job. Others did
theirs. It was my job to make Lanesboro happy, rain or shine. The crew
handled the rest. Steve Koeln, the stage manager, needed no guidance
from me, and when he went off to become a furniture maker we acquired
Albert Webster, who stayed to the end—between the two of them, forty
years of good spirit and dedicated competence. As an unreliable boss, I
know when I'm around competence.

real people in it. A man in blue and a woman in white were studying me up close, and Jenny sat at the foot of the bed, prepared for the worst. She'd been awakened a couple hours before by my convulsive thrashing in bed and called 911. The ambulance took me down the hill to United Hospital. I didn't remember a thing. I'd had a brain seizure.

I had no headache, no visual aura, and I still knew my birthdate and my mother's and could recite the eighty-seven counties of Minnesota, but I felt groggy and my legs were rubbery, like joke legs, and they put me on an anti-seizure medication, a big pill, the size you'd give a Percheron. I went home and sat out back on a reclining lawn chair and looked at the Mississippi below, my old tranquilizer, a body of moving water, and the Muse said, "This is your cue, my son. Don't ignore it. You have faithful listeners who've listened since college, now they're on the verge of retirement. They're not fans so much as they are cousins. Don't make people who love you watch you go to pieces in public view. Enough is enough. Respect your limits." It was similar to the speech she gave me back in 2002 when I quit drinking. The show started in 1974; I'd be 74 if I retired in 2016. The symmetry appealed to me. My hero Steve Cannon left WCCO at the age of seventy. The station planned a big to-do for his last day, invited the governor and so forth, and Steve got wind of it and called in sick. A classy guy. No Lucite plaque for him, no speeches about his iconic stature in Minnesota. He loved his work, and he left and hid out in his mansion on Lake of the Isles. I'd disappear too. I come from separatists, I'm good at quitting. So I told Jenny that 2015–16 would be my last hurrah. We were spending a weekend in northern Wisconsin, at the historic Nilsson lake cabin, built by her dad, Ray, and Grandpa Nilsson in the Forties, her grandpa's World War I bugle and helmet on the wall and the vest he wore at the battle of Verdun. She hugged me and said she would miss the show and so would Maia, but she was in agreement. "It's time," she said. "The show has never been better." The next week, I told the *Prairie Home* staff. Nobody begged me to reconsider.

It was a good show, even I had to admit: Fred, Sue, Tim, and Rich were syncopated and symbiotic, intuitively copacetic at turning simple cues into works of audio art. Sam and Thomas, Todd Behrens, Albert, Tom Campbell, and Alan Frechtman, the whole tech staff, was the best ever, a championship team, you could've written a textbook on positive group dynamics from observing those people in action.

Having been raised by women, I had naturally hired women to run the show—three of them over a period of forty years, Margaret Moos, Christine Tschida, and Kate Gustafson. That's why the show lasted so long. A male producer would've needed to call meetings so he could sit at the head and demonstrate authority; the women were not about authority but empathy—they accepted the confusion of impromptu changes and last-minute inspirations, they understood who does what. Kate ran the place for twenty-five years, knew every single person, from the newest intern to the old veterans, their history, family situation, ambitions, phobias, irritants, favorite beverages, musical tastes, and this familiarity encouraged people to give their best. Meanwhile, the host of the show sat in a dim room staring at a computer screen and seldom spoke to anyone unless messages were slipped under his door. If he walked into a room, the room got quiet, so he stayed in his quarters. The workers in the vineyard enjoyed socializing, enjoyed backstage life with performers, and Old Stone Face stuck to his stitching and was tolerated. It was a good arrangement. The comedy on the show leaned heavily toward senseless violence, man vs. whale, man vs. volcano, mutant dinosaur vs. attack pigeons, souped-up cars carrying crates of ducks at high speed across frozen lakes, men solving complex problems by blowing up stuff. But Lake Wobegon was about women—the observers, the gossips, the jury, the attendants at birth and illness and death, and the men were, like me, dogged hard workers in need of direction and desperate for affection.

Heather Masse played the cleaning lady Clarissa, who went around the house singing "Edelweiss" in a baritone voice. She sang the coffee jingle—*It's delicious all alone, it's also good with donuts. Coffee stimulates your urges, it is served in Lutheran churches, keeps the Swedes and the Germans awake through the sermons.* She was conservatory-trained and I learned to sing in a lavatory (for the reverb), but our voices blended well, according to my wife, and Heather is my height so I could read her lips when I forgot lyrics. She and I sang "Beautiful Dreamer" and the Stones' "Wild Horses" and even, in Honolulu, *Nani wale Puʻuanahulu i ka ʻiu ʻiu ʻaina pali kualana puʻu kinikini.* You could ask her to be a singing oyster or a singing vacuum cleaner and she would do it. She was

GK and Heather Masse. Two singers, close to the same height. She is much younger, a jazz singer, and never had the opportunity to sing "Sweet Hour of Prayer" or "Love's Old Sweet Song" until she met him.

fearless, and the show had been built on fearlessness, that's why we did a live show.

I was leaving behind a show that could accommodate opera singers, cowboy bands, blues piano, vocal swing, a Noah's ark of music, with lowbrow comedy and a monologue in which people raised children and watched for storms, a show with heart that loved the old songs, celebrated the familiar, and was capable of sharp satire when needed. In 2016, the biggest con man in New York City was slouching toward the presidency, an aging adolescent who enjoyed peeing in the political swimming pool. I tried to brush him away with a song, stealing a tune by Cole Porter:

> *Tycoons used to be more hesitant*
> *Now it's Donald Trump for president,*
> *So I suppose*
> *Anything goes.*
> *Mister Ducktail on his shelf he's*
> *Got a couple thousand selfies,*
> *Thinks he's hot,*
> *Believe it or not.*
> *The world falls apart today*
> *And dumb is smart today*

Junk is art today,
We're off the chart today,
And by a miracle
Old evangelicals
Think adultery's okay.
Must we every day contend
With having Donald's large rear end
In our face?
Guess that's the case.

I knew that duet-singing was the part of the show I'd miss most, so I booked my favorite partners for the last season. I could sing harmony okay, thanks to sitting next to my aunts on Sunday mornings, most of them altos, so I acquired an ear for intervals. I sounded pretty good for an older writer, especially when I'm singing with someone better than I. Equality was not in my favor. The woman shone and I reflected. We sang with tender feeling, nothing bitter, no breakup stuff: "If Not for You," Ann Reed's haunting "If You Were Mine," or Mark Knopfler's "Why Worry?" Once, before a show in LA, I saw a familiar figure sitting by the stage door, and I walked up, and said hello to Phil Everly. He had bought tickets to the show and was waiting for his date, an LA policewoman. He said he'd heard me sing "Why Worry?" on the radio and wished I'd sing it that night and dedicate it to his girlfriend. I'd been singing Phil's part on Everly songs for years, and now Phil Everly wanted to win points by having me dedicate a song to his girlfriend. It's the truth, Ruth. I did the job, Bob. I hope he scored, Lord.

32

An Easy Descent into Oblivion

THE SHOW BUSINESS HAS ITS moments—like standing eye-to-eye with Heather Masse and singing "Under African Skies" and feeling her voice take hold of my own, or seeing an audience fall apart as Tim Russell does Donald J. Trump singing "I Feel Pretty"—but there's also a lot of time spent sitting and waiting. You arrive early in case there are problems, and sound check is done at 2:30 and you sit in a dressing room waiting for a 5 p.m. show, try not to think about it, and soon it's 3. I didn't socialize backstage. I liked to sit still and become nobody, in keeping with LaVona Person's advice when I was fourteen: "It's not about you. It's about the material." When I walk out onstage, I'll be astonished by the applause, and then the material will spring to mind. Meanwhile, I sit in a room and empty my mind and odd things drift through it. My vacant chair at our family's dinner table as I stand outside looking through the window. Hitchhiking late at night on the West River Road, a car approaches, slows down for a look, and resumes speed. The feeling when the hockey team scores and we all jump up to sing "Minnesota, hats off to thee, to your colors true we shall ever be." And the prospect of retirement and decrepitude and not doing this anymore.

A Prairie Home Companion was wending its way toward the exit. We did a show in Baltimore at an open pavilion in the Inner Harbor, near where Francis Scott Key wrote the words, and a couple thousand people sang the national anthem in the key of A, with gusto, the sopranos floating up high over "O'er the land of the free." When the British attacked Fort McHenry in 1814, they were quite justified, American pirates having operated out of Baltimore harbor to prey on British cargo ships. The bombardment was their tit for our tat. Mr. Key wrote his lines in a fever of righteousness hardly supported by the facts. But it's a great rouser, and we all stand and feel good when the rockets go up and the bombs burst, and what would life be without mythology? Rather flat.

We were ten shows from the end, then nine, then five, an easy descent into oblivion, but in each of the cities a few reporters came backstage to ask, *How does it feel?* And *What do you see when you look back?* It felt good, of course. I loved the show. When I looked back, I remembered the Hopeful Gospel Quartet and the Red Clay Ramblers singing Carter Family songs and Ramblin' Jack Elliott the Brooklyn cowboy and Allen Ginsberg proclaiming Walt Whitman's "Song of Myself," like the prophet Isaiah of New Jersey—the mezzo Marilyn Horne singing her favorite tenor aria, "Celeste Aida," in the tenor key, an astonishing gender switch—Chet Atkins and Leo Kottke playing "Living in the Country" aboard an elevator rising slowly to stage level at Radio City Music Hall, the wave of applause that almost drowned out the tune, and the tune riding through the wave— Chet singing "I Still Can't Say Goodbye" to his dad and the show at St. Olaf College where the audience sang *Children of the heavenly Father safely in His bosom gather, nesting bird nor star in heaven such a refuge e'er was given* in pure four-part harmony, impromptu, which listeners thought was a choir, but it wasn't, it was just eight-hundred Lutherans. I made fun of Lutherans, for their lumbering earnestness, their obsessive moderation, their fear of giving offense, and I never felt so exalted as when I stood in the midst of a roomful of them (or Mennonites) and we all sang together.

And I remember Jearlyn and Jevetta Steele belting out "Natural Woman" as they boogied big-time at the microphone and the duo of Gillian Welch and Dave Rawlings and the sisterly harmonies of the DiGiallonardos with Rob Fisher bouncing at the piano with the Coffee Club Orchestra, and Soupy Schindler playing power jug and Peter Ostroushko's mandolin études and how astonishing it was, in the midst of our gumbo of comedy and mumbo-jumbo to hear haunting voices like Aoife's and Geoff Muldaur's and Helen Schneyer's. And then there was Fred Newman impersonating a man on a 50-below morning trying to start a car that only wants to die and praying through clenched teeth and hearing angel wings and ocean surf and tropical birds and the swing of a golf club and the *ohhhh* of an admiring crowd. Everything Fred did was masterful. I revised "Somewhere Over the Rainbow" for him:

Somewhere there's an old cabin
By a lake
Where I awoke to the bacon
Coffee and pancakes

Somewhere north of the Cities
Neath the moon
There I lie in the night and hear the distant loon (LOON CALLS).

Fred was the Birgit Nilsson of loon-calling, the state bird of Minnesota, and he made it into a work of art, filled with tender longing and bravery and the knowledge of mortality. His loon was luminous. He also did ominous ad hominem hums that were memorable and momentous.

Fred Newman calling a loon.

That last run of shows was a beauty, the mixed pleasure and regret of the audience. For years I'd been so busy writing the show that I didn't see the big picture until the show was coming to an end: *People listened, some of them from childhood into middle age. The show became a part of their lives like an oddball uncle who likes to natter and tell jokes. I set out to carry on the sort of show I loved as a kid, which was now a museum piece or close to it, and it moved me that the show was loved by people too young to remember the original. In years to come, younger people would put a hand on my shoulder and say, "Love your work," women would say, "I used to spend my Saturday nights with you." The show was not brilliant or revolutionary, but it had the genuine affection of its audience.*

The last show was at Hollywood Bowl, July 1, 2016, with Heather and Aoife and Sara Watkins and Sarah Jarosz and Christine DiGiallonardo as duet partners, and the duets were about enduring love and the Lake Wobegon monologue was about the dead—last monologue, so I get to talk about what's on my mind—Father Emil who died of a heart attack while on a tour of the Gettysburg battlefield and was distressed to fall behind Confederate lines, and Jack of Jack's Auto Repair whose ashes were put in his wife Loretta's coffin though she had made it clear she didn't want them there, being as tidy as she was, and my classmate Arlen who went through the ice on his snow machine, trying to impress Barb whom he was crazy about. She waved to him and he waved back and down he went. She married his twin brother, Arnie, which seemed to prolong the grieving process, sleeping with a man who looked exactly like your lost love, but he gained weight and his hair got thin and he turned out to be a good husband, which she eventually realized, and he adored her and Arlen was dead, and that made all the difference. Not a great monologue, which was fine, to let the audience down gently.

There was a half-hour encore of audience singing at the end—"I Saw Her Standing There" and "Swing Low, Sweet Chariot," "Can't Help Falling in Love with You," and "Auld Lang Syne," and a dozen others—and I bowed and took a wrong turn from the stage and wandered through the trees out into the crowd heading for the parking lots and was trapped there for an hour being manhandled by fans, a life-size male toy in their hands. I grew up an awkward misfit, no hugging or horsing around, but in the scrum of those fans I was extensively pawed over, an inert

object with no will of my own. People grabbed an arm, put a head on
my shoulder, crouched between my legs, planted themselves flat against
me as cameras clicked and hummed. Someone stuck a hand behind my
head to make my ears stick out, covered my eyes, I was hugged, squeezed,
clutched, patted, rumpled, fist-bumped, high-fived, groped—radio had
been an intellectual exercise, and now I was a physical object, to be
embraced, fondled, clasped, latched onto, poked, embraced, climbed on,
and heartily harassed. I was a prime rib at a piranha picnic. It was like the
winning team pileup on the football field. The mob grew, people gathered around to get a hand on me, whole families, children climbed into
my arms and stuck their fingers in my hair. A dignified lady almost my
age grabbed a buttock and gave it a good feel. I was not a distinguished
broadcaster, I was a beloved dotty uncle, exactly what I had wanted to
be without knowing it. No need for a Peabody or DuPont. No need for
MPR to throw a big party. (They didn't offer, so I didn't need to decline.)
That crowd was all the confirmation a man could want, the pushing
and pummeling of loving strangers. It was a transforming experience. I
accepted that I was loved.

I was in a taxi in New York a year later and heard my voice on the
cabdriver's radio talking about a baseball game in Lake Wobegon. The
cabdriver was a big man, African, wearing a dramatic black-checked
head wrap. I said, "I'm going to LaGuardia, Terminal D, please," and he
turned around and said, "Your voice is familiar." I laughed. On the radio,
I was telling about an exhibition game the Lake Wobegon Whippets
had played in 1942 against the Showboats and their one-armed pitcher,
Duke, and a catcher, Mark, who was legally blind, and a border collie
named Spike playing second base. It was wartime and the good ballplay-
ers were in the Army.

The cabdriver eyeballed me in the rearview mirror. The man on the
radio was talking about the dog coming up to bat with the blind man on
third. The dog held the bat between his teeth and his job was to get a base
on balls, his strike zone being about fifteen inches, shoulder to knees. The
driver said, "You're the man on the radio." I nodded yes. He said, "I'm
from Ethiopia. I learned my English from that show." He showed me a
bag of tape cassettes, labeled "Minnesota." He'd recorded them off the
air. The dog fouled off two bunt attempts, and we pulled up to Terminal

D. I gave the man a copy of my book of sonnets and he had me sign it to his wife, Sarah. I said, "It's an honor to meet you," and we shook hands. I gave him fifty bucks for a tip, and when I got into the terminal, I wished I'd given him more. I'd done the show for my own amusement, and it amazed me to find out I'd also been teaching English as a second language. My mother wanted me to be a teacher, and now I'd helped a man from Ethiopia learn English.

Usually on a flight home to Minnesota, the plane crosses the St. Croix and banks to the north and comes in low over farms and the Minnesota River, but coming home after the show in LA, the plane took a big loop around the metro area and made a tour of the geography of my youth, a dreamy celestial view of the town of Anoka where the Rum meets the Mississippi and where Mr. Andersen handed me a copy of *The New Yorker* as he said, "I thought this might interest you," and Mr. Buehler, worried about me and the power saw, dispatched me to LaVona Person's speech class where I recite an unrhyming limerick and get a big laugh, and Dr. Mork, who brought me into the world, decided to spare me from football and Mr. Feist gave me a desk in the front window of the Anoka *Herald,* the flatbed press rumbling down below. And then down the West River Road and Benson School, where Mrs. Shaver asked me to read aloud to her while she corrected papers, and over north Minneapolis where I biked past the factories and packing plant to go ruminate in the great sandstone library, long since demolished, but the great grassy Mall of the University is majestic below and the Union where I did a private daily newscast, and we descended over the blocks of little bungalows where Mother grew up, a glimpse of the Meeting Hall and 38th Street where I tried to buy a cheeseburger with stolen money, and then the wheels lowered and we sailed in over Don and Elsie's house and the old Met Stadium and onto the runway.

I came back from LA for the reunion of the Class of 1960. People asked, "What you been up to then?" and I said, "Not much." My classmates Marvin Buchholz and Wayne Swanson were still farming, Bob Bell looking young and fit, and so did Rich Peterson, having taught phys ed all these years. His parents ran Cully's Cafe out back of the *Herald* office where I worked, and I'd come in to eat a hot beef sandwich while reading galley proof. I hung out with Billy Pedersen, now retired as head of the

state hospital in St. Peter. Carol Hutchinson was a librarian, Vicky Rubis
a schoolteacher, Mary Ellen Krause had kept our hometown's enormous
Halloween parade going all these years. Liz Johnson, still a list-maker,
organized the thing, and I stood and talked to Don Carter and Wayne
West, whom I'd barely known in high school, and now, by the simple
fact of being 75, we were pals. Earl Krause had become a noted ocean-
ographer who had traveled most of the watery world and every conti-
nent. Some friends were missing, ambushed by old age. I thought about
Corinne, gone at 43, still a mystery. If she'd only survived that dark April
night on Cayuga Lake, she'd be here with us, laughing.

> *The secret is not a serene disposition,*
> *Or spiritual strength*
> *Or a strong core, regular exercise, or a good physician:*
> *The secret of longevity is length.*
> *Don't put rocks in your pockets.*
> *Every day take a long walk, it's*
> *Just that simple. By and by,*
> *Someday you'll be as old as I.*

When the show ended, I started to truly appreciate it, which you can't
do when you're in the thick of things, beating up on yourself to be better
than you are, and then in the small stillness that follows, you start to comprehend the miracle of the past forty years that a small staff and an enormous cast had created. Over time, the show had bonded in fellowship
with a diverse constituency of college profs and prison inmates, Republican moms, African cabdrivers, small-town teachers, renegade Baptists,
loony libertarians, soybean farmers, and countless etceteras, and one by
one they show up in my life with smartphones to take a picture, and I
stand beside them and put an arm around their shoulders and I think,
"How in the world did this ever happen?" A woman tells me her story:
In the hospital, her premature baby, 2 lb. 2 oz., with chronic pneumonia,
crying under an oxygen mask, and she put a boom box by him and played the
tape of my story about Bruno the Fishing Dog and the baby stopped crying; he
listened and relaxed and he survived and is now a junior in college. By way
of radio I became a friend of people who, as an old evangelical and liter-

ary gent, I'd likely have scorned mercilessly in real life. Scorn came easily to me. I am biased against tattooed people, grabby people, people who put oregano in everything, blowhards, emotional drunks, and scornful people like myself. (Also bolo ties, wind chimes, and mood music, but those vanished long ago.) But now a young woman gives me a long look and says, "I grew up listening to you." She went to MIT, majored in chemistry, writes scholarly articles about sanitation, raises her three kids, has a good life. (Also a spiderweb tattoo on her neck.) And then she pulls out a phone and I put my head next to hers, and she snaps our portrait. A miracle to be an intimate pal of a complete stranger.

Once a year or so, someone says, "I was at that show in Rochester where you leaped up into the ceiling." It was at a community college, a makeshift stage—plywood sheets on steel legs—which was moved back under a concrete overhang to make room for more folding chairs. The lights dimmed, I ran and leaped onto the stage and crashed my head into concrete and landed on my hands and knees, jumped up and said, "Happy to be here." I am bonded to those people by singularity, the only time a performer leaped up into the ceiling. Houdini did other things but never that.

But for every great leap into the ceiling, there are a dozen mistakes. A busy life is full of them. Whenever I go to Carnegie Hall, I remember the show I did there where I sang the New Orleans funeral march, "Just a Little While to Stay Here" and went parading into the house, waving a red umbrella, expecting the audience to sing along and they were embarrassed for me and averted their eyes. They wanted me to be funny, not do a charade of Mardi Gras in the French Quarter. I think about that night with sharp pain. "Forget about it," you say, I wish I could.

I've written some dull, pretentious material—like this sentence here—and that's why I never sit and read old work. I recently came across a folder from 1976, pages of single-spaced typing, that begins: *I am leaving this dark rattan Orlon Saran wrap wingtip apartment and this wickerbasket demitasse wingback risotto kitty litter life and mindless warp of numerals flashing twelve o'clock to go bopbopbop at the wheel of a big old fishtail car screaming west out of this catatonic cocktail freak show scene of Modigliani women with American Express eyes and collagen hearts and pituitaries like shotgun shells* and it goes on and on.

I regret that at the end of the last broadcast, July 1, 2016, I did not bring the *Prairie Home* staff out on stage at the Hollywood Bowl for a bow, the loyal veterans who'd kept the show running all those years, Deb and Kay and Theresa, Jennifer, Tony, Todd, Jason, Olivia, David and Noah and Tom and Alan, Janis, Ben, Ella, Kathryn, Albert, Sam, Thomas, and their leader Kate, and acknowledge them so they could hear the crowd roar. Why did this not occur to me to cue the staff for a bow? So simple. I forgot to do it, the man in the suit.

And most of all I grieve for the death the next spring of my grandson Frederick, seventeen, a funny boy of bottomless curiosity whose mind soaked up reams of information about cars, bugs, animals, India and China, the human environment, and unlike any Keillor I've known, he loved to talk, talk, talk. He had a compassion for all other creatures. He landed his first fish and then tried to revive it. A roomful of people in shock gathered for the memorial. I sat behind his brother, Charlie, and his mother, Tiffany, and his grandmother Julie. All I felt was a great heaviness, no tears, just shock. It simply wasn't possible to imagine Freddy absent from the world. I stood up with Bob and Adam and we sang "Calling My Children Home" and sat down. We all lose our parents, but losing a child is simply not supposed to happen. The brain goes numb, God's way of offering mercy. If we were fully cognizant, it would be unbearable.

Frederick, 6, and his cat Loretta.

33

The CEO

I GOT KICKED OUT OF public radio in November 2017, accused of an email flirtation with a freelance researcher, a friend who'd worked for the show for thirteen years, a woman of 55 who worked from home but who came to the office often to tell me about her troubles and who wrote me notes about my monologues, which she said were works of art, notes signed, "I love you" and "I miss you." A man whose job had been "eliminated" by MPR accused MPR of doing it because he knew some dirt about her and me and he demanded a larger severance payment. They declined to pay it, so the man got a lawyer and persuaded my researcher that he'd been eliminated on her account and she joined him in his demand, asking for an enormous sum of money with the implied threat that otherwise they would drag my name in the mud and put stones in my mailbox. They drew up a list of allegations against me and MPR, demanding cash and confidentiality.

The flirtation was not the classic #MeToo story of a powerful bully trying to extort intimacy. She wanted to go on working for me past my retirement, and I had said no, but she persisted. She wrote numerous affectionate emails and confided in me about her personal life. She wrote an email about wanting to ride a train with me and share a bunk; I wrote that I'd like to lie in a hammock with her. We never tried to catch that train or reconnoiter. There was no kissing, no unbuttoning, because we weren't attracted to each other, we were just two aging adults having an adolescent fantasy. I once, as she left my office, put my hand on her bare left shoulder by way of comforting her, and she winced, and I wrote her a note of apology the next day and she forgave me. The flirtation stopped. She worked for the show to the end and asked for a job recommendation, and I wrote her a good one and she got the job she wanted. We exchanged a few emails after the show ended. She said she had been afraid she wouldn't hear from me again and was glad to. She wrote to me in May 2017 to say she missed the show but enjoyed her teaching job and expressed condolences on the death of my grandson. She said that I had brought so much good to her life, that she would never say anything that would hurt me, which struck me as odd; I'd never imagined she might. She stayed friends until her attorney demanded the money.

MPR decided from the start that I was expendable. Their lawyer said, "There can be no mutuality or consent when there is a power imbalance," declaring me guilty, no need for discussion. I disagree. It was not a problem in physics, it was about two human beings, a flirtation that was manipulative on both sides, appealing to my vanity, proclaiming her loyalty. To say that a mature woman cannot, freely and of her own will and for her own pleasure, flirt with whomever she wishes is to make her a child. Over the years, there had been numerous romances at MPR, some of which wound up in marriage. When people are dedicated and work long hours, work life and social life may intermix. It's a simple story of proximity.

I don't blame her for trying to cash in: I suppose she needed the money and figured I could afford the damages. She never spoke to me through all of this and if she had, I would've apologized for offending her. I should have dismissed the notion of sharing a bunk on a train. I am truly sorry for her trouble. She only asked for money and confidentiality; I never had reason to believe she bore ill will toward me or the show and I still don't think she did.

MPR was named in the allegation, though she worked for me, and this may have made the CEO uneasy, knowing that, in December 1989, he had been accused of sexual harassment in Ramsey County District Court by his development director at KSJR where he'd been station manager. The case never came to trial and I assume he was innocent, but in the atmosphere of 2017, an accusation was the same as conviction, and certainly he didn't want the story to be MPR SLAMMED AGAIN FOR SEX OFFENSES and it wasn't. He threw me under the bus, and so it was not his picture that appeared on the front page of the New York *Times* in a story about men brought down by the #MeToo movement, but mine: the writer of flirtatious emails thereby linked to rapists and brutes who exposed themselves and threw women up against walls.

He kicked me out over the phone, a call that lasted less than two minutes. That's what hurt: the cool impersonal corporate tone of the execution. The executioner didn't show up in person to drop the trap, he did it by pressing *Delete*. An accusation of libidinous interest was handled as a piece of paperwork, like a real estate transaction except with no house or lawn. No voices were raised. I never saw my accuser face to face, nor the CEO, my co-accusee. There was no anger, no feeling expressed, nobody quoted Scripture or poetry or a line from a movie, there was nothing real about it. It was a play with no scenery and the script was deliberately boring.

It wasn't simply about money, a man's work was at stake, his vocation. The meeting should've taken place around a table in a tent in the woods, a bottle of vodka on the table, a crowd of the curious outside, crows screeching in the trees. The accuser wears a bandanna, a pistol in her belt, with a Rottweiler on a leash, slavering, it can taste my leg. She looks me in the eye and says, "You insulted and demeaned me but I was afraid you'd fire me and I needed the money so I feigned interest. I can never be the person I was, you hurt my soul, and I have a right to hurt you back."

I say, "I intended no harm. It was a game. It stopped when you said to stop." She says, "I'm taking your house."

The CEO says, "I never knew you. You're no part of anything. Your name will never be spoken in my presence again." And he walks out and mounts his horse and fires four shots in the air and rides away.

But it was all done quietly to the low hum of the AC. And when the bad news comes, it's by email. Viking-Penguin has canceled your book, the Washington *Post* has dropped your column, your upcoming tour is canceled and all of your dates from the lecture agency. Your daily show, *The Writer's Almanac*, which you did gratis for twenty-five years, with a poem a day, young poets, old, newcomers, classics, to millions of radio listeners, is gone, in the trash.

It was like what happened to Studs when Ed Clamage called him a commie, but I could also see a rough justice behind it: all my life I'd used subterfuge to avoid uncomfortable situations, and it had worked, and now someone else's subterfuge had dehorsed me.

What grieved me was the silence. Bill Kling called me and other friends, but none of the hosts of national talk shows where I'd been a guest in the past, and none of the station managers for whom I'd done benefits, nobody. It was a time of what Shakespeare called "puking cowardice," MPR News assigned three reporters to interview ex-employees of PHC, women who'd worked briefly for the show and then left, and they found several who felt unappreciated. No allegations of harassment, though a couple of them said I looked at them in a way that made them uncomfortable. In 2017, this accusation carried considerable weight. I once sat across a dinner table from Senator Ted Stevens of Alaska, who looked at me in a way that made me uncomfortable, but he looked at everybody that way, and his wife was wonderful to talk to so I ignored him. What the story didn't say was that I worked nonstop in small rooms and didn't need employees, male or female, to write Guy Noir or Lake Wobegon stories, so indeed they were not appreciated by me but if they were good at their jobs, they would've been appreciated by other employees. MPR News got a Sigma Delta Chi Award for locating five women who left the show feeling unhappy. Somebody could write the same story about former MPR employees and win a Pulitzer Prize.

The real news was not the unhappiness of five employees but the fact that for decades a staff of fifteen or so put on thirty-five broadcasts a year and another fifteen or twenty shows in a summer tour, plus a dozen *Prairie Home* cruises with 1,200 guests, plus marketing and *The Writer's Almanac* and much more, and did it quietly and stayed friends and took pride in their work.

MPR disposed of me without remorse and, oddly, life was better for it. They showed me the emptiness of corporate culture—everyone is disposable, forty years is a box of Kleenex. What endures is true friendship and thanks to the CEO, all false friendships are gone, all the hot buttered flattery, all the invitations to speak at graduations and receive a Distinguished Achievement award on a chunk of Lucite. The University took my picture down from its gallery of distinguished alums. I finally got the chance to live a quiet domestic life with the woman I love and write comedy. This is the beauty of misery—it invigorates you to work, work is what relieves misery. Good work rouses your heart to live another day: a good start means the job is half-finished.

It was a pleasure, in the midst of a week of corporate emptiness to go to the Mayo Clinic for a colonoscopy, and experience something real. The nurse decided I needed a bonus enema to make sure I was empty and in the middle of the procedure, with the nozzle in me and liquid gurgling, she said, "I have to tell you that I'm a fan of your show and I'm so sorry you retired. I think your singing has gotten so much better over the years." A classic Minnesota compliment: *you're getting better.* The doctor said I should have a prostate biopsy. A Russian urologist and his second banana did the job and their jokes were almost funny ("This will be like having wasps up your butt," said the banana, "except for the fact he's Jewish. And what we hope to find is a happy ending."), and then it was over, and I said, *Thank you* and prostate cancer was ruled out, which felt like a bargain—between slander and cancer, I choose slander—maybe the slander will scare some bully into behaving himself, and meanwhile *sticks and stones* and so forth.

I agonized over the #MeToo episode for a good long time, and then one Sunday morning I walked downtown to work at the New York Public Library on 42nd and was early so I walked by the Church of St. Mary the Virgin on 46th, and the door was open and I walked into the vast Gothic splendor, so stunning among the pawnshops and rummage sales. The priest was inviting people to come forward for healing, so I did. I didn't even stop to sit in a pew. I went forward and put myself in the hands of a tall Black deacon in vestments. She put her left hand on my right hip and her right hand on my left shoulder and her cheek against mine, and I whispered that I had been generously blessed in this life and I wanted to be healed of anger and bitterness at an injustice done to me. It was stunning to say this in the embrace of a stranger. I said, "I feel that this anger owns me, it's taken over my life, I can't talk myself out of it, I need to be free of it." I told her that I was a writer and had work left to accomplish and needed this stone to be removed. She did not blink at any of it. She simply laid her cheek against mine and prayed in a whisper that the poison of anger should be cleansed from my heart and my spirit go free. She prayed at some length and it was a powerful thing. I said Amen with her and walked over to Fifth Avenue to the Rose Reading Room and worked for a few hours.

That was two years ago and I still hear her voice, slightly Caribbean, and feel her hands on my hip and shoulder. I was in her embrace, her prayer in my ear: *Lord, release this man from the poison of injustice, relieve him of anger so that he may do the work You have put him here to do, in Jesus' name.* It was moving, a Black woman praying for me to be freed from anger and injustice, a woman who surely knew more about it than I ever will. I think of her whenever I sit in the Rose Reading Room, an anonymous old man among the college kids at their laptops. The room is like a church. Hushed. Everyone is occupied in her or his small space. I had my day and now my ambition is burnt away, but more than ever I love to work. Whenever anger whispers in my ear, prayer drives it away. I start by giving thanks for my wife and daughter and family and friends and colleagues, naming them one by one, and in two minutes, the darkness is gone, bitterness is washed away.

34

Toast

They love you still, your Mom and Dad.
You may not think so, but they do.
They gave you all the love they had
Though they were crazy, busy too.
Forgive the bungling of your folks,
Honor their memory through the years.
Turn your sorrows into jokes,
Water the flowers with your tears.
Everyone's life is in a mess,
Everyone did the best they could.
Treat your kids with tenderness,
Turn away wrath by doing good.

I WAS A WELL-LOVED CHILD with eighteen aunts and a string of teachers, Estelle, Fern, LaVona, Helen, who put an arm around me and told me I was smart, which obliges one to be a humorist, no way around it. It was your ordinary confusing and tumultuous childhood, but the road wound through the foothills and the red light on the water tower gave me my bearings, and I got where I was going. My dad wanted a garden so he could enjoy fresh tomatoes and sweet corn, and so I grew up a country boy and did not view the world as treacherous. At the age of ten, I rode my bicycle into downtown Minneapolis, past factories and Skid Row and two burlesque houses to the public library and enjoyed the scenery, the old bums, the bright lights, the flashy billboards, the

Egyptian mummy, the burger stands. I was a happy kid, no foreboding. Like Anne Frank, I believed that people are good at heart. The Brethren anticipated the end of the world and the Judgment, and I went to the ballpark and had a bratwurst. I wrote anguished inscrutable poems in my twenties and then my hero Berryman jumped off the bridge and I knew I would not, so why pretend? I quit drinking in 2002 because it was leading me to a dark place I was not entitled to. My aunts put me on the road to pastoral comedy. Why go to the town dump instead?

I earned money for my downtown explorations by hoeing corn for Fred Peterson, who did not think I was smart, and that was a good thing, too. He walked down the row and yelled, "What're you slowing down for?? Work!" I still hear his voice. I am a good worker. I don't remember vacations in any detail, but I remember my 15 x 20 studio in the woods, a box on stilts with windows looking out into the trees in winter, the desk a long shelf under the windows where I spread out my papers, a landscape so serene that the flight of a bird through the trees startled me. I remember every workroom clearly and restaurants and resorts not at all. I sit in the ornate reading room in the public library on 42nd Street and think of Leeds and Barry and Roger, whose lives snapped shut when they were the age of the men and women around me working at laptops, and I want to do good things in honor of my dead, and so I press on against the tide. The Internet has stupefied us, millions of songs available free, all of them XLNT, listen to one for 15 secs, move on. The culture rolls past me and I am a white grammar-centric binary atavistic dextromanual chauvinist, and so be it, the *Oxford English Dictionary* now includes the word "ish" and I feel the onrush of time and I wonder, What does my life add up to? Shouldn't a man who's written a memoir know this? I'm 78 and it feels like the outcome still hangs in the balance.

If there is a literary prize for diversity, I am a contender. I started out writing poetry, sports, and obituaries, have written short fiction, novels, sonnets (77), limericks (hundreds), essays, comedy sketches, newspaper columns, book reviews, straight reporting, an opera libretto (*Mr. and Mrs. Olson*), a play (*Radio Man*), radio monologues, songs (hundreds, some not bad), a movie (*A Prairie Home Companion*), speeches, campaign literature, an advice column for *Salon* called "Mr. Blue," children's books (*Cat, You Better Come Home*), and what this says about me is

(1) I'm not disheartened by failure; (2) I like to have three or four things going at one time; (3) I had plenty of time thanks to cleaning ladies like Lulu and Ritonia and had good children who played nicely with other children; and (4) I have no hobbies, no dog, no lawn to mow, I lead an uncrowded life.

I did hundreds of shows at which I walked into the crowd and sang, "My country, 'tis of thee," and because I'm not Pavarotti, the whole crowd sang with me and they enjoyed the communal feeling. We're all riders on the crowded school bus of life, eventually you find a seat, and the neighbors are nice to you and you're not an Untouchable. This happened to me in 1978, it's written down in my diary. A woman named Marilyn Heltzer walked into the radio studio and said, "You smell good." People had said nice things about stories I wrote but this simple approval of my creatureness touched me. My wife, Jenny, says this to me now and then: You smell good. Walking in Loring Park I saw a woman in a frilly white skirt and ratty old sweater, barefoot, singing to Jesus and dancing with one arm around a light pole, singing, *Jesus, I sing your praises. Jesus, I'm glad you're in my heart,* and letting out whoops at the ducks on the mucky lagoon, and then she stopped and yelled at me, "What you looking at?" and I'm sorry I didn't say, "You sound good." I walk farther and see a deranged man yammering to himself, talking a blue streak, a perfectly well-dressed lunatic having an episode, and then I notice the little device clipped to his ear. It's a free country, deranged, doing business, who can tell?

We're all in over our heads. I was a big shot at one time, and now I'm an old man who's done his share of dumb things, but at least I've not put my tongue on a frozen clothes pole, not so far.

I thought about death when I was young and saw Roger and Leeds and Barry go down in the dust. In hellfire gospel preaching, the prospect of imminent death was the main selling point. Now it's happening all around me. At the Class of 1960's reunion in 2000, I gave a speech, and during it, a classmate had a heart attack. He collapsed and three days later he died. I was reminiscing about Stan Nelson, our gym teacher who made us do chin-ups, and Ronnie was thinking, "Oh, God. This can't be a heart attack, can it?" and it was.

Seventy-eight is a good age: critical opprobrium is no longer a factor in my life. I no longer worry about being dragged off to jail. The goals of my sixties—to learn the tango, hike the Himalayas, win the Nobel Prize in Literature—have faded, and I am focused on other things, such as not tripping on a loose rug, not struggling when I rise from a chair, not telling a story and then forgetting her name, the girl who challenged me to wrestle when we were twelve, my first glimmer of heterosexuality—what a beautiful discovery!

Julie. Her name was Julie.

I feel good. My blood is thinned, a beta blocker suppresses atrial fibrillation, another pill prevents seizures and so I look normal, no collapsing on the floor, writhing and gibbering. People sometimes drop dead at this age on a moment's notice, I've known people it happened to. To go on living is a dangerous proposition and yet I never think about death. In fact, I believe my best work is still ahead, which is a lunatic notion, certifiably batty, but there it is. People give awards to old writers who've gone fallow and nobody's given me one so I feel I'm still in business. Many good friends have crashed, Arnie, Roland, Sydney, Arvonne, and my turn will come, meanwhile, there are good jokes about calamity. *Ole is dying when he smells Lena's rhubarb pie, his favorite, and he crawls into the kitchen and picks up a knife to cut a slice and she slaps him from behind: "That's for the funeral. Leave it alone." He says to Lena, "You've stuck with me through two heart attacks, a stroke, leukemia, brain seizures, and erectile dysfunction and now this dementia. I'm starting to think you're bad luck, darling."*

My friend Jim Harrison died at 78, at his desk, writing, pen in hand, in Arizona where he spent the winters, having spent enough of them in Michigan where he wrote *Legends of the Fall* and a great deal more, in a cabin in the woods. "Working every day of the week," he wrote to me. "I don't know what else to do. With age all my opinions drift away. Who am I to say for sure? My people thought they'd see Jesus when they died. Now that we know we have 90 billion galaxies, I'm not inclined to discount anything. The towering reality is death. I don't mind. I was never asked. On death, a tour of the 90 billion galaxies would be flattering. Yes? Our curiosity is still in the lead. Wittgenstein said that the miracle is that the world exists." He kept a radio in his cabin in the woods, and that's how we met: I was on the radio. Once, a women's quartet sang "Shall We Gather at the River (That Flows by the Throne of God)?" on the show, and he was moved to write a poem ("They say it runs by the throne of God./This is where God invented fish.") in which he said that maybe nothing happens after death, but if so, we won't know it. But maybe something does:

Maybe we'll be cast
at the speed of light through the universe
to God's throne. His hair is bounteous. . . .
We'll sing with the warblers perched on his eyelashes.

To which I replied:

Here's to old Harrison—Jim,
Who imagined the Lord as a limb,
Nothing fearful or horribler
But a place where a warbler
Would perch and perchance sing a hymn.

I wish you well, old man, as you fly around the galaxies. Maybe God will invite you to name a few of them.

I look forward to old age. My mother reached 97, and I hope for a cool 100. My heart got sewn up at the Mayo Clinic, solving the valve problem that wiped out two uncles in their late fifties, and I have faith that medical science will keep me upright for a while, though longevity is not nature's plan. Nature wanted me to beget offspring, raise them to be self-sufficient, then take the long walk across the ice before the young could acquire my deficits. But I intend to be useful. I blew away forty years amusing myself while other Keillors were trying to save the world. My brother Philip did research on shore erosion and thermal pollution on the Great Lakes, my sister Linda raised money for colleges, my brother Steve was a historian and brother Stan an attorney for the state appeals court, my sister Judy taught first grade. Meanwhile, I wrote:

There was an old man of Bay Ridge
Who cried out, Son of a bitch,
I got up in the night

And on came the light
And I find I have pissed in the fridge.

I invented a town "where the women are strong, the men are good-looking, and all the children are above average" and I said, "Nothing gets the taste of shame and humiliation out of your mouth like a piece of rhubarb pie." And sometimes people quote my line, "Nothing you do for children is ever wasted" and maybe that bucked up some parents and teachers who were sick of the little monsters and wished for a convenient orphanage to send them to.

What a person craves, more than money and fame, is to experience life in its fullness and the radio show was generous that way. Not many nerdy boys got to sing so many duets with women as I did. And singing the Whiffenpoof Song to the US Supreme Court sitting solemnly in a row—seriously, how many people get that opportunity? I spoke to the Harvard Phi Beta Kappa, my text Emily Dickinson's "Success is counted sweetest by those who ne'er succeed," and advocated failure as the surest means of education. I was joking, but they took me seriously so then I did too. I sat next to the famous critic Helen Vendler, who I don't think was fond of my work, and we carried on a friendly conversation—this is a privilege shared by few. I did a benefit for the Merce Cunningham Dance Company at which I said, "Merce believes there are no fixed points in dance, which is why he didn't become a professional ballplayer." I hung out with famous choreographers whose work I'd never seen and we got along fine. I went to Washington to lobby for the National Endowment for the Arts after they'd sponsored the famous Robert Mapplethorpe exhibit and how many old liberals have walked into a congressman's office prepared to talk about the value of letting schoolchildren hear Mozart and Chopin and he hands you a Mapplethorpe photograph of a naked man with a whip up his butt and says, "You call this art?" It's an experience more old liberals should have. (I walked into the office of Senator Alan Simpson (R of Wyoming) in his ornate Minority Whip's office, which looked like the King of Siam's personal chapel, and he told me about a contest cowboys waged, competing to see who could drop his jeans and pick up a silver dollar off a bench using only his bare cheeks.) I got to sing with the New York Philharmonic, a cycle of my own sonnets set to music, a pleasure denied to other writers of sonnets. On the other hand, for a show at the San Diego Zoo, I got to interview Murray the 400-pound sea lion who was trained, when a microphone was pointed at his mouth, to say: "BLEAUGHHH!" He never missed a cue. "BLEAUGHHH" was his opinion of the show and everything else. When Murray speaks, he tends to spray. Of all the writers I know, I daresay none has been spit on by a sea lion.

Murray the Sea Lion, San Diego Zoo.

Once, when the show was in Alaska, I went fishing for salmon on a commercial boat out of Juneau one chill summer morning and sat in the pilot house next to the captain as he maneuvered out of the anchorage and up the fjord, one ear to the radio, coolly observing the great gray whale surface on the starboard side. My daughter Malene was on board, and she came topside with a salmon she'd just hooked. The captain pulled out a knife and skinned a patch from the fish and cut two thin slices of raw flesh and offered it to us and she and I ate them. She was delighted. Snowy mountain peaks beyond the fjord, a chill wind, a gray whale alongside, a captain at the helm. And I felt a bond of captaincy with him, each taking responsibility for his own ship. I'd had fine crews, without whom there would've been nothing, people like David O'Neill who started out at the age of twelve as a volunteer and stayed to the end, and Debra Beck the Can-Do woman who managed everything that came her way, and Kay Gornick who did contracts and permissions and research and Caroline Hontz who liked to pretend she didn't love being a travel agent. I went out on stage and talked about my hometown, which people came to believe was real though they knew it wasn't. I was an oddball who never belonged in Anoka, so I had to invent a hometown. It happened accidentally, a story lost in the Portland train station men's room, the attempt to recapture it from memory, and I did this for a thousand-plus Saturday nights and when I told the audience, "Well, it has been a quiet week in Lake Wobegon," they sighed and closed their eyes and listened. I had been John and Grace's rebellious child, and yet the Lake Wobegon philosophy was simple and practical: *The way to do something is to do it. The secret of writing is rewriting. It's nice to dream, but the urge to perform is not in itself an indication of talent. Life is short and it's getting shorter—on the other hand, don't buy cheap shoes. Tall People cannot expect Short People to look out for us, so when you bang your head on the frying pan rack, it's your problem, nobody else's. Put a big dish by the door and put your car keys in it, your billfold, phone, extra glasses, and in the time you'll save not looking for them, you can write* War and Peace. *(On the other hand, it's already been written.)*

Cheerfulness is a fundamental American virtue. Some people look for euphoria, which I experienced once from a sedative an oral surgeon gave me for a wisdom tooth extraction, and I was euphoric for a whole day, but I only have three wisdom teeth left so the prospects are limited. So we sit and wait for redemption. Bases loaded, one out, our pitcher is struggling, disaster on the horizon, and then there it is—a squiggly grounder to the shortstop who underhands it to the second baseman who pivots and fires to first for the DP, catching the runner by a half-stride, and reflexively we jump to our feet and say, YES! Once again, the world is saved.

As the Psalmist said, it is God who hath made us and not we ourselves; we are His people and the sheep of His pasture. Come unto His gates with thanksgiving, and into His courts with praise. For the Lord is gracious; His mercy is everlasting; and His truth endureth from generation to generation. In other words, lighten up. It isn't about you. Improve the hour.

A Prairie Home Companion ended a month before my 74th birthday. When I invented Lake Wobegon in my thirties, I made the old people 75—Florian and Myrtle and the Norwegian bachelor farmers—and they stayed 75 for forty years—their grandchildren aged, old people didn't—I was fond of them and didn't want them to die. Now I'm older than either of my grandfathers. They died at 73, worn out from hard labor, and I avoided the labor and did work that I loved, a privilege unimaginable to them. I am a lucky man to live long enough to see how lucky I am.

I plan to become a living artifact like Albert Woolson of Duluth, the last living Union veteran whom I saw riding in a parade at the age of 105. I rode a hay wagon with my Uncle Jim, drawn by a team of Belgian horses, and saw New York City in 1953 and slept on a fire escape in a heat wave. I sang gospel songs on a street corner as a preacher hollered at passersby to give their lives to the Lord. I threaded 16 mm film in a movie projector. I sat in a car outside Anoka High School and mourned for Buddy Holly, who'd died the night before. I typed my first stories on an Underwood upright typewriter, using carbon paper. I was edited by the late William Shawn of *The New Yorker.* I hosted a live radio variety show. I refused induction into the Army during the Vietnam war. In my nineties, I will become an attraction, a man who can sing "The Frozen Logger" for you or "Frankie and Johnny" or recite the eighty-seven counties of Minnesota from Aitkin to Yellow Medicine and, if it is requested, I will tell how in 1947 I set out to ride a streetcar downtown to Dayton's and went into a luncheonette and was caught and not punished and my aunts were amused and that is how I got into comedy and radio.

I've been deeply troubled at times, like everyone else, but then I think of my college classmate who smoked some bad hashish and suffered a psychotic episode and was diagnosed as schizophrenic and went through various therapies and married a fellow therapee and illness became the main topic of her life. I have avoided therapy and sought grandeur. Therapy shows you that sadness is inexhaustible, and why would I want to know that? Hercules suffered insanity and purified himself by performing heroic labors, and I did the same by walking out on the stage, a sad man trying to be funny in front of thousands. I have a fundamentalist face and it was odd for the audience to see Cotton Mather singing "You Were Always on My Mind" with a woman standing next to him. Who wants to be on Cotton Mather's mind? Nobody. I had less stage presence than the average stone post, but audiences are polite and they gave me the benefit of the doubt. They looked around at the crowd and thought, "He must be good to attract this big an audience." So I made my way upstream. I made my mother laugh and taught African cabdrivers English and befriended a million strangers just as Jesus told us to do: love one another whether we want to or not, and for years thereafter, strangers walk up and say, "I liked your show," people smile at me in the airport, something Grandma never imagined as she and I knelt with our faces in the sofa as Uncle Jim asked the Lord's merciful blessing. He never prayed for me to be outstanding or celebrated, and now I'm over it. Minnesota is not a state of great poets or opera singers, much as we might wish to be, we are a choral state, people who enjoy ourselves more if we are surrounded by like-minded persons doing exactly what we're doing. I wanted badly to be gifted but instead I walked into a crowd and sang about how often at night when the heavens are bright with the light from the glittering stars and the crowd was amazed and asked as they gazed if their glory exceeds that of ours. That's what happens when you get old, your specialty fades, your uniqueness, you wade into the river of anonymous old age, the river of Jordan, Shenandoah, the beautiful beautiful river where bright angel feet have trod that flows by the throne of God, and you gather here and join your voices to the others, and this, you realize, is what you always wanted, life itself, why wish for anything more?

That time of year thou mayst in me behold
That which I see clearly in my peers
Who disappear at New Years' to escape the cold,
My classmates with white hair and gizmos in their ears.
In me thou see'st a former tennis player
And devotee of biking, hiking, sailing,
Now hesitate when heading down the stair
And take a firm hold of the railing.

In me thou see'st a formerly swift mind
Once given to riposte and repartee
Now he resorts to googling to find
The word for confusion that begins with D.
This thou perceiv'st, and regard with gentle scorn,
But your time will come, as sure as you were born.

Acknowledgments

My fervent gratitude to these two, Katharine Seggerman and Kate Gustafson. Katharine came aboard for the 27-city Farewell Tour of 2017 and stayed on to run The Writer's Almanac and as managing editor and Kate was managing director of PHC through half its history. They were trusty companions through my productive twilight and now that I've told my story, they're free to fill in the gaps.

The publisher and the author thank the following for permission to reprint copyrighted materials:

"Barnyard Dance" words and music by Johnny Copeland. Copyright © 1972 Happy Valley Music. Copyright Renewed. All Rights Reserved. Used by permission. *Reprinted by Permission of Hal Leonard LLC.*

"Bus Stop" from *Collected Poems* by Donald Justice, copyright © 2004 by Donald Justice. Used by permission of Alfred A. Knopf, an imprint of

Credits

177, Hopeful Gospel Quartet: Photo by Fredric Petters.

178, Jean Redpath: Photo by Stormi Greener, copyright © 1987.

179, Chet Atkins: Photo by Stormi Greener, copyright © 1987.

185, GK: Photo by Mike Zerby.

212, Jenny Lind Nilsson.

216, Tim Russell, Sue Scott, and Walter Bobbie: Photo by Prairie Home Productions, copyright © 2008.

220, Street Dance: Photo by Prairie Home Productions, copyright © 2007.

234, GK and Maia: Unknown.

246, GK and Jason Keillor: Unknown.

268, Maia and GK: Photo by Stormi Greener, copyright © 2001.

283, Richard Dworsky: Photo by Fredric Petters.

292, Jenny Lind Nilsson and Garrison Keillor: Photo by Nancy Kaszerman/ZUMA Press, copyright © 2006 by Nancy Kaszerman.

320, APHC on the stage: Photo by David Berg.

323, Sam Hudson and Thomas Scheuzger: © 2016 Minnesota Public Radio®. Used with permission. All rights reserved.

326, GK and Heather: Photo by Prairie Home Productions, copyright © 2009.

330, Fred Newman: Photo by Ralph Nelson, copyright © 2002.

336, Frederick Keillor.

349, Murray the Sea Lion: Unknown.